Bearing Right

Bearing Right

How Conservatives
Won the Abortion War

William Saletan

UNIVERSITY OF CALIFORNIA PRESS
Berkeley · Los Angeles · London

University of California Press
Berkeley and Los Angeles, California

University of California Press, Ltd.
London, England

Library of Congress Cataloging-in-Publication Data

Saletan, William, 1964–
    Bearing right : how conservatives won the abortion
war / William Saletan.
        p. cm.
    Includes bibliographical references and index.
    ISBN 0-520-08688-0 (cloth : alk. paper)
    1. Abortion—United States—Public opinion.
2. Public opinion—United States.   3. Abortion—
Government policy—United States—Citizen
participation.   4. Conservatism—United States.
5. Liberalism—United States.   I. Title.

HQ767.5.U5 S25 2003
363.46'0973—dc21

                                        2002035355

Manufactured in the United States of America

12   11   10   09   08   07   06   05   04   03
10 9 8 7 6 5 4 3 2 1

To my parents,
Jeanne and David Saletan

I am reminded of the picture of the giant, tied to the ground
by threads of resistance, secured by an army of Lilliputians.
The giant represents the force we fight against and the
Lilliputians represent the majority of American public
opinion, the efforts of thousands of individuals working
together.

> —Kate Michelman, address on becoming executive
> director of the National Abortion Rights Action
> League, Harrisburg, Pennsylvania, January 22, 1986

But I can tell you now that a sleeping giant is awakening and
is ready to change the face of the political landscape. . . . We
will organize this awakening giant into a politically powerful
grassroots constituency that will flex its political muscle in
the 1990 and 1992 elections.

> —Kate Michelman, announcement of NARAL's 1989–
> 92 political campaign, Washington, D.C., March 23,
> 1989

It is a common irony of transitions from one technology to
another, and from one social idea to another, that progress is
often blocked by unanticipated consequences of the rhetoric
of proponents of change.

> —Harrison Hickman, pollster for NARAL, memo to
> NARAL, March 4, 1991

Contents

Introduction

If you think that the abortion debate is over, or that you've heard all the arguments, or that you know which side you're on, think again. Ask yourself why the arguments seem so stale and irreconcilable. Ask yourself why first one side, then the other, appears to be winning the war. The moral monotony and the political mystery are related. They're clues that we're missing something. Our two-dimensional map of the abortion conflict—pro-life on one side, pro-choice on the other—oversimplifies the moral and political world in which abortion is being debated. That world isn't flat. It's round.

This book explores the many sides of the abortion issue. It explains who the various constituencies are, how they overlap, how they see the issue, and how the evolving relationships among them affect the progress of the war. It suggests new ways to think not just about abortion but also about politics, dialogue, and the communication of ideas.

To understand the abortion debate, you have to ask people not just whether abortion should or shouldn't be legal, but why. Some people believe the issue is about protecting human life. Others believe it's about women's rights. Some say it's about taking responsibility for sex. Others say it's about poverty and preventing unwanted children. Some think it's about preserving the family. Others think it's about limiting the power of the church or the government.

Every day, in Congress, courts, state legislatures, and informal conversations, people who see the issue one way try to engage people who see it a slightly different way. It's a labor of imagination and persuasion, and the stakes are enormous. Since no single perspective commands a majority, the right to abortion hangs on this struggle for alliances, this symphony of ideas.

In 1986, halfway between *Roe v. Wade* and the election of George W. Bush, a group of pro-choice strategists developed an idea that changed the course of this struggle. They feared that abortion restrictions would roll back women's rights and condemn many women to the poverty of untimely motherhood. But they understood that most voters didn't share that concern. So instead of talking about women's rights, the activists portrayed abortion restrictions as an encroachment by big government on tradition, family, and property. When the issue was framed that way, many voters with conservative sympathies turned against the anti-abortion movement. And the balance of power turned in favor of abortion rights.

From the beginning, the alliance was unstable. Only on the question of abortion's legality did voters who cared primarily about protecting traditional institutions from big government agree with activists who cared primarily about women's rights and poverty. As the debate moved to other questions—whether the government should spend tax money on poor women's abortions, or whether teenage girls should have to get their parents' permission for abortions—the alliance fell apart. Voters who believed in tradition, family, and property abandoned liberal advocates of poor women and teenage girls, leaving those advocates in the minority.

Many people think that the political struggle over abortion has been resolved and that feminists have won. They are mistaken. The people who hold the balance of power in the abortion debate are those who favor tradition, family, and property. The philosophy that has prevailed—in favor of legal abortion, in favor of parents' authority over their children's abortions, against the spending of tax money for abortions—is their philosophy. People who believe that teenage girls have a right to abortion without parental consent, or that poor women have a right to abortion at public expense, have largely been defeated. Liberals haven't won the struggle for abortion rights. Conservatives have.

The terms *liberal* and *conservative* appear throughout this book, so it's important to clarify what they mean. I use these terms as they're commonly used in the United States today, focusing on three distinctions.

First, conservatives tend to think of government as the principal threat to freedom, whereas liberals often view government as an ally in the exercise of rights. Liberals generally believe, for example, that food and health care are human rights and that the government should help poor people pay for these necessities. Conservatives frown on the notion that some people are entitled to such aid, since it requires the government to tax others.

Second, liberals tend to think that freedom belongs to the individual, whereas conservatives tend to think that freedom belongs to private or local institutions such as families, communities, and businesses. The debate over prayer in school, for example, pits individual freedom against community freedom. Child abuse laws pit the rights of children against the sovereignty of families. Consumer product safety laws pit the asserted rights of consumers against the freedom of businesses. In such disputes, liberals are more inclined than conservatives to distinguish the interests of the individual from the interests of private institutions and to enlist the government to protect the former from the latter.

These two differences between conservatism and liberalism were elegantly summarized by President Ronald Reagan in his farewell address to the nation in January 1989: "Man is not free unless government is limited. There's a clear cause and effect here that is as neat and predictable as a law of physics: As government expands, liberty contracts." This equation of freedom with government's absence, which I will refer to as Reagan's Law, lies at the heart of the story that follows.

Third, conservatives are more willing than liberals to subordinate freedom to traditional morality. Whereas liberals think of freedom as a prerequisite to sorting out one's values, conservatives think of values as a prerequisite to managing one's freedom. Conservatives are inclined to grant greater freedoms and privileges to model citizens than to sinners. They distinguish these two classes of people by means of moral or social conventions—heterosexual marriage, for example—as well as criminal laws. Conservatives are less concerned than liberals with the rights of felons and more concerned with the rights of law-abiding gun owners.

The terms *pro-life* and *pro-choice* also appear throughout the book. I use these terms not because they are unbiased but because, like *Democratic* and *Republican,* they are the terms by which the two principal factions of the debate refer to themselves. Every attempt at unbiased language—for example, reserving the term *anti-abortion* to describe those who would outlaw the practice, or calling them "anti–abortion rights" instead of "pro-right-to-life"—adds a new bias. The least biased solution is to let each side choose its name.

The central story of this book, the tale of the troubled alliance between liberal feminists and pro-family, anti-government conservatives, begins in Arkansas in 1986, during the administration of Governor Bill Clinton. Chapter 1 explains the predicament that forced pro-choice activists in that state to repackage abortion rights as a conservative idea. There weren't enough liberal voters to defeat an impending pro-life ballot measure. Clinton and other moderates refused to oppose the measure. So the activists hired a pollster to figure out how to win over moderate and conservative swing voters.

These swing voters didn't share the activists' concerns about women's rights or the welfare of teenagers and the poor, but they were willing to reject the measure on other grounds: the perils of big government; the sovereignty of families, as opposed to women or girls; and the rights of rape victims, as opposed to women who indulged in sex willingly. By appealing to these concerns rather than to their own principles, the activists attracted enough support to win. They proved that the abortion rights movement could escape unpopularity and defeat by bearing right.

Chapter 2 follows the progress of this idea from Arkansas to Alabama to the nation's capital. Impressed by the Arkansas campaign, the National Abortion Rights Action League (NARAL) hired the same pollster in 1987 to figure out how to rouse public opposition to Judge Robert Bork's nomination to the U.S. Supreme Court. NARAL's research on voter attitudes in Alabama confirmed that abortion rights, couched as part of a defense of traditional, private institutions against big government, could attract conservative southerners to the campaign against Bork. This "privacy" issue became, in effect, the right wing of the anti-Bork coalition. It attracted voters who were indifferent or hostile to the coalition's liberal concerns.

Chapter 3 examines how in 1988 and 1989 NARAL refined the lessons of the Bork campaign and its own public opinion research into a strategy for folding pro-family, anti-government voters into its electoral coalition. Girding for the political firestorm that would follow the Supreme Court's 1989 decision in *Webster v. Reproductive Health Services,* NARAL hired a team of pollsters, wordsmiths, and media consultants, who distilled the pro-choice message to five words: "Who Decides—You or Them?"

The value of this slogan was that, like "privacy," it could be interpreted in many ways. Voters could agree, for example, that "you" should be in charge of abortion decisions, without agreeing on whether "you" meant women or families, teenagers or parents. But the underlying tensions between these interpretations were beginning to emerge as cracks in the pro-choice coalition—between men and women, liberals and conservatives, ideologues and pragmatists.

Chapter 4 pursues the widening of these divisions as the conservative interpretation of abortion rights took on a life of its own. In summer and fall 1989, as the *Webster* decision propelled abortion to the center of American politics, Lieutenant Governor Doug Wilder of Virginia took hold of the issue. By advertising his pro-choice position, he attracted swing voters and became America's first elected black governor. To NARAL, Wilder was Frankenstein's monster. He proved that abortion rights could win an election. But the version of abortion rights he advertised, as a philosophy and a political strategy, contradicted liberal activists on two key points.

Wilder refused to challenge Virginia's ban on public funding of abortions for poor women, and he proposed to require teenagers to get their parents' consent before obtaining abortions. He thereby honored the conservative pro-choice doctrine that the government should leave private matters to the heads of families and shouldn't tax them to pay for other people's sexual carelessness. Wilder also distinguished women impregnated through such carelessness from those impregnated by rape, defending abortion more as a victim's than as a woman's right. As he adopted, adapted, and vindicated the strategy conceived by pro-choice activists, they lost control of the weapon they had deployed.

Chapter 5 charts the nationwide explosion of abortion as a political issue in the wake of Wilder's election. Pro-life and conservative strategists learned to use two wedge issues, parental control and public funding, to separate abortion rights activists from moderate voters. These counterattacks inflicted heavy damage in Michigan, North Carolina, Oregon, and Texas. Pro-choice politicians, wary of being separated from swing voters, adopted Wilder's version of abortion rights instead of NARAL's. The rift between pragmatism and ideological purity reached even into the leadership of the abortion rights movement, as activists in Georgia, Missouri, and other states wrote off battles for abortion funding and against parental control.

Chapter 6 shows how the politically defeated extremes of the debate—on one side, opposition to legal abortion, and on the other, insistence on abortion rights with public funding and without parental control—faded away during the 1992 election year. Pro-choice politi-cians, led by Clinton and Senator Al Gore, converged with pro-life poli-ticians, led by President George H. W. Bush, in a "middle ground" of re-stricted choice, consecrated by the Supreme Court's decision in *Planned Parenthood v. Casey.*

The next two chapters depart from this historical sequence to ex-plore, through other episodes of the abortion war, additional differences between liberalism and conservatism. Chapter 7 explores the implica-tions of reserving rights—both the right to choose and the right to life—to people who are deemed innocent of sin or crime. In 1990 and 1991 lawmakers in Louisiana debated and passed legislation to ban abortions. The balance of power in these debates lay not with pro-choice or pro-life absolutists but with ambivalent legislators and citizens, led by Gov-ernor Buddy Roemer, who favored abortion as an option for rape vic-tims but not for other women.

Unable to dissolve the basis of this distinction—the belief that women who willingly indulged in sex deserved the consequences—pro-choice lawmakers and activists turned the distinction to their advantage. They framed the issue in terms of crime instead of gender equality, rallying support for rape victims rather than for women in general. In the end, the strategy failed. Pro-life pragmatists isolated and conquered pro-choice feminists by exempting rape victims from the abortion ban, as the pivotal bloc of voters and legislators demanded.

Chapter 8 confronts the dark question at the far end of this line of in-quiry. If the voters who hold the balance of power in the abortion war revere neither a woman's right to choose nor an unborn child's right to life, then both rights are in peril. The principles that motivate these vot-ers—the rights of husbands, parents, businesses, and taxpayers—co-incide sometimes with the right to choose and sometimes with the right to life. But sometimes they coincide with neither and threaten both.

These threats take numerous forms. Some women are steered toward abortion by boyfriends, husbands, or parents. Others face similar pres-sure from employers. Still others are persuaded to end their pregnancies by welfare reforms that penalize childbearing. All of these perils coalesce in a narrative that spans from a famous Boston murder case to a noto-rious Virginia sexual mutilation trial to the evolution, from David Duke to Bill Clinton, of the use of financial threats to stop welfare births.

Chapter 9 draws together the preceding lessons to explain the abor-tion rights movement's eventual disillusionment. The movement declared victory on the arrival of a pro-choice president and Congress in 1993. But in campaigns for federal funding of abortions, federal legislation to protect abortion rights, and coverage of abortions under a national health insurance plan, activists discovered that conservative pro-choice voters and lawmakers were unwilling to embrace this agenda. Republicans captured Congress in 1994, exterminated the remnants of liberal abortion policy, and dispelled fantasies of a new era of government activism. Having vanquished the pro-life movement, conservatism vanquished the pro-choice movement as well.

The late 1990s brought new variations on established themes: the extension of parental rights to birth control and interstate travel for abortions, the withdrawal of public funding from international family planning, and the national embrace of welfare reforms aimed at discouraging births. These years also saw the rise of two creative pro-life strategies. Pro-lifers sidestepped the right to choose abortion in the womb by shifting the debate to "partial births," and they linked life to choice by protecting the fetus and its mother from violence aimed at both.

Chapter 10 suggests how all of these developments came to a head. In 1999 the pro-life movement embraced pro-choice conservatism in the person of George W. Bush. Al Gore defied that conservatism and lost the White House. As president, Bush continued to move the campaign for human life out of the woman's body by focusing on born-alive infants and in vitro embryos. He also broke with conservative doctrine on welfare reform by endorsing public health insurance for fetuses through prenatal care. Forced to choose between advancing the ability of low-income women to bear healthy children and preventing the assignment of value to unborn life, abortion rights activists chose the latter. They pursued that course even as stem cell research carried them out of the maternal body in which the right to choose was conceived.

Choice is sacrifice. That insight has always guided and defined the abortion rights movement. In every decision, even a decision to give birth, something important is compromised. If you think you're compromising nothing, you're overlooking what you're compromising. Thirty years after *Roe v. Wade,* the abortion rights movement must ask itself what kind of autonomy it has won, what kind it is fighting for, what kind it is sacrificing, and whether that sacrifice is, after all, the right choice.

CHAPTER 1

A Place Called Hope

LITTLE ROCK, ARKANSAS
SEPTEMBER 29, 1986

The room was half dark when the visitors took their seats. Before them, curtains framed a wall of glass. Beyond the wall, an identical row of panes loomed like an optical illusion. Staring into the glass, the visitors beheld their own faint reflections, the faces of women who had marched for civil rights in the 1950s and 1960s and for sexual equality in the 1970s. They were here to survey what they regarded as the next battleground in the fight for freedom.

The outlook was bleak. In Washington, President Ronald Reagan and Republican senators were in their sixth year of power. Three days earlier, William Rehnquist, armed with fresh reinforcements in his campaign to overturn *Roe v. Wade,* had been sworn in as chief justice of the United States. In little more than a month, voters in four states would decide whether to ban public funding of abortions for poor women. Among these four battlefronts, the weakest position for pro-choice forces, the line most difficult to hold, was here in Arkansas. The job of the women in this room, against Reagan's will and without Governor Bill Clinton's help, was to hold that line.

Peering through the double glass, the women discerned the contours of another room beyond it. Their own reflected images obscured the details of that room. From the opposite direction, the glass functioned as a mirror, rendering the women invisible to anyone on the other side. No sound breached the barrier between the chambers.

A technician twisted two dials on the wall behind the women, extinguishing the lights above them. The reflections in the glass vanished. Through the darkness, they beheld clearly the contents of the illuminated room. A dozen chairs surrounded a rectangular table. Above the table hung a microphone, through which sound could pass into the viewing chamber.

Through a doorway concealed from view, a line of women, and later a line of men, entered the illuminated room and filled its chairs. These miniature assemblies—"focus groups," in the parlance of the polling industry—had been culled from the hundreds of thousands of voters who would decide whether to amend the Arkansas constitution to ban abortion subsidies. They didn't think all abortions should be outlawed, but they were inclined to support the amendment.[1]

Each of the women watching from the darkness was here to absorb a hard lesson. She would have to win over these voters. She would have to respect their values and accommodate their prejudices. She would have to perceive them clearly, without projecting her beliefs onto them. She would have to see what was beyond the glass, past the illusory reflection of herself.

The man seated at the near end of the table, with his back to the viewing chamber, was Harrison Hickman, the pollster who had arranged this encounter. He led each of the focus groups through a discussion. In the first session, the women in the illuminated room agreed among themselves that taxpayers shouldn't subsidize abortions. It took Hickman three-quarters of an hour to find a question that gave them pause. What would you do, he asked them, if one of your own daughters were impregnated as a result of rape? In that case, they conceded, abortion might be acceptable. They were disturbed to hear that the amendment might deny them that option.

After the women left, Hickman brought in the group of men. They, too, thought abortion should be reserved for rape victims. But unlike the women, the men didn't address the issue in personal terms. They were more outraged by the general idea of government interference in family life. Several men nodded as one member of the group asserted, "We live in the U S of A and are supposed to have freedom of choice."

The women watching from behind the glass remembered what freedom of choice had meant to Arkansans not long ago. On September 23, 1957, before the eyes of a rapt nation, 1,000 segregationists had mobbed Little Rock's all-white Central High School, forcing nine black children to abandon their attempt to attend classes there. The black students hadn't returned until President Dwight D. Eisenhower dispatched 1,200 army paratroopers to protect them.[2]

Which legion was freedom's enemy that day—the segregationists or the soldiers? Most southerners said it was the soldiers. Arkansas governor Orval Faubus accused the federal government of trampling "individual rights" and "the rights of a sovereign state." South Carolina's governor and senior U.S. senator denounced the government's assault on white citizens' "personal and property rights," especially its "invasion of their homes." Georgia's governor vowed never to "surrender our liberty and our freedom."

In the view of liberals, the freedom at stake was that of the nine black students. The government might deny the students the right to enroll at Central High School, as Faubus had done two weeks before the mob arrived. But it might also guarantee that right, as Eisenhower did in the end. In theory, the Little Rock School Board had declared the students free to enroll at their leisure. But in practice, they couldn't have exercised that freedom without government intervention. As one white student put it, "If they don't have guards with them niggers, they're going to get murdered."

Conservatives saw it differently. For them, the freedom at stake was that of white parents. The government was denying those parents the right to direct their children's education. "We're not trying to tell others what to do," the vice president of the local Mothers League insisted. "That's what we dislike—people trying to tell us what to do about our own schools." To protect white families from government intrusion, segregationists proposed, in the wake of Eisenhower's invasion, to privatize the public schools. And to avoid subsidizing a practice they despised, they sought to ban the spending of state tax money on integrated schools.

Three decades later, a few miles from the scene of that confrontation, the women behind the glass perceived the same resistance. In the illuminated chamber, men decried government intrusion in their affairs, and women bristled at laws that in the name of universal justice would, as they saw it, allow their daughters to be defiled. Such entrenched convictions—suspicion of government, love of parental sovereignty, faith in easy distinctions between angels and animals—would probably strengthen the campaign against public funding of abortion, just as they had strengthened the campaign against public funding of integration.

But perhaps the effect could be reversed. Perhaps these attitudes about government, family, and good breeding could be turned against pro-lifers. Perhaps, one of the women mused in the dark, people who didn't like the government messing with their guns or schools wouldn't like it messing with their pregnancies. The same idea dawned on another of the women as she studied the strangers in the illuminated chamber. *Let's be them.* How easy it would be to adapt the rhetoric of abortion rights to the mind-set of these voters. How easy to adopt their logic and their language. How easy to pass from this side of the glass to the other.

And how hard to come back.

The battle of Arkansas unfolded little more than a decade after *Roe v. Wade,* when advocates of legal abortion, under attack throughout the country, were realizing that the courts wouldn't protect them. They would have to defend their cause in the electoral arena, not with the subtleties of law, but with the blunt weapons of politics. This was quite a challenge, since abortion rights had never been politically secured. Before 1973 only four states had legalized abortion outright. The Supreme Court's decisions in *Roe* and its companion case, *Doe v. Bolton,* created overnight a nationwide regime of abortion rights for which no consensus had been built.

Pro-lifers spent the next decade exploiting that weakness. Their principal target was public financing of abortions for poor women. They convinced lawmakers in many states to stop covering abortions under state Medicaid programs. In 1976 Congress passed the Hyde amendment, essentially abolishing federal Medicaid coverage of abortions. In 1977 and 1980 the Supreme Court refused to block these rollbacks.

By 1984 two-thirds of the states had banned or sharply restricted the use of their funds for abortions. Of those that still subsidized abortions, one-third did so only because courts had ruled that their state constitutions required it. Even then, pro-lifers held the ultimate trump card. Most voters opposed government financing of abortions. If they engraved that judgment in their state's constitution, even the state's highest court would have to give way.

With that in mind, pro-lifers launched several ballot measure campaigns against abortion funding. Arkansas hadn't paid for abortions since 1977, but in 1984 pro-life strategists decided to go a step further. They offered Arkansas voters a state constitutional amendment against abortion funding, onto which they piggybacked a declaration of the rights of the unborn. The amendment's funding clause said, "No public funds of this state shall be used directly or indirectly to pay for all or any part of the expenses of performing or inducing an abortion," except to save the woman's life. The unborn-rights clause said, "It is the public policy of the state of Arkansas to promote the health, safety and welfare of every unborn child from conception until birth."

Until 1984 pro-choice lobbyists in Arkansas had worked backstage in the legislature, relying on personal relationships to quash pro-life forays. The ballot measure, Amendment 65, rendered that strategy moot. Defenders of abortion rights could no longer rely on back rooms or courtrooms. They would have to fight this battle in the open.

Planned Parenthood's New York office dispatched one of its top political strategists, Lydia Neumann, to Little Rock to scout the terrain. In an internal report, she observed that in other states liberal and feminist groups such as the National Organization for Women (NOW), the American Civil Liberties Union (ACLU), and the National Women's Political Caucus were "well respected." In Arkansas, however, pro-choice activists were "viewed as espousing an agenda considerably more liberal than that of the community at large." To win the election, Neumann wrote, they would have "to shift people's perception away from the notion that pro-choice was necessarily a radical position to hold." They would have to mute their feminism and marshal "other more conservative voices" for abortion rights.[3]

Two weeks before the election, as polls showed Amendment 65 heading for a landslide victory, pro-choice activists got a reprieve. The Arkansas Supreme Court struck the proposal from the ballot on the grounds that its title, "The Unborn Child Amendment," was misleading. One last time, the ACLU and the courts had rescued abortion rights from a showdown with the electorate. But everyone knew the amendment would return to the ballot in 1986. Its supporters would have to change only its title. Its opponents would have to change the minds of hundreds of thousands of voters.

In their fight against Amendment 65, pro-choicers were up against more than the pro-life lobby. A simultaneous referendum on a similar amend-

ment in Colorado showed why. The strategist in charge of the campaign
for the Colorado amendment recognized that pro-lifers weren't a voting
majority. They needed help from anti-tax voters, many of whom viewed
abortion as a private matter.[4] With that in mind, newspaper ads for the
amendment told voters that according to the U.S. Supreme Court, "the
private right to an abortion does not mean taxpayers must pay for it."[5]
A campaign flyer for the amendment asked:

> Why should any taxpayer be forced to pay the bill for those who decide to
> have an abortion at public expense? This is an unfair burden imposed on
> Coloradans who each year see their taxes grow higher and higher. Those
> who choose to have an abortion should accept the personal responsibility
> of paying for it. They have no right to expect taxpayers to foot the bill for
> a personal, private decision.[6]

After the amendment passed, Colorado's leading pollster concluded,
"The winning percentage had to do with money, not abortion." The
amendment, by his estimate, had "probably picked up the support of
15–20 percent of the voters who don't care about abortion but are
against public expenditures no matter what." Observing that similar majorities could be assembled elsewhere, Planned Parenthood predicted
that pro-life groups in other states would try to duplicate the Colorado
campaign.[7]

A national poll commissioned in 1984 by Planned Parenthood, the
National Abortion Rights Action League, and other pro-choice organizations taught the same lesson. In that survey, pollster Tubby Harrison
found that many voters who opposed banning abortion also opposed
paying for it. These two positions struck pro-choice activists as contradictory, but in fact they were connected.

Philosophically, the anti-ban and anti-funding positions followed
from the principle of minimal government involvement in private life.
The poll showed that people made this connection spontaneously. "The
reasoning used (again on an *unprompted* basis) most often by opponents of federal funding," Harrison wrote, "is that abortion is a private
matter that the government should stay out of—confirming the two-
edged nature of this argument."[8]

Politically, the anti-ban and anti-funding positions were linked by
hostility to taxes and welfare. When interviewers introduced the word
welfare into the conversation, the margin of opposition to abortion subsidies doubled. As Harrison noted, "The public opposes the use of federal funds to pay for abortions for *poor women* by 55% to 42%, with

that margin growing to 62% to 36% when the words *women on welfare* are substituted for 'poor women.' . . . [I]n the case of 'poor women,' strong opposition outweighs strong support by a little over 2 to 1; in the instance of 'welfare women,' the margin leaps to slightly more than 4 to 1."

Economic rather than moral concerns seemed to account for this reaction. When the question was rephrased, with "poor women" replaced by "women on welfare," the percentage of respondents citing moral reasons for their opposition to abortion subsidies dropped by one-fourth. Meanwhile, the percentage who rejected these subsidies on the grounds that they imposed "a burden on taxpayers" or that if the "government pays, more people will want abortions" more than doubled. Harrison concluded that "opposition to federal funding of abortions for women on welfare seems to be a mixture of opposition to abortion and opposition to government spending."

The results were even more striking when broken down by race. Blacks narrowly favored abortion funding; whites broadly opposed it. Changing the language of the question from "poor women" to "women on welfare" didn't affect blacks' feelings about abortion funding. But among whites, the margin of opposition surged from 17 to 29 percentage points.

Confronted by this latent coalition of pro-life, anti-government, anti-tax, anti-welfare, and anti-black voters, abortion rights activists had two choices. They could declare war against all of these constituencies in the name of a broad liberal agenda. Or they could divide the coalition and isolate pro-lifers by seducing the other constituencies.

In spring 1986 Lynn Paltrow, a New York ACLU attorney, came to Little Rock to counsel the first course. In a speech to abortion rights activists, she argued that the movement should stand for a society "that respects privacy but also one that takes public responsibility for all its citizens—including women."[9] Government noninterference wasn't enough. "You need to make it a requirement to talk *now* about how we can do more than maintain the status quo," she demanded. "Here the status quo is that poor women—the poorest of the poor in this state—are denied funding for abortions. We need to win public funding so that *ALL* women have the right to choose to have an abortion."

Paltrow conceded what Harrison's poll and the defeat in Colorado had shown: To win public funding, pro-choice activists would have to challenge an array of conservative beliefs. So be it, she concluded. The

pro-choice agenda was indivisible. The resentments that stood in its
way—against abortion, against taxes, against welfare—must be swept
aside by a campaign of enlightenment:

> Our opponents can only win when they link their small anti-abortion con-
> stituency to something else. So they have had some success limiting inter-
> national family planning, including abortion, by linking anti-abortion con-
> stituencies with those opposing foreign aid. And they have succeeded in
> cutting off domestic funding by linking anti-abortion constituencies with
> anti-welfare and racist constituencies.
>
> This means that in order to achieve our long term goals we will need to
> address not only anti-abortion sentiments, but also anti-welfare sentiments
> and racism.

That was one view. The woman in charge of the campaign against
Amendment 65, Brownie Ledbetter, took another. She had spent much
of her life grappling with the resentments of which Paltrow spoke. In the
1950s Ledbetter had worked in the civil rights campaign that forced the
confrontation at Central High School. In the 1960s and 1970s she had
helped to lead the fight for the Equal Rights Amendment (ERA). And
when Planned Parenthood sought her aid in defeating Amendment 65,
she answered the call.

Ledbetter was no stooge. In 1978 President Jimmy Carter appointed
her to his National Advisory Committee on Women. The committee
was cochaired by Ledbetter's friend, former representative Bella Abzug,
Democrat–New York. Six months later, when the panel warned that
Carter's policies would hurt women by raising unemployment and gut-
ting social programs, Carter fired Abzug. Ledbetter and most of the
other panelists resigned. They blasted Carter for supposing that "women
should be seen but not heard."

But Ledbetter was no radical either. She had worked in more than
twenty campaigns for political office, usually as the chief strategist.
She understood that to stage a successful rally, her friends at Arkansas
NOW needed only a few dozen feminists. To score a victory in court, her
friends at the ACLU of Arkansas needed only a few liberal judges. But
to win a statewide political campaign, she needed the support of half the
voting public.

As the second showdown with Amendment 65 approached, Ledbetter struggled to impress this point on her fellow activists. She wanted to
hire a pollster. They wanted to spend the money on getting out the vote
among the faithful. Ledbetter replied that the faithful—"all 14 feminists," she jokingly called them—would hardly suffice. She worried that

feminist rallying cries would alienate the electorate. In 1984 a prominent pro-choice activist had urged voters to oppose Amendment 65 if "we value women's ability to control their bodies and their lives." [10] Most Arkansans didn't value that agenda, and insisting that they do so was a sure way to lose.

Sandra Kurjiaka, head of the ACLU of Arkansas, wanted to mount an ACLU "public education campaign" against the amendment. Ledbetter cringed at the idea. "When issues go before the voters it is very different from the courts," she told Kurjiaka in a February 1986 letter. The two arenas "require different strategies," Ledbetter argued.

> I have shared with you our firm commitment to broaden the constituency beyond those of us, ACLU, NOW, and [the Arkansas Women's Political Caucus], who have struggled to defeat these issues over the years. There are not enough of us to win. I believe that the only way to break through the current Arkansas voters' perception of "crazies opposed to abortion" on one side and radicals "for abortion on demand" on the other is to establish a very public mainstream presence.

In Colorado, pro-lifers had established that mainstream presence. In Arkansas, they hadn't. Their literature and campaign events focused on the unborn's right to life rather than the taxpayer's right not to pay for abortions. They also burdened their amendment with an unborn-rights clause that appeared to oblige taxpayers to subsidize the "welfare of every unborn child." This was no way to build a conservative coalition. The anti-government voters who had carried pro-lifers to victory in Colorado could sink them in Arkansas.

Ledbetter knew such a flanking maneuver was possible. Late in the 1984 campaign, Lydia Neumann had hired Tubby Harrison to test various arguments against Amendment 65. Neumann thought Arkansans would be upset to learn that the amendment would halt access to birth control at public clinics. She was mistaken. They were more interested in three other arguments—that abortion should be available to rape victims, that the government should stay out of the issue, and that by funding abortions, taxpayers could avoid subsidizing pregnancies and children.[11]

The findings were tenuous. Few people had been polled, and the invalidation of the ballot measure three weeks later spared Ledbetter the task of testing the arguments in a media campaign. She didn't think Harrison understood Arkansas, but she suspected he was on to something. She wanted a more complete analysis of what the electorate was prepared to hear and how to say it.

Ledbetter had a network of friends in Washington, D.C. Her son, who
worked for the Democratic Senatorial Campaign Committee (DSCC),
had a network of his own. They drew up a list of pollsters and interviewed several for the job. Many didn't understand the Bible Belt.
Others didn't understand that women differed from men in their per-
ceptions of abortion and other issues. Only one pollster understood
both.

Harrison Hickman had been born, raised, and educated in North
Carolina. He epitomized the South's cultural stubbornness, its reverence
for God, and its irreverence for liberal anti-religious snobbery. The
Quakerism of his grandmothers, refracted through the Methodism of
his parents, had inspired his dual faith in communal morality and its
individual interpretations. His philosophy of personal autonomy came
not from the sexual revolution but from the Protestant Reformation. He
had grown up learning about the separation of church and state among
Southern Baptists who worried less about religion polluting politics
than about politics polluting religion.

Hickman's parents raised him to believe in civil rights. He learned to
get along with neighbors who saw the issue differently. They might have
some bad ideas, but they were still good people. Hickman didn't just
make peace with this sort of paradox; he thrived on it. He developed
an acid taste for irony and an acid distaste for ideologues. In college he
scorned radicals who glorified the murderous Viet Cong. When male
leaders of the anti-war movement spoke of liberation, he cast a cold eye
on their sexist treatment of subordinates.

He disdained the left's naïveté about government. The state was con-
scripting Americans into a foolish war in Southeast Asia. Why did leftists assume it would beneficently oversee the welfare programs of the
Great Society? Hickman agreed that the government could help people,
but he worried that it could reach too rashly into their wallets and
homes. The Democratic Party, his party, had lost its ironic distance from
state power. It believed too casually that politicians could solve the nation's deepest problems.

Hickman loved to dissect ideas. But beneath the mind of a philoso-
pher lurked the soul of an engineer. He wanted to analyze other people's
beliefs, not his own. He wanted to comprehend the laws of political
thought and behavior in order to exploit them.

The profession to which this interest led him, political consulting,
wasn't purely mercenary. Every consultant was expected to confine his
clientele to one party or the other. Hickman chose the Democrats since

he believed that by and large they stood for the common man against the elite.

He also adopted a professional creed grounded in a theory of democracy and its limits. On the one hand, he considered himself an instrument of democracy. In an interview with *Campaigns & Elections,* Hickman argued that although candidates or activists paid for his work, his job as a pollster was to "represent the voters' interest." [12] The pollster didn't simply manipulate voters on his clients' behalf, as critics supposed. He helped his clients discern and heed the will of the voters.

On the other hand, his job was to win and get out of the way. The pollster's domain, according to Hickman, was "elections and not governments." How the client construed or executed his mandate wasn't the pollster's ultimate concern.

Statesmanship during the election was a delicate matter. If the client's position on the central issue of the campaign was unpopular, what should the consultant do? Candidates hated to swallow their convictions, particularly on moral issues. Many imagined that their charisma would bring voters around. Media consultants who made the candidates' television ads encouraged that idea. They believed in what they sold, the power of image and emotion to transform public opinion.

Hickman rejected this poetic conceit. He was a scientist, not an artist. Voters' attitudes weren't fluid, much less impulsive. They were structured. Conclusions rested on premises, and premises were difficult, if not impossible, to move. The South's resistance to integration taught that lesson. Too many politicians and ad makers, blinded by vanity, refused to recognize that they didn't think the way most voters did.

Hickman saw one way out of this dilemma. Voters reasoned thematically rather than deductively. Their premises might be set in stone, but their conclusions weren't. The trick was to extract the candidate's conclusion from the voters' premises. It didn't matter that the candidate's route to that conclusion differed from the voters'. What mattered was that the candidate didn't have to change his position. He could simply preach a different line of reasoning to the same result. Hickman had no compunction about this tactic. He sometimes joked that he didn't care why voters pulled the lever for his candidate, even if they did it by accident.

In the early 1980s, Democratic consultants often found that their clients were more liberal than the electorate. The young pollster worried that his party, while attracting blacks and women, was losing everyone else. He understood the logic of conservatism. In a debate rehearsal during the 1984 North Carolina Senate race, he played the part of Republican senator Jesse Helms so well that he flummoxed his own client, Governor Jim Hunt.[13] In newspaper interviews, Hickman warned that liberals weren't a majority, and he spoke enviously of Reagan's talent for "running against the government."[14]

Hickman realized that this anti-government message, properly exploited, could shatter the Republican alliance between libertarians and moral conservatives. In a 1979 essay, he wrote, "American conservatism is a broad spectrum, including members supporting tenets that are philosophically contradictory. . . . The libertarians support the idea that freedom is essentially the absence of political constraint; the traditionalists argue that freedom is to be found in a stable society. In this sense, their dual existence seems incompatible."[15] But Hickman's analysis of this contradiction, using the ideas of the libertarian thinker F. A. Hayek, also implied the reverse: The same anti-government wedge, applied from the opposite direction, could shatter an alliance between libertarians and liberals. As Hickman put it,

> Hayek rejects the basic ideas of later liberals . . . who align freedom with an active state creating the material conditions in which man can most fully enjoy the advantages of liberty. Hayek believes the principal threat to freedom comes primarily from the political arena or the state. . . . He does not consider economic deprivation a serious threat to freedom. . . . Thus, freedom must be maximized by limiting the areas in which a government can meddle.[16]

Abortion rights first caught Hickman's attention not as a cause but as a study in the nuances of polling. Perusing surveys as a political science student, he was struck by the superficiality of abortion questions. The surveys asked whether respondents were for or against abortion, or whether abortion should be legal or illegal. There was no allowance for Hickman's view: against abortion but in favor of keeping it legal. As a pollster in 1981 and 1982, he saw his clients paralyzed by this dichotomy. Afraid of being labeled "pro-abortion," they falsely pleaded that they wanted to ban abortion but were thwarted by *Roe*. They didn't realize that their distaste for abortion could be reconciled with the deliberate preservation of its legality.

Hickman never saw abortion as a feminist issue. Indeed, he never saw himself as a feminist. He believed that America had oppressed women and blacks, and he had favored the ERA when North Carolina's legislature debated it during his college days. But he considered the sexual revolution and the anti-war riots of the 1960s recklessly excessive, and he viewed their association with the abortion rights movement as an unfortunate accident. Mainstream America had needlessly come to regard legal abortion as a symptom of liberalism run amok.

Hickman might never have invested much thought in the issue had another accident not transformed his career. In 1983 Martha Layne Collins, lieutenant governor of Kentucky, hired him to counsel her campaign for governor. Her victory gave Hickman a decisive credential in an emerging political market: female candidates. Over the next three years, several prominent women enlisted his help, including Senator Barbara Mikulski of Maryland and former vice presidential nominee Geraldine Ferraro of New York. Hickman's talent for absorbing foreign ways of thinking served him well. He made himself an expert in voters' assumptions about women and "women's issues" and in differences between male and female political psychology. He devoured gender-related survey data and theoretical works such as Carol Gilligan's *In a Different Voice*.

But while absorbing this new culture, Hickman never lost touch with the old one. A few weeks before the Arkansas campaign, Terry Sanford of North Carolina told Hickman a story from his 1960 campaign for governor. One day, Sanford was introduced to a rural man who was thinking of working for him. The man told Sanford that the big controversy in those parts was the "nigger issue." He asked where Sanford stood on it. Sanford replied indignantly, "You know very well where I stand on that." Mistaking this for racist solidarity, the man thanked Sanford and helped to elect him. Only later would he learn that Sanford was an enemy of segregation.

The story amused Hickman for years. What a deliciously clever answer, he thought.

From the outset of the Arkansas campaign, Hickman looked for popular assumptions he could exploit. He liked the anti-government theme suggested by Tubby Harrison's 1984 survey, but it was tricky. The contexts in which this theme flourished in Arkansas were the same as in North Carolina: gun control and desegregation. White southerners feared, loathed, and furiously resisted attempts by outsiders to confiscate their firearms or bus their kids to black schools.

Hickman believed that these contexts could be separated from the theme. He believed that many Southern Baptists had resisted federal civil rights legislation not necessarily because they were racists but because they sincerely opposed federal intrusion into families and communities.

He believed that he could steal this theme and apply it to abortion. But he also believed that he had to start where the voters were. Ledbetter agreed with him. In their first survey questionnaire, with the help of Hickman's deputy, Rich Schreuer, they distilled the argument to one sentence: "The government is threatening to take away our right to own a gun and telling us where to send our children to school, and now they want to say that women can't have abortions—even if they're raped." [17]

This wasn't the first time pro-choice strategists had portrayed abortion restrictions as government interference in private life. But it was the first time they had embraced the broader conservative implications of that theme. They hoped the embrace would serve their cause. They didn't think it would change it.

Hickman and Schreuer conducted the survey in March and wrote up the findings in a report to Ledbetter. When asked about "social issues like abortion and school prayer," nearly half of those who planned to vote in the election called themselves conservative. Only a quarter called themselves liberal. By a margin of better than two to one, voters supported Amendment 65. Hickman stated the task bluntly:

> To win the election we need to sway all of the currently undecided voters, as well as a large portion of those who are now "soft" supporters of the Amendment. When weighing the effectiveness of different arguments it is important to keep this "target group" in mind. It is less important to consider how arguments affect voters already committed to their position, than to consider their effect on the "swing" constituency that is crucial to our victory.

A battery of questions posing rationales for the amendment teased out the attitudes of these swing voters. Half responded favorably to the argument that "the mother's rights" had been elevated too far above "the rights of the unborn child." Nearly four in ten responded favorably to the suggestion that abortions were "against religion and God's will." Many embraced the idea that the amendment would "save money because it will prevent our taxes being used to fund abortions." A substantial number liked the argument that the amendment would discipline a society that "has gotten too liberal." Many favored the amendment as a way to "cut down on teenage sex."

In short, Ledbetter's instincts were correct. Talking about abortion as an issue of women's rights, taxpayer funding, sexual freedom, liberalism, or freedom from religion would lose the election. Most respondents generally opposed "the right of women to have an abortion." More than six in ten favored efforts to make sure "no state funds could be spent to directly or indirectly pay for abortions." Messages and messengers that inflamed these hostilities had to be squelched, Hickman wrote. Pro-choice advocates should avoid the word *funding* when referring to the amendment, and they should "keep the public involvement of the ACLU and NOW to a minimum."

The most effective approaches were the least radical. One was to focus on rape. Only 11 percent of respondents said abortion was acceptable "if the mother is an unwed teenager." Just 9 percent said it was acceptable if "the parents can't afford to care for" the child. But 66 percent said it was acceptable "in the case of incest or rape."

The argument about busing and gun control turned out to be even more potent. "*Government intrusion* . . . is our most effective argument," said the report. "One-third of our target voters said they were definitely less likely to support the Amendment after hearing: 'The government is threatening to take away our right to own a gun and telling us where to send our children to school, and now they want to say that women can't have abortions—even if they're raped.'" While the mention of rape moved female respondents, "the government intrusion aspect of the message ha[d] the greatest impact among men," Hickman wrote. "Younger men, and men in general, will be motivated to oppose the Amendment primarily because of their concern about government intervention in their private lives."

These arguments attracted broad support because they meant little. Tolerance of abortion in rape cases didn't entail tolerance of abortion generally. Nor did opposition to government intrusion entail respect for women's autonomy. Voters who strongly favored Amendment 65 opposed "the right of women to have an abortion," yet nearly 40 percent of these voters agreed with the statement, "Abortion is a private issue between a woman, her family and her doctor. The government should not be involved." Just because they distrusted the government didn't mean they trusted a woman to choose abortion without the consent of her husband, doctor, or clergyman.

Hickman zeroed in on this conceptual gap between the feminist minority and the conservative majority. To win the election, feminists had to cross that gap. They had to reduce abortion rights to a negative proposition. "Our goal must be to redefine the issue away from a question of rights, to one of government intrusion, privacy, and the right to an abortion in a variety of circumstances," Hickman wrote. "We must not stress the individual's right to abortion, but rather, that the government *does not* have the right to say that abortion is *never* acceptable."

Hickman added that even if his clients redefined the issue this way, their opponents could win by pointing out that Amendment 65 didn't ban abortions; it merely banned state financing of abortions, in compliance with the electorate's belief that the government should stay out of the issue. He advised Ledbetter to unleash a massive blitz of television and radio ads two weeks before the election, allowing no time for an effective rebuttal. As to Lynn Paltrow's call for a crusade against Arkansas's statutory ban on public funding, Hickman recommended the opposite. He counseled his clients to "take a conservative position" and "claim that Arkansas laws are working well now."

In late April Ledbetter summoned other pro-choice activists to discuss the poll results and the battle plan. Fireworks ensued. A black friend angrily confronted Ledbetter over the poll's slap at desegregation. Ledbetter invoked her credentials as a civil rights activist and said she was only experimenting to see whether the segregationist mentality could be diverted to good use. Janet Pulliam, chair of the Arkansas Women's Political Caucus, fielded similar complaints. While assisting the campaign, Pulliam was also litigating a school desegregation case. Her friends worried that the campaign would stoke the same sentiments she was fighting in court. Other activists called for an education project to persuade voters to oppose Amendment 65 for the right reasons. They dismissed Hickman's strategy as degrading.

Hickman had no patience for this squeamishness. His target was a voting majority, not a marginal sisterhood of the pure. He despised idealists who preferred to lose the election standing for principle. More than that, he despised their contempt for the public's way of thinking. Did they regard ordinary people as stupid or dirty? Did they consider democracy an inconvenience? Did they imagine that "education" would wash away popular folkways? At times during the focus groups, Hickman felt more at home among the participants in the illuminated room than among the observers in the dark.

In the end, Hickman's view prevailed. Some activists agreed with his sober assessment; others grudgingly accepted his advice. Strategists for NOW and the ACLU purged their literature of references to their organizations. They called themselves the "Stop Big Government Committee of Arkansas" and distributed flyers proclaiming, "KEEP BIG GOVERNMENT OUT OF BEDROOMS." ACLU director Kurjiaka wrote to a right-wing lawmaker, reminding him that "government intervention" was a hallmark of "communist, socialist or Marxist societies." The headline over NOW's newspaper ads bragged, "NOT ONE RED CENT. THAT'S HOW MUCH YOUR TAXES PAY FOR ABORTIONS." The ads assured readers that no one in Arkansas was proposing to change that policy.[18]

Far from challenging the public's resistance to welfare spending, the activists exploited it. A NOW radio ad reminded voters that the money they saved by not subsidizing abortions would be dwarfed by the cost of subsidizing pregnancies, deliveries, and children. Planned Parenthood, the ACLU, and the Arkansas Women's Political Caucus told taxpayers that the amendment would force them to subsidize prenatal care for all pregnant women. A pro-choice fund-raising letter claimed that the amendment would require "tax-supported state maternity centers" to provide "free prenatal care." According to the letter, Arkansas would become a welfare magnet for "families of child-bearing age." [19]

The campaign also spotlighted the rights of families rather than the rights of women. This was another way to reduce abortion rights to a negative proposition. The sovereignty of "the family" defined the limits of government without asserting the independence of wives or daughters. To traditionalists, it connoted parents' and husbands' rights. As a male spokesman for the campaign put it, "I'll be hanged if I'm going to surrender my rights over family decisions to the government." [20]

Like the anti-welfare argument, the family-rights argument embraced attitudes antagonistic to much of the pro-choice agenda. Four years before *Roe v. Wade,* Arkansas had granted men the authority to deny abortions to their daughters or young wives. That authority had been enjoined by the courts but never repealed. Pro-lifers wanted to restore it. Throughout the 1986 campaign, they protested that Arkansas was failing to enforce parents' authority over minors' abortions. One member of the committee sponsoring Amendment 65 complained openly that adult women were being allowed to get abortions without their husbands' consent. Pro-lifers resolved to introduce legislation requiring teenagers to get parental approval for abortions.[21] The popularity of requiring at least parental consultation was clear from Tubby Harrison's 1984 report:

> In cases involving unmarried, pregnant teenage girls, the public, by almost 3 to 1 (it is better than 4 to 1 among people who have a teenage daughter)[,] favors requiring parental notification before the abortion. Furthermore, arguing against parental notification either on the grounds that it is unnecessary (because in most cases the parents have already been brought

into the picture by the girl herself) or that this will cause many teenage girls to endanger their lives (by going to someone other than a doctor for an abortion or waiting until very late in their pregnancy) is successful only to the extent of bringing opposition down to better than 2 to 1—with nearly half the public still strongly opposed even after the arguments.[22]

The third issue of the campaign was rape. The worst thing about Amendment 65, according to pro-choice activists, was that it would prohibit public clinics and hospitals from providing abortions or morning-after pills to rape victims.[23] Focusing on rape had always been an effective pro-choice tactic, but nobody quite knew why. The reason was that it changed abortion from a welfare issue to a crime issue.

Pro-lifers often spoke of abortions for "convenience." On the surface, this meant that most women who had abortions did so for trivial reasons. As one pro-lifer put it in the *Arkansas Gazette,* "Can we really trade a life for the risk of stretch marks?"[24] But the only abortions pro-lifers consistently excluded from the "convenience" category were those that resulted from rape or incest. The rape/convenience distinction had nothing to do with protecting life. It had to do with enforcing the consequences of the choice to have sex.

Speaking in Little Rock early in 1986, a senior official of the National Right to Life Committee (NRLC) affirmed that women should reap what they sowed.[25] An Arkansas columnist agreed:

> We often hear the propaganda, offered mainly by feminist groups, that every woman's body belongs to her and that she has the right to determine how it will be used. Well, from this writer's point of view she made that determination when she placed herself in a position to mandate what she sees as a need for an abortion. . . . No woman is forced to become pregnant unless she is forcibly raped. It simply gets back to choice and responsibility. Those who would dance usually have to pay the fiddler.[26]

The involvement of tax money compounded this argument. Even if abortion remained legal, the columnist observed, "it is another thing entirely to say that taxpayers should be required to pay to correct the mistakes of others." Responsible people shouldn't have to bail out irresponsible people. That was the rationale for opposing welfare in general and for drawing a rape/convenience distinction on abortion funding in particular.

Rather than confront this distinction, abortion rights advocates in Arkansas turned it to their advantage. They persuaded voters that Amendment 65 wouldn't punish bad girls, since they were already off the dole. As one pro-choice leader put it,

> The backers of Amendment 65 tell us that its only purpose is to limit the
> use of your and my tax dollar to provide abortions of convenience to irre-
> sponsible little trollops whom they feel get pregnant for the pleasure of a
> safe abortion at taxpayer expense. If the amendment said only that, neither
> I nor most of the others now doing so would be spending our time fighting
> this amendment, for the state is not now funding abortion.[27]

Instead, pro-choicers argued, the amendment would hurt the good
girls—the ones who hadn't chosen to have sex—by halting their access
to morning-after pills. Worse, it would reward the criminals who had
impregnated them. To law-and-order voters, this was an outrage. "I believe in a strong defense and fiscal responsibility," wrote one citizen in a
letter to the *Gazette,* "[but] I don't see how you can responsibly argue
that some leftover semen from a rapist or incestuous abuser has more
rights than the victim."[28]

No one seemed less likely to view the issue that way than the ACLU,
a longtime advocate of defendants' and prisoners' rights. Yet no one argued more loudly that Amendment 65 was soft on crime. One Arkansas
ACLU pamphlet screamed, "Protect Victims of Rape and Incest. Vote
No! on Amendment 65." Another asked whether a woman should "be
forced to bear a rapist's child." On a radio program, ACLU director
Kurjiaka warned that under Amendment 65, "never in the future can
these victims of violent crimes be helped by the state of Arkansas." In a
letter to newspapers, she wrote, "We've made a good beginning in helping crime victims—let's not stop now."[29]

Ledbetter held out hope that Governor Clinton would join the campaign. She knew he was pro-choice. Bruce Lindsey, Clinton's friend, had
drawn Ledbetter into the Amendment 65 fight in the first place by putting Planned Parenthood in touch with her. Betsy Wright, Clinton's chief
political operative, had secretly coached the campaign. And just before
the state supreme court announced in 1984 that it would strike the
amendment from the ballot, Hillary Clinton had phoned the campaign
headquarters to leak the good news.

Publicly, however, Bill Clinton positioned himself as a defender of
the taxpayer's right not to subsidize abortions. In 1984 and 1985 he declared Amendment 65 harmless but pointless, observing that Arkansas
didn't pay for abortions and, under his leadership, wasn't likely to do so.
In September 1986 he questioned the implications of the amendment's
unborn-rights clause but said he had "no problem with the stated purpose" of its funding clause. In deference to taxpayers' objections, he affirmed that Arkansas "shouldn't spend state funds on abortions."[30]

From Ledbetter's standpoint, these remarks were worse than unhelpful. She had it on good authority that Clinton wanted the amendment to lose but deemed it too popular to oppose. She pleaded with Wright and sent Clinton a memo urging him to come out against the amendment. The best she could wring from him was silence. Even after the referendum, Clinton refused to say how he had voted. Six months later, in their "Guide to the Presidential Candidates," Voters for Choice and the National Abortion Rights Action League would tartly recall that Clinton had "provided no leadership against" the amendment.

In late September 1986, while Clinton was endorsing the amendment's "stated purpose," Hickman and Schreuer completed a second poll that verified the popularity of Clinton's position. A week later, Hickman flew to Little Rock to conduct the focus groups. On October 10 he and Schreuer sent Ledbetter a summary of their findings. Little had changed. Conservatives still outnumbered liberals two to one. Likely voters still opposed state funding of abortions and rejected "the right of women to have an abortion." Rape and government interference were still the most effective arguments against the amendment. And the amendment was still likely to pass by a two-to-one margin. Polls released to the media on October 14 and 21 suggested that the margin would be even wider.[31]

The election was just two weeks away.

One of the women behind the glass on September 29 was Jill Buckley, Hickman's friend and fellow Washington consultant. Having helped to write the campaign plan, Buckley was now charged with executing the final stage, a blitz of television ads making the arguments that had shown the most promise. Three impressions from the focus groups reinforced patterns in the initial poll. One was the effect of the rape question on the women; another was the extent of antigovernment feelings among the men. The third was the mistaken belief—repeatedly cited by the women as grounds to vote for Amendment 65—that Arkansas was still subsidizing abortions.

Over the next three weeks, with help from Hickman and Ledbetter, Buckley fashioned these themes into a pair of television commercials. The task of the first commercial was to neutralize the strongest argument for the amendment. The ad informed viewers that Arkansas didn't subsidize abortions—and then falsely implied that the amendment might change that policy. Buckley, Hickman, and Ledbetter would later admit that they had designed this ad to deceive viewers.

The task of the second commercial was to deliver the strongest arguments against the amendment. Somehow, it had to integrate the rape scenario with the family-versus-government theme. A teenage virgin was the perfect vehicle. To stop her from getting an abortion, the government would have to overrule her father and mother. This was an affront to traditionalists as well as feminists. Ledbetter wanted to make clear that it was also an assault on the authority of the church and the medical profession.

On the morning of October 25, Ledbetter called a press conference to launch the ad campaign. The first commercial was too crudely dishonest to parade before reporters, so she showed them the second. It opened with a chastely dressed girl walking home from school with books under her arm. "Imagine," said the male narrator. "Your fourteen-year-old child, your own sweet daughter, is raped and pregnant. She's frightened, confused, and so are you." On the screen, the girl sobbed in her mother's arms.

The narrator went on: "Imagine, too, the government says *they'll* make the decision. Never mind the circumstances. You, your doctor, your preacher, your daughter have no say in this personal, private tragedy." As he spoke, this panel of authorities appeared on the screen. The girl sat between her father and mother as a gray-haired physician explained that he couldn't help them end the pregnancy.

As the narrator enumerated the people excluded from the decision— parents, doctors, preachers—the visual image switched from a wide shot of the family and doctor to consecutive close-ups of the dismayed father and mother. The nightmare dissolved as the narrator concluded, "Don't let this bad dream become reality. Vote against Amendment 65." [32]

Ledbetter announced that the commercial would begin running the next day. Pro-lifers called the ad "a straight-out lie," noting that the amendment didn't ban abortions.[33] But Hickman had calculated correctly. With a week remaining and just $24,000 available for their own commercials, pro-lifers had no chance to launch an effective rebuttal. Buckley and Ledbetter buried their protests under $115,000 worth of television and radio advertising. Commercials pounded the amendment fifteen to twenty times a day in every corner of the state.

Five days into the bombing campaign, National Right to Life Committee president Jack Willke flew into Little Rock in a desperate attempt to halt the damage. He conceded that support for the amendment was collapsing under the onslaught. "This campaign has nothing to do with a 14-year-old rape victim," he pleaded.[34] But Willke didn't control what

the campaign was about. Hickman, Buckley, and Ledbetter did. Thanks
to their ads, the election was about what they wanted it to be about: protecting families from big government, protecting good girls from criminals, and protecting the state's ban on abortion funding from clumsy
do-gooders.

Arkansas voters flocked to the polls on November 4. At midnight the returns were still too close to call. The next morning, with only two precincts remaining to be tallied, UPI reported that the amendment would
pass by about 1,600 votes. "We are grateful to the Lord for this victory,"
said a pro-life spokesman.[35] Then United Press International reversed itself, projecting a narrow defeat. The returns continued to fluctuate. By
evening, the Associated Press was reporting that the amendment had
failed by 623 votes. A correction cut the margin to 585. Another correction cut it to 418. It took the state three weeks to resolve the outcome.
More than 635,000 ballots had been cast. Amendment 65 had failed by
519 votes.

The defeat knocked pundits off their chairs in Little Rock and Washington, D.C. "Downright phenomenal," declared the state's top political columnist. "Here we sit, forming the buckle of the Bible Belt, where
Southern Baptists and scripture-quoting football coaches roam, and half
the voters, perhaps a few more than half, said 'no' to a two-sentence an-
tiabortion proposition." NOW president Ellie Smeal lauded Ledbetter's
performance. The head of the Religious Coalition for Abortion Rights
called the win in Arkansas a virtual "miracle." Planned Parenthood
hailed it as "a special triumph in a Southern state dominated by . . . fundamentalist Christians."[36]

The war would go on, but the battle was over. For Brownie Ledbetter and the Arkansas brigade, it was time to stop the campaigning, with
its ugly devices and deceptions, and begin the healing and helping. At a
press conference after the votes were tallied, Ledbetter pleaded that
abortion not be turned into a political wedge issue. "It's not a Democratic or Republican issue or a liberal or conservative issue," she insisted.
"It's not about those things."[37]

But, of course, it was.

CHAPTER 2

Privacy and Prejudice

In another illuminated chamber, Harrison Hickman sat at the near end of the table, his back to the reflective glass. It was another circle of southerners, another conversation about abortion. This time, the eyes that watched from the darkness belonged not to Brownie Ledbetter but to Kate Michelman, executive director of the National Abortion Rights Action League. She was here to figure out how to sabotage President Reagan's nomination of Judge Robert Bork to the U.S. Supreme Court. Through Hickman, and now through Michelman, the brain trust of the pro-choice movement was absorbing the lesson of the Arkansas campaign: Abortion rights, traditionally dismissed as a liberal idea, could be repackaged and sold to conservatives.

The voters in this focus group supported Reagan's agenda and wanted the Supreme Court to represent his views. When Hickman raised the possibility that Bork might ignore laws against racial discrimination, they were unmoved. Instead they worried that civil rights laws would lead to discrimination against whites. They thought stricter abortion laws would help to restore moral discipline. They chafed at the idea of letting high school students get abortions without telling their parents. But when Hickman suggested that Bork's ascent to the Court might threaten not just the right to abortion but the larger principle of privacy as well, they began to doubt Bork's fitness for the job.

Michelman, a newcomer to national politics, was making great strides in her understanding of public opinion. To begin with, she was recognizing a gender-based division in pro-choice thinking. Women in these focus groups spoke of choice in personal, affirmative terms. Freedom, as they saw it, meant that each woman could make her own decision. Men, on the other hand, interpreted freedom as the absence of state intervention. They spoke of choice in negative terms, reasoning that the government had no business prying into family affairs.

Michelman was also witnessing a troubling conclusion to which the latter interpretation of freedom could lead. As in Arkansas, some white participants in the Alabama focus groups criticized the government for presuming to tell them not only whether they could have abortions but also with whom they and their children had to socialize in schools and restaurants.

The racial allusion was ironic. Seven weeks earlier, Senator Ted Kennedy of Massachusetts had launched the liberal attack on Bork by declaring, "Robert Bork's America is a land in which women would be forced into back-alley abortions [and] blacks would sit at segregated lunch counters." The discussions in Birmingham implied the opposite. Kennedy, like Lynn Paltrow in Arkansas, had erred strategically in challenging the whole conservative agenda. If Bork's enemies attacked private segregation, they would alienate voters whose love of privacy might prove useful. The antigovernment spirit of segregation, properly cultivated, could defeat Bork's nomination and thereby preserve legal abortion. Robert Bork's America could be turned against itself.[1]

This was a hard lesson for Michelman. In 1964 she had brought a contingent of civil rights activists to Alabama. She had marched, alongside an amputee on crutches, from Selma to Montgomery. Pregnant with her second child and her first not yet a year old, she had endured her father's chastisement for endangering her family. She had slept in the home of a black woman whose hospitality later cost the woman her job.[2] To Michelman, the principles at stake then were the same principles at stake today: freedom, dignity, civil rights.

Battlegrounds of those days lay all about her. A few miles from this room, Birmingham police commissioner Bull Connor had shattered a civil rights demonstration with attack dogs and high-pressure hoses that ripped clothes from the bodies of onlookers. Forty miles to the west,

Governor George Wallace had stood in a doorway at the University of Alabama, denouncing the intrusion of the federal government and barring the entry of two black students and an assistant U.S. attorney general. Ninety miles to the south, the arrest of Rosa Parks had triggered the bus boycott that brought Martin Luther King Jr. to the forefront of the movement. On a nearby bridge, troopers wielding clubs and tear gas had battered a column of civil rights marchers.

Two decades later, the icons of that era remained. The Reverend Jesse Jackson, who had stood a few yards from King at the moment of King's assassination, had come to Alabama within the past month to pay his respects to the reformed and ailing Wallace. With the support of Alabama's present governor and two-thirds of the state's white voters—and against the wishes of a comparable majority of blacks—the Confederate stars and bars still flew over the statehouse in Montgomery where a century earlier Jefferson Davis had been sworn in as president of the Confederacy.

The tyranny and indifference of the past hadn't vanished. They had merely withdrawn behind a veil of privacy, a conviction that men had no business minding each other's affairs. That principle, with all its protections and perils, had survived the passage from the age of tradition to the age of freedom. The spirit of the state motto still reigned: We Dare Defend Our Rights.

Behind the veil of privacy, discrimination persisted. Alabama ranked last in the country in public school spending per pupil. Across the state's "Black Belt," white flight to private academies, known as "seg schools," had left many public school systems destitute. Political rights had failed to secure economic equality. Two decades after segregation by choice had replaced segregation by law, the percentage of businesses owned by blacks, compared to the black percentage of the population, was lower in Birmingham than in any other city in America.[3]

Religious bigotry, too, masqueraded as freedom. A few months earlier, a judge in Mobile, siding with Wallace and local parents, had banned forty-five textbooks from public schools on the grounds that they promoted "secular humanism" over Christianity. "It's a great day for religious freedom," the attorney for the Christian parents had exulted. His antagonist, former Birmingham congressman John Buchanan, now chaired the civil liberties group People for the American Way. Buchanan believed that the Christian parents were treading on the religious freedom of other parents and children. But at a press conference in Mobile, he charged instead, in the style of Wallace and Faubus, that "a federal court" had unduly "injected itself into the curriculum of the public schools."[4]

For women, little government meant little progress. In its seventy-four years, the Birmingham Rotary Club had never admitted a woman. Nor was poverty a public concern. The state's Medicaid rules for expectant mothers were the harshest in the nation. A family of three earning barely $1,400 a year failed to qualify for Medicaid coverage of the woman or her child. Ninety-seven percent of the families covered by Alabama's Aid to Dependent Children program were headed by single women. Ninety-four percent had no other source of income. For the average family in that program—a mother and two children—the monthly check was $118, about a third of the national average. Alabama led the country in infant mortality.[5]

Many women rued another double-edged corollary of privacy, the inviolability of the family. Absent a warrant, state law permitted police to arrest a man for domestic abuse only if they witnessed the assault or believed, as they seldom did, that it merited a felony charge. Women's requests for warrants in such cases were often rebuffed. Despite three years of debate in the legislature, marital rape still wasn't a crime under Alabama law.[6]

If, through some folly or misfortune, a young woman in Alabama were to get pregnant in the wrong circumstances, she could count on two things. No matter how poor she might be, the state wouldn't help her pay for an abortion unless the pregnancy threatened directly to kill her. That was Alabama's idea of keeping government out of the abortion business. And unless she was at least eighteen years old or a judge dared to intervene on her behalf, she couldn't get the abortion without the written consent of her mother or father. That was Alabama's idea of entrusting abortion decisions to families.[7]

An outsider looking into this world might imagine how such indifference to economic circumstance and such reverence for family authority would constrict the choices available to poor and young women. But Michelman didn't need to imagine that consequence. She had lived it.

In 1970, Michelman was raising three preschool daughters at her home in central Pennsylvania. One day her husband announced that he had found another woman. He walked out and took the family car, leaving his wife destitute. She discovered that the burden of single motherhood elicited not sympathy but stigma. Unmarried and without a financial record in her name, she was refused credit. She ended up on welfare.

She had hardly caught her breath when she realized she was pregnant. Another child? Now? The idea seemed absurd. She wasn't opposed to having a fourth child; she had wanted six. But months of pregnancy and another mouth to feed under these conditions would destroy what remained of her ability to support her family. Not in defiance of motherhood, but out of what she saw as respect for it, she resolved to stop the pregnancy.[8]

Hard as the choice was, effecting it was harder. Abortion was illegal in Pennsylvania, but at each hospital a committee of doctors held the power to grant exceptions. Before a panel of men she had never met, Michelman pleaded that she couldn't cope with an additional child. With their mercy secured, one final indignity remained. Under state law, she had to track down the man who had deserted her and get his written consent to the abortion.

Michelman had never cared much about the women's movement. Its leaders seemed hostile to men and motherhood, which she valued. Her crisis changed her. She saw how little respect a poor, single woman commanded. In her dilemma and her struggle to exercise her choice, she saw the plights of other women. Three years afterward, when she read the words of Justice Harry Blackmun's opinion in *Roe v. Wade,* she spilled tears for what she had endured, for what others had endured in the abortion underground, and for what her daughters would be spared. In a letter to Blackmun, she poured out her gratitude for the end of an era of degradation.

With help from her parents, Michelman climbed out of poverty. In 1978 she built a program for troubled preschool children in rural Pennsylvania. Budget cuts killed the project in 1980, so she turned to reproductive health care, a service she deemed crucial to family stability and child welfare. Her platform was the directorship of Tri-County Planned Parenthood in Harrisburg, the state capital. Her clients were largely poor and rural, with little access to medical care. She relished the opportunity to help. She frequented the clinics and counseled patients.

Tri-County Planned Parenthood offered contraceptives, but Michelman thought the moral and practical approach was to offer women the full range of reproductive options. She introduced services aimed at childbirth, such as prenatal care, genetic screening, and infertility treatment. Abortion proved the thorniest issue. The chapter's board feared controversy and fund-raising trouble. Michelman persisted, and the board gradually relented.

With her office just two doors from the governor's mansion, she became embroiled in the legislature's abortion wars. In 1981 Pennsylvania's leading pro-lifer, state representative Steven Freind, introduced the restrictive Abortion Control Act. Michelman fought it, only to see it passed and signed by Governor Dick Thornburgh in 1982. She discovered that Catholic Democrats could be her fiercest enemies and that secular Republicans, among them the president of the state senate and the chairwoman of the state Republican Party, could be her staunchest allies.

On November 15, 1983, the Pennsylvania House of Representatives considered a bill that would for the first time make the rape of one's spouse a crime like any other rape. Michelman watched from the gallery as Freind rose to speak in favor of an amendment to weaken the bill. He opened with a joke: "I have never forced myself on my wife; instead, I paid her each time." [9]

Michelman was outraged on behalf of every woman within earshot. What astonished her more, however, was the contempt of this man for his wife. To dehumanize women in the abstract was easy. But to dehumanize one's sworn life partner in such a public way reflected a pathology of a different order. As Michelman stared in amazement, Freind's next words slipped by her: "You know, people accuse me, on the pro-life bills, of trying to put government into people's bedrooms. Now, the last time I checked, you did not perform abortions in people's bedrooms. But this bill . . . places government right in the bedrooms of married couples."

A year later, when the legislature finally passed a marital rape bill, Thornburgh vetoed it. "I am concerned that with this bill [the government] would be entering into the privacy of the home and the sanctity of an ongoing marriage," he explained.[10] This cornerstone of conservatism—that the government should stay out of family matters—had long served Michelman's enemies. Now it would serve her.

In 1985 NARAL began searching for a new executive director. Michelman was on the board of its Pennsylvania affiliate. Her name was passed along, and she soon got a phone call. The idea of taking the job struck her as absurd, well beyond her ability. But her recruiters persisted, and by year's end she was preparing to take NARAL's reins.

In her farewell speech on January 22, 1986, the thirteenth anniversary of *Roe,* Michelman told her Harrisburg colleagues, "I feel like I have one foot in each world." Behind her lay the "world of providing reproductive health care." Ahead lay the "world of nationwide politics."

The old world, she recalled, had taught her to care most for the young and the poor.

> I have seen firsthand the great need for affordable, accessible family planning services and reproductive health care for women and men of all ages. I have talked with and counseled teen-agers who are ill prepared to become mothers. . . . I will do everything I can to preserve that right [to abortion]— and particularly to preserve and protect the rights of teenagers needing access to abortion and poor women, who are currently denied Medicaid-funded abortions in this and many other states.[11]

Drawing together her professional and personal history, she resolved to incorporate abortion rights in a feminist agenda. Abortion, she explained,

> is really about the value of women in our society. If a woman cannot plan her reproductive life, she is not free to make and carry out life-shaping decisions about work, education, marriage, family, home, health and happiness. . . . The pro-choice movement . . . has always understood the need not only for reproductive choice, but for fair wages, equal educational opportunity and other necessities for a full and productive life.

The organization Michelman inherited was recuperating from a three-year battle. Stung by the defeat of a federal abortion ban and a constitutional amendment to overturn *Roe,* pro-lifers had launched a campaign in 1983 to focus attention on the humanity of the fetus. Their central weapon was *The Silent Scream,* a film that depicted the abortion of a twelve-week fetus in wrenching detail.

NARAL countered in 1985 with an effort to draw sympathy away from fetuses and toward the women in whose bodies abortions took place. Organizers of the "Silent No More" campaign urged women to tell the stories of their abortions, legal or illegal. The campaign aimed to connect Americans personally with the difficulty of abortion decisions, the conscientiousness of the women who made them, and the horrors of illegal abortions. Sixty thousand women responded with letters to NARAL. Thousands told their stories in public forums. NARAL considered it a stirring success.

Michelman had participated in the "Silent No More" campaign and recognized its importance, but she wanted to move NARAL's rhetoric and image into the political mainstream. By "mainstream," she meant less emphasis on abortion and more on women's equality, birth control, and sex education. But two tremors in Washington during her first year awakened her to *Roe*'s precariousness and to the perils of coupling abortion rights with women's rights.

Pennsylvania's Abortion Control Act had followed her to Washington. Two months before her arrival, in *Thornburgh v. American College of Obstetricians and Gynecologists of Pennsylvania,* the Supreme Court had heard arguments over the law's constitutionality. No administration since 1954 had dared to ask the Court to overturn a landmark decision, but that was what Reagan's Justice Department now asked the Court to do to *Roe.*

On June 11, 1986, the Court struck down the Pennsylvania law and reaffirmed *Roe* by a single vote. Blackmun's majority had dwindled from seven justices to five. Michelman began to see that *Roe* was mortal. Six days later Reagan called a news conference to drop three more bombshells. Chief Justice Warren Burger had resigned. Reagan was nominating Justice William Rehnquist, a critic of *Roe,* to succeed him. And to fill the post vacated by Rehnquist, Reagan had chosen appellate judge Antonin Scalia, an adamant foe of the constitutional right to abortion.

While civil rights groups scrambled to derail the nominations, NARAL tried to bring *Roe* into the debate as a women's issue. Testifying before the Senate Judiciary Committee, Michelman and NARAL board chair Karen Shields depicted *Roe* as a crucial link in "the continuum of progress in women's rights." In August Michelman wrote to senators asking them to oppose Rehnquist out of respect for "women's health and women's lives." [12] Her appeals failed. Rehnquist won Senate confirmation on a 65 to 33 vote; Scalia sailed through 98 to 0. To make abortion rights a compelling issue, NARAL needed a message that reached beyond feminists.

That summer Michelman got her first taste of a common Washington dilemma—a debate between purists and pragmatists over the wisdom of compromise. The question on the table was how to get Congress to extend Medicaid to cover abortions for poor women. Strategists for several pro-choice organizations had crafted a plan to divide and conquer their opponents incrementally. In the first year, pro-choicers would propose to extend abortion coverage only to pregnancies caused by rape or incest. In subsequent years, they would try to extend coverage to other pregnancies.

Michelman liked the plan, but some NARAL officers objected that it would reinforce a simplistic distinction between "innocent" women—those who had been victimized by criminals—and other women, who were presumed to have engaged in sex irresponsibly. According to the objectors, the first stage of the plan, by isolating rape cases and justifying abortion coverage on grounds that applied only to those cases, wouldn't help and might hinder the second.

After giving it some thought, Michelman settled on a compromise. NARAL would support the incremental strategy but would pursue it in language that united women's reasons for abortions. In a memo to NARAL's state affiliates, she argued that legislation applying only to rape or incest "would appeal to the 'middle ground,' the group that most often waivers on abortion funding." [13] She explained, "Polling data consistently shows that there is not strong majority public support for funding. The incremental approach is designed to use those areas where there is strongest public support for the legality and morality of abortion as the foundation for a campaign that will restore *all* funding."

Michelman pledged to promote this legislation with "messages that talk about women taking control of [their] lives," adding that NARAL should "work to limit the use of women-as-victim images."

> This is an opportunity to make clear that the oppression of women which leads to rape and incest and other violence is the same oppression which wants to restrict women's control of our reproductive lives. We support funding for abortion for women pregnant as a result of rape and incest because it is a way for women to take control of our lives again, not because we are trying to focus on victims. We should avoid implying that there is a particular horror to these pregnancies that is not there for other unwanted pregnancies or that this is somehow a "better" reason for funding than other reasons.

The incremental strategy scored a partial victory. In August a Senate committee narrowly voted to exempt victims of rape or incest from the Medicaid ban. But in September the exemption was dropped in exchange for continued federal support of family planning programs.[14] A week later the Senate confirmed Rehnquist and Scalia. The year looked like a disaster.

Then, in early November, came the pro-choice sweep of the four state ballot measures. Michelman was ecstatic. How had activists in these states, particularly the beleaguered battalion in Arkansas, prevailed? Could the secrets of their success be exploited in future campaigns? NARAL invited strategists from each state to a conference in Washington in December. The contingent from Arkansas included Ledbetter, ad maker Jill Buckley, and Hickman's deputy, Rich Schreuer.

At the conference, Ledbetter explained how her team had steered the debate in Arkansas away from abortion toward the broader question of government intrusion. She stressed that the campaign's leaders had shunned feminist rhetoric. Instead, they had relied on a game plan designed by professionals, based on polls and focus groups. They had worked in concert with public opinion, not against it. They had won with their heads, not their hearts.

Schreuer described what his polls had found. Most Arkansas voters were in the middle. They considered abortion immoral but soured on abortion restrictions when the question was framed in terms of government intrusion. They opposed abortions for "convenience" but wanted exceptions in extreme cases such as rape. Talking about government interference was the most effective approach for persuading men; talking about rape was the most effective approach for women.

Buckley explained how she had used these findings to select themes and images for her ads. She admitted that her second commercial, which had portrayed Amendment 65 as a threat to Arkansas's preexisting ban on abortion funding, was designed to confuse voters. Essentially, the ad had encouraged people to vote against abortion subsidies. But Buckley emphasized that her first ad, the one about the teenage rape victim, had turned the tide. She said she had chosen the rape theme because of its powerful effect on women in Hickman's focus group.[15]

Michelman had kept an eye on the Arkansas campaign throughout the year. Its success greatly impressed her. She knew she lacked experience in national politics. She wanted a strategist on whose judgment she could rely—not a sidekick or a soul sister, but a professional who could tell her things she didn't know and would say things she didn't want to hear. The job required not just technique, but temperament: a mixture of diplomacy, audacity, realism, and faith. Hickman had it all. His reputation among Michelman's friends was superb, and his performance in Arkansas made the decision easy.[16]

A few weeks after the conference, Hickman got his first assignment. The task was to persuade politicians that the ballot measures amounted to a national referendum on abortion. "We believe the voters have spoken—and we are looking to you to support their mandate," Michelman told senators in a letter. She attached a memo from Hickman explaining the victory in Arkansas:

> Our polling determined that in late September 58% of the voters in
> Arkansas said they approved of the Constitutional Amendment restricting

abortion. . . . However, while most voters believe that there may be too many abortions, they do not favor government restrictions. . . . 65% agree with the statement: "Abortion is a private issue between a woman, her family and her doctor—the government should not be involved."

Prior to the November election an anti-Amendment coalition ran advertisements which demonstrated that if the Amendment passed it would take the power to make decisions about abortion away from the family. Following these advertisements voters no longer saw the initiative as a means to register a complaint about too many abortions, but accurately saw it as a means of giving the government power to restrict a family's options regarding abortion. When perceived in this light the Amendment went down to defeat.[17]

The political marriage of Michelman to Hickman—and, through it, the nationalization and systematization of this way of talking about abortion rights—was the most important turning point in the debate since *Roe*. *Government* and *family* had always been part of the lexicon of the abortion rights movement but never its fundamental dichotomy. Those words had anchored the rhetoric of the right, not the left. Hickman and Michelman would make them the watchwords of a new pro-choice regime. By April 1987, in a discussion at the American Enterprise Institute, Hickman was already formulating the strategy. He would change the abortion question from "Are you for it or against it?" to "Who should make the choice?"[18]

The marriage was happily incongruous. Hickman's gruffness sometimes pained Michelman, but she treasured his insight, candor, and faith in the moral seriousness of abortion decisions. Michelman's political naïveté sometimes amazed Hickman, but he respected the integrity that lay behind it. And when decisions had to be made, he found her instincts commendably practical.

Hickman shared Michelman's frustration with the movement's isolation. He, too, wanted to reconnect it to mainstream America. But his understanding of mainstream America differed from hers. She looked for common aspirations to which abortion rights could be related. He looked for common fears and resentments. She envisioned a coalition for high-minded reform. He envisioned a coalition against high-minded mischief. She wanted to polish the message. He wanted to sharpen it. She saw government as a guarantor of rights. He saw it, through voters' eyes, as a threat.

Hickman didn't mince words. He told Michelman that the average voter saw pro-choice activists as a bunch of nuts locked in a shouting match with the nuts on the other side. When she slipped into activist-speak—describing abortion decisions as empowering, for example—he winced and corrected her. Maybe that kind of talk would go over in feminist circles, but most Americans wouldn't stand for it. Like Ledbetter, Michelman would have to learn to communicate with people who shared few of her premises—feminism, public assistance, enforced integration—but could be persuaded, for other reasons, to keep abortion legal.

Michelman's expansive designs were in full bloom in the heady days after the 1986 elections. She and her staff spent spring 1987 developing a "Reproductive Bill of Rights" that would enlarge the term *pro-choice* to include "genuine concern for the quality of life of women, children and families." In a draft of the plan, Michelman's deputy, Debra Ness, rejoiced that pro-choice activists need "no longer devote all [their] energies to fighting off" bans on abortion.[19]

Meanwhile, NARAL was planning its annual conference. The theme was "Abortion Rights: A Vision for the 1990's and Beyond." Feminist theorists were invited to discuss the future of the pro-choice movement and its place in the march of progress. A workshop called "Beyond the Right to Privacy: Abortion in the Context of Women's Rights" was to address the question, "How do we move from privacy to equality, from abortion rights to full reproductive rights, from the rights of some women to the rights of all women?" The major practical topic of the conference was to be the restoration of abortion funding for poor women.

Two weeks before the conference was to open, Justice Lewis Powell resigned from the Supreme Court. So much for expanding the pro-choice agenda. In *Thornburgh,* Powell had provided the fifth vote to reaffirm *Roe.* To fill his place, Reagan selected Judge Robert Bork. A nominee more certain to overturn *Roe* could scarcely be imagined.

Michelman declared a "state of emergency," and NARAL transformed its convention to confront the crisis. The threat to *Roe* galvanized the activists in a way that marginal, incremental, and often losing battles, such as the fight for abortion funding, seldom did. Other issues vanished. The conference "was originally planned to map our strategy for the next ten years," Michelman remarked afterward. "Instead, we set our strategy for the next ten weeks."[20]

In her keynote speech, conceived before the change of plans, Michelman described the world of her dreams:

I have a vision. . . . It is a vision of a truly pro-choice America. Not just an America where women have the legal right to choose abortion, but an America where women have the social and economic freedom to choose from a full range of reproductive options. . . . [P]ublic funding of abortion has always, and will always, be such a top priority for our organization. We know the difference between a real choice and the least disastrous option. We know that for a welfare mother of six living on $400 a month, the "right" to have a $250 abortion is no right at all. She doesn't have the choice to have an abortion, just as she doesn't have the choice to go back to school or the choice to feed her children three square meals a day. . . . We must talk about the social and economic conditions under which choices are made.[21]

To address these conditions of choice, NARAL would fight not just for privacy but for government activity:

We must insist that contraceptives be safe, reliable, and accessible. We must help women get the counseling they need. . . . We must lend our voices to the demands for adequate pre-natal and post-natal care. We must join the call for improved health care for women and their children, for effective nutrition programs and for affordable child care. . . . When groups get together to talk about economic equity, we should be there. When groups get together to talk about child care and nutrition issues, we should be there.

Beyond this vision, and beneath the abstract principles Michelman invoked, lay a narrative way of thinking that few male politicians, campaign consultants, or legal scholars understood. "Yes, of course, we must continue to make the arguments about constitutional liberties that we've been talking about," she conceded. "But it is also our job to remember [each] woman. It's not really even an argument, but a collection of stories—stories of women who have faced the abortion choice thoughtfully, painfully, and morally."

But Michelman knew that in the political arena, such contextual moral appeals would never do. In search of a simpler and more familiar rationale for freedom of choice, she turned to the Constitution:

It guarantees our rights . . . in a sort of round-about way—by carving out those spheres of American life which are off-bounds to state regulation. It defines what we *can* do by telling the government what it *cannot* do. . . . We simply contend that it should be a woman and her family, not the state, who should provide the answers.

This was a trap. The argument's familiarity came from Reagan, and its simplicity led to Reaganism. By equating liberty's expansion with government's contraction, Michelman was embracing the fallacies of

Reagan's Law. First, "telling the government what it cannot do" hardly clarified "what we can do." Who was "we"? Was it everybody except the government? Or was it particular people? Was it just women, or did it include husbands? Was it just teenagers, or did it include parents? If a wife disagreed with her husband, or if a teenager disagreed with her parents, which side should prevail—the "woman" or "her family"? Michelman and her liberal colleagues agreed with conservative voters in Arkansas and Alabama that the government should stay out. What they didn't agree on was the meaning of "we."

Second, by defining "we" as the alternative to "the government," Michelman, like Reagan, was obscuring the plight of people who needed public assistance to exercise their rights. Why should "we" pay money to "the government" for their abortions? For that matter, why should we pay for their prenatal care? If women, not the state, were responsible for "providing the answers" to the abortion question, why shouldn't they provide the answers to the question of how to pay for it?

Had NARAL's conference focused on public funding, as originally planned, these perils might have stood out more clearly. But the threat of losing *Roe* overshadowed them. "We must concentrate all our immediate energies into defeating Bork," Michelman argued in her closing remarks to the conference. "We must stop the nomination at all costs." [22]

The coalition of interest groups arrayed against Bork wasn't eager to work with NARAL. The Leadership Conference on Civil Rights, a league of organizations that packed most of the coalition's clout, was led by labor unions and civil rights groups whose attitudes toward abortion ranged from discomfort to disdain. The backbone of the Leadership Conference, the National Association for the Advancement of Colored People (NAACP), relied on black clergymen, many of whom were morally conservative. Black leaders also remembered the eugenic bent of the early birth control movement. They knew that some support for abortion came from whites who wanted to suppress the black birthrate. Leaders of women's groups blamed the rift on a third factor: sexism in the hierarchy of the civil rights movement.

Unions dominated by Catholic, blue-collar men also frowned on abortion. The United States Catholic Conference, a powerful member of the Leadership Conference, refused to collaborate with abortion rights groups. All of these points of friction had been exposed the year before, when the Leadership Conference, in an effort to squeeze a civil rights bill through Congress, had pressured pro-choice groups to accept an amendment that excluded abortion rights from federally protected civil rights. Now, as Michelman angled for a prominent role in the anti-Bork coalition, the unpleasantness returned.

Bork's record suggested an obvious solution. He rejected not just *Roe* but also the 1965 decision on which it was based, *Griswold v. Connecticut.* In *Griswold,* the Court had ruled that the Constitution implicitly recognized a "right to privacy" that barred government intrusion into marital questions such as the use of contraceptives. Bork denied that the Constitution established this right. His judicial quarrel wasn't with abortion but with the underlying doctrine of privacy. Within hours of his nomination on July 1, People for the American Way, the NAACP, and Leadership Conference director Ralph Neas stepped forward to decry Bork's views on "privacy."[23] A new issue was born.

This formulation didn't satisfy Michelman. In meetings with pro-choice and feminist leaders, she weighed in for a forceful attack on Bork's threat to abortion rights. Some of the more seasoned players sympathized with her impatience. Others were annoyed. Several assuaged and coached her. They told her that compromise was necessary to preserve the coalition and that abortion rights could be included in the campaign through the language of privacy.

The woman who became Michelman's closest adviser was Ann Lewis, a consultant to the coalition and a member of its steering committee. Lewis was a left-wing feminist. Convinced that men were screwing up the world, she had spent much of her career working in Congress, interest groups, and campaigns to put women in power. She had just finished a stint as director of Americans for Democratic Action, an organization synonymous with liberalism.

Temperamentally, however, Lewis was measured and disciplined. Two decades in the political trenches, including four years as political director of the Democratic National Committee, had sharpened her tactical judgment. Her mind was quick and her wit biting, but prudence restrained her tongue when adjacent egos, usually male, threatened to rupture. Given the coalition's misgivings, privacy seemed to her an artful way to talk about reproductive rights.

Others in the Leadership Conference saw privacy as a way to muffle the abortion issue. They feared being portrayed as a gang of special interests. Abortion, with its patina of loose morals and militant feminism, struck them as the issue most likely to alienate middle America from their campaign. Some wanted to focus on Bork's criticisms of civil rights laws. Many thought the public would be outraged to learn that Bork had fired Watergate special prosecutor Archibald Cox on the orders of President Richard Nixon in 1973. Privacy, when raised as a possible theme at strategy meetings, was ignored.

Lewis didn't suffer this treatment gladly. She concluded that the men around the table didn't recognize the broad appeal of abortion rights and weren't listening to the women in their midst who did. The simplest remedy was to prove that appeal in focus groups. By commissioning this research and analyzing its findings for the coalition, NARAL could establish itself as a serious player.

Michelman liked the idea. She was tired of promising to be a good girl. It was time to take charge. She knew who she wanted to run the focus groups. The next question was where to convene them. Arlen Specter, the pivotal Republican on the Senate Judiciary Committee, was from Pennsylvania. But the key votes on the Senate floor belonged to southern Democrats, and the only southern Democrat on the Judiciary Committee was Howell Heflin of Alabama.[24]

On July 29 Michelman and Lewis accompanied Hickman to Philadelphia for the first two focus groups. Women in these sessions seemed more disturbed than men by the prospect of losing abortion rights. What bothered the participants most was the impression that Bork was an extremist. Two weeks later in Birmingham, Michelman saw what Ledbetter had seen: a roomful of southern white men poised, at the first hint of meddling, to slam their doors in the government's face.[25]

Other coalition pollsters reached similar conclusions. Focus groups in Atlanta, conducted by Peter Hart on behalf of People for the American Way, confirmed that government interference was a potent issue among southern white conservatives. A nationwide survey taken by Tom Kiley for organized labor found that Bork's rejection of the constitutional right to privacy damaged his standing with 73 percent of voters.

Kiley's data illustrated the importance of framing abortion as an issue of big government rather than women's rights. While slightly more than 60 percent of voters endorsed the Supreme Court's judgment "that a woman has a constitutional right to choose abortion," more than 80 percent agreed "that abortion should be a private matter, one that is not subject to government interference." In Alabama, only 42 percent endorsed a woman's right to abortion, but 71 percent agreed that the matter was "best left up to a woman and her doctor without government interference." In his summary, Kiley argued that the South, despite its love of Reagan, could be turned against Bork.[26]

Members of the coalition had been calling Bork a radical since July. But no group had claimed the mantle of conservatism more openly than NARAL had. In an August 10 *New York Times* commentary, Michelman and former NARAL board president Robin Chandler Duke charged that Bork wasn't "a mainstream conservative," since he respected neither privacy nor tradition. "Judge Bork's refusal to recognize *any* realm of personal privacy and autonomy," they wrote, "should be troubling to conservatives and liberals alike."

Kiley's poll, coupled with the reports from Hickman and Hart, turned these bipartisan forays into a full-scale assault. Hickman and Kiley presented their findings to the coalition in mid-August. Lewis and Michelman underscored the power of the privacy issue in a meeting with Nikki Heidepriem, the coalition's chief message strategist. By August 28 Heidepriem had translated Kiley's findings into a memo telling activists around the country how to make the case against Bork. Polls "suggest that the key to the public debate over the Bork nomination will be whether he is an 'extremist' or simply a conservative closer to the judicial mainstream," Heidepriem wrote. The way to isolate Bork from conservative voters and senators was to chastise him for rocking the boat. "Bork's writings," she explained, proved "that he intends to be an 'activist' judge, an attribute Senator Heflin said . . . he would object to in a nominee."[27]

On August 29 the American Civil Liberties Union voted to oppose Bork, calling him "more radical than conservative." Two weeks later Planned Parenthood argued in newspaper ads, "[Bork] thinks the government is free to dictate what you can and can't do in highly personal and intimate matters. . . . Bork sees the Court not as a problem-solver, guided by past decisions, but as a reckless trouble-maker, aggressively seeking ways to upset past rulings he thinks are wrong." In a television ad aired that week by People for the American Way, actor Gregory Peck cautioned viewers that Bork "doesn't believe the Constitution protects your right to privacy."[28]

As the confirmation hearings opened on September 15, liberal senators picked up the tune. Senator Howard Metzenbaum of Ohio asserted that whereas "Justice Powell was a conservative justice," Bork was "likely to tip the Court radically." Senator Kennedy, the prince of liber-

alism, called Bork "an activist" rather than "a real judicial conservative." Metzenbaum's opening statement zeroed in on privacy; Kennedy
began his interrogation of Bork with a long lecture on it.[29]

The man at the center of this strategy, and the key bridge from left to
right, was Senator Joe Biden of Delaware, the Democratic chairman of
the Judiciary Committee. Biden had been running for president for two
years. His advisers included Tom Kiley's partner, John Marttila, and Pat
Caddell, an eccentric pollster widely credited with masterminding the
1972 Democratic presidential nomination of George McGovern and the
1976 election of President Carter. Caddell had always believed that Reagan's traditionalism on sex and religion didn't sit well with most voters.
In Bork he saw the perfect foil, an opportunity to make Biden the pre-
eminent foe of an arrogant religious right.

Powell resigned two weeks after Biden announced his candidacy.
Thereafter, Biden used speeches, campaign events, and television ap-
pearances to stress the "social issues" on which Reagan ran afoul of
privacy. Liberal activists who met with Biden a week after Bork's nomination learned, to their surprise, that he was ready to lead the opposition. In August Biden invited Senator Bennett Johnston of Louisiana, a
conservative Democrat, to lead a vanguard of southern senators against
Bork. Toward the end of the month, Caddell arrived to help Biden prepare for the hearings.[30]

Two days before the hearings opened, Biden rehearsed his performance for six hours at his home. His aides videotaped the performance
to see how it would come across on television. When the hearings began, he repeatedly framed the Bork vote as a referendum on privacy and
the rights of the individual. He underscored concerns that Bork would
fulfill the agenda of the religious right. His reward was a prized spot on
the evening news, in which he charged that Bork's jurisprudence would
allow police to invade couples' bedrooms. Bork was no liberal, but,
Biden added, he was no conservative either.[31]

Michelman saw Biden's attack as smart politics. She and Duke argued
in a jointly written essay that privacy and choice had become "especially
important to those voters who [would] cast the deciding votes in the
next Presidential election: the less partisan, more independent, family-
centered young people who now comprise[d] the balance of power in
American politics." "Already skeptical with government's ability to perform," Michelman and Duke wrote, "they are not pleased to think
that bureaucracy might gain power over their private lives."[32] But

smart politics carried a price. Voters suspicious of government weren't likely to support tax-funded abortions. Nor were politicians who catered to those voters. Biden didn't support such funding. Neither did most of his Democratic presidential rivals. In Hickman's eyes, this caveat set Biden apart from liberalism and its stigma. In Michelman's eyes, it betrayed the meaning of choice. In an unpublished op-ed, she accused Biden and his fellow candidates of "sacrificing the health care needs of poor women" and "creating an artificial, political middle ground."[33]

Enthralled by the assault on Bork from the left, reporters and analysts overlooked the significance of the attack on his right flank. Most senators were looking for the safest way out of the conflict. Some had other reasons to vote against Bork and needed only a rationale that would satisfy their conservative constituents. Privacy offered them the ideal fig leaf. Others didn't care much about Bork but hated talking about sex or religion. Privacy promised to insulate them from abortion and similarly messy questions. Others just wanted to stay out of political trouble. For them, privacy turned aside a wave of Reagan voters who had been expected to rally behind the nomination.

The desertion of Bork by conservative voters was unmistakable. In a series of three *Washington Post*–ABC polls between early August and mid-October, his support dropped by only 15 net percentage points among liberals and by just 13 among moderates. Among conservatives, however, his support fell by 38 net points. By the week of his testimony in late September, opposition among southern whites had risen from 25 to 41 percent. A Roper poll in late September found that southerners opposed him 51 to 31 percent and even southern conservatives tilted against him by a margin of 44 to 39 percent.[34]

As one Texas political strategist put it, "[H]ere's a former Yale professor who wants to deny these people their right to privacy. He might as well be saying he wants to deny their right to bear arms." The National Rifle Association (NRA) seemed to agree. Unconvinced that Bork would fully respect the Second Amendment's protection of private gun ownership and disturbed by his narrow view of the Fourth Amendment's restraint on unwarranted seizure of firearms, the NRA refused entreaties from fellow conservatives to support the nominee. "Don't own a firearm if you choose not to," said an NRA newspaper ad that ran, by coincidence, on the first day of Bork's hearings. "But never let anyone deny or delay your constitutional freedom to make that choice."[35]

On Capitol Hill, lobbyists for the anti-Bork coalition exploited the conservative dilemma. NARAL and Planned Parenthood spearheaded the coalition's overtures to Republican senators who were less accessible to civil rights groups. Senator Bob Packwood of Oregon, the consummate libertarian Republican, met with Michelman within days of Bork's nomination and announced publicly that he would lead a filibuster against Bork if the nominee failed to affirm a constitutional right to privacy. That challenge deterred some other Republicans from consolidating behind Bork. Eventually, Packwood helped to lure four GOP colleagues to the opposition.[36]

Pro-choice lobbyists directed senators' attention not to abortion but to birth control and privacy. They presented *Roe* as the status quo and warned that by shattering it, Bork would drag lawmakers into an issue they dreaded. In the offices of many Republican and conservative Democratic senators, the reaction to those arguments, particularly privacy, was strikingly positive.

Nowhere was the attack on Bork's right flank more vigorous than in Alabama. Here, black ministers, black politicians, and black political organizations dominated the campaign against the nomination. To avoid a racial backlash, activists needed to persuade whites that they, too, had reasons to fear Bork.

Privacy became the answer. At a rally in Montgomery, the local NAACP president advised whites that Bork "rejects the principle of a constitutional right to privacy" and that "people who think this is just a minority issue are sadly mistaken." The ACLU of Alabama told conservatives that the nomination "puts the lie to the Reagan administration's pledge to 'get the government off the people's backs.'" The Alabama New South Coalition defended privacy alongside the racially coded freedoms of the Old South: "[Bork] opposes the U.S. Constitution's protection of State's Rights. He opposes the right of parents to send their children to private schools. He opposes the right of married couples to use birth control."[37]

Two other issues helped local activists to isolate Bork from conservative whites. In his youth Bork had dabbled briefly in socialism; and in July 1987 *Time* magazine had carelessly labeled him an "agnostic" because he had admitted he wasn't very religious. "This is not a civil rights fight, it's a fight for justice which crosses racial lines, state lines and political lines," said Joe Reed, chairman of the Alabama Democratic Conference, in a September interview with the *Birmingham News*. "I don't want anyone on the court who doesn't believe in God."[38]

A week later Reed told the *Montgomery Advertiser,* "I don't see this as a black-rights issue. I'm personally concerned about Mr. Bork's past connections. He was a socialist . . . who's got doubts about God. I don't see how folks in Alabama could be for him." At a news conference in Montgomery, Hank Sanders of the New South Coalition charged that Bork "began as a socialist . . . and now is on another extreme, not even accepting God's existence." A coalition memo noted that Alabama operatives had "mailed to a list of Baptist ministers and are recruiting their support primarily on the basis of Bork's agnosticism." [39]

Over the summer, the idea that Bork was unstable—as one local activist put it, a "Dr. Jekyll" with a "bizarre mind"—worked its way through the coffee shops of Alabama and into the ears of Senator Heflin. On a trip home shortly after the nomination, Heflin was struck by how many people told him they were put off by Bork's appearance, especially his beard. As Heflin toured the state during the Labor Day recess, community leaders and ministers raised concerns about Bork's alleged agnosticism. Meanwhile, the privacy issue divided the disloyalties of anti-government voters. At one town meeting, a Bork supporter told Heflin, "We southerners have been the target of too many court rulings by judicial activists." But a former steelworker warned, "If that Judge Bork gets in, it'll be just a matter of time before nobody in the country has any more freedoms." [40]

Heflin got the message. On the first day of the hearings, he underscored suspicions that Bork would practice "judicial activism" on behalf of a "radical" agenda. His opening statement dwelled at length on allegations "that Judge Bork is an agnostic or a non-believer." While ostensibly lecturing against judging Bork by his religious beliefs, Heflin noted that many critics deemed it "a legitimate area of inquiry, for in determining the fitness of a nominee, they argue, one must look to the total man—his reasoning process and the reaches of his values and views." The front page of the *Birmingham News* picked up the poisonous theme: "Heflin Says Religion Not a Bork Issue." [41]

On the second day, Heflin grilled Bork for fifteen minutes on privacy and *Roe.* Then he turned to the third issue that was bothering folks in Alabama:

> [I]n your early youth, they list you as being a socialist, that you stated that socialism sounded like a swell idea. . . . Then, there are writings in some of the papers to the effect that you succeeded in getting a young friend of yours to attend a Communist party meeting. . . . [And later] after coming

out of the Marine Corps, as I understand it, the second time, there was
some instance in which you still exhibited maybe some socialistic leanings.

Bork replied that the allegation about his later years was untrue. He explained that he had merely been a liberal Democrat. When Heflin finished his interrogation and ducked into the corridor, Michelman stepped
forward and thanked him for raising the abortion issue.[42] The feminist
and the old southern pol had converged.

By the time Bork finished his testimony, Heflin's rationale for rejecting him was taking shape. The senator suggested that Bork might be
a "kook" and told the Birmingham News that he was trying to decide
whether Bork had "a great intellectual curiosity to experience the un-
usual, the unknown, the strange" or was simply a "weirdo."[43] In an au-
diotaped statement distributed to Alabama radio stations in October,
Heflin told his constituents, "I was troubled by Judge Bork's extremism
and admission that he'd been a socialist, a libertarian, that he'd nearly
become a Communist and actually recruited people to attend Communist party meetings and had a strange lifestyle. I was further disturbed
by his refusal to discuss his belief in God or the lack thereof."[44]

Heflin's colleagues followed similar considerations to the same result.
On the Senate floor, many described Bork as a radical activist bent on
uprooting conservative principles, especially limited government and its
corollary, privacy. Half a dozen, some of them quoting Heflin, spoke dis-
approvingly of Bork's deviation into socialism. One pro-life Democrat
criticized Bork's "lack of occupation with morals and with religion."
Another accused him of lacking a "moral foundation."[45]

Behind the scenes, Joe Biden's pollster, Pat Caddell, and Caddell's
deputy, Mike Donilon, distributed their own analysis of Tom Kiley's
findings to southern Democratic senators. They wrote that the South
was fertile ground for defeating the nomination, in part because Bork
defied "a very strong pro-privacy sentiment among southern voters."
The results of the September Roper poll, distributed to southern senators later that month, backed up this analysis.[46]

With Biden's and Caddell's encouragement, Senator Johnston began
to counsel his southern colleagues who feared that a vote against Bork
would alienate voters back home. Johnston saw that this peril was van-
ishing. His reassurances confirmed the younger senators' impression
that conservative southerners were failing to rally behind Bork and that
visible opposition to the nomination had spread well beyond liberal
circles. Johnston, a pro-life traditionalist, found the privacy issue "very

big with everyone." Alabama's junior senator, Richard Shelby, cited privacy as one reason why Bork lacked "the overwhelming support [one] would have thought he would have gotten from the moderate to conservative electorate in Alabama." [47]

By October senators seemed convinced that privacy had struck a major nerve in the electorate. Of the fifty-eight senators whose votes sunk Bork, fifty-one advertised privacy among their reasons. Twenty depicted it as a primary consideration. Only five implied any sympathy for abortion rights. Sixteen of the eighteen southern Democrats voted against Bork; all sixteen cited privacy among their concerns. None spoke up for abortion rights. Some, while championing privacy, condemned abortion. [48]

In its October 13 report, the Judiciary Committee placed privacy first among its ten indictments of Bork. The seven pages devoted to that subject never mentioned abortion and referred to *Roe* only once in passing. Privacy, as many senators interpreted it, strayed far from what Michelman had in mind. It stood for the preservation of traditional relations "between a man and his wife" and "between parents and child." It could be cleansed of "the controverted abortion cases or the controverted homosexual rights case." [49]

Was this a perversion of privacy, or was it the original meaning of the term? Justice Powell's jurisprudence suggested the latter. In 1979 he had wrought the compromise that preserved laws requiring teenage girls to get their parents' consent before obtaining abortions. In 1980 he had cast the fifth vote to let states deny tax-funded abortions to poor women. In 1986 he had cast the fifth vote against gay rights, ruling that the right to privacy protected only traditional family and procreative relationships. This was the man whom the liberals of 1987, in their haste to isolate Bork, exalted as the true conservative. [50]

What did privacy mean? Bork raised that question repeatedly at his hearings. "Privacy to do what, Senator? You know, privacy to use cocaine in private? Privacy for businessmen to fix prices in a hotel room?" He reminded his inquisitors that decades earlier, a libertarian Supreme Court had used the principle of "a generalized liberty of contract" to strike down statutes that protected workers, such as minimum wage laws, caps on weekly work hours, and a federal law that barred interstate railroad companies from requiring workers to stay out of labor unions. [51] Would liberals support such limits on governmental authority to intervene in the private sector?

Bork believed that legal conflicts involved many kinds of liberty. Employees might demand the liberty to join unions or to bargain away that option. Their employer and its shareholders might demand the liberty to lay down conditions of employment or to resist union control of its workforce. A union and its members might demand the liberty to recruit employees or to represent their interests. The state and its residents might demand the liberty to regulate the employer or the union. The federal government and its taxpayers might demand the liberty to review the state law.

How did all these liberties fit together? Bork's answer was that one person's liberty, as "a matter of plain arithmetic," could be expanded only at the expense of another's and that as far as the Supreme Court was concerned, any kind of liberty not specifically mentioned in the Constitution was as good as any other. This theory struck his opponents as simplistic, and it was. But it was less simplistic than the theory put forward by Biden and his fellow Democratic presidential candidate, Senator Paul Simon of Illinois. They defined liberty as a single, indivisible entity that, through progressive enlightenment, had expanded throughout American history. As Simon put it with a counterfeit air of wisdom, "[W]hen you expand the liberty of any of us, you expand the liberty of all of us." [52]

Whose liberty should grow, and to do what? That question was lost in a confused barrage. In his testimony against Bork, the liberal constitutional scholar Laurence Tribe defended "the idea of family privacy and personal autonomy," as though the two were identical. To the battered wives and pregnant daughters of Alabama, they weren't. As Bork observed, "[L]egislatures do and can constitutionally regulate some aspects of family life. . . . We have divorce laws, custody laws, child beating laws and so forth." Were his critics willing to renounce such laws? Would the doctrine of privacy, he wondered aloud, "protect beating your wife in private?" [53]

The ambiguity of liberty unfolded vividly in an exchange between Simon and Bork over the Court's 1857 *Dred Scott* decision. In that case, a slave who had moved temporarily to a free state was denied the right to be released legally from the possession of his master. Simon suggested that the Court's mistake was in failing to accord the slave his full liberty under the Constitution. Bork disagreed. In deciding the case, he noted, the Court had expressly rejected "an act of Congress which deprives a citizen of the United States of his liberty or property"—in this case the property of the slave owner—"merely because he came himself or brought his property into a particular territory of the United States." [54] In the name of liberty, the Court had forbidden government intervention in a private property relationship between Dred Scott and his master.

Bork's critics argued that his irreverence for privacy and his neglect of civil rights went hand in hand. But their analysis of his career suggested the opposite. His criticisms of privacy had emerged during his current period of deference to government. His most pernicious statements on racial questions had emerged during his earlier, libertarian, period. In that earlier period, contrary to his current view, he had denied "that law should be used to overcome private immorality," such as a white person's refusal to sell his house to a black person. [55] The problem wasn't just that Bork had respected the liberty of blacks too little. It was that he had respected the private property rights of bigots too much.

In that mistake, he was far from alone. During Bork's hearing, Republican senator Alan Simpson of Wyoming pointed out that southern Democrats in the 1960s had been equally guilty. Chief among them was Senator John Sparkman of Alabama, the party's 1952 nominee for vice president. In 1964 Sparkman had tried to exempt eating establishments "situated within the residence of the operator or proprietor" from the Civil Rights Act. "Regulation of them is coming very close to regulating a person's own home" and threatens "an invasion of the spirit of the Bill of Rights," Sparkman had warned. [56] Surely, Simpson reasoned, Bork's misunderstanding was no worse than Sparkman's. But was it a misunderstanding of civil rights, or of privacy?

Speaking in Birmingham a day before the Judiciary Committee was to vote on the nomination, Heflin concluded that the question was whether Bork was "a conservative or an extremist." He worried about Bork's tolerance for regulating "what people do in their own home." Some people "equate privacy with abortion rights, but privacy goes beyond that," said Heflin. Joe McFadden, an Alabama political columnist, agreed. "As the hearings began, 'privacy' was merely shorthand for abortion," McFadden wrote. "But the more Judge Bork talked—and talked—the more people realized they value being left alone by the government in a lot of different ways." [57]

If to some people privacy meant more than abortion rights, to others it meant less. Five weeks after Michelman concluded her second journey to Birmingham, a seventeen-year-old girl appeared in court there to ask a judge for permission to get an abortion. Hers was the first request for a judicial waiver under Alabama's new parental consent law. She explained that she was afraid to tell her abusive stepfather about her pregnancy and that with her eighteenth birthday only a month away, she was mature enough to choose for herself. The judge listened politely but declined to intercede.[58] This was a matter for her family to decide.

And so it went, from state to state. While Bork's incineration mesmerized a movement and a nation, criminal codes in fourteen states still required women to notify or secure the consent of their husbands before getting abortions. The Supreme Court didn't allow those laws to be enforced, but it permitted the enforcement of laws requiring parental consent. Twenty-one states required parental consent, and fourteen more required parental notification. Only eight voluntarily extended Medicaid funds to cover abortions for poor women.[59]

In Washington, enemies of abortion rights were plotting not to thwart the ascent of privacy but to commandeer it. On Reagan's orders, the federal government published regulations barring abortion counseling at taxpayer-funded family planning clinics. White House aides talked about shaping a national consensus in favor of the private right to abortion but against public aid for it. "People have a right to drive, but the government does not provide them with automobiles," reasoned a White House strategy memo. "One may have an unrestricted right . . . to produce lascivious literature without being able to demand that taxpayers pay for it."[60]

Only years later would pro-choice advocates realize that rallying support for privacy had been the easy part. *Privacy* was a popular word because it was empty. It could be filled with whatever the speaker or the listener valued. The struggle between the conflicting values of speakers and listeners, between liberal and conservative understandings of privacy, was just beginning.

CHAPTER 3

Who Decided

WASHINGTON, D.C.
OCTOBER 9, 1987

Three days after the Senate Judiciary Committee dealt Robert Bork's nomination its mortal blow, Kate Michelman dispatched a distress call to her followers. The battle against Bork had distracted NARAL from threats elsewhere. Michigan lawmakers had approved a ban on using tax money to fund abortions. California's governor had signed a law giving parents the right to decide whether to grant abortions to their teenage daughters. The Reagan administration had quietly taken steps to evict abortion counseling from family planning clinics funded by federal tax dollars.[1] Abortion rights everywhere were under attack, in the name of privacy.

The acceleration of the 1988 presidential campaign heightened Michelman's anxiety that an intermediate pro-choice position, deferring to parental authority and withholding public aid for abortions, was taking shape. She worried not that *Roe* would be overturned outright but that "a conservative majority on the Court [would] permit the right to abortion to be chipped away at, so that [it would be] available only to white middle class women."[2] She decided to commission a national survey and more focus groups. NARAL's invitation to potential pollsters sketched the problem:

Some candidates, claiming a "moderate" position, say they are pro-choice
and anti-funding. They seek to identify themselves in the public mind with
both the right to choose and opposition to government funding of contro-
versial programs.

This dichotomy is not acceptable to NARAL, which is committed to full
equality of reproductive health care. To oppose it effectively, we need more
information about public attitudes towards funding.[3]

Harrison Hickman got the job. He was joined by a Republican pollster for the sake of bipartisanship. They found that although fewer than
40 percent of voters agreed that abortion should be "available to any
woman who wants one," twice that number—including nearly half of
those who said abortion should never be allowed—agreed that "abortion is a private issue between a woman, her family and her doctor [and
the] government should not be involved." Again, Hickman traced this
paradox to distrust of government. By a margin of 50 to 36 percent, voters were more afraid that "government will go too far trying to regulate
private personal decisions like abortion" than that "government won't
go far enough to uphold traditional family or moral values."

NARAL made much ado of the poll's finding that 70 percent of
self-described conservatives, 76 percent of likely Republican voters, and
65 percent of white fundamentalist southerners felt the government
should stay out of the abortion issue.[4] But NARAL kept another finding
to itself: Given a three-way choice among opposing all abortions, leaving all abortion decisions to women, and supporting the right to abortion but refusing to subsidize it, only 42 percent of respondents took the
solidly pro-choice position. Another 27 percent—enough to create a
hostile majority if combined with pro-lifers—took the pro-choice, anti-
funding position.[5] Contrary to NARAL's complaint that this middle position reflected a "dichotomy," Hickman traced it in part to white southerners' "reluctance to let the government intrude on what ought to be
private issues." He explained, "They often believe in the private right to
choose but oppose government interference in the form of funding."[6]

The poll confirmed that while women defined abortion rights in terms
of individual autonomy, men were more likely to define it simply as government inaction. Hickman wrote,

Some variations do show up in the language used by those who express a
pro-choice conceptualization of the issue. Among those using a personal
privacy justification most commonly are working women, women over 45,
women with children and political independents. . . . Opposition to govern-

ment interference is cited more often by single men than any other sub-
group of the pro-choice adherents.[7]

By May the presidential primaries had effectively winnowed the field
of candidates to two. Vice President Bush would carry the Republican
banner; Governor Michael Dukakis of Massachusetts would represent
the Democrats. Bush was pro-life; Dukakis was pro-choice. Dukakis
wasn't eager to raise the issue. In the last two weeks of August, Bush
branded him a big taxer, soft on crime and defense, and uncomfortable
with the Pledge of Allegiance. By the end of the month, Dukakis had lost
his lead and was struggling to escape this left-wing caricature.

On September 7 NARAL sent Dukakis a customized document explaining how to advocate abortion rights in popular terms. It opened
with a renunciation of liberalism: "The common perception of the pro-
choice position is that it is a 'liberal' position and a 'loser' with some key
groups of conservative swing voters. The common perception is wrong."
Next followed Hickman's poll findings about conservatives, Republicans, and southerners.[8]

Attached to the document was a memo from Hickman, addressed
to Michelman but intended for the Dukakis campaign's consumption.
Hickman suggested that Dukakis's strategists, fearing that his support
of legal abortion would make him look permissive, hoped to avoid the
issue. The pollster stressed that "the key for Dukakis is to neutralize
the issue as an indication that he is 'liberal.'" This could be done by
presenting abortion rights as a question of government intervention.
"The most important thing is to frame the debate in terms of who makes
the choice," Hickman wrote.[9] As the NARAL document put it,

> [T]he American public strongly agrees with the notion that government
> should play no role in decisions regarding abortion. They overwhelmingly
> oppose government interference in what they consider a very personal, pri-
> vate matter. Witness the widespread outcry over the nomination of Robert
> Bork to the Supreme Court, an outcry based in large part on the public's
> concern for his views concerning the right of privacy.[10]

Dukakis's advisers refused to make abortion rights a major issue, but
they bought Hickman's linguistic advice. On September 25 Dukakis met
Bush in Winston-Salem, North Carolina, for the first of their two debates. One of the appointed questioners, Anne Groer, a reporter for the
Orlando Sentinel, asked Dukakis about his "support for abortion on demand." Dukakis answered as Hickman had counseled: "The question
is, who makes the decision. And I think it has to be the woman in the

exercise of her own conscience and religious beliefs that makes that decision."

Next, Groer asked Bush whether women "should go to jail" for procuring abortions if, as he hoped, abortions became illegal again. "I haven't sorted out the penalties," Bush replied. He suggested, however, that "once that illegality is established, then we can come to grips with the penalty side, and, of course, there's got to be some penalties to enforce the law." [11]

The next morning, Bush's campaign chairman, Jim Baker, announced that on reflection Bush had decided "that he would not wish to see a woman labeled as a criminal" for having an abortion. "He thinks that a woman in a situation like that would be more properly considered an additional victim," said Baker. "That she would need help and love and not punishment." [12]

Michelman saw that this characterization of women as victims, though offered as a concession, undermined her efforts to portray women as competent deciders of moral questions. In a reply to Baker, she rejected Bush's poisoned pity: "The fact that George Bush characterizes women as 'additional victims' . . . is a significant clue to the way Bush views women. By treating women as victims, Bush is sending the message that he does not believe women are capable of making informed, conscientious decisions to determine their own destiny and protect the well-being of their children and families." [13]

If no one else would affirm the moral competence of women, Michelman would. In a September 28 speech, "Why Can't George Bush Hear Women's Voices?" she conveyed, in the first person, the words with which various women had explained their pregnancy dilemmas and their decisions to abort. These stories were what the word *privacy* glossed over. They were the moral substance that filled the void created by keeping the government out. "Listen to the women," Michelman pleaded. She concluded, "The voices of women are as varied as the reasons abortions are sought. But, in one voice and with one purpose, millions of women are saying to both presidential candidates: We must be free to make our own choices about the most intimate aspects of our lives. Why can't George Bush hear?" [14]

In a speech delivered in Chicago and other cities beginning two weeks later, Michelman framed abortion squarely as a women's issue:

> The common thread that weaves together the policies of George Bush, the votes of Congressmen who refuse to fund abortions for poor women victimized by rape or incest, and the actions of the fanatics who are trying to

close the clinics through "Operation Rescue," is a striking lack of concern for the lives of women. They are united by the conviction that their way is right for everybody. That women's lives have little value. That women should not be accorded the moral dignity to exercise their own conscience and religious convictions.

Bush "must not be voted into the White House," Michelman concluded, condensing her plea to a sentence: "Women's lives are worth too much." [15]

What followed was the worst week of Michelman's political career. On November 8 Bush swept forty states, winning the presidency in a landslide. Three Supreme Court justices who had voted with the majority in *Roe v. Wade,* now in their eighties, had survived Reagan only to be replaced, in all likelihood, by Bush. According to exit polls, more people voted for Bush because of his pro-life position than voted for Dukakis because of his pro-choice position.[16] NARAL lost two of its foremost allies in Congress, and pro-lifers swept referenda on abortion funding in Michigan, Colorado, and Arkansas.

Amendment 3, the anti-abortion-funding measure in Arkansas, was nearly identical to the previously defeated Amendment 65. Over the summer of 1988, with the help of a $5,000 grant from NARAL, Brownie Ledbetter had hired Hickman to take another poll. In a letter to him, she suggested that "hopefully, there has been some change" in local attitudes. Hickman's answer, delivered a month later, shattered that hope:

> Voters' attitudes and opinions about abortion have changed very little since the 1986 general election. . . . Arkansas remains a conservative state. Forty-four percent (44%) of all voters identify themselves as conservative on social issues like abortion and school prayer while only 16% say they are liberal. But even these liberals and those who call themselves "middle of the road" (31%) are not as *un*conservative as the label may sound: significant percentages of these two groups disagree with the pro-choice position on key questions.

Again, most Arkansas voters opposed "the right of women to have an abortion." Again, nearly two-thirds opposed "the use of government funds for abortions for women who could not otherwise afford one." And again, although a huge majority thought abortion should be allowed in the case of rape or incest, only a small fraction thought it should be allowed if the woman were an unwed teenager or couldn't afford another child.

Hickman repeated his previous recommendations: The pro-choice campaign should attack government interference, defend rape victims, and reassure voters that the state already prohibited the use of tax money for abortions. The principal change in Hickman's advice was that Ledbetter should focus even more aggressively on privacy, since it had worked so well against Bork.

At the same time, Hickman acknowledged that a conservative reading of privacy wouldn't protect public funding of abortions. Although Arkansans were pro-choice in the sense of opposing government interference, he explained, the amendment to ban abortion funding was still likely to pass because "the terms of the amendment do not violate voters' pro-choice tenets. They do not feel . . . their right to make a private decision [is] significantly threatened by the referendum." [17]

Ledbetter tried the same strategy she had used in 1986, flooding the airwaves in the final week with essentially the same commercials. But this time pro-lifers countered with radio spots telling listeners that the referendum was about the abuse of "your tax dollars." They also bought space in the state's biggest newspapers for an ad that depicted a husband, perplexed over an invoice, asking his wife, "Honey, who is this girl? I thought we paid for her abortion last month." The ad continued:

> You, too, can be forced to pay for an abortion on someone you don't even know. How? The nation's leading provider of abortions wants you to spend your hard-earned money, your Arkansas tax dollars, for abortions.
> In 14 states people are already being forced to pay for abortions with their tax dollars. If you want to keep your tax dollars from paying for unnecessary abortions, vote *yes* for Amendment 3.[18]

Ledbetter's opponents had figured out how to beat Hickman at his own game. Government could violate family privacy in more than one way. Ledbetter's ads depicted one kind of intrusion: "You, your doctor, your preacher, your daughter have no say in this personal, private tragedy." But her enemies had found another: "You, too, can be forced to pay for an abortion on someone you don't even know."

The ads for Amendment 3 dovetailed with a simultaneous ad campaign against the Fair Tax Amendment, a liberal proposal that shared the Arkansas ballot. With Bush promising Americans "no new taxes," opponents of the Fair Tax Amendment urged Arkansans to demand the same. On election day, Arkansas voters cast their ballots for Bush, rejected the Fair Tax Amendment, and approved Amendment 3.[19]

In its internal analysis of the referendum defeats in Arkansas, Colorado, and Michigan, NARAL observed, "In all three states the anti's were highly effective in translating the public funding debate into a 'tax-payers'' issue, simultaneously playing on voters' most negative attitudes about taxes and welfare recipients." NARAL legislative director Nancy Broff concluded that "in the current political climate," NARAL's congressional strategy "may need to move away from public funding as [its] primary focus."[20]

Events soon sealed that decision. Two days after the election, the Reagan Justice Department filed a brief at the Supreme Court in the pending case of *Webster v. Reproductive Health Services.* The brief invited the Court to use *Webster* to overturn *Roe.*[21] The Missouri law at issue in *Webster* banned the use of public health facilities for abortions, and it barred doctors from aborting a fetus late in the second trimester unless they first determined that it couldn't yet survive outside the womb. The Justice Department had asked the Court to overturn *Roe* in 1986, but this time the math was different. In Bork's place, Reagan had named Judge Anthony Kennedy to the Court. Pro-lifers were counting on Kennedy to cast the fifth vote against *Roe* when the time came. This was the time.

Michelman resolved to meet this assault head-on. On December 23 she announced plans for the Emergency Action Mobilization Campaign. Its initial goal was to get more than a million people to sign a pledge to defend abortion rights. But its ultimate purpose was more ambitious. "The campaign's goal, quite simply, is to activate the pro-choice majority and to create a climate in which it is unacceptable for the Supreme Court to overturn or chip away at *Roe v. Wade,*" Michelman wrote. "We intend to leave no doubt that any Court action to restrict or end a woman's right to choose abortion will create immediate social and political upheaval." Although the campaign would address the "need to keep reproductive choice free from government intrusion," its main thrust would be "to shift the focus of the debate from fetal rights to women's rights" and to "re-insert women's voices in this debate in a compelling way."[22]

On January 9, 1989, the Court announced that it would hear *Webster* during its spring term. Michelman called a press conference and read a statement full of feminist declarations: "[T]his is about much more than just abortion. It is about the lives and dignity of women. Women must control their reproductive lives in order to support themselves, care for families, and insure their health and well-being. . . . What is at stake now, in *Webster,* is the place women have won in this society and the degree of autonomy we have gained over our lives."

"Beginning today, women's voices will be heard," said Michelman. To illustrate the point, she released *The Voices of Women,* a book of letters in which women had described their illegal abortions. She read aloud from two of the letters. She also unveiled the campaign's theme: "Millions of Voices, Silent No More." [23] It looked like 1985 all over again.

Hickman had other ideas. If Michelman wanted to generate a groundswell big enough to scare the Court, preaching about women's rights wouldn't cut it. She needed another dose of reality. The prescription was another round of focus groups, starting in Tampa, Florida.

In his January 28 report on the Tampa focus groups, Hickman identified three messages that penetrated the apathy of the audience NARAL needed to reach. All were negative. Conspicuously absent was the message Michelman had been using: the value of women's lives. One effective argument was the prospect of back-alley abortions. Hickman was intrigued by the possibility of tapping into public anxiety about crime. He noted,

> One participant raised an interesting new angle to this argument, suggesting that those who would involve themselves in the trade of illegal abortions would likely be the very same people involved in the trade of illegal drugs. This specter of confused young pregnant women looking for abortionists in the open air drug markets of America's cities disturbed the participants and will likely leave a powerful impression.

A second message, that overturning *Roe* would put control of abortions in the hands of state lawmakers, elicited another cynical reaction from the focus groups. "These politicians, and the sleazy interests that would influence them, frightened the participants," the pollster wrote.

Hickman's weapon of choice, however, was "the slippery slope of government intrusion." The participants in Tampa, he noted, "were frightened by the intrusive direction of the same ideologues who promised to take government off our backs." He concluded, "This is the same fundamental issue of privacy which helped defeat Bork and should be the centerpiece of efforts to raise the volume about *Webster.*"

The remainder of the memo proposed a grand offensive to execute that strategy. "We must think of the coming process as if it were a political campaign," Hickman argued. "Our primary objective must be to mobilize the pro-choice majority in this country and frame the way the abortion issue is considered." The campaign would be orchestrated by a "Strategy Team" of professional political operatives and administered by a campaign manager under Michelman's direction. Ideally, it would provoke a popular uprising sufficient to deter the Court from tampering with *Roe*. But in the likelier event that the Court undermined or over-turned *Roe*, the campaign would rally the public against new abortion restrictions in the states.

The campaign would also have a private objective—to propel NARAL to the forefront of the abortion rights movement. The focus group participants in Tampa "don't want to be labeled feminists for supporting choice," Hickman observed. Their "negative reaction to NOW and similar feminist oriented groups" offered NARAL "a golden opportunity" to market itself as the nonfeminist alternative.[24] NARAL had found its niche and its constituency. It would become the master, and the servant, of conservative, pro-choice America.

Two weeks after the trip to Tampa, Hickman and Michelman returned to Birmingham. Again, Hickman gathered two successive focus groups around the table, one composed of whites and one of blacks. Again, Michelman watched from behind the glass. She sympathized with the black women, who feared that an erosion of abortion rights would lead to a broader erosion of civil rights. But the white group, dominated by Bush voters, spoke in the alien language she had heard in the same room in 1987. At one point, referring to Bush and his religious supporters, Hickman asked the group, "Aren't they the ones that want to keep government out of people's lives? Isn't that what they talk about when they run?" Heads nodded around the table. "But now they want to get in your bedroom," jeered a young man.[25]

Describing the conversation in a February 16 memo, Hickman struggled to make the logic of the Alabamans intelligible to the leftists at NARAL:

> The white participants in Birmingham demonstrated most clearly that voters need not be consistent in their political opinions, nor need they agree with the liberal Democratic position on non-abortion issues. They showed that pro-choice attitudes can come from a variety of sources and can be found among almost any group of people. . . .
>
> In a discussion that ranged from the Confederate flag to Martin Luther King's birthday, the participants minced few words to explain their displeasure with blacks and the way things had changed in the South. Their arguments were generally libertarian, claiming that things would be better if whites and blacks would leave each person alone to do as he or she

pleased. The sentiment was that people should not be told, especially by the government, how to live their lives, and in whose company they ought to live them.

Strange as it may seem at first glance to outsiders, this is just the line of thought that leads these people to be pro-choice. Nobody can tell them what to do, and that includes what to do about pregnancy. They were quite adamant and strongly committed to the idea that there should not be governmental intervention in such a serious and private area.[26]

Five days later Hickman distilled his findings to three messages that would resonate with the audiences NARAL needed to mobilize. The first message was that the loss of abortion rights could begin "a series of backslides." Blacks and liberals would envision voting rights and free speech as the next to go. But others required a different approach.

The trouble comes when communicating this to southern whites, some of whom we involved in our focus groups. For them the erosion of civil liberties is less troublesome than the interference of government into their right to do as they please. To them the idea of government telling them whether or not to bear a child is the first step toward the government telling them who has to live next door to them or what kind of flag they can fly.

"Who has to live next door to them" meant, of course, blacks. And "what kind of flag" meant the banner of the Confederacy.

Hickman's second message, that tearing down *Roe* would revive the grisly horrors of pre-*Roe* days, was a familiar mantra. But his third, a refinement of the question he had first sketched in 1987, coined the battle cry for a new era: "Who do you trust to make this decision, the pregnant woman or a state legislator[?] With our audiences the answer is obvious, but the question isn't, and raising it is crucial to NARAL's task of raising awareness about post-Roe life."[27]

Those two sentences drove home a lesson Hickman had been trying to convey for years. In politics, only the little fights are about answers. The big fights are about questions. Pro-choicers could never win a debate about whether to be for or against abortion, because everyone knew that abortion was bad. Once the issue was framed that way, the fight was over. The only way out was to change the question, ideally to one that was equally skewed in the opposite direction. The winning question was who should make the decision. The challenge was to drag the debate toward that question.

Webster made the task easier. Until now, pro-lifers had controlled the war's periphery. They had laid siege to the Supreme Court, demanding that it relinquish to the people and their elected representatives the power to regulate abortion. Now the people and their representatives would get that power. The new war, as Hickman envisioned it, would be between the people and their representatives. The siege would shift to the state legislature, and the movement that spoke for women and their families would control the periphery.

If Hickman could set up the conflict along these lines, he would face a political consultant's dream. The usual campaign configuration was one politician running against another, with each claiming that he or she represented the people and would handle the job better than the opponent would. Hickman would get to run a campaign in which his client literally was the people. The job at stake was making abortion decisions. The candidates were the pregnant woman and a state legislator. In effect, Hickman would be asking voters to elect themselves.

In Arkansas, where pro-lifers had entrusted the issue directly to voters, Hickman had labored to frame abortion rights as an anti-government proposition. But in an election between people and legislators, this proposition would be obvious. Hickman could run a traditional negative campaign. If he couldn't sell his candidate, he would attack the opponent. Voters who didn't trust women to make abortion decisions could at least be persuaded to trust state legislators less.

These three memorandums became the blueprint for NARAL's *Webster* campaign. Pursuant to Hickman's advice, Michelman hired a team of political consultants. First came Tony Podesta, who in 1987 had commanded People for the American Way, one of the principal armies in the battle against Bork. Next came Page Gardner, a veteran of two presidential campaigns and a term as political director of the Democratic Senatorial Campaign Committee. Gardner would run the campaign. She suited Hickman perfectly. She was blunt and deliberate, with no patience for dogma.

Gardner arrived at NARAL in mid-February and set to work digesting Hickman's memorandums. Her first task was to flesh out his sketch into a detailed battle plan. According to that sketch, the campaign manager would need absolute authority to command NARAL's resources in the execution of the plan. In a memo to her staff on February 24, Michelman announced that the *Webster* campaign was now NARAL's top priority and that all staffers were to coordinate their projects with Gardner. A new regime was taking over.

Gardner quickly forged an alliance with Jackie Blumenthal, a sardonic wordsmith Podesta had brought with him from the Bork campaign. The two women shared an aversion to pomp and an attention to business. When meetings bogged down, they pressed for decisions. They detested the campaign's theme, "Millions of Voices, Silent No More." Gardner found its tone hysterical and grating. To Blumenthal, it conjured up the image of millions of howling fetuses. Slogans such as "Remember, you can get pregnant until you're 50," were floating around NARAL's offices. NARAL's ad firm had even suggested buttons and stickers proclaiming, "Necessity is the Mother of Abortion." What this campaign needed was a more palatable theme, and fast.

The problem with "Millions of Voices" was its diffuseness. Women's reasons for choosing abortion were too complex and various to convey in a phrase. Moreover, some of these reasons wouldn't sit well with voters who otherwise agreed that politicians should stay out of the issue. NARAL's rhetoric "must not contain complicated concepts; and it must contain thoughts that are broadly acceptable," Blumenthal argued in an early outline of the campaign's communications strategy.[28]

In her outline, Blumenthal agreed with Hickman that the *Webster* campaign, like the Bork campaign, could "raise the related issues of government intervention and privacy." More than anyone else in NARAL's increasingly crowded junta of consultants, she recognized the power of the third message Hickman had recommended: "Who do you trust to make this decision, the pregnant woman or a state legislator?"

Rather than defend the trustworthiness of the pregnant woman, which many voters doubted, Blumenthal proposed to attack the comparative untrustworthiness of "legislators," "politicians," and other rhetorical "targets." Indeed, why mention the pregnant woman at all? It was safer to associate freedom of choice with the one chooser each person was certain to trust: himself or herself. By this chain of logic, Blumenthal condensed Hickman's work to five words: "Who decides? You or them?"[29]

Like privacy, "Who decides?" had the magic of plasticity. Each person could read into it what he or she preferred. Feminists could take it as an affirmation of women's right to control their bodies. "You" meant each woman; "them" meant fundamentalists and sexist legislators. Conservatives could take it as a rebuke to big government. "Them" meant nosy, corrupt politicians and bureaucrats; "you" meant families and communities.

Blumenthal devoted particular attention—far more than Hickman had—to associating abortion decisions with families rather than women alone. In her outline of the "Who Decides?" theme, she framed the candidates as "the politicians" on one side and "you and your family" on the other. In a memo to pro-choice groups, she explained, "The main thrust of the theme—'you or them'—is a populist message designed to reach a broad cross-section of Americans. The 'you' can be male or female or plural (as in family); the 'them' is generally nefarious." [30]

Everyone on NARAL's Strategy Team was impressed. No matter who might be asked the question, there was only one way to answer it: "You" should decide. "You" meant anybody and, therefore, nobody in particular.

Blumenthal and Gardner tried in two successive meetings to get the Strategy Team to adopt the new theme. Several staff members and minor consultants protested that "you or them" was ungrammatical. NARAL's board of directors was upset about it, too. Gardner and Blumenthal looked on with disgust bordering on amusement. *Roe* was on the chopping block, and its rescuers were bickering over grammar.

By late March the delay was becoming intolerable. On April 9 activists were going to converge on Washington for a massive pro-choice march. NARAL would be there with posters and buttons. What should those posters and buttons say? The staff favored "Millions of Voices." Posters bearing that message were being printed while the Strategy Team dithered. Gardner and Blumenthal could no longer wait. One Saturday when most of the consultants and top staffers were out of the office, they put out an order for thousands of posters and buttons splashed with the question, "Who Decides—You or Them?"

NOW had been planning the march for months. Its official theme was "Women's Equality/Women's Lives." Its original purpose had been to revive the ERA and to address issues such as the minimum wage and equal pay for equal work. Abortion rights didn't become its focus until the Supreme Court took up *Webster*.

In NOW's hands, it might have been dismissed as a fringe gathering. Five days beforehand, NOW president Molly Yard told the *Washington Post* that the march stood for women's "right to control their reproductive organs." At a rally concluding the march, she declared, "We won't accept the tyranny of men and the church." Her troops brandished stickers calling for "Abortion On Demand and Without Apology." Activists chanted and displayed slogans such as "Patriarchy's got to go," "Dead women can't cook your meals," "Keep your laws off my body," and "Hey Bush! We wish your mother had a choice!" NARAL took the opposite approach. On the instructions of Hickman and Blumenthal, its spokeswomen avoided confrontational language.[31]

NOW leaders insisted on control of the march. They kept NARAL organizers in the dark about the times and locations of events. Despite efforts to appease Yard, Michelman was banished to the end of a long series of speakers and couldn't get inside the VIP tent to mingle with celebrities and the press. Blumenthal earned a stinging rebuke for asking NOW's vice president to move Michelman up to the front line of the march, alongside Yard and the celebrities.

At sunrise NARAL's troops showed up at a prime staging ground near the White House. They set up signature collection tables, a mountain of placards, and a gigantic banner asking, "Who Decides—You or Them?" The size, theme, and location of the operation took NOW's march organizer, Alice Cohan, by surprise. She ordered the NARAL activists to pull down their banner and move away.

The turnout astonished everyone. At least 300,000 people showed up. That was more than three times the number that had marched for the same cause three years earlier and 50,000 more than had attended the famous March on Washington for civil rights in 1963. NARAL had printed more signs, buttons, and stickers than any other group. Volunteers handed them out to anyone who asked. Bold green placards bearing the organization's abbreviation, its Statue of Liberty logo, and its new slogan flooded the streets. The four-foot posts to which NARAL's troops had affixed the placards elevated "Who Decides?" above NOW's hand-held "Keep Abortion Legal" posters.

NARAL's backseat role in the march was forgotten. So was the "Millions of Voices" theme. In the streets, on television, and in the public imagination, a new message and a new leader emerged. NARAL's April 15 bulletin to its affiliates hailed the ascendant regime:

> To the media and the half million March participants, this was NARAL's March: NARAL posters, stickers, signs and buttons were everywhere! On every jacket, in every photo, behind every celebrity, loomed the ubiquitous NARAL logo and slogan, "WHO DECIDES? YOU OR THEM?" The new slogan appears to be a "winner" with everyone except high school English teachers.[32]

As NARAL's profile rose and the Supreme Court prepared to hear oral arguments in *Webster*, Michelman was deluged by interview requests. Three years earlier, when she first came to NARAL, she hadn't even owned a television set. Her media coordinator, Richard Mintz, had been aghast. How could she conduct herself properly on the *Today* show without having seen it? Mintz had resorted to clipping newspaper photographs of members of the Senate Judiciary Committee so that Michelman would recognize them when she testified against Bork. If only he could see her now. "People, come on!" she barked at one strategy meeting, clapping her hands impatiently as the evening news hour approached. "We've got to make the five o'clock feed!"

With Blumenthal's coaching, Michelman seized every opportunity to drive home the new theme. On CBS's *Face the Nation* on the day of the march, she emphasized that polls showed

> there is no ambivalence at all on the question of who should make the decision about abortion. . . . The solid majority of Americans believe that politicians should not make the decision, but in fact women and their families should weigh those ethical moral values. So yes, it's a complicated decision. Yes, there are moral questions involved. But politicians shouldn't be making the decisions.

Two weeks later she hammered this message again on ABC's *This Week with David Brinkley*. Over the next three months, she repeated "Who decides?" so religiously that NBC anchor Jane Pauley finally groaned, "I think we've heard your campaign theme."[33]

As she described a populist, pro-choice majority, Michelman was addressing two audiences. Many voters watching her on television needed to be persuaded that abortion restrictions were a bad idea. But her interviewers, CBS correspondent Lesley Stahl and ABC reporter Sam Donaldson, didn't. Such "opinion leaders," as they were known in the public relations business, needed to be persuaded that the new message would amass enough support to turn NARAL into a winner. To the pundits, success or failure, not right or wrong, was the story; and their judgment was self-fulfilling. By perceiving and reporting political momentum, they accelerated it. In this way, NARAL's moderation raised it above its rivals exactly as Blumenthal had predicted in her outline of the communications strategy:

> By choosing to distinguish between rhetoric designed to rally the troops and language that presents its arguments in a conventionally acceptable form, NARAL has the opportunity to reach not only these opinion leaders but also the very wide range of people who are pro-choice. Thus, the theme/message element of this campaign becomes a statement of intent to build an inclusive movement and sets NARAL apart from other pro-choice

groups in a way that speaks to NARAL's commitment to doing what has to be done to protect a woman's right to choose a safe, legal abortion.[34]

The sensation of power was intoxicating. NARAL's rallying cry was echoing in the far corners of the nation. Staffers' descriptions of themselves as "savvy," "sophisticated," and "heavyweight" were creeping into their press releases. They now routinely called themselves "the political arm of the pro-choice movement." But beneath this newly muscled exterior, they were beginning to worry about a change in NARAL's soul. Reaching out to a conservative audience was one thing. Suppressing beliefs that might challenge that audience was another.

What set off alarms among the staff was a March 22 memo from Hickman about "the kinds of language" they should use when talking about abortion. The memo was sent to NARAL's affiliates around the country as well as to its Washington staff. It began with the campaign's premise:

> Remember, there are millions of people out there who agree with us about the basic question of CHOICE who may not agree with us on any other issue, including those WE may assume are interrelated, i.e., civil rights, feminism, labor issues, etc. . . . With that in mind, we've included below some talking points and some points on which we ought to be silent.

In a gentle and understanding tone, Hickman proceeded to administer mouthfuls of the bitterest medicine:

> AVOID LOADED RHETORIC—You may actually believe it, just don't say it. Using phrases such as "don't put women back in their places," "a woman's body is her own to control," "having a child limits a woman's choices," etc., just triggers the hostility so many people still feel about women's issues. We may not like that fact, but it is unfortunately true and is a perfect example of a time when we have to find a way to talk with people who agree with us on choice and maybe not on anything else. . . .
> All too often we talk about "career women," and by and large people don't care that some women are interested in having a "career." And people are not interested in giving such a career top priority, even if it means the difference between survival and ruin for a single parent household. They just don't care, and in fact, they are hostile to the women for wanting to better themselves and for wanting to behave like men. . . . When you have the choice, talk about women who have "jobs" and not careers.[35]

Hickman commanded enormous respect among the staffers. They trusted him to understand and represent Main Street. They admired his political judgment and his ability to synthesize messages. Some of them revered him. But many found this medicine too harsh to swallow. Three months earlier they had launched a campaign to enlist millions of people to speak out for women's lives and health. Now they were being told to bite their own tongues.

Tensions between the staff and the consultants had been brewing since February. The staffers worked for a cause. Their pay was poor. At work, they valued discussion, consensus, and kindness. They shared a broad feminist agenda and were loath to separate abortion rights from it. They believed that they spoke chiefly for poor and young women. Having devoted their days entirely to abortion rights, they resisted concessions. Where public opinion thwarted them, they resolved to change it.

The consultants worked for a campaign. They were handsomely paid from the windfall of donations that the *Webster* shock had brought to NARAL. They valued what warriors valued: speed, decisiveness, and a clear chain of command. Busy with many clients, they lacked patience for consensus building. Where obstacles or quarrels surfaced, they preferred to split the difference and get on with other business.

All of the consultants were Democrats. They supported women's rights, and though they dreaded the word, most were liberal. But in their business, compromise was routine. Often, to win an office from which he could affect the issues he cared about most, a candidate would mute or modify his unpopular positions on issues that concerned him less. Every consultant knew the fundamental equation of politics: By narrowing its agenda, a campaign could broaden its base of support.

Broadening NARAL's base was the mission at hand, and the consultants fixed their attention entirely on it. They catered assiduously to the sensitivities of what they called "average voters," the "mushy middle," and "middle America." They seldom looked beyond the Supreme Court's decision in *Webster*—expected in June or July—and almost never beyond the November 1989 elections. In that span, there was no time to indulge illusions that society could be enlightened.

Such illusions, and the inflexibility that accompanied them, struck the consultants as not just foolish, but irresponsible. What good were ideals if one shunned the means necessary to realize them? Like adults beside children, they never doubted the superior wisdom of their own weather-beaten creed. It was, as Blumenthal had written, the simplest of all commitments: the "commitment to doing what has to be done."

As the two factions converged, the contrary gears in which they thought and worked ground against each other. The consultants scorned the deliberations that encumbered every NARAL decision; the staffers resented the decrees imposed on them by outsiders. The staff's naïveté exasperated the consultants; the consultants' bloated fees infuriated the staff. Having surrendered their management responsibilities to the consultants, the staffers were reduced to menial tasks. The consultants' very presence insulted them. At meetings, the two groups gravitated to separate areas of NARAL's conference room. Gardner, who worked out of NARAL's offices and was responsible for pushing the staff to meet deadlines, delivered and received the brunt of the bitterness.

The clash of cultures encompassed and overshadowed an important thematic shift. In a video created for the "Millions of Voices" campaign, NARAL had warned that "the decision about a woman's reproductive rights could soon be given over to judges, state legislators, panels of doctors and clergy—anyone except the woman herself." [36] But under its new regime, NARAL began rhetorically to give over much of that power. In meetings and memos leading up to the April 9 march, Hickman and other consultants instructed NARAL's staff to assure the public that in a pro-choice world, doctors, clergy, and family members would have a say in abortion decisions.

In the short term, this made sense. Polls showed that when people were asked whether abortion decisions should be left to the woman or the government, more and more respondents shifted toward the pro-choice position as the interviewer added more and more participants—families, doctors, clergy—to the woman's team of decision makers. This tactic worked for two reasons. Culturally, it reassured people that traditional moral institutions would continue to supervise women's decisions. Politically, it redistributed decision-making power so that many voters who might have been excluded—husbands, boyfriends, and parents—became direct beneficiaries of a pro-choice policy. It diluted feminism into populism.

In the long term, the dilution game threatened to dissolve abortion rights. The staff had bought into "Who Decides?" with the understanding that "you" meant the woman and "them" meant anyone who presumed to intrude in her decision. Now members of "them" were being smuggled into the woman's decision-making circle. "You" was getting crowded. If enough of "them" seeped into "you," the distinction would be reduced to a slogan.

The NARAL officers who had the most trouble digesting the new language were communications director Tamar Abrams and legal director

Dawn Johnsen. They were young, and neither had worked in a campaign before. Abrams's principal project in the weeks before the *Webster* buildup was the book of women's letters about their abortions. In its introduction, she wrote, "And what about the voices of women who have struggled, not with the abstract issue, but with the actual decision? Listen to their voices. They yearn to be heard[,] . . . not to apologize or even justify, but simply to inform. . . . They are voices filled with dignity and resolve, and sometimes with pain and anger." [37]

One of Johnsen's principal projects during *Webster* was a brief to the Supreme Court, cowritten with attorneys from the NOW Legal Defense and Education Fund. Two-thirds of the brief consisted of the names of nearly three thousand women who had undergone abortions, plus sixty-five letters in which the women or their friends explained the circumstances of their abortions. The remaining one-third was a defense of women's moral competence. The brief's summary began, "For compelling physical, economic, social and moral reasons, women have sought and will seek to have abortions." It concluded that women were "the people best situated to make this decision."

> Many women who believe that bearing a child would cause them to fail in deeply felt obligations to their own or other already existing lives decide against childbearing and consider themselves morally bound, indeed compelled, to act upon that decision. Whatever her decision, it is one that only the woman herself, aided by the advice of her physician, can make, given her unique position of knowledge and responsibility.[38]

The consultants were steering NARAL away from these themes: away from women's particular moral experiences, away from their collective welfare and moral competence, and toward the simpler and less challenging message that the government should leave abortion decisions to families. Abrams regretted this. She found the whole campaign mind-set dirty. She lamented the demotion of women's stories and bristled at the promotion of family members, doctors, and clergy as presumptive participants in abortion decisions.

Johnsen added practical experience to this concern. As an ACLU attorney before joining NARAL, she had defended women against boyfriends, husbands, and former lovers who sought court injunctions to prevent them from getting abortions. While the consultants were stretching NARAL's message to include family members, pro-lifers were orchestrating a legal campaign to encourage men to seek such injunctions.

Johnsen agreed that NARAL should include family members in its message, but she warned against any formulation that could be construed to grant husbands a right to participate in their wives' abortion decisions.

The concerns voiced by the two young women didn't go over well. Some of the consultants cringed at Johnsen's leftist rhetoric and legal exactitude. They pitied her innocence and tried to get her to see things their way. Abrams's misgivings drew a sharper rebuke. "Do you want to win this, or don't you?" one consultant demanded of her after a meeting. A month after *Webster,* by mutual agreement with Michelman, Abrams would resign.

The final phase of the *Webster* battle plan, a nationwide advertising campaign, was entrusted to Democratic adman Frank Greer and his deputy, Kim Haddow. Greer was tense and passionate, a Deep South evangelist trapped in the expensively dressed body of a Washington political consultant. He lacked Hickman's equanimity but shared his heritage. Raised in Alabama by liberal Southern Baptists, Greer, too, had seen the anti-government fervor of the segregationist resistance. In 1960 Greer's high school classmates had unanimously opposed his parents' presidential candidate, John F. Kennedy, on the grounds that the Catholic Church, through Kennedy, would control the U.S. government. Three years later the showdown between Governor George Wallace and black students at the University of Alabama, punctuated by Wallace's denunciation of the federal government, unfolded scarcely three blocks from Greer's house.

Out of this paradox of liberal values and conservative sensibilities, Greer, like Hickman, fashioned a career. While southern and Appalachian voters rallied behind Reagan, Greer helped to persuade them to elect Democrats to statewide offices in Alabama, Georgia, and West Virginia. No one surpassed Greer at stealing traditionalist symbols. In his 1986 television commercial for Senator Wyche Fowler of Georgia, a schoolteacher reminded her pupils that "Wyche" should be pronounced with a hard *ch,* "as in church."

Greer's wife, Stephanie Solien, had directed the Women's Campaign Fund from 1984 to 1988. She had raised his consciousness not only about feminism and abortion rights but also about libertarianism. Solien had grown up in Spokane, Washington, in a family of hunters. She believed in the right to own firearms. On that subject, she found in her family and neighbors the same hostility to legislation with which she regarded incursions on abortion rights. When her father, a supporter of the National Rifle Association, passed away, she brought back from his house a cap inscribed with the words "NRA—Freedom." The all-purpose appeal of that message intrigued Greer. Why couldn't supporters of abortion rights exploit the same theme?

Greer's account executive, Haddow, was sharp-tongued and voraciously inventive. Bidding for the NARAL account had been her idea. She was a radical feminist, but seven years in Louisiana had taught her to measure her words. As a radio reporter in New Orleans in 1978, she had seen supporters of the ERA antagonize local voters by threatening to boycott the city. She had resolved to avoid their two mistakes: They had behaved like outsiders, and they had threatened to take something away.[39]

Greer and Haddow were given two weeks to turn the team's strategic memorandums into television ads. With help from Hickman, Gardner, and Blumenthal, they developed a dozen scripts. One depicted a housewife, a male factory worker, and a male doctor being jailed for involvement in abortions. Another, entitled "Couple," emphasized marital privacy. A third portrayed a husband and wife with their daughters, saying, "We certainly don't need the politicians and state legislators interfering in our family."

Groping for a visual image that would pit government against the family, Blumenthal and Podesta came up with an ad called "Intervention." It would begin with a conversation between a woman, a man, and a doctor. The script didn't specify whether the man was the woman's husband or boyfriend. The camera would gradually pull back to reveal that the conversation was taking place in a legislative forum and being monitored by politicians and judges. Abortion is *"your* decision," the narrator would tell viewers—unless "politicians" managed to seize "the power to decide for you."

"Intervention" dramatized the danger as well as the allure of NARAL's theme. In juxtaposing "you" against "them," it represented "you" as a trinity. In the make-believe world of advertising, inserting doctors and a woman's husband into her decision-making circle was smart politics. In the real world, it was the nightmare to which Pennsylvania had subjected Kate Michelman.

In the first week of April, NARAL sent Celinda Lake, another pollster, to Iowa and North Carolina to test the ads in more focus groups. Like Hickman, Lake combined professional expertise in women voters with personal expertise in an anti-government culture. She had been raised in a Republican family on a Montana ranch and had belonged to the NRA. In 1972 she had organized the state chapter of Students for Nixon.

When the GOP's resistance to women's rights became too much for her, Lake quit the party. But she didn't quit the culture. She returned to Montana to work for Pat Williams, a libertarian Democratic congressman. To Williams's constituents, speed limits, drunk-driving laws, gun laws, and abortion laws were just different kinds of meddling. In Iowa and North Carolina, Lake saw the same thing. In her report to NARAL, she observed that during their abortion conversation, the focus group participants drew "analogies to a number of instances where the politicians have unnecessarily intruded in their personal lives—seat belts, gun control, and non-smoking laws." "Something very central to the American way of life is being threatened here," she wrote.[40]

Lake also confirmed and refined Hickman's theory of a conceptual gender gap in the pro-choice electorate:

> Men and women approach this issue from very different perspectives. For women "choice" is key and this is a very personal choice and decision— "my freedom," "my choice." . . . Women ask "why should someone else make such a personal decision for me."
>
> Women readily think of the consequences of botched illegal abortions for themselves and their daughters and the cost to women and families of unwanted children. . . . One woman noted[,] "[It] upset me to think that there might be a time a woman didn't have the right to her body."
>
> Women respond to this issue then in a deeply personal way. They relate to personal stories, women's voices, and first person accounts.
>
> Men respond more abstractly—in terms of rules and rights. They want to "keep the government out" and do not want the government to "take away our rights." . . . Men respond significantly less to the personal stories of women. They feel "sorry" for the individuals, but think of them as "isolated instances only." [41]

This was the fifth time in three years a NARAL pollster had noticed this duality. The pattern was becoming clearer. There were two faces of choice: feminine and masculine, contextual and abstract, affirmative and negative, empathetic and detached, personal and territorial, liberal and conservative.

The ads that worked best in the focus groups showed both of these faces. In television advertising, technique was often more important than theme. Although government intervention was a potent argument once the viewer was engaged, it didn't work as an attention grabber.

That was one reason the decisive ad in the 1986 Arkansas campaign had opened with a rape. It was also why the three ads favored by the NARAL focus groups opened with images of the abortion underground.

The first commercial began with a soft-spoken, white-haired doctor recalling how, before *Roe v. Wade,* his hospital had reserved a ward for women wounded by secret abortions. The second simulated a woman's walk down a filthy, dark alley and up a flight of stairs to a rusty metal door. Sirens wailed in the background. In the third, a slide show chronicled the happy childhood of a middle-class white girl. "She grew up in the fifties," said the narrator. "She died in the sixties—the victim of a back-alley abortion."

Those were the personal, female-oriented segments of the ads. Next came the abstract, male-oriented segment. Each ad dissolved to a white-on-black screen featuring NARAL's name and phone number. Duplicating the words on the screen, a male announcer warned that the Supreme Court was threatening to "let politicians take away your right to choose." He urged viewers to call NARAL to find out how "to keep government out of your private life." [42]

Michelman unveiled the ads at an April 19 press conference. The event demonstrated Blumenthal's idea of using the campaign's resources and sophistication twice: privately for their actual value and publicly for their intimidation value. "LEADING PRO-CHOICE GROUP LAUNCHES TWO MILLION DOLLAR MEDIA CAMPAIGN," roared the press release. "NARAL TV, Radio And Print Spots Focus On Consequences Of Letting Politicians Decide."

The ads were broadcast through the end of May in Washington and four other cities. They also aired nationwide on CNN. In the midst of this blitz, on the day the Supreme Court heard oral arguments in *Webster,* NARAL brought out its ground troops. In thirty-six states, pro-choice activists staged "speak-outs."

Like the ads, the speak-outs reflected a gender duality. In the spirit of the 1985 "Silent No More" campaign, they were contextual, affirmative, and feminist. To "speak out" meant to tell a story, usually the story of a woman's pregnancy, her circumstances and moral considerations, and her struggle to get or survive an abortion.

But NARAL didn't want the abstract, libertarian aspect of its message to get lost in these stories. The passion of 1985 had to make room for the strategic discipline of 1989. "Who Decides?" placards and stickers were boxed up and shipped off to NARAL's state affiliates for the speak-outs. Two days beforehand, NARAL sent the affiliates a sheet of talking points. All media questions about letters in which women had told their abortion stories were to be answered with a generic line: "We don't want politicians and judges taking this private decision away from us."[43]

Three weeks after the speak-outs, NBC aired *Roe v. Wade,* a film about Norma McCorvey, alias Jane Roe, whose battle to end her pregnancy had triggered the 1973 decision. NARAL invited reporters to watch the movie at "house parties" organized by its members. Nothing could have been more personal than this tale of one woman's abortion. Yet in its instructions for handling the press, NARAL advised its members, "The movie is essentially irrelevant to our comments. We should look at this as an opportunity to get our message out. . . . What is universal and important about this movie is the fundamental question: Who Decides?"[44]

The contest between the two faces of choice wasn't confined to ads, rallies, and strategy memos. It was building inside the Court on April 26 as the speak-outs raged outside. Frank Susman, the attorney for the clinic challenging the Missouri law, was telling the justices why *Roe* should be preserved:

> I suggest that there can be no ordered liberty for women without control over their education, their employment, their health, their childbearing and their personal aspirations. There does, in fact, exist a deeply rooted tradition that the government steer clear of decisions affecting the bedroom, childbearing and the doctor-patient relationship as it pertains to these concerns.[45]

These two sentences, spoken as though parts of the same thought, implied very different things. Control of one's life was an affirmative principle. It would direct and possibly compel states to promote the elements of women's liberty Susman had enumerated. Steering clear was a negative principle. It foreclosed state involvement in procreative matters, for good or ill. Beyond that, it assigned no rights or responsibilities to any person or private institution.

The Court had chosen the negative over the affirmative principle in 1977 and 1980. In *Maher v. Roe* and *Harris v. McRae,* it had ruled that the constitutional right to abortion didn't require states or the federal government to subsidize abortions for women who couldn't afford them.[46] Missouri claimed that it was simply extending that logic by ban-

ning the use of its state-financed health facilities or employees to perform, procure, or suggest abortions.

Susman's adversary, Missouri attorney general Bill Webster, argued
that this foreclosure of state participation was compatible with *Roe*. Activist judges, he told the Court, had "contorted *Roe* to create an abortion right in public hospitals." That interpretation was false, he said.
Roe stood for state neutrality, and so did Missouri: "We contend the
Government is certainly not obligated in and of itself to become an advocate for abortion." Indeed, Missouri's law was arguably milder than
the abortion funding bans the Court had upheld. Webster called it "a
convoluted result to suggest that if you can afford an abortion we have
to provide one for you in a public facility, but if you lack the financial
capacity to provide an abortion the state and other public governmental entities are not obligated to provide those services for you."[47]

Webster had a point. If Missouri had bitten off too much of *Roe,* so
had *Maher* and *McRae*. The tempting response was to agree and ask the
Court to throw out *Maher* and *McRae* as well. But that was folly. Instead, Susman defended those decisions and sought to distinguish them
from *Webster*. Missouri's ban on state-subsidized abortion counseling,
he reasoned awkwardly, presented a "new obstacle" to abortion rights,
whereas bans on public funding of abortions didn't:

> I think the suggestion that the physician say to the woman[,] . . . now you
> must go elsewhere because the state tells me I can't talk about it, is a new
> obstacle. It is not the kind of obstacle such as subsidy that we saw in *Maher*
> and *McRae*. . . . I cannot in my mind compare this with the withholding
> of funding which created, as this Court said repeatedly, no new obstacle.
> Women were poor before and by denying them a subsidy we are not creat-
> ing any obstacle that did not previously exist.[48]

With those words, the abortion rights movement's de facto legal representative embraced libertarianism. At a speak-out across the Capitol
lawn, Kate Michelman did the same. "Government has no part in the
most private decisions women and families ever face," she told the
crowd.[49]

In its resolution of *Webster* on July 3, the Court agreed. Writing for the
plurality, Chief Justice William Rehnquist concluded,

> Just as Congress' refusal to fund abortions in *McRae* left "an indigent
> woman with at least the same range of choice in deciding whether to obtain
> a medically necessary abortion as she would have had if Congress had cho-
> sen to subsidize no health care costs at all," . . . Missouri's refusal to allow

public employees to perform abortions in public hospitals leaves a pregnant
woman with the same choices as if the State had chosen not to operate any
public hospitals at all. . . . Nothing in the Constitution requires States to
enter or remain in the business of performing abortions.[50]

Had the Court stopped there, *Webster* would merely have extended
the line of cases affirming a conservative theory of privacy. But in upholding Missouri's demand for fetal viability testing, Rehnquist went
further. He granted states new authority to ban abortions, not just de-
fund them, in the sixth month of pregnancy. *Roe*'s author, Justice Harry
Blackmun, concluded that "*Roe* would not survive" this decision and
that state lawmakers were now free to recriminalize abortion. Justice
Antonin Scalia agreed that Rehnquist's opinion "effectively would overrule *Roe v. Wade.*"[51]

Like Bork, Rehnquist had overstepped public opinion by inviting
government interference in the family. At an afternoon press conference,
Michelman declared war.

> For months we have posed the central question in this debate: Who de-
> cides? America's answer has been clear: We do. But the Court today said
> no, politicians will decide.
>   The Justices cracked the foundation of privacy that has been the basis
> for personal decisions about abortion, contraception and other freedoms in
> America for decades. We are now careening down the slippery slope toward
> government control of our most fundamental right.[52]

What a difference NARAL's new regime had wrought. Six months
earlier, in her four-page statement announcing the "Millions of Voices"
campaign, Michelman had used the word *woman* or *women* thirty-three
times. Now, in her four-page statement concluding the "Who Decides?"
campaign, those words appeared just seven times. In their places were
the words *Americans, voters,* and *families.* In place of the old references
to "women's voices" and "every woman's right to make her own decision" were references to "privacy" and "government control."[53]

"NARAL will launch the most sophisticated, hard-hitting political
campaign in American history to preserve our right to choose," said
Michelman. Mimicking the bravado of George Bush and Clint East-
wood, she warned, "To politicians who oppose choice, we say: Read our
lips. Take our rights; lose your jobs."[54]

Within hours, NARAL's opening salvo, a television commercial prepared by Frank Greer, was on the air. From just above, the camera approached the face of the Statue of Liberty. She overwhelmed the screen.

The camera's downward angle, backed by a disjointed piano rendering of "America the Beautiful," evoked a look of tragedy in her gaze. A male narrator sounded the alarm: "On July third, Americans lost a fundamental liberty. The Supreme Court took away your right to choose and gave it to state politicians. . . . Now it's up to you to win back this fundamental right. Help the National Abortion Rights Action League elect public officials who believe this personal decision should be yours—not theirs." [55]

To liberals, the ad depicted a rollback of civil rights. To conservatives, it depicted a coup against tradition and families by a meddlesome elite. In Lady Liberty's unfinished eyes, it was impossible to see which conception of freedom would prevail. But that hardly mattered now. Abortion's very legality was in peril. On the screen, three terse sentences declared the end of an era of jurisprudence and the dawn of an era of wholesale political war. "Who decides? You decide. With your vote."

CHAPTER 4

The New Mainstream

LYNCHBURG, VIRGINIA
MARCH 14, 1989

The Moral Majority would end where it had begun. On the stage of a high school auditorium in the Reverend Jerry Falwell's hometown, the Republican candidates for governor, joshing and preening, gathered for their third debate. One of these four men would win the nomination and with it, in all likelihood, the governorship. Four months earlier, the Republican presidential ticket had carried this state for the ninth time in the last ten elections. Falwell, with a congregation of twenty thousand, was the fifth-largest employer in this part of the state. Each of the men onstage had sought his endorsement. The audience was full of his faithful.

Emboldened by the setting, the candidates preached traditional values and served up red-meat tirades against the presumptive Democratic nominee, Lieutenant Governor Doug Wilder. Marshall Coleman, the former state attorney general, charged that Wilder talked like a conservative but behaved like a liberal. Paul Trible, the former U.S. senator, joked that Wilder was "sprinting to the right as fast as he can." Stan Parris, the northern Virginia congressman, sneered that contrary to his moderate pretensions, "Doug Wilder's for freedom of choice for abortion." With a nod to school prayer, capital punishment, and other moral

84

issues, Parris promised, "All these differences are going to be pointed out in the general election." [1]

The exchange was grotesquely shortsighted. Within twenty months, the careers of all three men would lie in ruins. Two of them would be destroyed by the abortion issue, which they had dismissed as an embarrassment to the left. On their political graves, Wilder, a man misjudged throughout his career, would found a pro-choice empire sustained and controlled by the pro-family, anti-government conservatives on whom the abortion rights movement had staked its hopes. To everyone's surprise, he would become the movement's leader—and its usurper.

From his cluttered apartment in Washington, D.C., Wilder's pollster, Mike Donilon, chuckled into the phone as Wilder's chief strategist and alter ego, Paul Goldman, conveyed the latest news from the campaign trail. The two men were a Laurel and Hardy team, Goldman with his slight frame, vacant expression, and disheveled hair, Donilon with his stocky physique, gentle eyes, and pudgy, mustachioed face. For months they had been concocting a recipe to steal the election from the Republicans. They had lacked one ingredient, and the enemy was now providing it. [2]

Back in fall 1988, when Goldman and Donilon began charting the campaign, the facts were grim. Wilder was black; eight out of ten Virginia voters were white. Wilder was a Democrat; most people who planned to vote in the general election were Republicans. Wilder's boss, Governor Gerry Baliles, a Democrat, had imposed record taxes and spending.

Donilon's first poll, taken in December, brought reassuring news. Wilder was well known, well liked, and trusted. Solid majorities believed that he was qualified and was a leader. His life story dispelled whites' usual doubts about black politicians. He had fought for his country in war and had served sixteen years in the legislature. The grandson of slaves, he had earned every step forward in life. Yet only a quarter of white voters were ready to support him. What Wilder needed was a threat, an issue capable of distracting whites from their fear of electing a black man. He needed to affix that threat to his Republican opponent and to convince Virginians that only he could save them from it.

Goldman and Donilon believed that threat could be found in the religious right. Goldman had helped to defeat Marshall Coleman in his first race for governor in 1981. He believed that Falwell's embrace of

Coleman in the campaign's final days had frightened away moderate voters. In the 1985 governor's race, Donilon had tracked the desertion of the Republican nominee by moderates upset over his support for teaching creationism in public schools. Virginia was growing more Republican each year, but the new, libertarian Republicans—young adults and immigrants from the Northeast—viewed the Christian right as an odd stepbrother.

Several issues might turn the libertarians against the cultural conservatives, but Goldman and Donilon were most intrigued by abortion. Donilon remembered the panic that had engulfed George Bush's campaign in September, when Bush suggested that women should face "penalties" for getting abortions. It was the only time the Bush team had looked scared. After the election, Donilon's poll confirmed that abortion remained a hot issue in Virginia. When the Supreme Court agreed to hear *Webster*, Goldman and Donilon saw that *Roe* might be dismantled—and with it, the judicial barrier that had shielded pro-life politicians from a collision with voters.

Goldman worried that Wilder might look soft on family values. Donilon believed the strait could be navigated. Throughout the presidential election, he had badgered his friends in the Dukakis campaign to use the abortion issue against Bush. They found the suggestion absurd. Abortion rights was a liberal concern, they reasoned, and Dukakis's problem was that voters thought he was too liberal. Donilon knew that abortion rights, framed in terms of privacy, could be purged of liberal associations. He had seen it done in the campaign against Robert Bork. But Dukakis and his advisers were unlikely candidates for the experiment. They lacked the imagination and the gall.

No one could accuse Wilder or Goldman of deficiency in those departments. Wilder had spent his life bulldozing the received unwisdom about what a black man in Virginia could aspire to. He was admired and despised for the same reason: he would do whatever it took to win. In 1985 he had used his cachet with blacks and liberals to capture the Democratic nomination for lieutenant governor, only to repackage himself as a crime-busting war hero in the general election.

Goldman was a pale, bony, Jewish vegetarian with a New York accent, a fondness for raw potatoes, and a conspicuous disregard for grooming. He approached politics animated by the insights of dead thinkers and statesmen, from Adam Smith to Theodore Roosevelt to Martin Luther King Jr. On his arrival in Virginia in 1976, he had taken on the absurd task of electing Jews and liberals to major offices. Wilder was his most absurd project and his most appreciative employer. Both men were attracted to the impossible, and they never ceased scheming.

The coincidence of Wilder's ascent with the Supreme Court's rollback of *Roe* was fateful. Unlike other politicians, Wilder was willing to defy strategists who considered the issue too risky to raise in the South. He was willing to defy activists who demanded pro-choice purity. He was willing to bet millions of dollars' worth of television advertising on the issue, which no candidate had ever done. But if Wilder was the father of a new kind of pro-choice campaign, necessity was its mother. There was no other way to win.

In Goldman's view, the chaos over abortion presented an opportunity to reorient the Democratic Party. He believed that the party's constituency was the middle class and that its enemy was a wealthy elite that would just as soon milk big government as starve it. In the 1977 governor's race, Goldman had urged his client to forswear any tax increase. In 1980 he had watched with disgust as Ronald Reagan branded Democrats the party of big government and seized the banner of the overtaxed middle class. Goldman believed that Reagan had tapped a deep American fear of losing one's freedom and livelihood to a self-serving bureaucracy. Now the threat of a Falwellian Big Brother policing sexual matters gave Democrats a chance to mine that fear.

In Virginia, Goldman had come to terms with cultural conservatism, a widespread antipathy to labor unions, feminists, and other agitators. He had concluded that a politician who implicitly threatened social change would do well to repudiate it rhetorically. Thomas Jefferson's Declaration of Independence was a perfect example. Although the colonists had decided to break with the crown, Jefferson dwelled painstakingly on their reluctance. They had hoped to remain loyal subjects, Jefferson explained, but the king's abuses had forced them to resist. They had sought no revolution.

By March 1989 Goldman and Donilon had sketched a plan. The competition for right-wing votes in the Republican primary would pressure the candidates to juice up their rhetoric against abortion. If they went all the way, advocating a ban even in cases of rape or incest, Wilder would draw the line there, sealing them off from Bush and 85 percent of Virginia voters.

Any effort by the Republicans to pin down Wilder's position or to open new fronts on other abortion questions would be resisted. Wilder would run as the safe choice. He would pledge to leave Virginia's abortion laws alone. That meant abortion would remain legal, but the state wouldn't pay for the procedure except in medical emergencies or cases of incest or rape. The government would stay out of it.

Goldman wanted Wilder to advocate one change: a new law requiring parental consent. That position was favored by a clear majority of pro-choice voters. It would draw a second line, this time between Wilder and feminists. Wilder supported parental consent anyway, but Donilon's poll showed that he had much to gain and little to lose by advertising his position. The people most likely to object were conveniently omitted from the poll, not to mention the election. They were old enough to get pregnant but too young to vote.

On April 9, just across the river from northern Virginia, thousands of pro-choice activists marched through the streets of Washington. They carried posters asking, "Who Decides—You or Them?" In a newspaper interview that day, Wilder gave his answer: You, the head of the household, should decide. "How would you feel if one of your children . . . were to slip off someplace" for an abortion? Wilder asked the interviewer and, implicitly, the parents of Virginia. A parental consent law, he argued, was "the only way to keep the family intact." [3]

The Republicans played into Wilder's hands. In an April 21 debate, the top three contenders called for a ban on abortions except to save the woman's life.[4] Coleman's performance was particularly gratifying. In a June 5 letter to Christian ministers, he pledged "to work to prohibit all abortions in Virginia, except to protect the life of the mother." [5] His extra effort to win pro-life votes arguably bought him the nomination. The price would prove dear. In the afterglow of his victory, a copy of the letter circulated among Wilder's advisers, awaiting its encore.

Like Falwell, Coleman sought to blend evangelism with contempt for government. "God gave *us* the responsibility for our children, not the government of Virginia," he declared in a campaign brochure. On the reverse side, he paraphrased Reagan: "How can families and family values flourish when big government . . . has absorbed their wealth, usurped their rights, and too often crushed their spirit?" Yet in the same brochure, Coleman promised "[a]ctive use of the office of governor to awaken Virginians to the need to value and protect the most vulnerable members of the human family." [6] The contradiction didn't escape Wilder's strategists. They would make Coleman's pro-life activism a symbol of the intrusive style of government he had condemned.

Goldman and Donilon developed this plan in ignorance of the un-folding campaign at NARAL. Not until June 1989 did Goldman realize that the media consultant Wilder had hired in March, Frank Greer, was also working for NARAL. Greer found the coincidence fortuitous. A victory for Wilder, coupled with a win by Democratic representative Jim Florio in the New Jersey governor's race, would parlay NARAL's research and mobilization into a sweep of the November elections. It would awaken politicians and pundits to the power of the pro-choice majority. Conversely, NARAL's research clarified how Greer's candidate could most profitably handle the issue: When the *Webster* decision was released, Wilder should issue a statement defending the rights of women, families, and doctors to make abortion decisions without government interference.

After explaining the political logic of this position to Goldman and to Wilder's press secretary, Laura Dillard, Greer considered the matter resolved. But Greer's NARAL affiliation made Goldman and Dillard nervous. Their loyalty was to Wilder, to whom abortion rights was a means, not an end. NARAL was the kind of advocacy group against which Goldman hoped to define Wilder's moderation. To Dillard, Greer was a newcomer with deeper roots at NARAL. Where did his loyalty lie?

Goldman and Donilon conferred several times a day about how Wilder should respond to the Court's decision. They agreed that he should take exception to it but not too stridently. Goldman was emphatic that Wilder keep his distance from NARAL and NOW. The best way to do that was to avoid NARAL's language and to underscore Wilder's support for mandatory parental consent.

Donilon agreed, for different reasons. He was less interested in Goldman's triangulation strategy than in staying on the attack. Wilder mustn't let his views distract attention from Coleman's. The cross Coleman had shouldered in the primary was his pledge to ban abortion in cases of rape or incest. It was essential to nail him to that cross now, before he could wriggle away. Donilon also worried that the Virginia press was framing the abortion debate as left versus right, with Wilder on the left. Positioning Wilder as the critic of government intervention would confound that framework.

On July 3, the day the *Webster* decision came down, Wilder was on vacation, and Greer was in a studio assembling material for a NARAL teleconference. Goldman edited the campaign's statement and released it to the press. It opened with an attack on Coleman for advocating a ban on abortion in cases of rape, incest, or fetal deformity. "In all these tragic cases," Wilder was quoted as saying, "this most personal of decisions ought to be made by a woman in consultation with her loved ones, her religious advisers, and her doctors—without governmental coercion. And yet, a need exists for appropriate limitations on abortions." One appropriate limitation, the release noted, was parental consent. As to Wilder's views on the more than 90 percent of abortions that didn't involve sexual assault or fetal abnormality, the statement said only that he supported Virginia's current laws.[7]

Greer was in his studio when the statement arrived by fax. He didn't take the surprise well. Goldman's answering machine suffered the brunt of the explosion. "Well, we've just blown the campaign," Greer ranted. Months of polling had shown that abortion rights was a winner in Virginia, the Supreme Court had tossed the issue back to the states, and Wilder was seizing the banner of "appropriate limitations." Goldman had used the phrase about women, families, and doctors, but he had confined it to cases of rape or deformity. To Greer, that wasn't even a pro-choice position. And parental consent wasn't what NARAL had meant by entrusting abortion decisions to families.

When Goldman returned home, he played back Greer's tirade, ejected the tape, and saved it to amuse friends. Greer didn't own the term *pro-choice*, NARAL didn't own the meaning of the phrase "a woman and her family," and nobody owned Wilder. For the next five months, the eyes of the political world would be on Virginia. If a black man won this election on the abortion issue, his campaign would become the national model. NARAL no longer defined abortion rights. Wilder did.

For the next two days, Wilder tried to slalom through the issue, dodging invitations to clarify his views. On July 5 reporters confronted him after a speech in Richmond. He declined to say whether he would veto restrictions on first-trimester abortions. While defending abortions for rape victims, he added, "I don't think that abortion for purposes of birth control should be available."[8]

Birth control, like *convenience,* was a pejorative term for all abortions in cases other than rape or incest. In the 1986 Arkansas campaign, pro-choicers had focused on rape victims in order to circumvent the popular assumption that women who had consented to sex should "pay the fiddler." Wilder wasn't just circumventing that assumption; he was embracing it. This was too much for NOW president Molly Yard. Her tart verdict—"wimpy"—thundered out over the AP wire.[9]

Goldman savored the slap. "Molly Yard is not happy with us, apparently," he chuckled in a note to Greer. "We are therefore somewhat to the right of her on this thing and comfortably to the center of Coleman. Can we make it stick?" Greer wasn't amused. He warned that Wilder's advocacy of parental consent would cut him off from NARAL's money and credibility. Goldman was unmoved. NARAL and NOW had been bellowing for years. What had they accomplished?

Something deeper was driving this quarrel. Greer had made his share of negative ads, but he believed that Wilder could win by appealing to the moral aspirations of white voters. He viewed abortion rights as a cause, something that a statesman should stand *for* and that voters would rally *to*. Goldman and Donilon took a darker view. Goldman had studied the history of racism and anti-Semitism. Donilon remembered how white opponents had turned white voters against his previous black clients. He and Goldman believed that whites would vote against Wilder because he was black, unless something about Coleman scared them more. That something was Coleman's abortion position. Defining Wilder's position would only give Coleman something to shoot at.

Wilder, as usual, settled on a compromise. He would stay on the attack, but when forced to define his position, he would use Greer's language. He unveiled that strategy at the nominees' first debate on July 15. "It's clear that your position on abortion is out of step with Virginia values and law," Wilder told Coleman at the first opportunity to pose a question. "How can you justify saying to a woman who's a victim of rape and incest that she cannot have an abortion?"

Coleman replied that "we ought to protect the lives of the pre-born." He joked that Wilder had modified his position twice during the previous week. "I never had but one view," Wilder shot back, "that government should not interfere." Returning to the attack, Wilder asked, "How can you say to a woman who's a victim of rape and incest that you can say what's best for her? How can your judgment supersede hers?" At this, Coleman retreated. He assured voters, "I'm not going to propose legislation outlawing abortion in cases of rape and incest during my term." [10]

While others fretted over the *Webster* statement and the debate, Donilon conducted a statewide poll and three focus groups. As in the 1986 Arkansas campaign, the idea was to find out how voters would respond to arguments from both sides—essentially, to play out several campaign scenarios and choose the one that turned out most favorably. At the outset, Wilder trailed Coleman 50 to 41 percent. Donilon tested four strategies. One was to emphasize Wilder's qualifications; another was to present him as the heir to the past two Democratic governors; the third was to cast him as a fighter against crime and drugs. None of these arguments attracted enough voters.

Then the survey respondents were told that Coleman favored a constitutional ban on abortion, even in cases of rape or incest, whereas Wilder supported a parental consent law but otherwise favored leaving Virginia's abortion laws alone. That news capsized the race. Two-thirds of the respondents leaned toward Wilder's view; only one-fourth leaned toward Coleman's. When they were asked to vote again, 51 percent chose Wilder; only 39 percent chose Coleman.

The focus groups were equally striking. Donilon and his colleague, David Petts, began each session by asking the participants which of the state's issues or problems concerned them. In most elections, the answer given was jobs, taxes, or schools. This time, four or five people in each group, primarily younger women, brought up abortion. They pointed to the Supreme Court's decision to allow new restrictions, and they expressed fear that their right to abortion would be taken away.

Donilon recognized the same fixation on privacy that he had seen during the Bork campaign. But now two other patterns struck him. Without being told about Coleman's position, several participants, most of them older men, raised the subject of rape. They argued that the government shouldn't tell the victim of such a crime what to do about her pregnancy. In the focus groups, as in the poll, support for abortion rights evaporated as the discussion turned to other scenarios, such as an abortion for a woman who had already had one or for a teenager without her parents' knowledge.

Then Donilon and Petts confronted the participants with various criticisms Coleman might raise against Wilder. The participants replied that such faults paled next to the prospect of losing abortion rights. Donilon concluded that an early assault on Coleman's abortion position would keep voters anchored to Wilder throughout the subsequent storm of character attacks—and that an emphasis on rape victims would keep the abortion debate from straying into tougher questions.

From the poll data, Donilon drew up a plan. Assuming unanimous black support, Wilder needed 43 percent of the white vote to win. Using abortion, he would target whites between the ages of eighteen and forty, carrying 60 percent of women and 55 percent of men. That would be enough to offset a 2 to 1 loss among white voters over forty. Donilon spent much of July and August persuading Wilder, Goldman, and Greer that the plan would work, or at least that nothing else would.[11]

Goldman spent much of August weaving the team's strategic threads into a theme. Younger voters were happy that the legislature no longer regulated private life. Accordingly, Wilder should underscore the danger of returning to the bad old days. In that vein, he could subsume his racial novelty under the theme of going forward. But the forward motion had to be steady. It couldn't connote a lurch toward government activism that might alarm whites or threaten the economy. As the kickoff of the fall campaign approached, Greer, Dillard, and Wilder added their ideas. Goldman spent the Labor Day weekend holed up in his apartment, working their points into a speech.

By the time Wilder rose to speak before his first Labor Day audience, the finished text lay on the podium before him. He stood for Virginia's "New Mainstream," a force that looked "forwards, not backwards," and sought "to unify people, not divide them." The "greatest responsibility of government," he proclaimed, was "to protect our individual freedoms." His adversary was the "New Extremism," a "self-righteous, moral majority" movement that dared to assert that "government should dictate the most personal of personal decisions."[12]

Among other things, navigating the New Mainstream meant steering clear of eddies on the left. On August 24 Dillard, Wilder's only senior female aide, met secretly with feminist leaders in the Arlington living room of NOW's Virginia coordinator, Georgia Fuller. The activists were familiar with Wilder's aversion to feminist groups. In 1985 his staff had asked NOW to delay its financial contribution to him until the end of the campaign so that the public wouldn't find out about it until after the election. This year was no different. Dillard would later deny to the press that the meeting she was now attending had occurred.

Dillard's message to the activists was blunt. The campaign welcomed their help but would keep them at arm's length in public. Furthermore, Wilder didn't want to be called pro-choice. For one thing, said Dillard, nobody understood what the term meant. For another, it would be misleading since Wilder rejected what feminists regarded as the pro-choice position on parental consent.

Alice Cohan, NOW's national political action director, told Dillard that Wilder's support for parental consent legislation was unacceptable. Dillard refused to budge. Yes, she acknowledged, Wilder had switched from opposing to supporting parental consent. Yes, he would sign a

tightly drawn consent bill if it arrived on his desk. No, he wouldn't ini-
tiate legislation on this or any other abortion issue. If feminists wanted
to liberalize the abortion laws, they shouldn't expect leadership from
Wilder. And no, he wouldn't change his position.

Cohan left the meeting unmollified, but Fuller, mindful of the Republican alternative, put her trust in Dillard and in the candidate who had
given this young woman such an important role in his campaign. Maria
Briancon, head of NARAL's Virginia affiliate, attended the meeting and
agreed reluctantly to help Wilder. Although Coleman was worse, Briancon knew that Wilder had made a career out of playing the left and
right against each other. She suspected that Wilder's sudden outspoken-
ness on abortion rights was mere opportunism. And she knew that the
one abortion restriction that came close to passing the Virginia legislature every year was parental notice.

Across the river in Washington, D.C., NARAL faced a similar dilemma. Kate Michelman and her deputies had regarded Wilder coolly
since April, when he began to advertise his interest in parental consent.
Three months later, when he endorsed that restriction in response to
Webster, Michelman told the press that Wilder's apostasy would cost
him NARAL's support. Instead, she announced, NARAL would cast its
lot with Florio in New Jersey. "Wilder needs to understand that his position on consent and notification undermines the entire area of a woman's right to choose," she argued.[13]

There was a political catch, too: While Florio coasted toward victory,
Wilder trailed in Virginia. By campaigning for Wilder, NARAL would
risk taking blame for his defeat and diluting the perception of pro-choice
political strength. For these reasons, NARAL initially planned to ignore
Wilder and confine its activity in Virginia to the race for lieutenant
governor.

On the other hand, mail, phone calls, and money were flooding the
organization. The press was demanding to know what NARAL would
do next. Michelman felt that she had to do something to make a difference and to demonstrate the power of abortion rights. Like it or not, the
nation's eyes were on the Wilder-Coleman contest. Coleman proposed
to ban abortion; Wilder didn't. How could NARAL sit it out?

Michelman regarded Wilder as a deeply calculating man. She judged
that he was championing parental consent primarily for political advantage. That motive reflected poorly on his character but also meant that
he might be susceptible to pro-choice lobbying if elected. And despite

Wilder's flaws, Michelman, like the young feminists on her staff, yearned to play a role in the struggle to install America's first elected black governor.

When the question of endorsing Wilder arose in staff discussions and at a NARAL Political Action Committee (PAC) meeting that summer, fierce debates erupted. NARAL's standing policy was to endorse pro-choice candidates only if they also opposed parental notice and consent laws, on the principle that "all women, no matter what their age, should have access to safe and legal abortions." [14] Purists argued that if one group of women—in this case the young—were abandoned, others would soon be in jeopardy. Some reasoned that if NARAL, the flagship of the abortion rights movement, declined to fly the banner of teenagers' rights, why would anyone else? Pragmatists replied that *Webster* had spawned a new world of threats and opportunities and that NARAL had to step forward quickly to strike a decisive blow. Sitting out Coleman's election was unacceptable.

Two memorandums that circulated among NARAL's consultants and staff in early September crystallized the question at the heart of this debate: To what extent should NARAL treat policy as a means to politics rather than the other way around? Those responsible for policy took one view. Those responsible for politics took another.

Speaking for those who refused to subordinate policy concerns, NARAL legal director Dawn Johnsen and staff attorney Marcy Wilder drew a hard line against legislative compromise on parental involvement. Unlike NARAL's campaign consultants, Johnsen and Wilder dealt with the effects of legislation. "In practice, both consent and notification laws amount to a parental veto power over a minor's decision to have an abortion," they wrote. "Do not, as part of an affirmative legislative strategy, introduce even a liberalized version of a parental consent or notification law." [15]

A week later, Page Gardner, the consultant who had managed the *Webster* campaign, outlined the opposite perspective. She proposed to transform NARAL from an advocacy group into a "party committee" modeled after her previous employer, the Democratic Senatorial Campaign Committee. This meant two things.

First, rather than treat elections as a means to winning legislative fights, NARAL would treat legislative fights as a means to winning elections. It would focus on campaigns rather than government, as Harrison Hickman had put it in his creed of political consulting. "Our decision to

become involved in defensive legislative efforts should be dictated by our
political and electoral objectives," Gardner wrote. On this principle,
NARAL might support bills crafted to "give our friends 'cover' on issues
such as parental consent." Better to pass a diluted parental involvement
bill than to jeopardize the careers of pro-choice lawmakers by forcing
them to oppose the idea altogether.

Second, NARAL would judge candidates not in absolute but in
relative terms. The DSCC supported Democratic nominees even if they
strayed from the Democratic platform. Likewise, Gardner argued,
"NARAL should be involved in all races where one candidate is better
than another on choice," even when NARAL had "disagreements" with
the pro-choice candidate. "[W]e must not allow ourselves to be 'fringed'
by an unyielding concept of what constitutes the pro-choice position,"
she wrote. In practical terms, she explained, this meant that NARAL
should get off the sidelines and into the Virginia governor's race.[16]

Strategically, Gardner's plan impressed NARAL staffers. Morally,
it disturbed them. They bristled at her talk of being "fringed" and were
alarmed by her advice to relax the definition of *pro-choice*. Part of their
mission, as they saw it, was to teach politicians and voters that "choice"
entailed more than the legal right to abortion, that it included subsidies
for women who couldn't afford the procedure and excluded mandatory
parental consent. If NARAL came to Wilder's aid, other politicians
would take it as an invitation to hedge.

The NARAL officers caught at the center of this struggle were Michelman and the director of her legislative and political department, Nancy
Broff. Broff was a pragmatist and a cynic. She had worked in the coalition against Bork and in the campaign against the 1988 Arkansas referendum. Her judgment might be clouded by jealousy—it was her turf,
politics, that the consultants had invaded—but not by squeamishness
about doing what it took to win.

Broff's concern was that the ostensibly pragmatic course, supporting
Wilder, would hurt NARAL in the battles ahead. The Supreme Court,
she observed, was just months away from upholding parental notice
laws in Minnesota and Ohio. That ruling would invite every state that
didn't already have such a law, including Virginia, to enact one. Pro-
choice lobbyists were also sure to face parental notice proposals in Congress during upcoming debates over federally funded clinics and legislation to guarantee abortion's legality. If NARAL rewarded Wilder's
calculated compromise, how could pro-choice lobbyists ask state legis-

lators and members of Congress to endure the political price of resisting the country's most popular abortion restriction?

Broff's cynicism extended to NARAL's friends as well as its enemies. Her job was politics *and* legislation. To her, winning elections was a means to passing pro-choice measures and defeating abortion restrictions. Gardner and the other consultants didn't share the latter responsibility. In that respect, their agenda diverged from NARAL's.

Broff and Michelman had worked together since the Bork campaign. They shared a feminist philosophy, an institutional loyalty, and even a birthday. But as Michelman came around to the consultants' view that NARAL should enter the Virginia race, Broff pushed back. She reminded Michelman that the consultants had other clients, politicians who didn't want to take unpopular positions on issues such as parental consent. She warned Michelman to beware this ulterior agenda. She even called it a conflict of interest. At this, Michelman erupted. The consultants were part of NARAL's family, she replied, and Broff's insinuation to the contrary was baseless and unseemly.

Across town, Greer and Haddow spent the latter part of August building the Wilder campaign's A-bomb, a television ad that would pack the power of abortion rights into thirty seconds of video. Greer was irked that Republicans were campaigning to amend the Bill of Rights to let states ban the desecration of the American flag. He wanted to reclaim the flag as a symbol of the liberties that the Bill of Rights protected. The image he had used in his July 3 NARAL ad, the Statue of Liberty, didn't fit the South. But Virginia had its own icon of freedom: Thomas Jefferson.

Greer had studied Jefferson's life and work for years. Jefferson's portrait hung on the wall beside his desk; copies of Jefferson's writings graced bookshelves in his offices. Greer's brother, an author of books on the revolutionary period, taught history at Virginia Commonwealth University and knew the director of Monticello, Jefferson's estate. Greer had made the trek to Monticello before, a two-hour drive that, for a political consultant, amounted to a pilgrimage.

Greer wanted the abortion ad to evoke lofty traditions and to position Wilder clearly as the pro-choice candidate. Donilon wanted it to attack Coleman. Goldman wanted it blunt and brutal. "Hang the bastard with his own words," he urged in a note to Greer.[17] To complicate matters, Wilder insisted that he had never run a purely negative commercial and wouldn't start now, a policy with which Donilon was losing pa-

tience. "That posture is putting us in a suicidal position," Donilon
warned in a memo.

By the first week of September, the ad was finished. It opened with a
profile of Monticello illuminated against the night sky, followed by cin-
ematic sweeps of Jefferson's towering statue and the marble columns of
his memorial. As the scenes passed, the stripes of an American flag veiled
the screen. "In Virginia," a male voice began, "we have a strong tradition of rights and individual liberty—rights that are now in danger in
the race for governor."

The flag and the icons gave way to a corpselike photograph of Coleman accompanied by an ominous background hum so deep the cycles
were audible. "On the issue of abortion," the narrator continued, "Marshall Coleman wants to take away your right to choose and give it to the
politicians. He wants to go back to outlawing abortion, even in cases of
rape and incest." The last three words were spat with revulsion.

Coleman vanished, replaced by a video clip of Wilder wearing a concerned, sympathetic expression. "Doug Wilder believes the government
shouldn't interfere in your right to choose," said the narrator. "He wants
to keep the politicians out of your personal life." Coleman reappeared
and then vanished again as a smiling, handshaking Wilder filled the
screen. "Don't let Marshall Coleman take us back," the ad concluded.
"To keep Virginia moving forward, Doug Wilder is the clear choice." [18]

In those thirty seconds, Greer and Haddow had refined years of polling and strategy into the definitive abortion commercial of the post-
Webster era. It reached across ideological lines and beyond the abortion
issue, framing a whole election. It embraced southern tradition, condemned government interference, and focused its outrage on rape. Apart
from a fleeting handshake at the end, no women appeared, nor were any
mentioned. The choice wasn't between conservatism and feminism. It
was between "politicians" and "you."

On the evening of September 19, television studio technicians across
the state loaded the ad onto their stations' airwaves and dropped it into
the living rooms of Virginia. Wilder trailed in Donilon's polls. His game
plan hinged on this issue. If the ad didn't work, the campaign was basically over.

Seven days later, at around five o'clock in the morning, Donilon went
to his office and printed out tables of numbers that had been sent to his
computer overnight. They were the results of his first poll since the ad's
debut. For three months, Donilon had told Wilder to stake his twenty-

year career on this ad. Donilon figured that if the tables showed no improvement, Wilder would fire him.

It was a full two hours before Wilder received the phone call from his pollster. "My God," he replied. "We've got to keep these numbers quiet." Donilon hung up the phone and dragged himself across the street to Greer's office. Greer saw the despair in Donilon's face. "What are the numbers?" Greer asked. Donilon said nothing. He shook his head in dismay. "Frank," he groaned. Greer grew frantic. "What?" he barked. "What?" After another pause, a mischievous smile crept across Donilon's face. Wilder had surged ahead. The abortion ad had turned the race upside down.[19]

NARAL's strategists had known since the first week of September that Wilder was preparing an abortion ad. This put an end to their debate about the political wisdom of associating the issue with his troubled candidacy. Wilder had resolved that question. They decided that if his commercials propelled him into the lead, NARAL should move in with its own media campaign. There remained the moral question of whether to endorse a candidate who wasn't fully pro-choice. Gardner urged Michelman to set aside her misgivings and do everything possible to help Wilder win. Michelman consented but with a caveat: technically, NARAL would neither endorse nor campaign for Wilder; its stated objective would be to defeat Coleman.

By law, Greer couldn't participate in NARAL's Virginia campaign while working for Wilder. Tony Podesta took his place at the helm of NARAL's media strategy. On September 20, the day after Wilder's abortion ad premiered, Podesta submitted a plan to reinforce Wilder's offensive. The plan assumed that Coleman would respond to Wilder's ad. As Wilder moved to attack Coleman on other fronts, NARAL would bombard Coleman's abortion position again with its own ads.[20]

Michelman approved the plan. Within a week, Podesta returned with drafts of a newspaper ad and two scripts for television commercials. One commercial, designed for female voters, featured a woman on camera. The other, crafted for men, featured a male doctor. The newspaper ad would feature either the doctor or the woman. Podesta suggested that using the doctor would help NARAL attract men's votes.[21] The NARAL team agreed and chose the doctor.

By and large, Podesta followed Gardner's advice to stick to the "Who decides?" message. NARAL's mid-October newspaper ad asked, "WHO

DECIDES? YOU . . . OR MARSHALL COLEMAN?" Its final television ad began: "The fundamental question in the abortion debate is: Who decides?
You or the politicians?" In a flyer distributed to Virginians, Michelman
boasted, "For months, NARAL has posed the question: Who Decides?
For most Americans, the answer is evident. We want intensely personal
decisions about abortion left to women and families." 22

Coleman spent the end of September and the beginning of October trying to change the subject. He criticized Wilder's record on crime, touted
his own values in television ads, and hosted a visit from Bush. Nothing
erased Wilder's lead.

The problem wasn't just abortion, but Wilder's carefully cultivated
immunity to charges of liberalism. He was dead set against raising taxes.
He supported Virginia's right-to-work law, which protected nonunion
workers in unionized industries. And in a reversal of his 1985 position,
he now favored the death penalty. Apart from the color of his skin—and
even that looked curiously pale in his television ads—Wilder had rendered himself almost indistinguishable from his opponent.

The anti-government approach to abortion blended into that strategy. Late in the campaign, the NRA aired radio ads portraying Wilder
as a threat to gun owners. Greer had seen the gun issue hurt Democrats
in other southern states, but this time his client had a credible rejoinder.
"Doug Wilder believes the government doesn't have any business in
your personal life," Greer's new radio ad replied. "And that includes
your constitutional right to keep and bear arms."

Wilder's treatment of abortion also deflected Coleman's efforts to la-
bel him soft on crime. In Virginia, as in Arkansas, traditionalists sympathized with rape victims who didn't want to carry their pregnancies
to term. To stand up for such women was to stand up for morals and
justice in the face of crime. To some, this connoted the protection of
whites from blacks. As Coleman's vanquished primary opponent, Congressman Stan Parris, had put it five years earlier, "If a black man rapes
a white woman, I don't think God meant for her to have that child." 23

In 1988 supporters of Bush's presidential candidacy put a face on this
nightmare. It belonged to Willie Horton, a black convicted murderer
who, after being furloughed from a Massachusetts prison, had raped a
white woman in Maryland and stabbed her fiancé. Bush's television ads
didn't include pictures of Horton. But a group called Americans for
Bush, employing a Republican adman connected to the Bush campaign,

aired a commercial that used Horton's menacing visage to scare a largely white audience.

Bush held Dukakis responsible for Horton's furlough and, by implication, the subsequent rape. Dukakis tumbled farther in the polls when he refused to endorse the death penalty even if a man were to rape and kill Dukakis's wife. (Bush slam-dunked this gaffe by replying that "some crimes are so heinous" that the criminal had to die.) Republicans portrayed Horton's rape as a crime not against one woman but against the sanctity of the family. A flyer distributed by the Maryland GOP, depicting Dukakis and Horton together, asked, "Is This Your Pro-Family Team for 1988?" [24]

Wilder was no Dukakis. He remembered the beating he had taken in 1985 for opposing the death penalty. It hadn't helped that Wilder was black. Knowing that in 1989 he would again be accused of coddling criminals, Wilder renounced his opposition to the death penalty. And he used the issue of abortion for rape victims to turn public concern about moral decency and criminal justice against his opponent.

Coleman's advisers understood that Wilder's emphasis on rape tapped the same fear and loathing of criminals that Bush had exploited. During a strategy session late in the 1989 campaign, Coleman's media consultant put the point acidly to a pro-life activist: "If Willie Horton raped you, and you became pregnant, what would you do?" [25]

Within a week of the debut of Wilder's abortion ad, Coleman's team had prepared his reply. Coleman's commercial ignored the context of Wilder's attack—abortion—and instead addressed the underlying theme of criminal justice. It depicted a rape victim sobbing as she recalled her brutal cross-examination by her assailant's attorney. The narrator told viewers that contrary to his professed compassion for survivors of sex crimes, Wilder had once "introduced a bill to force rape victims age thirteen and younger to be interrogated about their private lives by lawyers for accused rapists."

The candidates' quarrel over which of them was insensitive to sex crimes continued all the way to the election. In answer to Coleman's rape ad, a new Wilder commercial maintained that Wilder had "supported the Virginia law that protects the victims of rape." Wilder's commercial repeated that Coleman intended "to outlaw abortions even in the case of rape or incest." In another ad, Coleman charged that Wilder had voted three times against legislation to shield rape victims from interrogations. In a spot two weeks later, Coleman asserted again that Wilder had voted "to allow rapists and their attorneys to grill the victim."

Wilder and his advisers relied throughout the latter part of the month on a commercial in which a white, middle-aged woman declared that she would break her tradition of voting Republican because Coleman threatened to ban abortions even for "victims of rape or incest." NARAL's strategists reinforced this theme. Podesta's newspaper and television ads hammered Coleman for threatening to ban abortions for sex crime survivors. One NARAL newspaper ad repeated the rape-and-incest mantra four times.[26]

Michelman had understood the risk of dwelling on sex crimes since 1986, when NARAL sought Medicaid coverage of abortions in those cases. The risk was that abortion would be construed as a victim's rather than a woman's right and that "choice" would be reserved for these victims. On October 16 that risk became reality, as Eddy Dalton, the pro-life, female Republican nominee for lieutenant governor of Virginia, declared in a television ad that in cases of rape, incest, or danger to a woman's life or health, "a woman should have a choice" to abort. Pro-choice lawmakers cried foul. Dalton, they charged, was stealing "the language of pro-choice champions."[27] But if Dalton had stolen the language of Wilder's July 3 statement, the reason was that she was saying the same thing.

Days after Dalton's ad premiered, a pitched battle erupted across the Potomac, propelling sex crimes to the forefront of the abortion debate. On October 21 Bush vetoed a federal spending bill on the grounds that it included Medicaid coverage of abortions in cases of rape or incest. He explained,

> My intense personal concern for those women who are victims of the crimes of rape and incest is as strongly felt as my position on abortion. Rape and incest are crimes of violence which must not go unpunished, and those convicted of such crimes must be brought to justice.
>
> The question raised by H.R. 2990, however, involves whether the Federal Government and American taxpayers should be forced to pay for [abortion] in the case of rape or incest.[28]

This would be quite a fight. It pitted two conservative principles—criminal justice and taxpayers' rights—against each other. In their campaign for a congressional override of the veto, pro-choice lobbyists stressed the vileness of rapists and the innocence of their victims. A fact

sheet distributed to lawmakers by NARAL and its allies quoted a the-
ologian's defense of abortion as a kind of "help" for victims "pregnant
as a result of crimes." Likewise, the tag line of NARAL's ad in the October 22 *New York Times* and *Washington Post*—"Don't you think
poor women who are pregnant because of rape and incest have suffered
enough?" [29]—implied that motherhood was a punishment and that rape
victims, unlike other women, had met their quota of suffering.

In the days leading up to the override vote, pro-choice lawmakers
smothered questions about women's rights and fetal life under a gravy
of breast-beating about crime and punishment, innocence and guilt.
In an hour's worth of speeches from the House floor, they mentioned
victims 135 times and crime 46 times. Denying abortions to rape survivors would "sentence the victim" and "punish the victim twice," they
charged. The rights of each woman hinged on her role as victim rather
than perpetrator of intercourse, and the worth of each unborn life hinged
on its father's guilt. Any fetus conceived by force was dismissed as the
"child of a rapist," "the unborn of that hateful act," and "the fruit of
that terrible crime." One speaker called it "Rosemary's baby." [30]

Pro-choice legislators didn't hesitate to frame the debate in terms of
sexual responsibility. Louise Slaughter, a New York Democrat, asked,
"Is it morally right to tell a poor woman who becomes pregnant by violence that she must pay for a crime she did not commit?" Nancy Pelosi,
a California Democrat, pleaded that women shouldn't have to "take responsibility for other people's actions." [31] Olympia Snowe, a Maine Republican, echoing Wilder, called for a legal distinction between abortions for rape victims and abortions for "birth control":

> Women who are victims of rape or incest find themselves in a situation not
> of their own making; these are instances far beyond their own control.
> They have become pregnant unwillingly. . . . Opponents to this exemption,
> however, are effectively saying that a pregnancy resulting from rape or in-
> cest is no different from any other pregnancy. Reality, though, is quite to
> the contrary: These situations are a far cry from so-called abortion as birth
> control. . . . It is a distinction worth making in our policy, and I urge my
> colleagues to make this distinction by voting to override. [32]

Pro-choice legislators were equally emphatic that abortion for rape
victims was a matter of criminal justice, not abortion rights. "We are
not opening the floodgates for abortion," said Nancy Johnson, a Connecticut Republican. "We are providing justice for victims of terrible
crimes." Slaughter agreed: "As long as Government cannot protect
women and children from the crimes of rape and incest, Government

should not compound that felony by denying those victims the right of some recourse." To uphold Bush's veto, said George Miller, a California Democrat, would be to "come down on the side of the perpetrators of these crimes." Jim McDermott, a Washington Democrat, seconded by Ron Wyden, an Oregon Democrat, added, "For a President who said he would be tough on crime, he is being awfully tough on victims."[33]

Several speakers resurrected the soft-on-crime attack with which Bush had torpedoed Dukakis. Tom Sawyer, Democrat-Ohio, recalled that Dukakis, when "asked his reaction if his wife were raped," had betrayed insensitivity to crime. In the same spirit, Sawyer said, "We ask President Bush what he would do if his wife or daughter were raped or the victim of incest."[34] Steny Hoyer, a Maryland Democrat, completed the regression to 1988 by bringing back Willie Horton: "[I]t was in Maryland that Willie Horton raped that innocent woman. God was gracious. And Willie Horton did not impregnate that woman that he raped in Maryland. But if he had, colleagues, if he had, which one of us would have stood before her and said, 'Carry Willie Horton's baby to term'?"[35]

The anti-crime invective was so unrelenting that Henry Hyde, Republican-Illnois, a pro-lifer and normally a law-and-order firebrand, concluded, "This is a question about love and vengeance. Do we hate the rapist so much, are we so intent on wreaking vengeance that we go beyond the criminal and we will impose on the child of the criminal capital punishment? . . . Vengeance, vengeance, we must extirpate, eliminate, not only the criminal . . . but the child of the rapist."[36]

When the debate ended, the House voted 231 to 191 against Bush— not enough to override his veto, but enough to demonstrate the power of framing abortion as a crime issue.[37]

Besieged by that issue in Virginia, Coleman spent the final two weeks of his campaign trying to redirect attention to his conservatism on other matters. First, he accused liberal governors of leading the state to the brink of a fiscal crisis. In a cruelly inept stroke, the National Right to Life Committee simultaneously endorsed him, stealing the day's media coverage and thrusting abortion back into the spotlight.[38] Coleman also aired a television spot in which the head of the Virginia Federation of Republican Women declared, "I'm pro-choice, but I'm not a single-issue voter." She praised Coleman's positions on taxes, day care, and crime.

In another ad, Coleman, following Dalton's example, told viewers, "I'm not going to restrict abortions for rape or incest." But unlike Dalton, Coleman had already said the opposite. Greer taped Coleman's earnest-looking denial and paired it with a copy of the June 5 letter in which Coleman had pledged "to work to prohibit" such abortions. Within hours, Greer had this mocking rebuttal, entitled "Promise," on the air. Coleman responded by yanking his ad and replacing it with a visibly desperate message. "Let's stop spreading fear on abortion and start making sense," he pleaded.

But spreading fear turned out to be Coleman's best recourse. Throughout the campaign, he had chafed under the impression that journalists were giving Wilder a free ride. On the Thursday before the election, when the *Washington Post* buried Coleman's latest criticism of Wilder under an upbeat story about Wilder's historic ascent, Coleman exploded. "Any one" of Wilder's known misdeeds "would disqualify me from high office," Coleman charged in a press conference. "I think that a double standard applies to Doug Wilder." [39]

In Wilder's camp, mayhem broke loose. Coleman was surging in the polls, and now he had lit the racial fuse. Wilder's advisers again argued over whether to bet on hope or fear. Greer believed that to motivate his supporters and avoid antagonizing other voters, a candidate should halt his negative ads in the last four days of the race and rinse out their bitter taste with an uplifting message. Accordingly, Greer had prepared an ad entitled "Rise Above," which implicitly called for racial progress. "On November 7th, we can lead the way again," said the ad. "To keep Virginia moving forward, for all of us, Doug Wilder is the clear choice."

Goldman and Donilon detested the idea. Donilon flashed back to the final days of the 1983 mayoral races in Chicago and Philadelphia, when undecided white voters had rallied unanimously to white candidates. If that happened now, Wilder would be a hair's breadth from defeat. Asking white Virginians to "lead the way" would only remind them of their basic anxiety about Wilder. Goldman envisioned years of toil collapsing in this swoon of idealism. People were deciding which candidate to vote against, he reasoned, and the candidate who loomed largest in their minds would lose.

Greer wouldn't buckle. He persuaded Wilder that the ad had to go on. Goldman, equally vehement but unable to thwart Greer, ended one argument by dashing his telephone against a wall. Throughout the weekend Donilon and Goldman watched Greer's buoyant finale with despair.

Soon after the polls closed on Tuesday, television stations announced that an exit poll showed Wilder winning in a landslide. The euphoria among his advisers, gathered with him in a Richmond hotel suite, was short-lived. As vote tallies trickled in, it became clear that many whites had lied to the exit pollsters. By 10:30 P.M. Coleman was less than half a percentage point behind. Watching victory slip away, Wilder sensed that his appeal in the final days had been a mistake.

Shortly after 11:00 P.M., however, an analyst on one broadcast estimated that the precincts remaining to be counted were too few to tip the balance. "That's it," Wilder announced. He and his bodyguard made their way to a ballroom packed with supporters. "I am here to claim to be the next governor of Virginia," he declared as a wave of jubilation engulfed him.

Minutes later Wilder maneuvered backstage to a cluster of rooms where four television networks stood ready to interview him. Here he would address his biggest audience of the night, the viewers of ABC's *Nightline*. Democratic Party chairman Ron Brown was already on the program, trumpeting the party's victories in mayoral and gubernatorial races. The election of Wilder and two other black Democrats, said Brown, proved that Americans "vote their hopes rather than their fears."

As Wilder joined the discussion, host Ted Koppel zeroed in on his innovative use of the abortion issue. "You turned it, in effect, into kind of a libertarian issue," Koppel observed. "And therefore you found yourself with a considerable number of conservative Republicans voting for you," voters who "don't want the government interfering" in personal matters. Wilder welcomed the compliment. Looking ahead to the 1990 elections, Koppel asked, "Is this something the Democrats around the country are going to be able to use in the months and years ahead?"

The question seemed astute yet naive—astute because it grasped the irony of Wilder's conservative abortion message, naive because it treated that irony as an isolated ploy, an aberration from Wilder's platform. Koppel's colleague on the show, commentator Jeff Greenfield, had just finished arguing that Democrats couldn't win back the presidency based on abortion alone, because their liberal views on economics and crime remained serious liabilities.

Wilder paused. Didn't his interviewers see that the right to abortion was connected to these other issues, that his pro-choice position was part of a conservative platform? "I would think more that [Democrats] would be looking to candidates who can run and not be accused of tax and spend, who will not be accused of being weak on crime," he told

Koppel. "And I had a very tough crime message and a very good record in terms of cutting taxes and trying to find tax relief."[40]

A CBS–*New York Times* survey taken at Virginia polling places that day confirmed Wilder's analysis. More than 60 percent of those who had voted for him described him as moderate. One-third had supported Bush in 1988; fewer than six in ten had supported Dukakis.[41] For a black Democrat in the South, those numbers were phenomenal. What Virginians had voted for, Wilder told the ABC audience, was a candidate who had catered not to a pro-choice "litmus test" but to "mainstream people." "And if it takes place in Virginia," he concluded, "it can take place anywhere."[42]

A new breeze was in the air—not a liberal revival, not a feminist enlightenment, but a revolt of conservative voters against pro-life politicians who usurped family authority and ignored criminal justice. Hoisting his sails before that breeze, Wilder, the captain to whom NARAL had entrusted its quest for power, was sweeping the abortion rights movement forward into the New Mainstream.

CHAPTER 5

Triage

On the morning after Doug Wilder's victory, Kate Michelman made a triumphant appearance before a swarm of reporters at NARAL's Washington headquarters. "To politicians everywhere," she proclaimed, "we say with conviction: if you're out of touch with the pro-choice majority, you're out of office."

Wilder had proven that the abortion rights strategy pioneered in Arkansas and refined in the Bork and *Webster* campaigns could win a major statewide election. Now it was time to capitalize on that win. The lessons drawn by pundits and politicians in the days after the 1989 elections would establish the climate for 1990. In the coming year, one-third of the nation's Senate seats, two-thirds of its governorships, and all of its House seats were at stake. In her postelection statement, Michelman made sure everyone got the message: By framing the abortion issue "skillfully," Wilder had won "a southern conservative state" with "significant support from pro-choice Republicans." [1]

Media strategist Kim Haddow, a veteran of the *Webster* and Wilder campaigns, set to work consolidating the lessons of those campaigns into a manual for politicians. Harrison Hickman, Frank Greer, and other consultants helped to shape the draft. It become the *NARAL Guide for Candidates and Campaigns,* published in early 1990. It comprised three sections. The third consisted of model press releases and position papers. The second offered technical advice on field organization and media.

The opening section of the *Guide,* divided into chapters, was the most important. It distilled the work of the past year into a canon of pro-choice rhetoric, a chronicle of the genesis of that rhetoric, and a record of the events that had proven its power. The chronicle and the canon were interwoven. It was, in short, a bible of the politics of abortion rights. This bible became NARAL's chief means of propagating its message and its interpretation of the 1989 elections.

The first chapter told candidates how to deliver "the Message." The fundamental commandment was to "frame the issue as a matter of keeping the government from interfering in personal decisions." Wilder had shown the way. According to the manual, he had "discussed abortion rights in the context of NARAL's 'Who Decides?' message." [2]

Next came the story of the *Webster* campaign and the truth it had revealed to the world: "NARAL's strategy was to develop a message that broke through to the 60% of the voters who defined themselves as neither pro-choice nor anti-choice. NARAL's goal was to develop a message that helped Americans in the middle who were, in fact, pro-choice, to define themselves, to find their voice, to articulate their position."

According to the manual, "Who Decides?" attracted this audience for three reasons. First, it represented the conservative position, since "[c]onservative politicians historically have opposed government interference." Abortion rights followed naturally from the premise that "the government has no business in a free market place or controlling the rights of private citizens to bear arms." Second, "Who Decides?" avoided the drawbacks of feminism. "It does not appeal to one sex over another," said the manual. Third, it appealed to American individualism. As the manual put it, "Americans have historically answered the question, 'Who Decides?' whatever the issue, with the same response, 'I do.'"

This was the third appearance of NARAL's pronoun fallacy. Like the "we" whose rights Michelman had defended in her speech to NARAL's annual conference in July 1987 and the "you" whose authority Jackie Blumenthal had exalted in her "you or them" slogan in March 1989, the "I" whose territorial claims Haddow now celebrated was a vast, empty word.

The reason pro-choice strategists spoke of "we," "you," and "I" rather than "women," "poor women," and "teenagers" was obvious. Most people, encompassing nearly all the country's wealth, weren't

poor. Most people, encompassing all the country's votes, weren't teenagers. Half, encompassing the bulk of the country's political power,
weren't women. But everyone was a "you" and an "I." Everyone belonged to a "we." Pronouns were politically useful because they appealed to everybody. They appealed to everybody because they excluded
nobody. And because they excluded nobody, they meant nothing. They
were open to alternative and even hostile interpretations.

Haddow was correct that Americans thought "I" should decide every
issue. But the meaning of that word was in the "I" of the beholder. As
a matter of social logic, for every person to whom the issue was "my
pregnancy," there were others to whom the issue was "my daughter's
pregnancy," "my wife's pregnancy," or "the use of my tax money to
abort that woman's pregnancy." Who decides what to do about that issue? I do.

NARAL also propagated its rhetoric through ads and public statements. In commercials on behalf of some candidates and against others, Greer and Haddow recycled phrases from the *Webster* and Wilder
campaigns, plugging in new names. In 1989 their ad for Wilder had begun, "In Virginia, we have a strong tradition of rights and individual liberty." In 1990 their ad for congressional candidate Mike Kopetski began, "In Oregon, we have a strong tradition of individual liberty and
personal freedom." Against Governor Terry Branstad of Iowa, NARAL
argued, "He wants to take away your right to choose and give it to the
politicians." Against Representative Craig James of Florida: "He wants
politicians to decide." Against Texas gubernatorial candidate Clayton
Williams: "He wants the politicians to decide." Against Representative
Denny Smith of Oregon: "He believes politicians—not women and their
families—should decide." In North Carolina: "Jesse Helms wants the
government and politicians to make this personal decision for you."
Against Ohio gubernatorial candidate George Voinovich: "Tell him—in
Ohio, it's the people, not the politicians who decide."

In the North Carolina Senate race, NARAL's ad said, "Harvey Gantt
believes the decision should be yours, not the politicians'. Who decides
in North Carolina?" In the Iowa Senate race, NARAL's ad said, "Tom
Harkin believes the decision should be yours, not the politicians'. Who
Decides in Iowa?" In North Carolina: "On November 6, vote to keep
Jesse Helms and the government out of your private life." In Oregon:
"Vote to keep Denny Smith out of your personal life." In Ohio: "Use
your vote to keep Voinovich out of the governor's office and out of your

personal life." In Michigan: "On November 6, you can vote to keep the government out of your most personal decision."

A week after Wilder's election, pollster Celinda Lake followed up her work on the *Webster* campaign by conducting focus groups and a nationwide survey for another pro-choice organization, EMILY's List. In her report, distributed to NARAL and its allies, Lake noted that abortion rights advocacy by Democratic politicians "changes somewhat voters' definitions of being conservative":

> Most startling was the shift in perceptions of which party "most opposes government interference in your private lives." Before the discussion of abortion, more voters thought that description applied to Republicans (39 percent) than Democrats (29 percent). By the end of the survey, more voters thought that description applied to Democrats (43 percent) than to Republicans (31 percent).[3]

This shift confirmed that abortion was more than a single issue, that it could be made to represent the larger question of the role of government and could thereby shatter the Republican coalition. "The *Webster* decision has already reshaped agendas and restructured alliances," Michelman proclaimed on January 22, 1990, the seventeenth anniversary of *Roe v. Wade*. A month later that reshaping of agendas and alliances crystallized in a NARAL-funded radio ad in Alabama, where Michelman had first stared into the eyes of the voters who would become NARAL's prize converts. "This isn't Communist China or Romania," said the ad. "This is America, and the government shouldn't be involved in my freedom of choice."[4]

At the same time, Lake's report revealed strains within the new alliance:

> As in other surveys, voters overwhelmingly support parental consent, 68 percent in favor, to 27 percent opposed. However, voters do not see this as an abortion issue. For parents today, parental consent is an issue about control, authority, responsibility, and the difficult time that even good parents have. When voters express support for parental consent they are thinking about affirming parental responsibility and control—not about limiting women's right to choose.[5]

By tracing the problem to adults' concerns about "control" and "authority," Lake meant to comfort advocates of abortion rights. But her distinction between the two issues was a mistake. The compatibility voters perceived between parental "control" and the "right to choose" signified not that the two principles were separate but that they were affirmatively linked. What linked them was the belief that rights belonged to families and that "you," as an adult and parent, should decide. While winning the battle to define abortion as an issue of choice, NARAL was losing the battle to define what choice meant.

Other surveys confirmed Lake's findings. Most polls published in the year following *Webster* showed that about 70 percent of voters favored parental consent laws and an additional 13 to 14 percent supported parental notice laws. The pivotal bloc of voters, 30 to 40 percent, opposed outlawing abortion for adults but supported laws requiring teens to notify their parents. Surveys also suggested that only half the electorate was willing to spend public money on abortions for women who couldn't afford them.[6] Although this degree of support wasn't bad, it wasn't good enough to protect public funding, in part because it was concentrated among liberals rather than swing voters and in part because many politicians, having rejected abortion bans in order to distance themselves from the right, were inclined to reject abortion funding in order to distance themselves from the left.

Pro-life strategists studied these cracks in the pro-choice coalition and set to work exploiting them. Six weeks after their November 1989 losses, NRLC officials disclosed plans for a counteroffensive. They proposed to advance the political debate from the vague theme of choice to specific restrictions backed by polls, such as parental and spousal notice.[7]

Within two months, the National Right to Life (NRL) PAC answered NARAL's *Guide for Candidates and Campaigns* with its own *1990 Handbook for Political Candidates*. The pro-life handbook was subtitled *Balancing the Rights on Abortion*. Opposite its opening page was a two-frame cartoon that illustrated the strategic significance of this theme. The first frame depicted a seesaw perched atop the dome of a legislature. At one end sat a woman, labeled "the woman's right to privacy." At the opposite end lay a fetus, labeled "the unborn's right to life." The seesaw was evenly balanced—an acknowledgment that pro-life rhetoric, by itself, had failed to win the abortion war.

In the next frame, several people were added to the fetus's end of the seesaw. They were labeled "the parent's right to be consulted," "the husband's or boyfriend's right to have a say," and "the taxpayer's right not to pay for an abortion." The weight of these rights tilted the seesaw in their favor, leaving the woman suspended in the air. What would defeat the abortion rights movement wasn't the right to life but the pro-family, anti-government version of the right to choose.

The handbook's authors, NRL PAC director Sandra Faucher and NRLC associate director Darla St. Martin, exposed the fragility of the pro-choice coalition mathematically and rhetorically. First, they summarized the polls:

> Although many people may say they are "pro-choice," this does not mean what the pro-abortionists would like you to believe it means. Polls have shown that when asked about specific pro-life proposals a majority favor them. Over 80% of the public oppose using abortion as a method of birth control, 70% favor parental consent for minors before an abortion is performed, and over 60% oppose public spending for abortion.[8]

To substantiate the popularity of these restrictions, the handbook cited a September 1989 CBS–*New York Times* poll showing 70 percent supported parental consent, a July 1989 Gallup-*Newsweek* poll showing 61 percent opposed public spending on abortion, and a December 1989 *Boston Globe* poll showing 61 percent supported mandatory notice to husbands. The handbook also reported the findings of NRLC's fall survey, which showed an advantage of more than 40 percentage points for politicians who "favored a law requiring parental consent" and an advantage of nearly 20 points for politicians who "opposed the use of tax dollars for abortion."[9]

Next the authors explained how candidates could use the language of "choice" to promote these restrictions. "[I]f women have rights, so do men, fathers, parents," and taxpayers, they reasoned. Thus, a pro-life candidate could tell conservative pro-choice voters that his liberal pro-choice opponent stood for "unrestricted abortion . . . performed on your daughter without your consent or knowledge . . . and paid for with your tax dollars."[10] The winning question, in effect, was: Who decides? You, the parent and taxpayer, or politicians?

Pro-life and conservative advocates took up that question. NRLC headlined its new fact sheet on public funding "Getting Government Out of the Abortion Business." Conservative activist Phyllis Schlafly expanded on this theme in her syndicated column: "The pro-abortionists who claim they are so eager to keep the government out of a woman's bedroom are at the same time demanding that the government actively get into the abortion business by subsidizing it with our tax dollars. The taxpayers should not be forced to aid or finance this shameful, profitable industry." [11]

As the 1990 elections got under way, pro-life politicians capitalized on this contradiction. In Texas, a gubernatorial candidate attacked the idea that "the government should spend any money" on abortions. In Illinois, another accused his opponent of championing an "active role for government in the promotion of abortion through direct taxpayer funding." Talking about taxes brought home the trusty conservative message that liberals would use big government to rob the little guy. In Pennsylvania, literature for a pro-life state senator told voters that his pro-choice challenger "really liked the idea of taxpayer funded abortions. So, instead of going out and getting a real job, she decided to open an abortion clinic and worked to make you pay for the abortions." [12]

The word *taxpayer* became a succinct way to restore the alliance between hostility to abortion and hostility to big government. In Iowa, a congressman under fire for supporting a ban on abortion replied that his opponent was "out-of-step with the vast majority of the people on issues like taxpayer funding of abortion." In Maryland, a pro-life congressman who had been accused of promoting "government interference" responded by emphasizing his vigilance against abortions on the taxpayers' tab. In Indiana, a Republican challenger argued that unlike their Democratic congresswoman, his district's constituents "don't believe tax dollars should pay for abortions." [13]

Pro-life politicians also seized on parental rights as a wedge issue. In Michigan, South Carolina, and New York, legislators promoted parental involvement bills as "pro-family" and pro–"parental rights" rather than "anti-abortion." [14] Nowhere was this strategy more aggressively pursued than in Texas. Anticipating a battle over his opposition to legal abortion, Clayton Williams, the Republican gubernatorial nominee, launched a preemptive strike against the Democratic nominee, state treasurer Ann Richards. Immediately after their first joint appearance, in May 1990, Williams devoted an entire press conference to parental consent.

Williams presented the issue as a symbol of the difference between Richards's "far-out liberalism" and his own "modern Texas conservatism." "Unlike me and most Texas families," said Williams, "Ann Richards thinks it's OK for a 13- or 14-year-old to have an abortion . . . without the knowledge of her parents." Promising to make a parental consent law his first priority as governor, he charged, "Ann Richards has

allowed the liberal, feminist pro-abortion groups to set her agenda."
When reporters tried to change the subject, Williams refused to relent.
"I came here today to talk about parents' consent to an abortion,"
he said.[15]

Richards and the Texas Abortion Rights Action League (TARAL)
spent months grappling with the parental consent problem. TARAL director Phyllis Dunham understood that Williams was trying "to concentrate on parental rights because he's wrong on choice." Dunham
tried out the liberal rejoinder: "We support parental rights, but they
should not take precedence over teenagers' lives."[16] But that answer
was a loser, since it defended people who couldn't vote while offending
people who could.

Richards explored two other ways of responding to Williams. While
endorsing parental rights, she pointed out that through "judicial bypass" clauses, most parental consent bills actually gave judges the ultimate power to decide whether to require parental consent in a given
case. "It's not a question of parents, it's a question of judges," she argued. "Every bill I've ever read had to do with courtroom consent. It
didn't have to do with parents' consent."[17] This was a fine argument
against judicial bypass clauses, but it didn't answer the demand for some
kind of parental authority.

Richards's other response was that "government has no business
interfering in our lives any more than is necessary." But most voters
didn't see parental consent laws as interference. They saw them as cer-
tificates of authority. Williams mercilessly exploited this theme. "Ann
Richards says parents don't have the right to know if your teenage
daughter is about to receive an abortion," he charged. "Don't let Ann
Richards tell you that your child's future is none of your business."[18]

Though he had changed the lyrics, Williams was singing the same
populist tune—Don't let politicians take away your right to make family decisions—that NARAL had popularized in 1989. Distressed by
Williams's strategy and fearful that he would extend it to television commercials, Richards tried to avoid the abortion issue throughout the summer. She even asked TARAL not to advertise that she would veto abortion restrictions.

The Texas Republican Party reinforced Williams's attack with its own
media campaign. In April the GOP announced a "legislative action
plan" that featured mandatory parental consent and omitted any talk of
outlawing abortions in general. The party's chair promised to protect
the rights of "parents of minor children." In July the GOP began airing

a radio ad against Richards in West Texas and on Houston country music stations. "The real Ann Richards doesn't believe the parents of a 13-year-old girl should be told that their daughter is seeking an abortion," said the ad. Richards, it concluded, was simply "a liberal Democrat in a conservative state." [19]

In the midst of Williams's onslaught, the Supreme Court gave its approval to two more parental notice laws. On June 25, in *Ohio v. Akron Center for Reproductive Health,* the Court ruled 6 to 3 that Ohio could require notice to one parent while providing a judicial bypass option. Meanwhile, in *Hodgson v. Minnesota,* the Court ruled 5 to 4 that Minnesota could require notice to both parents as long as a judicial bypass was available. [20]

Hodgson demonstrated the losing politics of children's rights and the winning politics of parents' rights. The justices split into three camps. On the left, Justice Thurgood Marshall, joined by Justices Harry Blackmun and William Brennan, protested that Minnesota's laws "significantly restrict a young woman's right to reproductive choice." To begin with, wrote Marshall, "the notification requirement destroys [her] right to avoid disclosure of a deeply personal matter." In addition, he argued, since a parent, "once notified, can exert strong pressure on the minor," the notification requirement sometimes "usurps a young woman's control over her own body by giving either a parent or a court the power effectively to veto her decision to have an abortion." [21]

Marshall declared flatly that the case pitted parents against children and that he sided with children. "Parental authority is not limitless," he wrote. "Certainly where parental involvement threatens to harm the child, the parent's authority must yield." He added, "No person may veto *any* minor's decision, made in consultation with her physician, to terminate her pregnancy. An 'immature' minor has no less right to make decisions regarding her own body than a mature adult." [22]

This radical, intrafamily individualism was exactly what Minnesota attorney general Jack Tunheim had argued against. He had cautioned the Court against any attempt "to significantly limit parents' rights and responsibilities by finding that minors have constitutional privacy rights as against their parents and a right to withhold important information from parents." As Tunheim saw it, both parents had "a protected liberty interest" in "knowledge about important events" in their children's lives, whether or not the parents' decisions would best serve their children's interests.[23] A parent's right to know about her daughter's pregnancy superseded the daughter's right to keep it secret.

Justice Anthony Kennedy, joined by Chief Justice William Rehnquist and Justices Byron White and Antonin Scalia, agreed with Tunheim. Kennedy scolded his liberal colleagues for disrespecting "our most revered institutions." "The common law historically has given recognition to the right of parents, not merely to be notified of their children's actions, but to speak and act on their behalf," Kennedy wrote. Thus Minnesota's law "rests upon a tradition of a parental role in the care and upbringing of children that is as old as civilization itself." By "giving all parents the opportunity to participate in the care and nurture of their children," states were simply taking "reasonable measures to recognize and promote the primacy of the family tie."[24]

But to justify Minnesota's demand that minors notify two parents rather than one, Kennedy had to change costumes. He shed the vestments of tradition and clothed himself in women's rights. "In this century, the common law of most States has abandoned the idea that parental rights are vested solely in fathers, with mothers being viewed merely as agents of their husbands," he wrote. "[I]t is now the case that each parent has parental rights and parental responsibilities."[25]

Politically, this was an ingenious argument: Both parents had to be notified because mothers had equal rights. Rather than reject the woman's perspective, Kennedy had complicated it. A "young woman's control over her own body" collided with a mature woman's "parental rights." In Kennedy's calculus, the elder woman prevailed, enshrining gender equality alongside generational authority.

Unfortunately for Kennedy, Justice John Paul Stevens trumped him with an even more ingenious argument. Responding to Minnesota's assertions of parental rights, the attorneys opposing the Minnesota law had suggested that by requiring the notification of a second parent, "[t]he statute interferes . . . with the ability of single parents to control communication, association, and the flow of personal information to the minor's other parent. . . . Contrary to defendant's arguments, a statute like Minnesota's which compels minors and their single parents to communicate private information to an estranged second parent may in fact violate, rather than protect, parents' constitutional rights."[26]

In oral argument, Janet Benshoof, director of the ACLU Reproductive Freedom Project, reinforced this point. "The heart of our case is the two-parent requirement . . . which tramples on the integrity of many families," she told the Court. The state had no authority "to force the parent who has been a sole custodian for 16 years to go to an ex-husband and reveal this personal information" about her daughter's pregnancy.[27]

In a centrist opinion joined by Justices Blackmun, Brennan, and Marshall and in part by Justice Sandra Day O'Connor, Stevens developed this ironic observation into a lethal indictment. He pointed out that in a voluntary setting, the mechanism that transformed one-parent notice into two-parent notice was the first parent's decision to notify the second. Each parent had the authority to decide whether to notify the other. By insisting that the other parent be notified, Minnesota had usurped that authority.

Just as Kennedy confounded women's rights by turning woman against woman, Stevens confounded parents' rights by turning parent against parent. While purporting to protect the rights of one parent, Stevens explained, the state was encroaching on the rights of the other. "[T]he State has no legitimate interest in questioning one parent's judgment that notice to the other parent would not assist the minor or in presuming that the parent who has assumed parental duties is incompetent to make decisions regarding the health and welfare of the child," Stevens wrote. Minnesota's requirement that the first parent notify the second or seek a court's permission to be excused from that obligation was an "unjustified governmental intrusion into the family's decisional process."[28]

The recognition of two contrary parental rights also changed the Court's calculus of interests. A parent's interests generally outweighed his child's. But since everyone agreed that the child's interests counted for more than zero, Stevens logically deduced that "the combined force of the separate interest of one parent and the minor's privacy interest must outweigh the separate interest of the second parent." On the bottom line, this theory changed the calculus that mattered most: Whereas Marshall could muster only three votes, Stevens mustered five.[29]

Even so, Kennedy prevailed when the fifth justice, O'Connor, voted to uphold the Minnesota law if it were softened by a judicial bypass. Three months later, Kennedy explained that Ohio, like Minnesota, had "acted to protect families against unilateral action by a child and her doctor."[30]

In Texas, Clayton Williams applauded Kennedy's opinion and used similar arguments to give NARAL strategists fits. Though Williams managed, through a series of unrelated gaffes, to fumble away the advantage he had gained on parental rights, that issue helped to sink at least two other prominent pro-choice politicians. One was Joseph Strohl, majority leader of the Wisconsin state senate, whose pro-life challenger unseated him with the help of pro-choice voters, in large part by attacking Strohl's obstruction of a parental consent bill.[31] The other was Harvey Gantt, the Democrat nominated to replace Senator Jesse Helms in North Carolina.

Gantt was no Wilder. In two televised debates during the Democratic primary, Gantt highlighted his opposition to parental consent laws and proudly distinguished himself as the only candidate who supported unrestricted abortion coverage under Medicaid. "It is the only way to assure that poor women have the same rights, concerning abortion, as women who can afford to pay for abortions," he lectured an opponent.[32]

North Carolina was Harrison Hickman's turf. In July NARAL announced that according to a poll by Hickman, 59 percent of North Carolina voters believed "government should stay out of the abortion issue." Based on that finding, NARAL launched a media campaign against Helms. "Six years ago, Jesse Helms ran for reelection saying he would keep the government out of your private life," said one television commercial. But on abortion, the ad continued, "Jesse Helms wants the government and politicians to make this personal decision for you."[33]

Helms and the conservative voters of North Carolina, many of whom NARAL had claimed as part of its anti-government majority, had a different notion of the kind of "private life" the government should respect. Helms answered NARAL's attack with a television commercial that criticized Gantt for endorsing the use of tax money for abortions. The ad also asked viewers, "Should teenage girls be allowed to have abortions without their mothers being informed? Harvey Gantt says yes, it's a teenage girl's right."[34]

By appealing to parents and taxpayers, Helms blunted NARAL's assault and avoided losing the election on the abortion issue. He violated the conservative policy on sex crimes—in banning abortions, he made no distinction between innocent and guilty women—but NARAL couldn't exploit that violation to the extent Hickman had hoped. To sow confusion among racists, Hickman wanted to run an ad telling voters, "Jesse Helms wants your daughter to have Willie Horton's baby." Only one inconvenience prevented the pollster from playing this angle: Gantt was black.

One Helms ad called Gantt a tool of "the gay and lesbian political groups, the civil liberties union—all the extreme liberal special interests." Another showed Gantt's face and told viewers that even if "you were the best qualified" for a job, Gantt would force the employer to hire "a minority" instead. The racial ad destroyed Gantt in the campaign's final days.[35] The abortion issue, defined as such, didn't win the election for Helms. But the issue of the rights of upstanding white parents, taxpayers, and job applicants—which Helms's abortion ads, like his other ads, underscored—did.

While liberals fell, moderates flourished. At the outset of the election year, in its *Guide for Candidates and Campaigns,* NARAL presented its anti-government, pro-family rhetoric as "a foundation on which candidates can build—a message to refine, to make their own." Dozens of politicians took up that offer, making the message their own at NARAL's expense. Like Wilder, they endorsed the caveats favored in polls. "I voted for parental consent," boasted a pro-choice candidate for lieutenant governor of South Carolina, adding, "Read my lips, no public funds for abortion."[36]

Politicians everywhere proclaimed that abortion decisions "should remain in the family," where they could be made according to "traditional values." Like Wilder, many interpreted this to include a guarantee of parental authority. The day after Wilder's victory, Kansas's pro-choice governor kicked off his reelection year by proposing to require parental notice. In California, a candidate for lieutenant governor promised to leave the abortion decision to each woman "with her doctor, her God and her family," which in the candidate's view included parental consent. In Kentucky, the leading candidate for governor took the same position, explaining that the decision "ought to be made by family members, the family physician and family minister." In Florida, a pro-choice Republican candidate for governor defended the state's parental consent law, which she had sponsored, as an expression of her commitment to the family. The two top pro-choice Democrats in that race likewise endorsed parental consent. So did the NARAL-funded Republican candidate for governor of New Hampshire and the front-running pro-choice gubernatorial candidates in Illinois and Massachusetts.[37]

Pro-choice candidates who pledged to get "big government out of our private lives" shunned abortion funding on the same grounds. In Texas, Republican gubernatorial candidate Tom Luce argued, "[G]overnment officials should not be involved in that decision. And I take the same neutrality position with respect to financing of abortion." In Florida, Representative Bill Nelson, a Democratic candidate for governor, was accused of violating "choice" by opposing federal funding of abortions. Nelson's campaign manager replied that Nelson, although pro-choice, "will not favor people willy-nilly depositing themselves at Uncle Sam's doorstep and saying 'Give me an abortion. It's my right.'" In Arizona, all seven candidates for governor, four of them pro-choice, refused to spend state money on abortions. In California's gubernatorial race and Colorado's U.S. Senate race, pro-choice Republicans who opposed public financing of abortions defeated Democrats who supported it.[38]

Republicans even formed a PAC to cater to conservative pro-choice voters. In November 1989, after watching the abortion issue wreck Republican campaigns in Virginia and New Jersey, Republican National Committee chairman Lee Atwater met with conservative activist Ann Stone over dinner to propose a new venture. As Stone later described the conversation, "Lee said that the only people who were urging the party to back off of its anti-choice position were people who were against everything the party leadership was for, anyway. . . . [What we need] is somebody from the conservative wing of the party, who agrees with the leadership on most things, but not on abortion. A woman, preferably. Lee looked at me and said, 'Do we know anybody like that?' I said, 'I get the message.'"[39]

Stone named the PAC Republicans for Choice. "As Republicans, we oppose government interference in our private lives," she declared in an April 1990 manifesto. But to maintain a partisan edge, she advised Republicans "to shift the abortion debate to the question of individual restrictions." Stone called this "an important difference between the parties and a crucial element of a 1990 campaign strategy." A pro-choice, pro-restriction position, she calculated, "will appeal to the vast majority of voters who favor a woman's right to choose a legal abortion but are troubled by wholesale abortion on demand." Conservatives should "compromise and win reasonable restrictions on abortion," she concluded. "Let the Democrats be the party of abortion on demand."[40]

In the face of these defections and with polls running against them, what could feminists do? Feminist Majority president Eleanor Smeal pledged to rally one million "young women" in high schools and colleges to fight parental consent measures. NOW president Molly Yard announced a "Campus Caravan" that would "organize the youth of this nation, in high schools and colleges," to "fight rollbacks of their reproductive rights." As Yard envisioned it, lawmakers would "hear directly from the young people these laws affect." "I want to see teenagers and young adults in every state house in the nation, and outside every polling place on election day, whether or not they can vote," she said.[41]

This was the army that stood ready to battle pro-choice conservatism: the moral authority of the young, armed with the voting strength of the disenfranchised, backed by the money of the financially dependent. Not a sleeping giant but a herd of besieged, defenseless, doomed Lilliputians.

In war, medics overwhelmed by wounded soldiers sort them into three categories. Some don't need prompt attention. Others can't be saved. Those who need prompt attention and can be saved take priority. Doctors call this logic "triage." If there were more help, some of the patients deemed unsalvageable might be rescued. But there isn't. Among pro-choice activists, a nationwide pattern of triage was emerging, and the young and the poor were its losers.

In his annual address to the South Carolina legislature on January 17, 1990, Republican governor Carroll Campbell urged lawmakers to pass a parental consent bill. "We cannot—we must not—diminish the role of parents in rearing their children," said Campbell. "Government must undergird parental responsibility, not interfere with it. This applies to abortion." Four weeks later, when the bill came before the state senate, a pro-life senator affirmed, "This is not really an anti-abortion bill. It's a pro-family bill. It restores the family situation back into a very serious surgical procedure." [42]

Thus framed, the debate was over before it began. Who would interfere in the natural order of the family? Not the state's pro-choice lawmakers. After amending the bill slightly, they waved it through without dissent. At most, they reasoned, it would trouble a few hundred girls each year. "I can live with or without the bill," shrugged a pro-choice floor leader in the house.[43]

Two days after South Carolina legislators passed their parental consent bill, a committee of West Virginia lawmakers considered legislation to outlaw state funding of abortions. Exceptions would be allowed in cases of rape, incest, fetal deformity, or danger to the woman's health. The bill also included an ingenious concession: It would allow taxpayers to check a box on their state income tax forms assigning a few dollars of their tax money to an abortion fund for poor women.[44]

As in South Carolina, the bill's pro-choice tint made it hard to resist. Who would oppose a taxpayer's right to choose whether to subsidize abortions? Not West Virginia's pro-choice legislators. They joined pro-lifers in a lopsided vote to advance the bill. Within two weeks, the house and senate voted to strip abortion subsidies from the state budget. The president of West Virginia NOW conceded the futility of resistance. Poor women "have no voice," she lamented. "The Legislature could care less."[45]

Fresh from victory in Virginia, Frank Greer headed south to Georgia, where Atlanta mayor Andrew Young was running for governor after a career in the civil rights movement and Congress. Though the color of Young's skin invited comparisons to Wilder, the content of his character distinguished him. Wilder enjoyed strategy for its own sake; Young focused on what strategy might achieve. Wilder had chosen a career in the law; Young had chosen a career in the ministry. Wilder had watched the civil rights movement from the sidelines; Young had walked in its vanguard.

Young took risks Wilder would have considered imprudent, in which nothing but principle stood to be gained. In 1979 he lost his post as U.S. ambassador to the United Nations for meeting with officials of the Palestine Liberation Organization. A decade later, when President Bush proposed a constitutional amendment to ban the desecration of the American flag, Young declared his opposition to it without consulting his political advisers. Wilder endorsed the amendment.[46]

Young was renowned among pro-choice activists for energetically promoting women's rights and abortion rights during his two decades in Congress and city hall. In 1988 he enlisted city attorneys and law enforcement to break Operation Rescue's siege of Atlanta abortion clinics. In April 1989, while Wilder was hedging his bets on abortion, Young stepped forward at a NOW rally in Atlanta to support the pro-choice march on Washington.[47]

Young's principal rival for the Democratic nomination was Lieutenant Governor Zell Miller. In 1987 and 1988 Miller had supported parental notice legislation, brushing aside pro-choice lobbyists who tried to dissuade him. In April 1989 he declared himself "strongly opposed" to abortion and insisted that it be allowed only "in the early stages of pregnancy." After *Webster,* Miller concluded that "the decision ought to be in the hands of a woman, her pastor, her doctor and her family," but he added that by the same token, a girl's family had to be notified of her plans to get an abortion. He welcomed *Webster* as "an opportunity to come up with some sensible restrictions."[48]

Throughout the campaign that followed, Young assailed Georgia's

parental notice law and other abortion restrictions. He promised as governor to "support the right of minors to obtain abortion services confidentially without their parents' permission or a court or agency order."
Miller refused to support that right. Young insisted that the state provide abortion and other medical services to women "regardless of their
income." Miller rejected abortion subsidies. Young aggressively courted
pro-choice activists. Miller dodged the activists' overtures and failed to
answer their surveys or return phone calls seeking his response.[49]

Young tried to make abortion a central issue. He raised it in his
first television ad, returned to it in later ads, and spotlighted it in a campaign aimed at women. In one commercial, Greer borrowed images and
phrases from the ads he had made for NARAL and Wilder. But whereas
Greer had been able to tar Wilder's opponent as a big-government persecutor of rape victims, his ad for Young could only plead that Young,
unlike Miller, was "strongly and consistently pro-choice." [50] The idea of
using Wilder as a model for Young's campaign against Miller was absurd, for a reason that would have been obvious but for the blinding,
cosmetic resemblance of race. The true heir to Wilder's conservative prochoice philosophy wasn't Young. It was Miller.

Far from disputing Young's attacks, Miller and his aides advertised
them as proof of the lieutenant governor's moderation. "I guess Andy
has modeled himself as the most pro-abortion candidate in the race,"
shrugged Miller's campaign manager, James Carville. When Young accused Miller of inconsistency on abortion rights, Miller proudly replied
in a press conference and in a television commercial that he had always
stood on a moderate pro-choice platform of legal abortion, mandatory
parental notice, and no public financing of abortions.[51]

Repeatedly, Young's strategists warned him that his positions on
parental notice and public funding would cost him votes. They advised
him to stick to the theme of keeping government out of the issue. Repeatedly, Young ignored that advice. In the campaign's final televised debate, Young reiterated his stand against parental notice legislation and
blasted Miller for opposing state funding of abortions. Miller was delighted. He affirmed his support for parental notice and used the quarrel to underscore his posture as the candidate of moderation.[52]

Miller surged past Young and trounced him in a runoff. A poll taken
a week before the runoff showed that two-thirds of pro-choice Democratic voters supported Miller. More surprising was the indifference of
the abortion rights establishment. Two statewide pro-choice groups did
endorse Young—a Georgia NOW official explained that Miller wasn't

"pro-choice for pregnant women who are young or poor," and the Georgia Abortion Rights Action League noted that Young had pledged a far greater commitment to abortion rights than Miller had—but neither group had enough money to help Young.[53]

Two other organizations had the money but decided not to use it. One was Vote Choice, a well-endowed PAC run by a circle of wealthy Atlanta women, each of whom put up $1,000. These women weren't the sort to let sympathy cloud their judgment. They sized up Young as a potential investment, not as a hero. They flunked him for two reasons. First, they expected him to lose because of his color and his liberalism. Why alienate the next governor, Miller, by backing his opponent? Second, they deemed Young's differences with Miller trivial compared to the central task of electing a pro-choice governor. Miller was good enough.[54]

The other group capable of helping Young challenge Miller was NARAL. This wasn't the first time NARAL had met a Georgia politician with a different idea of abortion rights. In 1976 then-governor Jimmy Carter had won the presidency on a conservative pro-choice platform. In July 1977 Carter had endorsed and institutionalized the end of federal Medicaid coverage of abortions, arguing that the government had no business trying to give poor people equal access to every option available to rich people. Two months later, Carter's policy had claimed its first casualty, a woman named Rosie Jimenez who had sought an illegal abortion because she couldn't afford a legal one.[55]

In October 1988, a decade after Jimenez's death, Kate Michelman went to Atlanta to speak at a memorial service for her. "The death of Rosie Jimenez must remain with us" as a reminder to protect financial access to abortions, said Michelman. "Our opponents don't seem to care, but we will always remember." And NARAL did remember. In October 1989 Young was included on a list of candidates the organization expected to support in 1990.[56]

Over the winter, however, a frost of political calculation settled over NARAL. The reception of Wilder's victory as a triumph for abortion rights proved that the nuances of choice were lost on the press. Meanwhile, the movement's strategic framework was evolving from combat to deterrence. NARAL's new challenge was to use its victories to project pro-choice power and intimidate politicians. This was a game of perception, not reality. And in that game, the differences between pro-choice liberalism and pro-choice conservatism, between Young and Miller, didn't count.

On the second weekend of 1990, NARAL's board of directors met in Washington and approved the "NARAL-PAC Criteria for Support of Candidates." The statement, refined from the strategic blueprint that Page Gardner had drafted in September, stipulated that the PAC's goal was to elect politicians who favored "full public funding for abortion services and minors' access." But other criteria reflected the new emphasis on backing winners. "Is the more pro-choice candidate viable?" asked one question. "Can NARAL take credit for its involvement?" asked another.[57]

In March, Young applied to NARAL-PAC for support, spelling out his agreement with NARAL on every issue.[58] NARAL headquarters responded with skeptical inquiries about his chances in the election. Pro-choice activists in Georgia tried in vain to persuade NARAL that Young could win. By July it was clear that he couldn't. NARAL had refused to give him money because he was going to lose. And he was going to lose because he had run out of money.

In Virginia, Michelman had set aside her differences with Wilder in order to defeat the larger threat of criminalization. But in Georgia, that threat was absent. The Republican nominee for governor stood on a conservative pro-choice platform identical to Miller's. Furthermore, banning abortion was a dead issue in Georgia. The two abortion issues in play—parental notice and public funding—were precisely those on which Miller and Young disagreed. In terms of policy, nothing was gained and much was lost by conceding the Democratic nomination to Miller. The payoff was purely political: NARAL avoided being associated with a loser. The following year, under Governor Miller, Georgia would wage a successful legal battle to reinstate parental notice.[59]

NARAL wasn't always the voice of resignation in such decisions. It took the opposite side of a triage debate in Missouri, for example. After being routed in the referenda of 1988, NARAL strategists had sworn off voter initiative campaigns. But in fall 1989 they were tempted to launch an initiative to overturn the Missouri law upheld in *Webster*. Such a bold slap in the face of the pro-life movement would surely reverberate throughout the nation.

To test the idea, Harrison Hickman polled Missouri voters. On November 7, the day of Wilder's victory, Hickman delivered his report. Most Missouri voters would support an amendment to enshrine abortion rights in the state constitution but only if the debate were framed "in the larger context of 'who should decide' and preventing unnecessary government regulation." If the debate turned to whether families or individuals should control abortion decisions, liberals would lose. "Only 28% of voters would still favor the proposals if they would allow [women to obtain] abortions without their husbands' consent; only 19% would still favor them if they enabled teenagers to obtain abortions without their parents' consent," Hickman wrote. "Clearly, any broadly worded pro-choice proposal could be easily defeated by a well-financed and strategically-designed opposition campaign."[60]

Hickman's report chilled the enthusiasm of Missouri's pro-choice activists. In December they voted to scrap the initiative idea and focus instead on Missouri's 1990 elections. Pro-choice lawmakers, however, dismissed this retreat as folly. The legislature, they warned, was firmly in enemy hands and would soon ban abortion unless voters intervened through a referendum.[61]

Into this breach stepped Judith Widdicombe, president of the St. Louis abortion clinic immortalized in *Webster*. Widdicombe was a devout pragmatist. She saw in Hickman's findings an opportunity for compromise. If Missourians wanted a conservative version of abortion rights, she would give it to them. Better that, she reasoned, than outright criminalization by the legislature.

With the support of moderate lawmakers and a Republican financier who had helped to elect Missouri's two pro-life U.S. senators, Widdicombe formed a bipartisan "citizens' group" called STOP!PAC, shorthand for People Working to Stop Government Interference. On January 17 she launched an initiative campaign to amend Missouri's constitution. The proposed amendment declared that "no government or law shall restrict" abortion decisions. In view of Hickman's findings, however, the amendment included a caveat: "State laws in force before [1986] shall remain effective so long as they are not hereafter amended or repealed."[62]

This was a monstrous loophole. It preserved twenty restrictions, including parental consent and a ban on abortion funding. Widdicombe and her allies made this loophole a major selling point. They stressed that Missourians favored restrictions on funding and teenagers' abortions, and they assured parents and taxpayers that the amendment would honor their demands. "Our poll shows that people want regulation, and we've got to listen to where the people are," said Widdicombe.[63]

Other pro-choice activists disavowed STOP!PAC, deeming the initiative bad policy as well as bad politics. Since its gaping loophole would be written into the state constitution, they viewed it as a permanent sell-out of the young and the poor. Legal strategists were particularly sensitive to this problem. In a letter to STOP!PAC, Kathryn Kolbert of the ACLU Reproductive Freedom Project pointed out, "[O]ur constituency also opposes parental involvement statutes as well as Medicaid restrictions." She warned that the amendment would certify these restrictions as "constitutional under Missouri law." In an April visit to St. Louis, NARAL legal director Dawn Johnsen agreed. "We don't believe that it's time for us to contemplate any type of compromise on abortion, sacrificing some women to [preserve] protections other groups of women have," Johnsen said.[64]

True, NARAL was making precisely such a compromise by refusing to support Young in Georgia. But neglecting the young and the poor for a single election was one thing. Writing them out of a constitution was quite another. In a letter to STOP!PAC on June 6, Michelman, Planned Parenthood president Faye Wattleton, and two other national pro-choice leaders told Widdicombe, "We cannot support a constitutional amendment that sacrifices the rights of the most vulnerable women and writes into the constitution restrictions on choice against which we have long fought, including restrictions on minors and public funds for abortions."[65]

Widdicombe replied with the logic of triage: "We can lose everything by not being willing to compromise." She charged that her purist critics were "willing to sacrifice safe and legal abortion in Missouri to get 100% of their agenda." Without the amendment, STOP!PAC's director warned, Missouri lawmakers would outlaw abortion while pro-choice purists "play amateur politics."[66]

The concessions that rankled Michelman and Wattleton were necessary to attract moderate voters, Widdicombe explained. She illustrated her point by using these concessions to discredit the pro-life opposition campaign of which Hickman had warned. In June pro-lifers distributed flyers alleging that the amendment would force taxpayers to subsidize abortions and would let teenagers get abortions without their parents' knowledge. But Widdicombe reassured voters, "There have been no taxpayer-funded abortions since 1977, and there won't be, even if the referendum passes. Parental consent will stay as it is, unless it is repealed or amended to be more liberal."[67]

Widdicombe didn't stop there. She repudiated the abortion rights movement altogether, calling it a "fringe camp" of "extremists." She even resorted to the slander favored by many pro-life activists: "The pro-choice groups say all abortions, no restrictions. The pro-life groups say no abortions, no exceptions. STOP!PAC says let's keep it legal, but let's keep it regulated."

Widdicombe wasn't just quarreling with pro-choice purists. She was advertising that quarrel to endear her initiative to moderate voters. What offended groups such as Planned Parenthood and the ACLU, she charged, was her "mainstream moderate approach." "STOP!PAC will not cave in to extremists at either end of the spectrum," she pledged.[68]

Ultimately, logistical misfortunes prevented STOP!PAC from gathering enough signatures to put its initiative on the ballot. A judge threw out many of the signatures on a technicality, and the group's principal financier died in an accident. But in conceding defeat, Widdicombe laid much of the blame on "opposition from both ends of the abortion spectrum."[69] The purists had done her in.

With the collapse of the Missouri campaign, attention shifted to a referendum battle in Oregon. This time it was pro-lifers who were divided. While hard-liners proposed an initiative to ban abortions, Oregon Right to Life crafted a ballot measure that would require only parental notice. Polls showed that three-fourths of the state's voters favored such a measure. NRLC ponied up $25,000 to pass the parental notice proposal, Measure 10, but nothing to pass the abortion ban, Measure 8. The pro-life DeMoss Foundation spent $200,000 on behalf of Measure 10.[70]

A poll taken in August accented the political gap between the two measures. While more than six in ten voters opposed Measure 8, a commensurate majority favored Measure 10. One respondent explained that she supported "the parents' rights to be in on a decision" about abortion. Another agreed that a law requiring parental involvement "brings doctors, husbands, fathers, parents and education into an important decision for a woman and her family."[71]

To attract these pro-choice voters, Oregon Right to Life delegated its sponsorship of Measure 10 to a spinoff group called United Families of Oregon. One spokesman for the campaign declared that passage of Measure 10 would "send a resounding affirmation across the nation of a parent's right to participate in their minor daughter's life." Another stressed that the proposal was "primarily not an abortion-related measure" but sought to protect "parents' rights." The DeMoss Foundation's newspaper ads framed the parent, not the pregnant daughter, as the subject of the decision: "Should a parent have the right to be notified by a physician before an abortion is obtained by a minor?"[72]

The enemy of parents and families, according to supporters of Measure 10, was the same enemy identified by pro-choice activists: the government. At one press conference, an advocate of Measure 10 defended it as an antidote to previous divisive intrusions by the state into the family. At another press conference, two women, one of whom headed a national organization called Mothers Against Minors' Abortions (MAMA), described how government workers and agencies had conspired to arrange abortions for their daughters "behind their parents' backs."[73]

For three advisers to the campaign against Measure 10—pollster Celinda Lake and media consultants Frank Greer and Kim Haddow—this was an education in the abuse of their rhetoric. In January Lake had told EMILY's List that parental control was a separate issue from the right to choose. Now she was watching pro-lifers frame parental control as part of the right to choose. At a minimum, this tactic neutralized the choice argument. That became clear in March 1990, when Bob Packwood, the Oregon senator who had led the Republican opposition to Robert Bork, announced that he wouldn't be "dragged into the parental notification" debate. Measure 10 wasn't an "up or down" question of abortion rights. "I don't intend to take a position on it," said Packwood.[74]

Oregonians for Choice—a coalition that included the state's NARAL, NOW, and Planned Parenthood affiliates—tried to stop other pro-choice politicians from defecting. "The true pro-choice position on the initiatives proposed for the November 1990 ballot opposes both the ban on abortions and mandatory parental notification," the coalition argued in a letter. But in April, when NOW's Molly Yard toured the state to speak out for teenagers' rights, a pro-life strategist pointed out that pro-choice voters disagreed with Yard about parental involvement laws. "Molly Yard knows the numbers, and so do you," the strategist told reporters.[75]

Unable to defeat Measure 10 on its own, pro-choice operatives tied it to Measure 8. Having an abortion ban on the ballot lent rare credibility to their charge that parental notice was part of an attack on the right to choose. In July Oregonians for Choice announced a "No on 8 and 10" campaign. All of the television ads crafted by Greer and Haddow closed with the image of a double "No" vote on "8 and 10." Some of the ads misrepresented Measure 10 as a ban on abortions. One commercial claimed, "Measures 8 and 10 virtually eliminate safe abortions." Two others showed a doctor asserting, "Measures 8 and 10 are the same."

Pro-lifers protested this strategy, calling it a "deliberate attempt to muddy the waters between the two measures." But it worked. By the end of October, Measure 10's margin of support had evaporated. Measure 8 lost by a 2 to 1 margin, dragging Measure 10 down to a narrow defeat.[76]

The clearest demonstration of what pro-lifers could accomplish by targeting conservative pro-choice voters and avoiding blunders such as Measure 8 emerged from a four-year war in Michigan. In the decade after Congress banned federal funding of abortions, the Michigan legislature voted seventeen times to stop spending state tax money on abortions. But each time, the governor—first Republican Bill Milliken, then Democrat Jim Blanchard—vetoed the bill.[77]

In 1987 a coalition led by Right to Life of Michigan, the smartest pro-life organization in the country, decided to circumvent Governor Blanchard. The coalition gathered nearly half a million signatures for an initiative to end state funding of abortions for welfare recipients. Since the measure had been initiated by citizens, it couldn't be vetoed. When it passed the legislature in 1987, pro-choice activists mounted a petition drive to block it. The petitions, certified a year later, called for a statewide referendum on the abortion funding ban. The vote was scheduled for November 1988.[78]

As in Colorado and Arkansas, polls taken in Michigan identified a crucial segment of the electorate that favored abortion rights but opposed public funding of abortions. As one respondent put it to the *Detroit News,* "[Abortion] should be an individual issue, not government's. If one decides to have an abortion, I don't think other people should have to pay for them with tax dollars."[79]

To woo these voters, Michigan pro-life activists set up a front group, the Committee to End Tax-Funded Abortions, which was housed in Right to Life's offices and chaired by Right to Life president Barbara Listing. At a press conference kicking off the committee's campaign, Listing assured pro-choice voters that "abortions [would] still be legal" under the funding ban. "It is an abortion-funding issue; it's not an abortion issue," she explained. "What we're looking at is who should pay for elective abortions." Listing told reporters that the committee would craft its advertising to appeal to the "10 to 15 to 18 percent" of Michigan voters who, while demanding the right to choose an abortion, objected "to paying for somebody else's abortion." Committee strategists stressed that their campaign would focus on the rights of taxpayers rather than the rights of the unborn.[80]

The committee's first television commercial depicted a group of young well-dressed professionals seated around a dinner table, debating whether their tax money should subsidize abortions. Though they disagreed about abortion, they all agreed with the point made by one of the men at the table: "This isn't about abortion. This is about who pays for it." The ad concluded that "it's not fair to force taxpayers to pay for" abortions. Another commercial pointed out that one Michigan doctor, depicted as a welfare profiteer, had collected nearly half a million dollars in state abortion subsidies in one year. A third ad warned parents that without the funding ban, Michigan law would continue to let their daughters get tax-funded abortions without parental consent. Pictures of fetuses and talk of killing were scarce in the campaign. Instead, committee spokesmen stressed that it was "a tax issue" and referred to their opponents as "the pro-tax forces." [81]

NARAL and Planned Parenthood chipped in $50,000 apiece to fight the funding ban. Pro-choice strategists did their best but complained throughout the election's final weeks that their opponents were diverting attention to "the tax issue and the welfare system" and "playing into taxpayer resentment" of welfare recipients. That observation served merely as an epitaph for public financing of abortions in Michigan. On November 8, 1988, the funding ban passed easily. [82]

Eight months later, when the Supreme Court handed down *Webster,* Listing announced that Right to Life would make parental consent its top issue for 1989. She noted that a parental consent bill "might very well attract support from legislators who have opposed [Right to Life]" on abortion but who "agree that parents should be able to be involved in a minor's medical decisions." When Listing's allies introduced such a measure in the state senate a week later, she urged them to separate it from other pro-life bills in order to associate it with parental rights rather than with abortion. [83]

It was a lopsided fight. Blanchard defended abortion as a teenager's right, insisting "that girl has to make that decision." Meanwhile, supporters of the parental consent bill exalted mothers and fathers. The bill's chief sponsor entitled it the Parental Rights Restoration Act. "This is not just an abortion issue. It is parents' rights," he argued. When the state senate opened hearings on the bill, Listing released a poll showing that three out of four Michigan voters favored it. "To oppose this legislation is to say that every adolescent has a right to abortion which supersedes the right of her parents to know about it," she warned Blanchard and his allies. "To oppose this legislation is to conspire against parents [who seek] to raise their children within their own value systems." [84]

Blanchard and the pro-choice activists who stood with him denied that they were fighting "a parental involvement bill," "a family-rights bill," or "a family communication bill." "This bill is not about a parent's right to know," said one activist. "[T]he people who introduced this bill want only to stop abortion." But in Michigan, unlike Oregon, there was no Measure 8 to make that charge credible. On October 25 the state senate easily passed the bill. [85]

In November Right to Life strategists spent $100,000 on television ads promoting the bill. In December they aired a half-hour video urging viewers to contact their legislators in support of it. Listing framed the debate as a conflict between families and outsiders, between NARAL's "you" and "them." Opponents of the bill wanted "to circumvent parental authority," she charged in a *Detroit News* essay. "Opposition to parental consent laws comes from those who feel clinics offer better guidance than do mothers and fathers." [86] On December 6 the *Detroit News* published a poll showing that five of every eight pro-choice voters in Michigan supported mandatory parental consent. That day, the house passed the bill by a wide margin. [87]

Blanchard vetoed the bill in February. In a newspaper ad, NARAL thanked him and branded the bill "an effort to chip away at the right of all women in Michigan—young and old—to choose whether or not to have an abortion." [88] But in an editorial published the same day, the *Detroit News* explained how Blanchard, by elevating government above families, had affronted conservative pro-choice voters: "Gov. Blanchard has had the temerity to tell the parents of Michigan that the state will not allow them the legal authority to be parents. Instead, that authority is to be effectively vested in assorted third parties—school officials, abortion counselors . . ."

Referring to Blanchard and other politicians who resisted parental consent, the *News* asked NARAL's question: "Who are they to substitute their judgment for the judgment of a parent? They are government apparatchiks." Rather than protect families against government, the *News* argued, Blanchard "has acted to diminish parental authority and expand the hand of the state or outsiders in the affairs of the family." A referendum on the issue might remind Blanchard "that families are too important to be left to the control of the state government." [89]

That was precisely what followed. Lacking the two-thirds house majority necessary to override the veto, Right to Life leaders returned to the petition strategy by which they had passed the 1988 funding ban. Pro-choice pragmatists offered an alternative bill that would allow girls to get permission from adults other than their parents, but Listing dismissed this as a scheme to "circumvent parents." Meanwhile, pro-choice radicals, led by Eleanor Smeal, tried to mobilize Michigan high school girls in a campaign of marches, rallies, and sit-ins modeled on the student anti-war movement of the 1960s. "We will have young women facing down the legislatures and governors of this country," vowed the campaign's organizer.[90]

Listing wasn't impressed. Teenagers, she observed with maternal weariness, "want to make all their own decisions." Against this insubordination, her forces erected a front group called Citizens for Parents' Rights. By July more than 330,000 adults had signed the group's petitions for a parental consent law. In September, a week after the initiative reached the legislature, lawmakers approved it overwhelmingly.[91]

Already consumed by preparations for the November elections, pro-choice activists now had to decide whether to mount a petition drive to force a referendum on the parental consent law, as they had done on the funding ban. They had spent more than a year and more than $1 million on the funding referendum, in vain. On parental consent, the polls again predicted defeat. This time the activists decided that their resources would be better spent elsewhere. In the cold logic of triage, girls under eighteen—one of every four women seeking abortions in Michigan—lost out.[92]

Instead, the activists dedicated themselves to reelecting Blanchard. Nowhere in the country did the abortion rights movement have a better ally. He had thwarted seven attempts to ban state-financed abortions and had done his best to sabotage the parental consent bill. In October 1989 he was the keynote speaker at NARAL's annual conference in Washington. His pro-life challenger, John Engler, was one of five state senators who had signed a newspaper ad promoting the 1988 funding ban.[93]

NARAL strategists thought that Blanchard, like Wilder, could use abortion rights to sell himself as the pro-family, anti-government candidate. "We've seen what happened in gubernatorial races in Virginia and New Jersey . . . and that is going to happen in Michigan," said the director of NARAL's Michigan affiliate. In a newspaper ad that landed on Michigan doorsteps on January 23, 1990, NARAL applauded Blanchard's efforts "to keep the government from interfering in our private and family lives." Three weeks later, on the morning of his first official campaign appearance, Engler awoke to find an ad accusing him of refusing to "trust" Michigan women.[94]

Engler wasn't fazed. It was Blanchard, not he, who refused to trust parents and families. At a campaign stop in Detroit that day, when asked about the parental consent bill, Engler called it "an important statement of family values." Two days later, after voting for the bill, Engler said, "This is just one more issue where the governor is on the wrong side of the majority of the people of Michigan." When Blanchard vetoed the bill on February 23, Engler charged that Blanchard was "more than misleading when he infers that [the bill] will infringe on a woman's right to make a choice. . . . His decision undermines the rights of parents and the foundation of Michigan families."[95]

In September, when the parental consent bill became law, abortion rights activists predicted that financially secure pro-choice voters would punish pro-life politicians. As one pro-choice lawmaker put it, "Following the Medicaid ban, [parental consent] is merely step two in the process of terminating all abortion rights in Michigan. Step three is just around the corner. If you're not young and you're not poor, you're next." Listing disagreed. The voters of Michigan, she suggested, wouldn't lift a finger for a governor who "is in favor of teens keeping secrets from their parents."[96]

NARAL's Michigan affiliate invested nearly all its campaign time and money in a drive to reelect Blanchard. NARAL's television ads urged voters to defend the governor against "politicians who want to take away your right to choose." But many of Blanchard's supporters deserted him. He lost by fewer than twenty thousand votes. According to an exit poll, Blanchard's abortion position attracted fewer votes than Engler's did. That alone was enough to account for the governor's defeat.[97] A year after Michelman issued her warning to politicians everywhere, Blanchard had proven her horribly correct. He was out of touch with the pro-choice majority. And he was out of office.

Middle Ground

PHILADELPHIA, PENNSYLVANIA
APRIL 4, 1991

Ten miles from its destination, the twin-engine Aerostar turboprop veered south over Lower Merion township, one thousand feet above the ground. The helicopter crew shadowing the plane had just finished checking the plane's landing gear when the helicopter's rotors brushed the plane's fuel tank. A black-orange blast ripped through the sky. Flaming metal rained into the elementary school yard below, killing two first-graders and injuring five others. It took hours to identify the charred remains of the five men who had fallen to earth. Two were pilots of the plane; two were pilots of the helicopter. The fifth man, the plane's sole passenger, was identified by his wristband and his American Express card. He was U.S. senator John Heinz.[1]

With Heinz's death, an era of warfare ended. The election to replace him ushered in a season of convergence, marked by the rise of the Democratic Party's moderate wing and its capture of the presidency. The combat that had consumed 1990—left against right, pro-choice against pro-life—gave way to a consolidation of the center. The Supreme Court, in a pair of landmark decisions, secured a conservative constitutional theory of abortion rights. And the Democratic and Republican presidential tickets joined to galvanize that theory into a political consensus.

Heinz was a pro-choice Republican, but the task of replacing him fell to Bob Casey, the pro-life Democratic governor who had frustrated abortion rights activists in Pennsylvania since Kate Michelman's departure. Casey selected his labor secretary, Harris Wofford, to take over the seat and defend it against the Republicans in a November 1991 special election. Wofford's challenger was Michelman's old nemesis, former governor Dick Thornburgh. He had just resigned as President Bush's attorney general on the assumption that he would easily defeat Wofford. With Bush's prestige invested in him, Thornburgh set to work portraying Wofford as a liberal relic. "If Wofford's for unlimited abortion on demand, our views differ greatly," said Thornburgh.[2]

Wofford refused to be relegated to the left. He hired James Carville, the consultant who had helped Casey and Georgia governor Zell Miller win by rejecting their opponents' liberalism on social issues such as abortion. Like Miller, Wofford advocated parental consent and other "reasonable regulations." Specifically, he endorsed Pennsylvania's 1989 Abortion Control Act, which required parental consent, husband notification, and a detailed informed consent procedure followed by a mandatory twenty-four-hour waiting period.[3]

Michelman faced the same dilemma she had confronted in Virginia. At first, she refused to help Wofford. NARAL "cannot be in this race," she told one reporter, "as long as Sen. Wofford supports the state's abortion-control law." To another, she reiterated, "We can't. It's the principle. It's not even up for grabs." But eventually she settled on the same compromise as in Virginia: NARAL would mount an independent campaign against the greater of the two evils.[4]

In Washington, D.C., the Supreme Court was extending the libertarian line it had drawn in *Webster*. On May 23, 1991, in *Rust v. Sullivan*, the Court upheld a ban on abortion counseling at federally funded family planning clinics. In its legal challenge to the counseling ban, Planned Parenthood had portrayed the ban as government interference in the right of clinic personnel to speak freely to women about medical options.[5] The Court disagreed. Writing for the majority, Chief Justice Rehnquist construed the ban as a policy of state inaction rather than state action:

> That the regulations do not impermissibly burden a woman's Fifth Amendment rights is evident from the line of cases beginning with *Maher* and *McRae* and culminating in . . . *Webster*. Just as Congress' refusal to fund

abortions in *McRae* left "an indigent woman with at least the same range of choice in deciding whether to obtain a medically necessary abortion as she would have had if Congress had chosen to subsidize no health care costs at all," . . . and "Missouri's refusal to allow public employees to perform abortions in public hospitals leaves a pregnant woman with the same choices as if the State had chosen not to operate any public hospitals," . . . Congress' refusal to fund abortion counseling and advocacy leaves a pregnant woman with the same choices as if the government had chosen not to fund family-planning services at all.[6]

Seen in that light, the counseling ban comported with a conservative theory of abortion rights. The government wasn't overreaching. When women reached out for help to get abortions, the government merely sat on its hands. Rehnquist simply quoted from *McRae,* which held that the state's failure to subsidize abortions "places no governmental obstacle in the path" of the pregnant woman. "The financial constraints that restrict an indigent woman's ability to enjoy the full range of constitutionally protected freedom of choice," the chief justice wrote, continuing the quotation, "are the product not of governmental restrictions on access to abortion, but rather of her indigency."[7]

In late October and early November, two political tremors erupted from Pennsylvania. One was Wofford's upset victory over Thornburgh, widely hailed as a triumph of mainstream Democratic populism and a warning to Bush. That warning extended to abortion. Analysts noted that Wofford's moderate pro-choice position had attracted the crucial support of suburban Republicans. Within a month, Lieutenant Governor Mark Singel, preparing to run for Pennsylvania's other U.S. Senate seat, took heed and abandoned his opposition to legal abortion. Like Wofford, Singel supported the Pennsylvania restrictions and advertised his position as "moderate" and "reasonable."[8]

The other tremor erupted on October 21, when a panel of the United States Court of Appeals for the Third Circuit in Philadelphia upheld all but one of the Pennsylvania restrictions. The court ruled that Justice O'Connor's "middle ground" theory of abortion rights was "the narrowest grounds in the [Supreme Court] majority in *Webster* and *Hodgson*" and was therefore the new "law of the land." O'Connor's position was that federal judges shouldn't scrutinize abortion restrictions too closely unless those restrictions imposed an "undue burden" on women. The Court's previous doctrine of abortion rights—the "strict scrutiny test of *Roe, Akron,* and *Thornburgh,*" under which the Court had struck down virtually the same Pennsylvania restrictions in 1986—was "no longer governing and the results no longer binding." [9]

What did this mean? Was *Roe* dead? On November 7, two days after Wofford's victory, lawyers representing Planned Parenthood of Southeastern Pennsylvania and five other abortion providers asked the Supreme Court, in *Planned Parenthood v. Casey,* to review the Third Circuit ruling and to state clearly whether the Court had "overruled" *Roe.* Pro-choice legal and political strategists calculated that a blow to abortion's legality would at least provoke the electorate's wrath. [10]

Anything short of *Roe*'s reversal seemed unlikely to alarm the public. Most Americans continued to oppose government funding of abortions. A May 1992 poll asked whether federal money should be used for abortions for low-income women; 56 percent said no. A July 1992 survey found that by a margin of 52 to 42 percent, voters opposed the use of tax dollars to pay for abortions for indigent women. In a September 1991 poll, a 48 percent plurality went further, endorsing a law that would prohibit nearly all abortions at "any publicly financed medical facility." [11]

Surveys taken in 1992 continued to show that about 70 percent of the electorate supported parental consent laws and about 80 percent supported parental notice laws. Approval of husband notice laws ranged from 63 to 76 percent. Five of every eight Americans said would-be fathers deserved a legal right to prevent abortions of their potential offspring. The same proportion agreed that "a pregnant married woman should be required to get the permission of her husband before obtaining a legal abortion." Women favored husband notice laws and husband consent laws by clear majorities. [12]

Without these voters—those who defined choice in terms of family authority and limited government—what was left of the pro-choice constituency? A nationwide study released by the University of Michigan in 1991 answered that question. Of the 40 percent of voters who clearly favored abortion rights, more than half supported parental notice laws, and one-third favored the prohibition of public funding. With those factions removed, the "pure" pro-choice vote dwindled to 17 percent of the electorate. [13]

Bush saw these findings as an opportunity to seize the middle ground. His pollster and his chief of staff worried that the outright demise of abortion rights, possibly triggered by *Casey,* would drive suburban voters out of the GOP. [14] The Republicans would be hard-pressed to defend their official position that abortion should be banned. They needed a moderate position from which to attack the Democrats. They found it in Pennsylvania's restrictions and the issue of public funding.

In his annual speech to the national March for Life Rally on January 22, 1992, Bush didn't call for the overturn of *Roe,* as he had in previous years. Instead, he pledged, "I will continue to oppose and fight back attempts by Congress to expand Federal funding for abortions." [15] On March 3, speaking to the National Association of Evangelicals, Bush again spared *Roe,* focusing his fire on two other issues more likely to endear him to conservative voters:

> Six times the Congress has sent me legislation permitting Federal funding of abortion, and six times I've told them no and vetoed these bills.
>
> Now we've got another fight. The Democratic Congress . . . call[s] it the Freedom of Choice Act. . . . It would block many State laws requiring that parents be told about abortions being performed on their young daughters, even though the Supreme Court has upheld such laws five times. . . . This is not right. And it will not become law as long as I am President of the United States of America. [16]

In April White House officials embarked on a coordinated campaign to shift the abortion debate from prohibition to restrictions such as parental consent and spousal notice. Their dual objective was to deflect attention from the GOP's pro-life platform and, by seizing the middle ground, to put the Democrats in a posture of pro-choice extremism, driving a wedge between Democratic moderates and liberals. [17] Vice President Dan Quayle launched the attack in an interview with *USA Today* just before the Supreme Court heard oral arguments in *Casey:*

> I look at that Pennsylvania statute, and I think their governor and state legislature are probably more in tune with the American people than the media and some of our critics think. The Pennsylvania statute is a reasonable statute. Look at what it is: 24-hour waiting period, parental consent for someone under 18, informing the spouse when an abortion is to occur. Is that unreasonable? Is that out of the mainstream? I don't think it is. [18]

Weeks later, in a speech to the National Right to Life Committee's annual convention, Quayle encouraged pro-lifers to join the administration in moving the debate toward "reasonable" restrictions such as Pennsylvania's. [19] On ABC's *This Week,* Senate minority leader Bob Dole suggested that rather than attack the pro-choice position, Republicans could commandeer it. "There might be certain shadings you could do as far as abortion for sex selection or birth control or notification, spousal notification, parental notification," said Dole. "I think when people say pro-choice, you should define what they mean by 'choice.' Does that mean A, B, C and D? And you'll find many people saying, 'Well, I don't mean that when I say I'm pro-choice.' " [20]

While Bush approached the middle ground from the right, his principal Democratic challenger, Arkansas governor Bill Clinton, approached it from the left. In Arkansas's 1986 and 1988 referenda, Governor Clinton opposed public funding of abortions. In February 1989 a two-parent notification bill swept through the Arkansas house on a 90 to 1 vote and passed the senate with almost a two-thirds majority.[21] The culture of family authority was so strong in Arkansas that the director of the state ACLU, hoping to generate opposition to the bill, argued not that it was too harsh on teenage girls but that it wasn't deferential enough to parents:

> I think everybody ought to be really aware that it's not a parental notification bill, it's a judicial notification bill. The law does not require notification of the parents if the child doesn't want to notify the parents. There's a bypass, and that option is to bring in a third party. Now, what you have is a situation in which the state is interfering in what in essence is a family matter. I don't think that the sponsors of this legislation took into consideration the numbers of parents who may not . . . want their family business broadcast to the world by having a judge in essence interfere in that family's business.[22]

Clinton endorsed the bill in principle and, after securing a minor change, signed it into law.[23] Eight months later, in October 1989, he spelled out his general position on abortion: "I just think that government's done about all government should do on this issue. We've protected the life of the child that can live outside the mother's womb. We have said there won't be public funds for discretionary abortions, and we've required parental notification in cases of minors." [24]

In March 1990 Clinton became chairman of the Democratic Leadership Council, a centrist, anti-liberal group openly sympathetic to parental notice laws and restrictions on the use of "taxpayer money" for abortions. By October 1990 he had distilled his philosophy to a sentence: "While I have also supported restrictions on public funding and a parental notification requirement for minors, I think the government should impose no further restrictions." [25]

In January 1991 Clinton suggested that *Roe*'s premise that "the government shall not take a position on abortion" didn't mean that the government had to confiscate citizens' "tax dollars" for abortions. In the tradition of President Carter, Clinton argued, "[T]here are lots of rights, like the right to travel, that are not exercised equally because there is no governmental obligation to provide everyone with money so they can all travel to the same degree as everyone else. Abortion is in this category. Guarantee the right, but leave the question of who pays largely to the states." [26]

Speaking before the National Women's Political Caucus and the American Bar Association in summer 1991, Clinton endorsed "choice" but didn't define the term. When activists and reporters back home interpreted his remarks as a wholehearted embrace of abortion rights, Clinton reminded them that he also "supported parental notification and restrictions on public funding for abortions." In October, as he launched his bid for the presidency, he clarified what he meant by choice: "There's a big difference between being pro-choice and being for spending tax dollars for any kind of abortion. I don't think that's appropriate." Answering a NARAL questionnaire in November, Clinton defended Arkansas's parental notice law and endorsed public financing of abortions only in cases of rape or incest. [27]

The first battle among the Democratic candidates, the February 18 New Hampshire primary, solidified Clinton's position as the candidate of moderation. Supporters of his principal antagonist on the left, Senator Tom Harkin of Iowa, distributed literature protesting, "Governor Clinton's position on funding in the state of Arkansas punishes poor women and his position on minors punishes young women. He has created an atmosphere where only women who can afford an abortion have a right to one." Shortly before the primary, Harkin repeated on national television that Clinton had signed a parental notice bill and that such laws were not "in the best interests of the young woman." Clinton replied, "I did sign a parental notice bill." But that legislation, he argued, didn't contradict his consistent support for "the right to choose." [28]

Clinton and his advisers understood the complexity of the issue. Clinton had seen it in the 1986 and 1988 Arkansas referenda. His media consultant, Frank Greer, had exploited it for NARAL and Wilder. His pollster, Stan Greenberg, had helped Jim Florio to exploit it in New Jersey. Another Clinton media adviser, Mandy Grunwald, had seen Jesse Helms use the issue against her client in North Carolina, Harvey Gantt. Greer and Greenberg had seen Zell Miller use it against their client in Georgia, Andrew Young. And James Carville, the man who had masterminded Miller's campaign and Harris Wofford's election in Pennsylvania, was Clinton's chief strategist.

Seasoned by these battles, Clinton's team understood that while he couldn't afford to appear hostile to abortion rights, he also couldn't afford to look too liberal on parental consent or public funding. If he did, the Republicans would punish him in the fall. That peril was made clear six days before the New Hampshire primary, when the National Right to Life PAC took out a full-page ad against him in the state's leading newspaper, the Manchester *Union Leader*. The ad featured two large boxes labeled "Parental Notification" and "Abortion Funding." The text read:

> But on the issues of parental notification before a minor's abortion and tax funding of abortion . . . Bill Clinton has taken positions on both sides of these issues. . . .
>
> You can't have it both ways, Mr. Clinton.
>
> You can't be for parental notification and also for the so-called "Freedom of Choice Act," which would nullify all parental notification laws.
>
> You can't oppose taxpayer funding of abortion and also favor a taxpayer funded national health insurance that pays for abortion for all women.[29]

Clinton finished second in New Hampshire; Harkin finished fourth and soon dropped out. Victories in other states over the next six weeks established Clinton as the prohibitive favorite for the nomination. Abortion hardly figured in these primaries, for three reasons: most voters were preoccupied by the economic recession; few felt the right to abortion was directly threatened; and Clinton's careful statements avoided offending pro-choice Democrats who favored restrictions.

Complaints from the left persisted, but they hardly damaged Clinton and arguably helped him. NOW president Patricia Ireland hounded him for restricting "young women's rights to an abortion" in Arkansas. Later, during an MTV forum, a young woman asked Clinton how he could call himself pro-choice when he had signed a parental notice bill. He replied that "protecting the right to choose for a minor who couldn't get a tooth extracted without parental notification is a very different" question from protecting that right for an adult.[30]

During the New York primary in April, Clinton's sole remaining competitor, former California governor Jerry Brown, complained on national television that Clinton had said "he would not mandate the federal funding for poor women to get an abortion." The *New York Times* scolded Clinton for signing Arkansas's parental notice law. Clinton's radio ads in New York ignored such quibbles, reminding voters that Clinton stood firm against "extremists" who "would let the government interfere in your private life." Exit polls found that Brown did well among liberals, but Clinton thrashed him among moderates and conservatives and easily won the primary.[31]

Clinton locked up the Democratic nomination only to find a third candidate awaiting him and Bush in the political center. Texas businessman Ross Perot, sporting a $2 billion bankroll and an air of homespun wisdom, launched a petition campaign to join the ballot as an independent. By May polls showed him in a dead heat with Bush and Clinton. Temperamentally, Perot appealed to voters who didn't trust politicians. Ideologically, he appealed to pro-choice Republicans and independents who saw Clinton as a tax-and-spend liberal but couldn't stand to vote for Bush again.

Perot preached and exuded American pragmatism. Abortion should be a personal choice, he reasoned, but requiring a woman to notify her husband also seemed like a good idea. In a discussion with reporters, Perot explained, "[S]ince they both created this potential new life, it seems to me—and they're married—they should discuss it." Parental notice laws made sense to him, too: "We're saying a 15-year-old girl? Sure. I think her parents should have a vote in that."[32]

Pro-choice activists struggled to sabotage this convergence. In their brief to the Supreme Court in *Casey*, Planned Parenthood's legal strategists denied that Justice O'Connor's "undue burden" standard offered "an acceptable middle ground" on abortion rights. They insisted that the Court couldn't uphold the Pennsylvania law "without overruling *Roe* or so eviscerating its core holding as to render it meaningless." Pennsylvania's attorneys disagreed. *Roe* established only "a limited right," they suggested, and therefore could accommodate Pennsylvania's restrictions.[33]

As in *Hodgson*, both sides in *Casey* purported to defend families against government. In a brief supporting the Pennsylvania law, four conservative pro-family groups called the spousal notice requirement "a legitimate effort to protect parental rights and familial relationships." Planned Parenthood disagreed, contending that the requirement "flies in the face of" its stated pro-family purpose by "subjecting marital discussions to state surveillance, censorship, and control."[34]

In an argument reminiscent of Justice Kennedy's opinion in *Hodgson*, the conservative groups maintained that until *Roe* American law had "protected the right of *both* spouses to participate in decisions that are central to the destiny of the family." Not until the 1970s, they asserted, did federal courts usurp fathers' rights by entitling women to get abortions without consulting their husbands. In rectifying that "intrusion into a settled matrix of family responsibilities," Pennsylvania was "protecting a husband and father's fundamental liberty interest" from "governmental action by the judicial branch." [35]

Conversely, borrowing the logic of Justice Stevens's opinion in *Hodgson,* Planned Parenthood's attorneys construed Pennsylvania's parental consent requirement as an encroachment on parents' rather than minors' rights. By forcing a parent to appear in person at the clinic twenty-four hours before his daughter's abortion, they argued, Pennsylvania "presents so insurmountable an obstacle that even parents who have participated in, support, and consent to their daughter's abortion may be unable to comply with the law." [36]

The pro-choice strategy to force an all-or-nothing decision on *Roe* produced the bizarre spectacle of activists declaring defeat months in advance. In March Kathryn Kolbert, the lawyer in charge of Planned Parenthood's case, asserted that *Roe,* "as we know it, is dead and gone." A month later Kolbert promised, "I can predict I'm going to lose." Kate Michelman agreed: "*Roe* will be an empty shell and every American woman will lose a fundamental freedom." The public, according to Michelman, had to understand that "*Roe* is doomed" and that "this right is gone." Pro-choice activists put out the word that at least thirteen states would ban abortions soon after *Roe*'s demise. [37]

On the morning of June 29, the Court issued its decision. Four justices—Rehnquist, Scalia, Clarence Thomas, and White—voted to overturn *Roe.* But the majority opinion, coauthored by Justices Kennedy, O'Connor, and David Souter and joined in part by Justices Stevens and Blackmun, concluded that "*Roe*'s essential holding [should] be retained and reaffirmed." [38] After two decades of struggle and five Supreme Court appointments by ostensibly sympathetic presidents, pro-life activists tasted bitter betrayal. Pro-choice activists faced a hell of their own: They found themselves engulfed in the superficial victory parade they had dreaded.

Casey pronounced a grand compromise. Acknowledging the political conflict at stake, the three moderate justices observed that "pressure to overrule [*Roe*], like pressure to retain it, has grown only more intense." While purporting to ignore politics, the moderates promised a resolution that "calls the contending sides of a national controversy to end their national division by accepting a common mandate rooted in the Constitution." [39]

The "common mandate" was twofold. The Court would stand by "*Roe's* essential holding," but that holding would now be defined as the right to obtain an abortion "without undue interference from the State." As pro-choice activists had feared, this "undue burden" rule would allow restrictions that had previously been struck down. While reaffirming *Roe,* the justices noted that their reinterpretation of it obliged them to "overrule in part" subsequent decisions that had extended it.[40]

Much of the Court's reasoning flowed from two stated premises. First: "The fact that a law which serves a valid purpose, one not designed to strike at the right [to abortion] itself, has the incidental effect of making it more difficult or more expensive to procure an abortion cannot be enough to invalidate it." The legal right to abortion was immune to attack; the material ability to exercise that right wasn't. Second: "What is at stake is the woman's right to make the ultimate decision, not a right to be insulated from all others in doing so."[41] The Court would protect individuals from a state-imposed abortion ban but not from each other.

These two premises led the Court to uphold most of the Pennsylvania law. The parental consent requirement enabled parents to express pro-life values to their daughters, said the Court, and the waiting period subsequent to counseling offered the "parents of a pregnant young woman the opportunity to consult with her in private, and to discuss the consequences of her decision in the context of the values and moral or religious principles of their family."[42]

The four justices who preferred to overturn *Roe* agreed with these conclusions. But why pretend that *Roe* could accommodate such restrictions? Why not put it out of its misery? Writing for the dissenters, Rehnquist mocked the pretense that *Roe* had survived:

> *Roe* decided that a woman had a fundamental right to an abortion. The joint opinion rejects that view. *Roe* decided that abortion regulations were to be subjected to "strict scrutiny" and could be justified only in the light of "compelling state interests." The joint opinion rejects that view. . . .
>
> While purporting to adhere to precedent, the joint opinion instead revises it. *Roe* continues to exist, but only in the way a storefront on a western movie set exists: a mere facade to give the illusion of reality. Decisions following *Roe* . . . are frankly overruled in part under the "undue burden" standard expounded in the joint opinion. . . .
>
> *Roe v. Wade* stands as a sort of judicial Potemkin Village, which may be pointed out to passers-by as a monument to the importance of adhering to precedent. But behind the facade, an entirely new method of analysis, with-

out any roots in constitutional law, is imported to decide the constitutionality of state laws regulating abortion.[43]

The clearest evidence that *Roe* had been gutted was that despite their
quarrel about preserving *Roe,* the moderates and dissenters reached opposite conclusions on only one part of the Pennsylvania law. The dissenters voted to uphold the husband notice requirement in the name of
husbands, fathers, and the family:

> First, a husband's interests in procreation within marriage and in the poten-
> tial life of his unborn child are certainly substantial ones. . . .
>   In our view, the spousal notice requirement is a rational attempt by the
> State to improve truthful communication between spouses and encourage
> collaborative decisionmaking, and thereby fosters marital integrity.[44]

The moderates, however, rejected the old idea that "a woman had
no legal existence separate from her husband, who was regarded as her
head and representative in the social state." Women had attained a right
to "bodily integrity," they argued, and the spousal notice rule violated
that right. States "may not give to a man the kind of dominion over
his wife that parents exercise over their children," the moderates concluded.[45] By a single vote, the justices struck down that provision. The
Court's rightward march had reached its limit.

For the abortion rights movement, the next twenty-four hours were
disastrous. The press consecrated *Casey* as the new pro-choice middle
ground. Within seconds of the decision's release, television reporters outside the Court announced that *Roe* had been upheld. From an NBC studio, Governor Casey told the nation that with huge majorities supporting each of the Pennsylvania restrictions, the decision "moves us . . .
in the direction of a national consensus." CBS reporter Bruce Morton
agreed: "[T]hat's the kind of approach that the public opinion polls say
the voters like. Most people, asked if a woman should have the right
to choose, say yes. But asked if they approve those kinds of restrictions,
they say yes, too. So the justices . . . may have come down just about
where the country is on this one." [46]

    In the hours following the decision, activists fought a high-stakes
battle to shape the public's understanding of what the Court had done.
The pro-choice message was threefold. First, Rehnquist was right: *Roe*
had been "gutted," "overturned," and made "meaningless." Standing
before reporters outside the Court, Kolbert declared, "The Court has

taken away the fundamental right that women possessed prior to today." Across the street, Representative Pat Schroeder, a Colorado Democrat, announced, "*Roe v. Wade* is dead." Second, the threat posed by the four justices who wanted to scrap *Roe* overshadowed the details of the Court's controlling opinion. "We are one George Bush appointment away . . . from a complete criminal ban on abortion," said Michelman. Third, many poor and young women would be thwarted by the "burdens" imposed by Pennsylvania. Their right to choose had become useless.[47]

The pro-life message was simpler and more persuasive. First, the Court had explicitly reaffirmed *Roe*. Second, the approved restrictions were "moderate," "reasonable," "minor," "modest," and "common sense." While conceding that "a majority of the American public does not support a complete and total ban on abortion," pro-lifers emphasized that more than three-fourths of Americans favored each of the restrictions in question, "including spousal notice." Third, pro-choice activists who opposed these restrictions and denounced the ruling were "extreme," "radical," and "out of step" with America.[48]

Again, each side claimed to stand for families against government. On PBS, Michelman argued that *Casey* authorized the intrusion of "politicians and government" into a decision that "belongs to a woman and her family." But on NBC, Governor Casey suggested, "[Spousal notice] goes to the whole question of expanding rights to all members of the family. The *Roe* case, you know, knocked out the husband and knocked out parents," thereby trampling the "traditional rights of members of the family." The Court was simply acting "to reestablish" some of these rights.[49]

By evening it was clear that pro-choice activists were losing the message battle. At 5:00 P.M. National Public Radio's *All Things Considered* opened with the words, "The Supreme Court upholds *Roe v. Wade*." At 6:30 P.M. NBC's Tom Brokaw declared *Casey* a "compromise" in which "both sides came out winners." An hour later, Michael Kinsley, the designated liberal commentator on CNN's *Crossfire*, described Pennsylvania's restrictions as "very moderate." "They certainly do not deny anyone the right to abortion," he said.

The next morning's front pages and network news broadcasts solidified this conclusion. "The Supreme Court, defying predictions that it was prepared to eliminate the right to abortion, yesterday adopted a middle-ground approach," began the lead story in the *Washington Post*. The *New York Times* reported that the decision "redefined and limited the abortion right to some degree. But it left it stronger than many abortion-rights supporters had expected and opponents had hoped for." The *Los Angeles Times* concluded that the ruling "undercuts for now the movement to enact ever-stricter regulations on abortion." Anchors on ABC's *Good Morning America* and CBS's *This Morning* reiterated that the Court had secured a "middle ground."

That evening, ABC and CBS reporters cited polls showing that *Casey* "may reflect where this country really stands on abortion." CBS reporter Rita Braver told viewers that "legislatures now understand they must take a moderate approach to regulating abortion." Braver concluded that "even though there will be lots more shouting from the most extreme advocates on both sides of the abortion issue, yesterday's Supreme Court decision may result in a national policy that truly reflects the will of the people." By week's end, the conventional wisdom was settled. As ABC's Cokie Roberts put it, "[*Casey*] was the perfect ruling. The Court basically came down exactly where the American people are"— that is, "abortion should remain legal, but reasonable restrictions can apply." [50]

In their reactions to the ruling, Bush and Quayle embraced this consensus and associated it with their emphasis on family values. Bush declared,

> I am pleased with the Supreme Court's decision upholding most of Pennsylvania's reasonable restrictions on abortion, such as the requirement that a teenager seek her parent's consent before obtaining an abortion.
> The Pennsylvania law supports family values in what is perhaps the most difficult question a family can confront. [51]

Quayle added, "The American people support reasonable limitations on abortion on demand. That may not be the Democratic Congress's position, but that's America's position." [52]

The Democrats showed no interest in taking on this fight. In a July 7 interview with PBS journalist Bill Moyers, Clinton suggested that "Americans can differ on what restrictions" should be imposed on abortions. When Moyers asked whether Clinton opposed the Pennsylvania restrictions, Clinton said he was "very reluctant to get into a great deal of detail on that." As for the suggestion that Clinton had "stood back and accepted" the 1988 ballot measure that banned abortion funding in Arkansas, Clinton denied that he had sat idle but declined to pass judgment on the measure. [53]

At this same time, Clinton was interviewing potential running mates. He promised that his selection would be pro-choice but refused to say whether that entailed opposition to Pennsylvania's restrictions. One of the men on Clinton's short list, Wofford, supported those restrictions. Clinton declined to say whether Wofford was pro-choice. Another finalist for the job, Representative Lee Hamilton of Indiana, pronounced himself "comfortable" with the Pennsylvania law. When asked whether he favored abortion rights, Hamilton answered that he stood "exactly where most Americans are." "I want to see government not play a major role with respect to abortion," he explained. "I don't want it to ban the abortion, and I don't want it to encourage it through the providing of funds." [54]

On July 9 Clinton named Senator Al Gore of Tennessee to his ticket. Gore claimed to be pro-choice, but reporters pointed out that he had opposed federal funding of abortions, and pro-lifers called attention to a letter in which he had said so. Three days after Gore's selection, ABC's Sam Donaldson asked him to explain the discrepancy between his opposition to abortion funding and his support of abortion's legality. "It's the difference between imposing your beliefs on someone else and giving the American people the opportunity to make their own choices in their lives," Gore replied. "That's what freedom is all about." Infuriated by such comments, NOW officials announced that they wouldn't endorse Clinton and Gore "unless they [came] out strongly on the right to abortions by young women and poor women." [55]

Meanwhile, the Republican ticket evacuated its position that abortion should be outlawed. On July 22 CNN's Larry King asked Quayle what he would do if his daughter, as an adult, were to seek his advice about a problem pregnancy. "I would counsel her . . . and support her in whatever decision she made," Quayle answered. King persisted: "And if the decision was abortion, you'd support her, as a parent?" Quayle replied, "I'd support my daughter. I'd hope that she wouldn't make that decision." Afterward, Quayle's aides reinforced the impression that he was accepting abortion rights. One spokesman affirmed that "apparently he [Quayle] believes it's her decision." Another pointed out that Quayle's position was "consistent with individual responsibility. Right now in this country she has that choice." [56]

Bush soon joined the retreat. On August 11 he told NBC interviewer Stone Phillips that if his granddaughter were to consult him about an abortion, he would "try to talk her out of it" but would "stand by" her.

Phillips asked, "So in the end the decision would be hers?" Bush replied, "Who else's could it be?" Five days later, Bush gave the same answer to ABC's David Brinkley: "I'd try to talk her out of it. What am I going to do, other than that?" In his August 20 address to the Republican National Convention, Bush's only allusion to abortion was that he believed "in the worth of each individual human being, born or unborn." Quayle's only allusion was that he had taught his children "about family issues like adoption." [57]

Jack Kemp, Bush's housing secretary and an important figure in the GOP, added to the impression that the Republicans weren't serious about banning abortion. In a CNN interview on August 16, Kemp said that although Bush and Quayle wanted to "protect human life," they intended "to respect ultimately the decision of their daughter or granddaughter." A week later, Kemp assured viewers of NBC's *Meet the Press* that while he favored a constitutional amendment to ban abortions, "there's not going to be one." [58]

Quayle was explicit about confining pro-life evangelism to a pro-choice legal framework. On August 27, when asked again in an ABC interview what he would do if his daughter chose an abortion, Quayle answered, "I respect my daughter's decision. Others that have made a decision like that, I wish they hadn't, but I'm not going to challenge their decision. What I'm going to do is try to change attitudes in America, try to change the behavior." Three days later, CBS reporter Lesley Stahl suggested to Quayle, "[U]ltimately you want this decision to be illegal." Refusing to assent, Quayle replied instead, "Ultimately we want the decision to be life and not abortion." A week after that, on a television show in Los Angeles, Quayle added, "The issue of abortion is one where reasonable men and women disagree. I believe abortion is wrong. The choice should be life and not abortion. We're trying to get more reflection on the issue of abortion before the decision is made." [59]

But while accepting the principle of choice, Quayle and his wife, Marilyn, insisted on a conservative reading of that principle. In July, a day after Dan Quayle suggested that he wouldn't thwart an adult daughter's abortion choice, Marilyn Quayle insisted that if her daughter became pregnant while still a minor, "she'll take the child to term." When asked who would make the final decision, Mrs. Quayle answered, "We'll make it with her." The press thought she had contradicted her husband, but a spokesman explained that the Quayles didn't accord a teenager the same rights as an adult. From their perspective, it was liberals who were inconsistent about opposing government interference in the family. As one editorialist put it, "Dan Quayle's fatherly reaction shows why it would be wrong for the government to deny him and Marilyn the right to make such decisions of conscience for their minor daughter, not to mention her right to make them for herself as an adult." [60]

Throughout the campaign, the Republicans steered discussions of abortion toward middle-ground restrictions such as Pennsylvania's. In three televised interviews during the fall, Quayle dodged questions about banning abortion by changing the subject to Pennsylvania's restrictions, which he praised as "bipartisan," "rational," and "proper limitations on abortion on demand." In the October 13 vice presidential debate, when Gore called for "common ground" on abortion, Quayle proposed parental notice as part of that ground. Bush's campaign literature omitted his earlier opposition to legal abortion, suggesting instead that he "favors reasonable restrictions." [61]

The Republicans laid particular emphasis on the notion that Clinton and the Democrats were trying to undermine parents. In an ABC interview on August 23, conservative activist Pat Buchanan said of Clinton, "He is in favor, as I understand it, of 15-year-old girls getting abortions without telling their parents. Now, that is not in the mainstream." Four days later, on ABC's *Prime Time Live,* Quayle asserted that Democrats "don't even want parents to be involved" when a thirteen-year-old girl seeks an abortion. "We're saying the parents should be involved," said Quayle. In speeches and interviews, Bush pointed out that in some states, a thirteen-year-old girl needed parental consent to get her ears pierced but not to get an abortion. He called this "crazy" and "obscene." [62]

By the time Bush appeared on Larry King's show on October 4, he had completed his evolution from the candidate of prohibition to the candidate of reasonable restrictions. When King asked him about the pro-life Republican platform, Bush replied,

> I support the platform, but here's my position: I am against abortion. I am against federal funding, except for the life of the mother; and I am against abortions except for rape, incest, and the life of the mother. . . . One other thing on this question bothers me. A 13-year-old girl cannot get her ears pierced in some places without permission of her parents. And yet Gov. Clinton and those people want to pass an abortion law that doesn't require parents to be notified if the child's going to have an abortion. I find that appalling. I find that is something that is not good for families. We're trying to strengthen families. [63]

To reinforce their contention that Clinton would subvert family values, the Republicans turned their fire on his wife, Hillary Rodham Clinton. In a series of legal essays during the 1970s, Mrs. Clinton, then known as Hillary Rodham, had made three arguments about the culture of family sovereignty. Her first argument was that the doctrine of absolute parental authority deprived children of certain rights based on the same paternalistic logic that had been used to justify the oppression of women, slaves, and Native Americans. In a 1973 article, Rodham wrote,

> The basic rationale for depriving people of rights in a dependency relationship is that certain individuals are incapable or undeserving of the right to take care of themselves and consequently need social institutions specifically designed to safeguard their position. . . . Along with the family, past and present examples of such arrangements include marriage, slavery, and the Indian reservation system. The relative powerlessness of children makes them uniquely vulnerable to this rationale.

Rodham's second argument was that children's rights were a losing political cause. In the 1973 article, she examined one side of this equation: the "powerlessness" of children. In addition to their "physical, intellectual, and psychological" weakness, children suffered from "the organization and ideology of the political system itself. Lacking even the basic power to vote, children are not able to exercise normal constituency powers, articulating self-interests to politicians."

In 1977 Rodham explored the other side of the equation: the power and anxiety of parents. Noting "the rising debate over public intervention in family life," she observed that "politicians, not wishing to appear as advocates of interference with the family," succumbed to "a cultural reluctance to make children's needs a public responsibility." Two years later, Rodham wrote, "The fears that many people have about the formulation of a family policy or a law of children's rights arise from their concern about increasing government control over such intrafamily disputes."

Rodham's third argument was that despite this cultural resistance, the government should sometimes intervene in families to protect children. While conceding that the state occasionally "abused" its powers, she warned that "too often, on occasions when intervention is necessary, it does not occur because of the decision maker's extreme reluctance to interrupt family life." To avoid erring too much either way, she proposed what she regarded as a balanced intervention policy:

> I prefer that intervention into an ongoing family be limited to decisions that could have long-term and possibly irreparable effects if they were not resolved. Decisions about motherhood and abortion, schooling, cosmetic surgery, treatment of venereal disease, or employment, and others where

the decision or lack of one will significantly affect the child's future should not be made unilaterally by parents. Children should have a right to be permitted to decide their own future if they are competent.[64]

This analysis turned the argument made by Bush—and Bill Clinton—on its head. Rodham agreed with Bush and Clinton that for a teenage girl, having a baby or an abortion was vastly more serious than getting her ears pierced or her tooth pulled. But in Rodham's view, that was why parental consent should be waived in the former case rather than the latter.

Hillary Rodham Clinton's writings first surfaced as an issue in spring 1992, when her husband emerged as the front-runner for the Democratic presidential nomination. On March 16, three days after Mr. Clinton trounced his rivals in the Super Tuesday primaries, *Wall Street Journal* columnist Paul Gigot quoted from Mrs. Clinton's essays and labeled her "a feminist and an ardent liberal," unlike First Lady Barbara Bush. "Smart Republicans," Gigot predicted, would run "two races this autumn: Bill vs. George, and Hillary vs. Barbara."[65]

Two weeks later, when Mr. Clinton proposed to give his wife a "high-level" role in his administration, conservative activists sounded the alarm. "She'd be a danger in any position where she has influence over family decisions," charged Beverly LaHaye, president of Concerned Women for America. "She really feels decisions about abortion, schooling, motherhood, and treatment for VD should not be left up to parents. She'd totally rip the heart out of any family." Gary Bauer, president of the Family Research Council, warned that Mrs. Clinton "has radical views on children, families and the law."[66]

On August 12, as Republicans met in Houston to prepare for their national convention, party chairman Rich Bond distributed Mrs. Clinton's writings to the media and blasted her in a speech:

> Now, of course, advising Bill Clinton on every move is that champion of the family, Hillary Clinton, who believes that kids should be able to sue their parents, rather than helping with the chores as they were asked to do. She's likened marriage and the family to slavery. She's referred to the family as a dependency relationship that deprives people of their rights.[67]

Six days later, on the convention's opening night, Pat Buchanan carried the attack to the podium before tens of millions of television viewers:

> Elect me, and you get two for the price of one, Mr. Clinton says of his lawyer-spouse. And what does Hillary believe? Well, Hillary believes that

12-year-olds should have the right to sue their parents, and she has compared marriage and the family, as an institution, to slavery and life on an Indian reservation. Well, speak for yourself, Hillary.

Friends, this is radical feminism.[68]

The next evening, religious broadcaster and former presidential candidate Pat Robertson completed the indictment, connecting Bill Clinton's abortion views to his wife's pro-government, anti-family philosophy:

> He told *People* magazine that he wouldn't let his 13-year-old daughter get her ears pierced, but he wants your 13-year-old to be able to have an abortion without your permission. . . .
>
> When Bill and Hillary Clinton talk about family values, they are not talking about either families or values. They are talking about a radical plan to destroy the traditional family and transfer its functions to the federal government.[69]

Bill Clinton refused to take the bait. "This is not about restrictions in the Pennsylvania law," he argued. "That's what President Bush wants people to think it's about. This is about whether the minority opinion [for overturning *Roe*] should become the majority opinion." On September 29, when Marilyn Quayle accused Clinton of opposing parental notice, Clinton's spokeswoman replied that he supported Arkansas's parental notice law. Six days later, when Larry King asked him whether he supported "abortion unequivocally," Clinton cleared himself of that charge by noting twice that he had signed the Arkansas law. He repeated that point in a televised forum three weeks afterward.[70]

Gore followed the same strategy. In a nationally televised interview on September 23, he reaffirmed his opposition to "the use of taxpayer funds for abortions." The following evening, in a PBS broadcast, Gore dismissed abortion funding as a "separate" issue from abortion rights. In the October 13 vice presidential debate, Quayle reminded Gore of his 1987 letter "saying that [he] oppose[d] taxpayer funding of abortion." Gore didn't flinch. "And I still do," said the senator.[71]

Around the country, dozens of pro-choice gubernatorial, senatorial, and congressional candidates took a similar approach, using public funding and parental consent to present themselves as "classic conservatives" rather than liberals.[72] Even pro-choice activists played this game. In the two statewide abortion referenda that came before voters in 1992, activists jettisoned the interests of teenage girls and poor women in order to protect the legal right to abortion.

In Maryland, pro-choice forces passed Question 6, a ballot measure that guaranteed abortion rights but also reactivated the state's enjoined parental notice law by making it constitutional. When opponents raised the issue of parental involvement in television ads, supporters called a press conference at which a lawmaker promised that the measure would protect parents' rights. Far from "liberalizing" Maryland's abortion laws, he argued, "[j]ust the opposite is true." Over the next month, pro-choice spokesmen made this point again and again. "If Question 6 passes, Maryland will have an enforceable parental notification law for the first time in 20 years," they told voters.[73]

To make the measure look moderate, its supporters even bragged to voters that pro-choice activists were unhappy with it. When opponents suggested that Question 6 must be radical because Maryland NARAL supported it, a pro-choice lawmaker corrected them:

> During the 1990 session, the first time a codification of *Roe vs. Wade* was attempted, NARAL repeatedly threatened to scuttle the bill because it had a parental notification provision. NARAL capitulated only after I and other bill leaders insisted that we needed a moderate compromise bill to address the concerns of the public.
>
> Its current support of Question 6 is in deference to the political realities and not the pure codification of *Roe vs. Wade* it would wish.[74]

While pro-choice strategists in Maryland severed abortion rights from teenager's rights, their colleagues in Arizona, battling a ballot measure called Proposition 110, severed abortion rights from funding. Like Amendment 65 in Arkansas, Proposition 110 piggybacked a challenge to abortion's legality on a ban on abortion funding, even though the state already prohibited such funding.

Pro-choice activists first tried to split the issues in court. The League of Women Voters filed a lawsuit claiming that Proposition 110 unconstitutionally combined two distinct issues, abortion rights and abortion subsidies. The only witness summoned by the league's attorney was a pollster who testified that just three in ten Arizonans would ban abortion, whereas half would ban public financing of abortions. The league's attorney cited other polls that yielded the same discrepancy. By combining the two issues, she argued, Proposition 110 would confuse the pivotal bloc of voters who didn't want to ban or pay for abortions. "They will have to vote against their principles on one issue in order to vote in alignment with their beliefs on the other," she concluded.[75]

The league's suit failed on a technicality, and within a month, backers of Proposition 110 launched a half-million-dollar television ad campaign. As anticipated, their commercials alluded to polls showing that "a solid majority of Arizonans" favored minimal abortion rights but opposed abortion subsidies.[76]

Again, pro-choice strategists separated the two issues. Summarizing the opposition's case, NARAL's state political director dismissed abortion funding as a "non-issue" and assured voters that "no tax dollars are being used" for abortions. The opposition's first television ad took the point further, warning viewers that Proposition 110 "forces the government and politicians to meddle in a family's life. And it wants to use millions of taxpayers' money to pay for it."[77] As in Arkansas, the allusion to "taxpayers' money" was left ambiguous, suggesting to uninformed viewers that the ballot measure might restore tax funding of abortions. The safe, libertarian course was to vote "No."

The opposition's second television commercial featured Mr. Conservative, former Arizona senator Barry Goldwater. "We Americans share a heritage of freedom guaranteed us by our Constitution," he reminded viewers. Proposition 110, he declared, "is not good for our freedom." The ad concluded, "Keep government out of our personal lives. Vote no on Proposition 110."[78]

What a reversal time had wrought. In 1964, from the podium of the Republican National Convention, Goldwater had championed "extremism in the defense of liberty." Twenty-eight years later, the country had shifted so far to the right that pro-choice strategists were flaunting Goldwater's endorsement as proof that they rejected extremism in their defense of liberty. "Barry's very credible," crowed the manager of the campaign against Proposition 110. "You can't call him an extremist."[79]

On November 3 Arizonans rejected Proposition 110, Marylanders approved Question 6, and Americans replaced Bush with Clinton. The long march begun by the abortion rights movement in the late 1980s had at last arrived at America's middle ground. From opposite sides, Bob Casey and Harris Wofford joined hands to celebrate what Wofford called the new "common ground," a safe distance from what Casey described as "the far left, extremely radical NARAL line."[80] Pro-choice activists had reached the summit of victory stripped of the cumbersome weight of much of their agenda. They had conquered the middle ground, and the middle ground had conquered them.

CHAPTER 7

Victims and Villains

People who oppose abortion are often accused of caring more about punishing women for having sex than about protecting life. At the same time, they're accused of cruelty for trying to prohibit abortion in cases of rape or incest.

The accusations contradict each other. If you're trying to save unborn children, there's no reason to discriminate between those conceived in rape and those conceived in consensual intercourse. The reason to treat rape survivors differently is to discriminate between women who choose to have sex and those who don't.

Every woman who seeks an elective abortion sees it as an escape from the unwanted consequences of intercourse. If you grant abortions to rape survivors but not to other women, you're enforcing the unwanted consequences of sex on women who choose to have intercourse while sparing other women those same consequences. In short, you're punishing women for having sex. You can't claim that you're just letting nature take its course, since you're disrupting nature by letting rape survivors abort their pregnancies. You, not nature, are deciding which women are entitled to abortions and which aren't.

Harping on the plight of rape victims is an easy way to score points against pro-lifers. Pro-choicers often use this tactic to attract morally conservative voters and politicians who can't stomach pro-life absolutism. But when moral conservatives part company with pro-lifers, which group is cruel, and which is compassionate? What kind of choice do moral conservatives believe in? And what kind of life?

ANGOLA, LOUISIANA
MAY 18, 1990

It was time to kill the prisoner. He had spent a decade on Death Row at the Louisiana State Penitentiary for slaying a taxi driver and a state trooper. It didn't matter that he had killed both men while still a minor. It didn't matter that no state had ever executed anyone for a crime committed at such an age. It didn't matter that he had been beaten and brain damaged as a child and was mildly retarded. It didn't matter that he was black and that every member of the jury that had convicted him and had recommended his death sentence was, like the trooper he had killed, white. It didn't matter that he had repented and had behaved well in prison.[1]

Dalton Prejean's attorneys had made each of these points as they pleaded for his life. Twice in the previous six months, the State Pardon Board had asked Governor Buddy Roemer to commute Prejean's sentence to life in prison without possibility of parole. Twice, Roemer had rejected that advice, citing the "brutality" of Prejean's crimes. Prejean had sent Roemer a videotaped plea for mercy and had requested a meeting. Ninety minutes before Prejean's execution, Roemer had telephoned him in the Death House. Only by forfeiting his life, the governor told him, could Prejean serve society and send the proper message to those contemplating similar crimes.[2]

Around the world, Prejean's plight had inspired outcries. Amnesty International had petitioned the state for clemency. The Reverend Daniel Berrigan, the Catholic anti-war activist, had implored Louisianans not "to redress or avenge a crime by committing another crime." *Washington Post* columnist Richard Cohen had called the killing of Prejean, "at the mental age of 13," a retaliatory "abortion" at the behest of "an electorate crazed with fear of crime."[3]

In Louisiana, however, calls to Roemer's office and to talk radio shows conveyed enthusiasm for the execution. Here, the rights of victims came first. If expunging their injuries entailed taking a life, so be it. "It's the punishment for a crime," explained the widow of the trooper Prejean had killed, as she awaited Prejean's execution. "It's kind of like a book. It will be the end of the book, the last chapter. And you can put the book on the shelf."[4]

Standing in shackles before the electric chair, Prejean told the assembled witnesses, "Nothing is going to be accomplished." He turned and took his seat. His limbs were strapped down. A hood was lowered over his head. Four massive shocks convulsed his body.[5] The story of his crime, and of his life, was over.

Two weeks later Louisiana plunged the nation into another debate over guilt and punishment, life and death. This time the subject was abortion.

Before *Roe*, Louisiana boasted one of the nation's toughest abortion bans. When the Supreme Court rolled back *Roe* in 1989, Louisiana was the first state to act. Within hours, Roemer met with lawmakers to discuss stiffening the abortion laws. Three days later, the state house overwhelmingly passed a resolution, introduced by Representative Woody Jenkins, asking district attorneys to resume enforcement of the abortion ban *Roe* had voided.[6]

As measured by polls, Louisiana was the most anti-abortion state in the country. It was also the most sexist, with no women in its senate and only three in its 105-member house.[7] Whether these two characteristics were related was open to dispute. What was certain was that tackling them together, by defending abortion as a woman's right, was a losing proposition.

There were other ways, however, to crack the state's anti-abortion majority. According to polls, three out of four Louisiana voters would refuse to grant an abortion if the woman simply didn't want a child. If the child would be born with a severe handicap, nearly half would grant an abortion. But if the pregnancy had resulted from rape or incest, 70 percent would allow the abortion. Only 10 percent of voters would spend public funds on an abortion for a poor woman who simply didn't want a child, but 63 percent would do so for a victim of rape or incest.[8]

This discrepancy betrayed the chief standard by which Louisianans decided who was entitled to an abortion. Some women were perpetrators of sex; others were victims. The distinction wasn't just that a rape survivor had suffered but that she didn't deserve to suffer. The person who deserved to suffer was the perpetrator, her rapist.

Sex wasn't a sin in itself. It became sinful when performed outside traditional institutions. That was why Louisiana had banned sex education in its public schools until 1979 and why, even in 1990, only six of its school districts taught the subject.[9] The same logic applied to rape. What was violated in rape wasn't just a woman but womanhood and the whole fabric of traditional sexual morality. Abortion purged that violation.

This logic was on display in summer 1990 as the legislature debated a bill to criminalize a husband's rape of his wife. In the house, the bill triggered hoots, jokes, and laughter and was promptly voted down. Two of the three women in the chamber denounced the vote, provoking more laughter.[10]

The bill's opponents complained that it would let women seize their husbands' property by falsely accusing them of rape and sending them to jail. They also argued that women tacitly consented to sex by getting married. "Women know what a man is when they marry him," said the bill's chief antagonist, state representative Carl Gunter. If the woman stayed with her husband after forced intercourse, that was proof of consent. As Gunter put it, "[T]he second time it happens it wasn't rape." Summarizing the sentiments of his colleagues, Gunter called the bill an "attempt to destroy the home and destroy family life." Legislators later reconsidered and passed the bill only after exempting husbands from prosecution for "simple" rape—nonconsensual sex with a woman who was too drunk or drugged to resist—on the grounds that wives could gain too much "leverage" by accusing their husbands of that offense.[11]

If rape was a crime against a woman, a rapist's marriage to his prey wouldn't excuse him. But as the debate made clear, most Louisiana legislators assumed that to some extent it did excuse him. Sex was a wife's duty and a husband's right. Sex between husband and wife couldn't be rape, because it couldn't violate the ideal woman, the dutiful wife.

Furthermore, what went on between husband and wife was private. As Robert Bork had observed, privacy could mean many things. Feminists believed in the privacy of each woman. Louisiana lawmakers believed in the privacy of the traditional family. Fear of losing the latter kind of privacy had so eroded Bork's support among Louisiana voters in 1987 that the state's senior U.S. senator, Bennett Johnston, had led the movement to reject him. This understanding of privacy still echoed in the slogan of the late governor Huey Long: Every man a king.

Two politicians stood at the center of Louisiana's abortion war. One was Roemer. As a congressman, he had maintained that unborn children possessed full human rights. In 1985 and 1987 he cosponsored bills to prohibit abortion in facilities and programs that received federal funds. In 1987 he sponsored a constitutional amendment to ban abortion outright. His 1985 legislation declared that "abortion takes the life of a preborn child who is a living human being." His constitutional amendment declared that all "unborn offspring" were persons under the Constitution and that except to save a pregnant woman's life, "[n]o unborn person shall be deprived of life" by abortion.[12]

Throughout the 1980s Roemer's commitment to unborn life circumscribed two other convictions. One was respect for women. In Congress he encouraged female advancement in business. As governor, he was recognized by the National Women's Political Caucus for appointing women to three of his ten cabinet positions. But in 1980 he opposed Medicaid coverage of abortions for rape victims on the grounds that it offered other women a "loophole" through which to get money for elective abortions. And in 1983 he voted against the Equal Rights Amendment primarily "because it would permit the use of tax money for abortion."[13]

The other principle circumscribed by Roemer's commitment to unborn life was his belief that violent felons should be punished. In Congress he cosponsored bills to stiffen criminal penalties and cut off federal benefits to inmates. He also sponsored a bill to systematize the death penalty. The bill outlined factors that should determine whether a killer was to die. It also proposed to abolish the federal death penalty for rape, since only the taking of one life could justify the taking of another. And because no unborn child deserved to die for its parent's crime, the bill declared, "In no event shall a sentence of death be carried out upon a pregnant woman."[14]

Roemer entered the Governor's Mansion in 1988 promising a "revolution" against Louisiana's wheel-and-deal style of politics. But in 1989 voters crushed his fiscal reform plan, and his second wife moved out of the mansion. Roemer turned to a Baptist minister and longtime friend, from whom he learned a new philosophy based on "honor." As Roemer explained it, honor had to do with valuing "relationships" and "the journey instead of the destination." To honor others meant to "make time" for them, to listen to them, to "respect their values, learn to appreciate their differences."

From 1989 to 1990 Roemer changed. He dictated less; he listened more. He admitted that he didn't have all the answers. Hoping to heal his marriage, he took long afternoons away from his job to be with his wife. Addressing the legislature in April 1990, he apologized for his arrogance over the preceding two years and asked lawmakers to "hold hands" and "find common ground" with him.[15]

No one could have imagined such words issuing from Woody Jenkins. On his election in 1971, Jenkins became the legislature's chief advocate for Louisiana's fundamentalist Protestant churches. He fought the ERA and joined an elite network of moral conservatives that included Pat Robertson, Phyllis Schlafly, and Jerry Falwell. Trained as a radio and television speaker, Jenkins resembled the young Robertson in outlook, eloquence, and appearance.[16]

Jenkins understood the hatred of crime that suffused Louisiana. He sponsored a bill that would force judges to consider a victim's injuries when sentencing the assailant. He also orchestrated passage of a "shoot the burglar" bill that granted residents the right to kill intruders. Opponents protested that the bill legalized murder, but Jenkins insisted that citizens' "right to defend their homes" was paramount.[17]

Where Roemer sought consensus, Jenkins demanded victory. "He doesn't swap votes," marveled one colleague. "He doesn't make deals at all." When his friend, White House aide Oliver North, was caught selling arms to Iran and funneling the proceeds to Nicaraguan rebels, Jenkins, a fellow activist in the Nicaraguan conflict, staunchly defended him. And in his 1978 campaign for the U.S. Senate, Jenkins prophesied that he would beat the moderate incumbent because "strong-willed people prevail. They run right over those who vacillate."[18] The election that fall proved Jenkins wrong. And the abortion war of 1990–91, pitting Jenkins's pro-life absolutism against his constituents' deference to criminal justice, would prove him wrong again.

Sex crimes had always been the most difficult challenge for pro-lifers. All of the fourteen states that relaxed their abortion bans from 1967 to 1970 created exceptions for rape and incest.[19] Throughout the 1970s and 1980s pro-choice advocates harped on these cases to persuade conservatives of the injustice of outlawing abortion. In 1986 pro-choice activists in Arkansas made sex crimes a central issue in their campaign against Amendment 65. In 1989 sex-crime rhetoric helped Doug Wilder to compete with Marshall Coleman for law-and-order voters in Virginia. It also persuaded the U.S. House of Representatives to endorse Medicaid funding of abortions in rape and incest cases.

Polls published from July 1989 to March 1990 showed that while roughly half of all U.S. adults thought abortion should be banned in cases of voluntary intercourse, only a small fraction would extend a ban to cases of rape or incest. Recognizing this gap, NRLC embarked on a strategy to remove sex crimes from the abortion debate. In several states, NRLC engineered legislation that would ban abortion except in cases of rape, incest, profound fetal deformity, or danger to the life or health of the woman. Pro-choicers managed to shoot down this legislation in every state but Idaho.[20]

NRLC and Right to Life of Idaho described their bill as a ban on "abortion for birth control."[21] Like "abortion on demand" and "abortion for convenience," this phrase denoted abortions for less than compelling reasons—for example, that pregnancy or motherhood would derail a woman's education or career, or that she felt financially unable to raise a child, or simply that she didn't want to add another child to her family.

The exceptions for rape and incest divided Idaho's pro-life activists. Four pro-life groups asked Governor Cecil Andrus to veto the bill on the grounds that abortion was murder regardless of the manner of conception. But NRLC's regional director explained, "The reason for pursuing this type of legislation is a general consensus that abortion is all right in these [exceptional] cases." Right to Life of Idaho released a poll designed to show that a ban with such exceptions offered a popular middle ground.[22]

Andrus claimed to oppose legal abortion except in cases of rape or incest. But when the bill arrived on his desk, he complained that by requiring victims to report their rapes to police within seven days in order to get abortions, it might deter them from obtaining the procedure.[23] On March 30 he vetoed the bill in the name not of women's rights but of victims' rights.

> The bill is drawn so narrowly that it would punitively and without compassion further harm an Idaho woman who may find herself in the horrible, unthinkable position of confronting a pregnancy that resulted from rape or incest. . . .
> What do we do in a circumstance in which a 12-year-old girl becomes pregnant as a result of incest? If, for whatever reason, she does not or cannot report the identity of the perpetrator to the authorities, she will violate the law if she or her family cause the pregnancy to be terminated. This law would demand that this 12-year-old girl, who has already been the victim of an unspeakable act, compound her tragedy.[24]

Pro-choice leaders hailed the veto. Kate Michelman called it "the most significant demonstration to date of the power, depth and intensity of the pro-choice movement." She added that NARAL might campaign for Andrus in the fall against a pro-life challenger. But Andrus reiterated that he opposed legal abortion. He had rejected this bill only because it confused the innocent with the guilty. Under the bill, he explained, a rape survivor seeking to end her pregnancy a week after the assault "ceases to be the victim and becomes a criminal."[25]

The veto in Idaho transformed the Louisiana debate in two ways. First, it raised the stakes. Idaho had represented pro-lifers' best shot at passing an abortion ban that would force the Supreme Court to reconsider *Roe*. Although Guam, a U.S. territory, had enacted such a ban, experts doubted the Court would rewrite the nation's abortion jurisprudence unless challenged by a state. "Louisiana is the last state to meet in a session this year that could provide the Supreme Court the opportunity to consider a statute that would overturn *Roe v. Wade*," said Jenkins.[26]

Second, Andrus showed Roemer a way to reject an abortion ban without endorsing a woman's right to choose abortion. Before Andrus's veto, Roemer had asked only for "consideration" of rape or incest. But after Andrus's veto and the favorable nationwide reaction to it, Roemer declared that he would veto any attempt to ban abortion in Louisiana in such cases.[27]

In the legislature, the balance of power lay with those who supported exceptions for rape or incest. Lawmakers justified this compromise on the political grounds that polls showed it was popular and on the moral grounds that abortion in cases of forced sex wasn't "a form of contraception."[28] When the director of the Louisiana Pro-Life Council asked legislators why they insisted on these exceptions, they explained that since a rape victim hadn't consented to sex, she shouldn't have to suffer the consequences.

Pro-life activists thought they could overcome this resistance. National pro-life groups advised them to introduce model legislation similar to the Idaho bill, but the Louisiana activists insisted that they could pass an abortion ban without such compromises.[29] The Louisiana Right to Life Federation, well connected to the state's powerful Catholic churches, joined forces with Jenkins and his fundamentalist Protestant following. Together, they crafted a bill that would ban all abortions, with a penalty of up to ten years in jail.

Pro-choice activists had no such confidence. Only a handful of the 144 legislators supported a woman's right to abortion.[30] Most agreed that abortion should be allowed to save a woman's life or in the case of rape or incest. But when pro-choice lobbyists urged them to extend that sympathy to other scenarios, the lawmakers balked, invoking the unborn child's innocence. The lobbyists got the message. Rape victims could match that innocence. Other women couldn't.

If pro-choice activists couldn't dissolve this distinction, neither could their opponents. The governor would veto an abortion ban that ignored the distinction. One-third of the senate, enough to sustain his veto, would stand with him. Accordingly, pro-choice lobbyists instructed friendly legislators to vote against amendments to allow abortion in cases of rape or incest. They asked pro-life legislators, on grounds of moral consistency, to do the same.[31]

The leaders of Louisiana's pro-choice lobby were Terri Bartlett, director of Planned Parenthood of Louisiana, and Robin Rothrock, president of the state League of Women Voters. Arriving in Louisiana in 1983, Bartlett had been taken aback by the state's overt, church-sanctioned sexism. She had dedicated herself to earning women not just control of family and sexual matters, but society's trust to make thoughtful decisions about such matters.

Rothrock had been running an abortion clinic in Shreveport and promoting sex education for a decade. New Orleans, Bartlett's cosmopolitan port across the water in the state's far southeast, seemed to Rothrock an island of tolerance. When Jenkins's resolution steamed through the legislature after *Webster,* Rothrock told the press why few lawmakers would speak up for abortion as a women's issue: "In this state to say that is political suicide."[32]

In 1989, when Rothrock invited pro-choice organizations to consolidate under the banner of the Louisiana Coalition for Reproductive Freedom, she unveiled coalition stationery proclaiming, "Privacy is the Issue." Bartlett found this slogan hollow. Whose privacy was at stake, and how? Bartlett recommended an alternative theme that seemed to her more personal, moving, and affirmative: "Trust Women." Wasn't that what this fight was really about? Society trusted women to raise its children; surely it could learn to entrust them with abortion decisions. Legislators trusted their wives and daughters; surely they could extend that trust to other women. If not, shouldn't pro-choice activists use this debate to challenge the state's pervasive sexism?

Rothrock was mystified. Didn't Bartlett appreciate the power of the privacy message? Rothrock considered "trusting women" a nonstarter as a lobbying pitch. She spoke of family authority rather than women's authority, since lawmakers might sympathize more easily with a father's wish to choose abortion for his teenage daughter.[33] Other activists who had lobbied the legislature on women's issues shared Rothrock's pessimism and advised their pro-choice allies not to talk about women's rights.

To substantiate their assertion that Louisianans trusted women, Bartlett and her sympathizers commissioned a statewide poll. In their summary of the results, they boasted that "53 percent of respondents favor allowing a woman to decide for herself, in consultation with a physician," whether to have an abortion.[34] The survey question that produced this narrow majority had been edited by Planned Parenthood's national media strategist. By mentioning doctors' authority, it elicited the approval of many people who wouldn't grant women sole authority over abortion decisions.

National polls taken after *Webster* had proved the effectiveness of this tactic. In a 1989 Voters for Choice poll, support for abortion rights rose by 22 net percentage points among conservatives when the question was rephrased from allowing "choice" to allowing choice "with physician consent." In an ABC–*Washington Post* poll later that year, respondents agreed by only a 9-point margin that a woman should be allowed an abortion "if she decides she wants one." But in a CBS–*New York Times* poll, respondents agreed by a 39-point margin that permission should be granted "if a woman wants to have an abortion and her doctor agrees to it." [35]

In another CBS–*New York Times* poll, 53 percent of adults said that abortion should be banned entirely or restricted to cases of rape or incest. The respondents were then asked, "If your state restricted the number of abortions performed, who should decide which women would be allowed to have abortions?" Sixty-nine percent chose to confer this authority on "the woman's own doctor" rather than a judge or state functionary.[36] By rhetorically coupling doctors' authority with women's authority, pro-choicers could appease roughly half of those voters who refused to leave abortion decisions in women's hands alone.

On June 4, 1990, Jenkins's ally, state senator Mike Cross, presented Jenkins's bill to a Louisiana senate committee. Only one of the committee's seven members was pro-choice, but three others voiced concern about the bill's inflexibility in cases of rape or incest. Two of the three said they would oppose the bill unless such cases were exempted. They couched this demand as a matter of conscience, but they also referred to public ambivalence about rape and incest, as reflected in polls.[37]

Against these exceptions, Cross pointed out that if the fetus was a person, permitting abortions in cases of rape or incest amounted to "sanctioning killing." He conceded that rape was a terrible crime but pleaded that a child's life was sacred regardless of "the sins of its fathers." To dramatize the point, Julie Makimaa, a young Illinois woman allegedly conceived in rape, appeared before the committee and declared that no child deserved to die because of the manner of its conception.

Jenkins also testified against the rape exception. He argued that it was unnecessary since a rape victim could go to a hospital within a few days of the crime to get a pill or injection that would prevent pregnancy. He stipulated, however, that he didn't support the use of such morning-after pills in cases other than rape.[38]

This was an odd caveat. Why shouldn't a woman who knew immediately after consensual sex that she was at great risk of pregnancy— for example, because a condom slipped off—have the same access to a morning-after pill? From the standpoint of preventing pregnancy and abortion, there was no difference. The only difference was in the nature of the sex.

Two days later Jenkins presented his bill to a house committee. As television cameras and an overflow crowd looked on, Jenkins explained how abortion for "birth control" tempted young men and women to sin:

> [L]ook at what has happened since 1973. Teenage pregnancy has skyrocketed. Illegitimacy has skyrocketed. Welfare has skyrocketed. . . . Abortion has become birth control of last resort. [Teenagers] knew that if all else went wrong and there was a pregnancy, they could get an abortion. The young boys, the young males, have known that and so have the young females, and so they have been much more lax and much more liberal in their sexual practices. . . . They're having teenage pregnancies, and they're having illegitimate children and they're putting children on welfare.[39]

To most Louisiana lawmakers, this was a persuasive argument. But it didn't apply to victims of rape or incest. Indeed, the logic of sin and consequences justified exceptions for sex crimes. A pregnancy caused by rape was unnatural and criminal and therefore ought to be aborted. As one pro-life lawmaker put it, "My God is not for rape, my God doesn't cause rape to happen. That is caused by Satan himself."[40] The termination of such a pregnancy would partially restore the victim's honor, just as Dalton Prejean's termination had partially compensated his victim's widow.

Taking a life in order to restore a rape victim's honor wasn't just a hypothetical idea. Until the U.S. Supreme Court intervened in 1976, Loui-

siana law had mandated the death penalty for men convicted of aggra-
vated rape, even if they didn't kill their prey. Jenkins had voted against
executing rapists, reasoning that rape wasn't as grave as murder. But
during the 1990 abortion debate, he never denied that rapists should be
put to death. Instead, he urged conservatives to oppose a rape exception
on the grounds that if anyone deserved to die, it was the rapist, not his
offspring. "The rapist doesn't get the death penalty, but if we have an exception . . . the innocent unborn child will get the death penalty," Jenkins said.[41]

This argument raised a moral dilemma but failed to solve it. Even if
the abortion of a rape-induced pregnancy took the life of an innocent
child, at least it relieved the suffering of an innocent woman. One victim's rights countered another's.

Jenkins and Cross solved this dilemma by applying an old pro-life
tenet: Abortion itself was a kind of rape. To kill an unborn child inside
a woman was to rape her. As Cross put it, "Just as being raped and becoming pregnant is a traumatic experience, so is aborting a child."[42]

Sharon Fontenot, chief lobbyist for the Louisiana Right to Life Federation, explained to the house committee that "there are two victims of
abortion," woman and child. Jenkins agreed. Two other witnesses told
the committee about "post-abortion syndrome," a theory according to
which abortion, as a brutal violation of the mother-child bond, scarred
women emotionally and often injured them physically. Abortion was no
remedy for a pregnancy caused by rape. A pro-life rape survivor and
postabortion counselor pointed out to the committee how perverse it
would be to inflict on the rape victim a second trauma, "the trauma that
follows abortion."[43]

The idea that women were victims rather than perpetrators of abortion had been established in Louisiana law in the nineteenth century.
Louisiana courts had ruled in 1948 and 1970, and the legislature had
reaffirmed in its statutes, that a woman was "not criminally responsible"
for being "the subject of an abortion." Jenkins and Cross followed this
tradition. Their bills prescribed a penalty of up to ten years at hard labor for anyone who performed an abortion but no penalty for the
woman procuring the abortion.[44]

Superficially, this was a good deal for women: They could break the
law without being punished. But the victim theory reduced them to ob-
jects. Women weren't above prosecution; they were beneath it. The idea
of choice melted in the warmth of this paternal embrace: A woman
would no more choose abortion than she would choose rape. What she

needed was protection from such assaults. If pro-choicers wanted to portray women as damsels in distress, pro-lifers would oblige them.

The following morning, pro-choice witnesses testified against Jenkins's bill. A doctor told the story of a girl impregnated by rape at age fourteen and asked members of the committee what they would do if their own daughters faced such a crisis. Then Sally Donlon, a New Orleans businesswoman, told lawmakers about her own rape. She presented herself as a virtuous woman defiled by a vicious crime. "I was raised in a middle-class Louisiana home by Roman Catholic parents," she began. "[At seventeen] I was raped at gunpoint. I became pregnant and agonized over what to do." She explained to the committee that she had ultimately decided to expunge her rape through abortion: "I do believe that a woman's body is sacred. An unwanted fetus force-fathered by a violent and aggressive man can do terrible physical and psychological damage to that body. Finally, I decided that I couldn't allow the sanctity of my body to be sacrificed to vindicate an act of aggression." [45] Donlon later repeated that her objection was to "validating acts of violence." "I am not a feminist," she declared.[46]

   The committee passed the abortion ban without dissent. Many pro-choice witnesses left in disgust. Afterward, Terri Bartlett complained that the committee didn't "trust the women of Louisiana." [47] But maybe it didn't have to. Maybe pro-choice activists, taking a cue from Donlon, could defeat the ban by repackaging it as a crime issue, in which the conservative perception of duty was to protect the victim and expunge her violation.

   They would find an ally in Governor Roemer. As the bill advanced through the legislature, Roemer singled out rape and incest as "violent," "degrading," and "illegal." He demanded that the abortion ban provide "hope and constructive opportunity to the victims of those crimes." [48] To win over the governor and the public, pro-lifers would have to resolve the question of rape.

On June 13, the day before his bill was to come up on the house floor, Jenkins took out a full-page ad in the Baton Rouge *Morning Advocate* and *State Times*.[49] He headlined the ad "Rape—False Issue in the Abortion Debate." Jenkins warned readers that women would lie about being raped and that men would pay the price: "If rape is the only exception, hundreds—perhaps thousands—of women will claim they are

raped each year . . . and an equal number of men will be falsely accused
of rape."

Jenkins noted that Norma McCorvey, the Jane Roe of *Roe v. Wade,*
"claimed that she had been raped" but later "admitted publicly that she
had not been raped at all." "The irony is that 25 million unborn children have been killed as a result of this fraudulent rape case," he asserted.[50] But Jenkins cautioned that McCorvey was hardly the first to
pass off such a lie:

> In the late 1960s, California Gov. Ronald Reagan signed what was at the
> time the most liberal abortion law in America. It was liberal in that it al-
> lowed abortion in cases of rape. Like most of us, Reagan assumed that it
> was "only fair" to allow abortion in rape cases. But . . . California soon ex-
> perienced a flood of false rape accusations. . . . Real rapists suddenly had a
> new defense—"The only reason she's claiming I raped her is so that she can
> get an abortion!" The rape exception rapidly became abortion-on-demand.

Not only had women lied, and not only had men suffered for that treach-
ery, but Reagan's attempt to help victims had helped criminals instead.

Jenkins also challenged the innocence of rape survivors who failed to
get morning-after medical treatment to prevent pregnancy:

> If the victim fails to seek medical attention, she knows that she is *risking*
> pregnancy. In those cases where the victim has taken that risk and later de-
> cided to seek an abortion, the situation is now different. A tiny boy or girl
> is now growing within her[,] . . . innocent of any wrongdoing. Does this
> little boy or girl deserve a death sentence? . . . *Remember this: The rapist
> doesn't get capital punishment, if he is convicted. The only person executed
> is the innocent unborn child!*

The next afternoon, three hundred activists showed up to watch the
house floor debate on Jenkins's bill. Armed with plastic models of unborn children, Jenkins told his colleagues, "[W]e're not talking here only
about a woman's rights. We're talking about the rights of these little
boys and girls." He repeated that Jane Roe had lied about being raped
and that other women would do the same if rapes were exempted. "Rape
is too easy to fabricate," he warned.[51]

Like Roemer, Jenkins promised to rescue women from rapists and
murderers. But in Jenkins's view, the ultimate rapists and murderers were
abortionists: "What kind of man or woman would reach into a woman's
womb, pull out her baby and destroy it? Can you imagine the hatred
they must have for women and the perversion of what they do? What
worse thing can be done to a woman, I would say, than to kill her child

before her eyes." [52] Pro-choice advocates who objected to men's inter-vention in abortions missed the point, Jenkins said. Men were simply de-fending women against predators. "The one role men have played through history is that of protector," he explained.[53]

Pro-life moderates tried to amend the bill to exempt cases of incest or rape. But the house's small pro-choice faction, scheming to keep the bill unpalatable, voted with Jenkins and other purists to defeat the amendments. Even without the rape exception, 74 of the 105 repre-sentatives voted for the ban. Only 27, including the house's 3 women, voted against it. From pro-life activists in the balcony came a wave of applause.[54]

Jenkins's arguments in the *Morning Advocate* and on the house floor exposed a fatal flaw among Louisiana's anti-abortion crusaders: They were incapable of detaching their rhetoric from invocations of guilt and innocence, which in turn demanded a rape exception. A week after the house vote, in a senate hearing on Jenkins's bill, Mike Cross argued that a fetus was innocent even if its mother wasn't. Jenkins protested that a rape exception would encourage women to "clog up" the criminal jus-tice system with "false rape reports." [55]

Carol Everett, a former abortion clinic operator, offered a gentler ar-gument: Denying abortion to rape victims was a mercy, not a restriction. "Abortion is a skillfully marketed product sold to a woman when she needs help," Everett told the committee. "The mother is already the vic-tim of that crime [rape], and we don't traumatize that victim a second time by aborting her." But Everett, too, spoke of chastity and sexual re-sponsibility as larger objectives in the war against abortion. "Ninety-eight percent of abortions are for birth control—*birth control,*" she ex-claimed with dismay. While confessing that she had gotten pregnant in her teens by becoming "wrongfully sexually active," Everett credited herself for marrying the father of her unborn child and thereby "taking responsibility for [her] actions." Only later had she shirked responsibil-ity, aborting a child simply because it "was not convenient." [56]

Allusions to chastity and wantonness littered the hearing. Cross and another senator accused pro-choice witnesses of "advocating abortion as a method of birth control." Cross challenged the extent of a woman's authority over her body, protesting that if she were granted a right to abortion, she would have to be granted "a right to prostitute her body" and perhaps to use illegal drugs. Another lawmaker agreed: "We do not allow women to prostitute themselves. We do not allow them to be illegal drug users. There is no absolute freedom to use one's body as you so desire." [57]

This line of reasoning only made the rape exception more compelling. "I'm pro-life, but I believe there ought to be some exceptions," said a Methodist minister. "Why should we burden a young mother with an unwanted child if it wasn't the result of her own misconduct? She's blameless, so why should she be punished?" One senator bluntly said he wanted to ban most abortions but would vote against the bill because it failed to exempt rape and incest. Another distinguished abortion in rape cases from abortion for birth control: "I do not believe that we should use abortion as a form of contraceptive. . . . But I do think that there are certain circumstances where a woman should have the right, the opportunity to make a decision: Life of the mother. . . . Rape and incest. . . . I cannot in good conscience say to a woman that if you are raped by some thug on the streets, you must have that thug's baby." [58]

The votes of those two senators, combined with the committee's lone pro-choice member, produced a 3 to 3 deadlock. The full senate voted to keep the bill alive, but some senators who joined in that vote signaled that they, too, would demand a rape exception.[59] The alliance between moral conservatives and pro-life purists was coming apart.

On June 26 a swarm of activists and national journalists crowded into the capitol to watch the senate take up the Jenkins bill. Cross kicked off the debate with a half-hour reprise of Jenkins's floor speech, complete with the same plastic models and the same talk of men's duty to protect women from abortionists. "What kind of man or woman would reach inside a woman and kill her unborn child?" Cross asked. And again: "What is the worst thing you can do to a woman? Kill her child before her eyes." [60]

Only two senators argued that abortion should be a matter of choice. The real fight centered on a series of amendments to exempt sex crimes from the bill. "Rape and incest are heinous crimes and we ought to have some sort of exceptions," demanded one senator. Cross resisted such amendments on the grounds that women could feign rape and thereby procure "abortion on demand." Other senators reiterated that concern. Again, a small pro-choice faction teamed up with the absolutist pro-life faction to defeat the amendments.[61]

After numerous attempts to exempt rape and incest failed, the senate passed the ban, 24 to 15. Throughout the chamber, pro-life activists rejoiced. Several pro-choice onlookers wept. Amid the talk of protecting life, Robin Rothrock mused, "I'm beginning to wonder if women constitute life in the state of Louisiana." But Rothrock's sabotage had worked. The defeat of the rape and incest exceptions had alienated not only the governor but also a moderate bloc of senators who would sustain his veto. To override that veto, Jenkins and Cross would need twenty-six of the thirty-nine senators. Failure to exempt rape and incest had cost them at least three votes.[62] They were now two short.

What had doomed the abortion ban in the senate wasn't a newfound appreciation of women's rights but the ghost of Dalton Prejean. One senator who had voted against the ban because it didn't exempt rape victims explained, "I just don't believe that if a 14-year-old minor is raped by an individual with an IQ of 10, that the parents should have no say-so over whether she has an abortion."[63] What riled the senator wasn't just any unwanted pregnancy, but pregnancy by rape; not just any rape, but the rape of a virgin; not just the virgin's plight, but the honor and authority of her parents; and not just any rapist, but a stupid, subhuman brute. At times, Bartlett and Rothrock detected in such remarks the odor of the Scottsboro Boys, an old southern myth of black rapists defiling the white race through its women.

There was much embarrassment in the Louisiana house the next day, when Carl Gunter, who had rallied his colleagues against the spousal rape bill, pleaded that pregnancies caused by incest shouldn't be exempted from the abortion ban. "When I got to thinking, the way we get thoroughbred horses and thoroughbred dogs is through inbreeding," said Gunter. "Maybe we would get a super-sharp kid." Gunter's colleagues covered their faces at his monstrous gaffe.[64] It was absurd to subject humans to the sex practices of animals. It was equally absurd, to many, that a young virgin should bear the spawn of a beast such as Dalton Prejean.

On July 6 Roemer vetoed the bill. He framed his decision in terms of law and order, innocence and justice. Victims "must be protected against such horrible crimes," he argued. "As a member of Congress, I consistently voted to curb abortion on demand[,] . . . but over the years of struggling with this issue I became acutely aware of the need to except those instances where conception occurred because of rape or incest. Women cannot and should not be forced to bear the consequences of these traumatic, illegal acts."[65]

In a statement replying to the veto, Jenkins and Cross observed, "Perhaps the governor feels that an openly 'pro-choice' argument against the bill would have little support in Louisiana. But by using the sympathy that we all feel for rape victims, the governor is able to make a plausible case for opposing the legislation."[66]

Again, however, Jenkins and Cross entangled themselves in contrary images of women. In some passages, they spoke of women as anguished victims: "Persons who counsel rape victims say they typically recover from the physical and emotional trauma of the rape in weeks or months, but they often never recover from the effects of the abortion, especially from the guilt of having killed their unborn child." In other passages, they spoke of women as ruthless murderers: "Imagine, 25 million unborn children killed—because one woman lied about being raped! The fact is that anyone who is in a state of mind to kill her unborn child will have few qualms about lying about how that child was conceived."[67]

Kate Michelman seemed equally torn. In a statement, she tried to portray the veto as an endorsement of women's authority. But it was more consonant with Roemer's strategy to depict women as damsels in distress. Jenkins's bill, she said, "would have consigned countless women—including the most vulnerable, desperate victims of rape and incest—to the back alleys for health care."[68]

That night, as expected, the Louisiana house voted to override the veto. The next day, four thousand demonstrators mobbed the capitol to hear the senate debate. Addressing his colleagues, Roemer's floor leader, Senator Sydney Nelson, laid the issue bare:

> You've seen and read and heard of cases of a 15-year-old who is kidnapped, held prisoner for a week or so, repeatedly raped and released. This bill . . . would say she would be required to carry that child for nine months. . . . I'm not for abortion on demand or for gender selection or birth control. But . . . to say to the women of this state, that we don't care how you get pregnant, you must carry to term—I just can't do that.[69]

Nelson's concluding words distilled what moral conservatives couldn't stomach: pro-life absolutism, like pro-choice absolutism, implied that "we don't care how you get pregnant." Again, several conservative senators refused to support the bill.[70] The vote to override Roemer was 23 to 16. By a margin of three, the veto held.

The first year of the *Webster* era was drawing to a close. Louisiana had offered pro-lifers their best hope of enacting an abortion ban. They had one more chance to override the veto, but the legislative session would end on July 9. They had forty-eight hours to pick up three votes in the senate. They quickly secured the twenty-fourth vote and a pledge from another senator to provide the twenty-sixth if they could come up with the twenty-fifth. On July 8 Louisiana Right to Life leaders Bob Winn and Sharon Rodi went to Baton Rouge to meet with the three senators most likely to provide the needed vote. All three refused. One, senate president Sammy Nunez, told them flatly that a rape exception was necessary and sufficient to win his vote.[71]

Winn and Rodi were willing to make that deal, but Jenkins and Cross, who controlled the pro-life bills, weren't. It was too late to file a new bill. Rodi begged a friendly senator for ideas. He returned with an odd proposal. A bill to protect the American flag from desecration was still on the calendar. If it were gutted and converted into an abortion ban with exceptions for rape and incest, it would pass. Winn scribbled a series of amendments that would do the job. Within minutes, the bill flew through both chambers with veto-proof majorities.

The bill was still about purging violence through violence. A year earlier, the Supreme Court had ruled that states couldn't ban flag desecration. The bill had sought to circumvent that ruling by inviting private citizens rather than the state to punish flag burners. It had done so by reducing to $25 the penalty for assault and battery on anyone desecrating the flag. The penalty for any other kind of assault and battery was up to six months in jail. The point had been to let citizens commit one offense in order to remedy another.[72] As an abortion ban with exceptions for rape and incest, that was still its point.

At his press conference the next day, Roemer was flustered. He called the new bill "a step in the right direction," but he didn't like its details, particularly the requirement that a rape victim report her crime to police within seven days in order to qualify for an abortion. The morality of abortion had seemed so simple when the Supreme Court had stood in the way. Now that the Court had dumped the issue back to the states, it seemed vastly more complicated. Standing before an array of television cameras, Roemer repudiated his endorsement of *Webster*. "I speak for 49 other governors," he said. "That decision has been a disaster. To have this country checkerboarded is not in the nation's best interest."[73]

Roemer had three weeks to sign or veto the bill. He spent that time listening to his wife, his daughter, his female cabinet officers, and other women, including a nun who, before delivering the prayer at a business meeting, leaned over to him with the advice, "Veto it."[74] From all of these women, as Roemer later described it, he heard variations on a theme: "I'm not looking for an abortion. I'm looking for a place in the decision process. It's my body and my family and it ought to be my choice." The depth of these reflections touched Roemer. He began to think that the issue wasn't just about the unborn, that it was also about the moral competence of women.

The lesson Roemer drew from these conversations was that "there ought to be some freedom" for women on the abortion question. But how much? He still bristled at "abortion as a substitute for birth control." He construed the women in his life as having disavowed not just casual abortion for themselves, but "abortion on demand." The only thing he was prepared to say for certain was that women "whose lives are threatened" or "who have been illegally violated" deserved the right to choose abortion.[75]

Politically, the safe course was obvious: Stick to the rape issue. Although the bill purported to exempt rape victims, its seven-day reporting deadline rendered that exemption dubious. The New Orleans *Times-Picayune* gave Roemer further ammunition by announcing on its front page, "Bill would still ban abortion in some rape cases." Apparently, the bill's rape exception didn't apply to cases of simple rape.[76]

On July 27 Roemer vetoed the bill. Nowhere in his statement did he speak of the rights of women in general. His principal objection was that "the bill fails to provide adequate protection for rape victims. . . . Forcing a rape victim to report to law enforcement officials and seek medical treatment, all within seven days of the crime, is an onerous burden. Under this bill, sheer trauma or ignorance would force a woman to bear and give birth to a child conceived in brutality."[77]

After devoting four paragraphs to rape, Roemer scolded the legislature for changing the bill's subject from flag burning to abortion. He spent his final two paragraphs warning that the bill might condemn to prison the very women whom pro-lifers called victims of abortion.

> Under general criminal law, accomplices are liable for criminal behavior. . . . [T]he woman herself or anyone who helps her, counsels her or pays for her to have an abortion (such as her husband, her parents, her friends, or her minister), could be exposed to the same penalties as the doctor inducing the abortion. . . .
>
> Others have raised questions concerning whether the victim of the "battery" is the mother or the fetus. . . . If the mother is the victim, can she still be prosecuted as a principal? The answers to these questions are crucial if we are to expose women, their doctors, and their families to severe criminal penalties.

Roemer announced the veto at a press conference packed by twenty-one television crews and fifty reporters from around the country. The hushed and solemn session, including Roemer's statement and his replies to questions, was broadcast live on CNN. The governor spoke of women "illegally violated" and "brutalized and molested by rape and incest." He decried the bill's omission of simple rape and demanded a more lenient reporting period for "a crime this heinous." [78]

Occasionally, Roemer let slip a phrase that hinted at a broader faith in the moral wisdom of women. But he focused on distinguishing between women who were "illegally violated" and those who used abortion "for birth control."

> I consider myself pro-life in the belief that abortion on demand and as a substitute for birth control must be—in the name of the unborn—sharply curtailed.
> I have, however, grown in the personal belief that common sense, common decency and respect for women require that exceptions in an anti-abortion bill are required. [79]

Since legislators had adjourned for the year, Roemer's veto couldn't be overridden. But he offered to work with pro-lifers to draft a new abortion ban in 1991. [80]

Feminists anointed Roemer a hero. Bartlett praised him for defying Louisiana's tradition of "oppression against women." At a press conference in the capitol, Norma McCorvey, alias Jane Roe, raised her arm in a victory salute. Planned Parenthood president Faye Wattleton declared that Roemer had "set an example for other politicians." The president of Louisiana NOW acclaimed his veto as proof of "the power of the pro-choice majority." That weekend, when Roemer went to Mobile, Alabama, for the annual meeting of the National Governors Association, a woman approached him and said, "On behalf of all women, thank you." [81]

The truth was less profound. Roemer hadn't embraced abortion rights for all women. Nor had the pro-choice majority. Half of all Americans favored outlawing abortion in cases other than rape or incest. Significant majorities told pollsters that women shouldn't be allowed to get abortions to protect their careers or their families' financial viability. [82] Pro-choice politicians and strategists learned, like Roemer, to bypass public doubts about women's moral competence by separating crime from birth control, innocence from guilt.

Some candidates charged their pro-life adversaries with coddling the guilty. In Illinois, Rosemary Mulligan, a NARAL-funded Republican, made crime and abortion the central issues of her campaign against right-wing state representative Penny Pullen. In mailings to Republican voters, Mulligan called Pullen "weak against crime" and promised to fight "for victims' rights—not criminals' rights." Not only had Pullen refused to "toughen jail sentences for sex offenders whose victims are under 13 years old," said Mulligan; she had voted to "give a rapist the right to prevent his victim from seeking an abortion." [83]

Other candidates faulted their opponents for punishing the innocent. Barbara Hafer, the Republican nominee for governor of Pennsylvania, aired a television ad that depicted a woman screaming for her life on a deserted street as a rapist threw her against a wall. The ad told viewers that Bob Casey, the incumbent Democrat, was "committed to outlawing abortions—even for victims of rape and incest." [84] In Texas, a television ad for Democrat Hugh Parmer questioned the law-and-order reputation of Republican senator Phil Gramm: "If a victim of rape or incest becomes pregnant, shouldn't she have the right to choose what to do? Phil Gramm would take away that right. Five times Phil Gramm sponsored a law so extreme it denies women a choice even in cases of rape and incest. Phil Gramm's law would treat victims like criminals." [85]

Michelman, too, relied on this message. In 1992 NARAL featured the rape issue in its direct-mail campaign against Representative Bob Dornan, Republican-California, and in its television ads against Senators Al D'Amato, Republican–New York, and Bob Kasten, Republican-Wisconsin. The Democratic National Committee and congressional challengers in other states also raised the issue in television commercials. In one ad, aired by a Democratic congressional candidate in New York, a hospital official told a man that although his wife had been raped, the Republican nominee wouldn't grant her an abortion. The woman was the victim; the husband was the protagonist. [86]

The strength of these attacks—that they focused on crime, not abortion rights—was also their weakness. Politicians didn't have to accept abortion rights in order to answer the charges. Some, such as Senator Jesse Helms, responded by calling their opponents soft on sex crimes. A week after Roemer's veto in Louisiana, NARAL released a television ad in North Carolina that accused Helms of trying "ten times" to "outlaw abortion, even for victims of rape and incest." A NARAL radio ad warned, "Jesse Helms would take away a rape victim's right to make her own decision about whether or not to have an abortion." In a second NARAL radio ad, a woman added, "I don't know if I would ever have an abortion. But I do know, if I were raped, I would want to be the one making the decision." [87]

Realizing that these attacks challenged his sensitivity to criminal justice rather than to women's rights, Helms responded with an ad that focused on rape rather than abortion. As paraphrased in the *Charlotte Observer,* Helms's ad asked, "If somebody brutally rapes someone in your family, do you think he should get the death penalty?" The ad pointed out that whereas Helms favored the ultimate punishment for such violations, his "liberal" challenger didn't.[88]

Other pro-life politicians neutralized the victim issue by conceding exceptions for rape or incest. In 1990 California attorney general candidate Dan Lungren announced that because society failed to protect and help victims of violent crime, he would grant such victims abortions. In 1992 Senator D'Amato, under fire from NARAL on the rape issue, attacked his opponent for opposing the death penalty and retracted his own opposition to abortions for victims of sex crimes. Vice President Quayle executed a similar retreat under fire from challenger Al Gore. In an interview just before his speech to the 1992 Republican National Convention, Pat Robertson claimed that the death toll from U.S. abortions "exceeds the Holocaust." But in the next breath Robertson added, "[I]f you can believe it, I think that there should be rape and incest exceptions." [89]

What emerged from these retractions was a creeping consensus that women impregnated by sex crimes deserved abortion privileges. This consensus didn't lead to legislation banning abortions in cases other than rape; such bans passed only in Utah and Louisiana and ultimately failed in the courts. But victims' rights became the middle ground in disputes over parental consent and public funding of abortions.

In 1989, after years of rejecting Medicaid coverage of abortions, the House of Representatives approved such coverage for victims of sex crimes. Meanwhile, Virginia voters rejected Marshall Coleman, who opposed abortion rights for rape and incest victims, and instead elected Doug Wilder, who endorsed public funding of abortions only for such victims. Two years later, many pro-lifers in Congress opposed the Bush administration's ban on abortion counseling at federally funded clinics because it failed to exempt rape or incest. And in several states that had set up funds to compensate crime victims, lawmakers introduced bills to spend some of those funds on abortions for survivors of sexual assaults.[90]

Incest, usually an afterthought to rape, became the strongest argument against parental involvement laws. In 1990 Planned Parenthood aired a television ad featuring Karen Bell, the Indiana woman whose daughter had died from an illegal abortion rather than obey such a law. In the ad, Bell agreed that parental consent "sounds good" but cautioned that it was a bad idea in "cases of little girls that have been raped" or violated by incest. Kate Michelman and NOW's Molly Yard pleaded that parental involvement laws endangered "abused" teenagers. They told the story of an Idaho girl whose father had shot her dead after learning that she intended to abort a pregnancy he had caused.[91]

Politicians who opposed parental involvement laws used the same argument. Campaigning for governor of Texas in 1990, Attorney General Jim Mattox recalled, "When I was a prosecutor in Dallas County, I sent to prison parents and step-parents who carried out immoral and illegal incest and sexual abuse of their children. So I have a great deal of difficulty believing that such adults should make a decision on abortion for their teenagers."[92] Months later in North Carolina, at a debate among Democrats vying to replace Helms, one candidate denounced Helms, a critic of tax-funded abortions, for opposing "compensation for the victims of rape and incest" and thereby forcing women "to bear the child of a criminal rapist." Another candidate endorsed the idea of parental involvement legislation but dismissed most parental involvement bills as insensitive to victims of sex crimes. "As a prosecutor," he asserted, "I have seen 12-year-old girls who have been raped by their father."[93]

Sex crimes, parental rights, and abortion funding collided most directly in a 1991 congressional race in Massachusetts. During a debate, the pro-life candidate, Steven Pierce, blasted his pro-choice opponent, John Olver, for supporting the state furlough program that had released Willie Horton. Pierce also accused Olver of helping "12- and 13-year-old daughters to get abortions without their parents finding out about it." Olver responded by framing his abortion position as an anti-crime policy: "As for 12- and 13-year-olds, very often the sexual abuser happens to be a member of the family. That is why parental consent cannot be required." Then Olver assailed Pierce for opposing the use of the state Victims' Compensation Fund to subsidize abortions for rape victims. Pierce was left sputtering at the insinuation that he lacked "sensitivity to women who suffer that most heinous of crimes."[94]

As in the case of abortion bans, however, pro-lifers could defuse these objections by exempting sex crimes from parental involvement and abortion funding bills. And in state after state, they did just that.

The wisdom of the exemption strategy wasn't lost on Louisiana's more pragmatic pro-life activists. They spent fall and winter 1990 studying their defeats and conferring with legislators. They emerged with a bill that allowed abortions in cases of incest or rape—but only if the victim reported the crime to police within a week and was examined to certify that her pregnancy hadn't preceded the rape. NRLC, the Louisiana Catholic Conference, the Louisiana Pro-Life Council, and leaders of the Louisiana Right to Life Federation endorsed the bill.[95]

The pragmatists entrusted their bill to state representative Sam Theriot and state senator Allen Bares, who had defended the rape exception in 1990 while Jenkins and Cross were sabotaging it. They presented the bill to Jenkins and requested his forbearance, if not his support. He turned them down. Instead, he again introduced what he called a "clean" abortion ban, in contrast to their "exceptions" bill. With the support of fundamentalist churches, traditional-values groups, and most chapters of the Right to Life Federation, Jenkins lambasted the exceptions bill. On April 14 he told a pro-life rally that exceptions violated the right to life. A week later he called a press conference at the capitol to denounce the exceptions bill and pledge his opposition to it.[96]

The bill faced little resistance from the left. Eight politicians, including Roemer and former governor Edwin Edwards, were running for governor in 1991. None of them maintained that abortion decisions should be left to women. Edwards defended doctors instead: "I would have more faith in the medical profession than apparently Mr. Theriot has." Only three candidates said they would ban abortion completely, but all eight said they would sign a ban if rape and incest were exempted. "They've come to my position," Roemer gloated. "I was alone last year and obviously I'm not alone this year. We're making progress." [97]

On May 9 activists packed a house hearing to watch the purists savage the exceptions bill. While pragmatists stressed the bill's political advantages, purists attacked it on moral grounds. Speaking for the pragmatists, Louisiana's Catholic bishops touted polls showing that Americans opposed indiscriminate abortion. In response, the purists brought forward a priest who pleaded, "A child conceived by an act of rape is as much a child as one conceived in an act of love . . . or as a result of the failure of contraception." A pastor representing the Louisiana Baptist Convention entreated lawmakers to accord children conceived in rape the same rights held by "any legitimately conceived child." And in a brutally incisive speech, Jenkins said that abortion foes who permitted exceptions showed they were "not sincere" in proclaiming the personhood of unborn children.[98]

The committee passed the exceptions bill and the clean bill. Four days later, so did the house. On May 29 senators again heard testimony from Julie Makimaa, the woman conceived in rape who had appeared before the same committee a year earlier. A rape survivor told the committee that bearing and raising a child conceived in rape had healed her. She held the two-year-old girl in her lap as she spoke. Pro-choicers countered with an incest victim and a woman who testified that she had regarded her rape-begotten son as "a living, breathing torture mechanism that replayed in my mind over and over the rape." [99]

Despite their contrary conclusions, all four women had been taught to regard pregnancy as punishment. Makimaa recounted the advice given to her mother by friends who knew she was pregnant by rape: "You do not deserve this. It's not your fault." The pro-choice rape survivor recalled that she had felt guilty about her pregnancy until she realized that she "was not responsible" for it. Sex-crime victims were different from other women. As the incest survivor put it, "We've been violated enough." [100]

The senate agreed. The committee killed the clean bill but deadlocked on the exceptions bill. When pro-lifers asked the senate to force both bills through the committee, senators voted resoundingly for the exceptions bill but rejected the clean bill.[101] The clean bill was dead.

The next morning, when the committee reconvened, a pro-choice senator, Cleo Fields, offered an amendment to abolish the death penalty. He described it as a test: "You have to make a decision [as to] whether or not you are anti-abortion or pro-life." A pro-life senator, Richard Neeson, rose to the challenge: "Several springs ago, I saw David Dean Martin put to death at Angola. The experience left a real impression in my mind about life and death. At that time, I was very much for the death penalty. . . . I have moved 180 degrees in an attempt to be consistent on both points. Life is very important, so I am going to support your amendment." Neeson's six colleagues split evenly on the amendment. With his vote, it passed.[102]

The bill's sponsors, Representative Theriot and Senator Bares, pronounced Fields's amendment "unacceptable" and vowed to strip it. As for Fields's suggestion that pro-lifers were hypocrites to support the death penalty while opposing abortion, Theriot replied that Fields was a hypocrite to support abortion while opposing the death penalty. "If he cares about guilty convicted criminals, why doesn't he care about babies?" Theriot demanded.[103]

The dispute wasn't about whether human life was sacred. Fields and Theriot agreed that in some cases it wasn't. The dispute was about what made some lives more sacred than others. To Fields, the death penalty was worse than abortion because its victims were fully alive; they had experienced the world. To Theriot, abortion was worse because its victims were innocent; they had *not* experienced the world. Liberals who dismissed the fetus as unarticulated didn't understand that this lack of articulation was what made it precious to moral conservatives. The unborn child was untainted by sin. Unless, perhaps, it was the product of a crime.

Buddy Roemer opened the 1991 legislative session on that theme. "If a woman is raped or incest [is] committed against her, it's an illegal act," he declared. "I will not have a law reward an illegal act." But Roemer soon added a new demand, an exception for deformed fetuses. He also began to weave pro-choice language into his answers. He pledged to evaluate the exceptions bill "in terms of honoring women and families, in terms of making sure that women who are abused have a chance to gain their self-esteem and self-respect, to have power of choice, them having been abused." He added, "I said I would sign a bill like that, even with some reluctance that the government is interfering. I felt that reflected the vast majority of Louisiana citizens. I still feel that way. The polls clearly show that."[104]

Roemer's understanding of choice, nurtured by conversations but pruned by politics and discomfort, had grown into the philosophical equivalent of a bonsai tree. He acknowledged the complexity of abortion decisions but offered to permit such decisions only in extreme cases. While speaking vaguely of women's rights, he confined these rights to women who carried deformed fetuses or had been "illegally abused." Privately, he indicated to Bares and Theriot that their bill would probably suffice.[105]

Again, pro-choice and pro-life activists formed an uncoordinated alliance. On June 4 they tried to remove the exceptions on the senate floor. Pro-life pragmatists defeated them. Roemer's floor leader proposed further exceptions in cases of fetal deformity or danger to the woman's health. The pragmatists thwarted this move as well. Cleo Fields resubmitted his amendment to abolish the death penalty. This, too, failed. Twenty-nine senators, a veto-proof majority, voted the bill through.[106]

Roemer vetoed the bill a week and a half later. His conclusion had
changed, but his rationale hadn't. "The open window for abortions
must be closed in order to protect the life of the unborn, but *meaning-
ful* exceptions must be drawn in order to protect the life and rights of
the woman involved," the governor wrote. He conferred these "rights"
on victims of rape or incest and women with tubal pregnancies or
gravely deformed fetuses. He devoted two-thirds of his statement to
rape, protesting that the bill's tight reporting deadline for that crime
would force victims to bear children "conceived in brutality." [107]

Roemer concluded that the bill "dishonors women, shows great mis-
trust of doctors and their professional judgment, and unduly burdens
the traumatized victims of rape." He explained:

> The proponents of this bill also maintain that any expansion of the report-
> ing period will "open the door" for women to lie and doctors to conspire
> with women to obtain abortions. They ignore the fact that rape is a terrible,
> pervasive reality in this country. . . . More importantly, they ignore the ba-
> sic dignity and trustworthiness of women as well as the honor and profes-
> sional ethics of the doctors with whom these women consult. Women need
> more time to make a real, meaningful choice in a traumatic atmosphere.[108]

The governor would make his last stand here. He trusted women
to speak honestly in reporting rapes. He trusted them to restore their
dignity in that circumstance. Pruning the language of choice to bonsai
proportions, he added that in the case of a deformed fetus, the decision "should be up to the woman and her family—not the Legislature."
What he didn't trust women to do was to decide in which other cases, if
any, the decision should be theirs.

The day after the veto, delegates to the state Republican convention
repudiated Roemer, a recent convert to their party, by endorsing an ul-
traconservative pro-life congressman to replace him. Many delegates
waved placards bearing the word "Override." In his acceptance speech,
the congressman questioned whether Roemer truly opposed abortion.
He pledged to be more "concerned with the rights of victims than with
the comforts of violent felons." [109]

Roemer implored voters to urge their representatives not to override
the veto. "I stand like a man in a hole in the levee," he pleaded. "Not
just my finger, my whole body, and the hole is bigger than I am. Help."
His entreaties fell on deaf ears. Now that rape victims were exempted,
pro-choice lawmakers were reduced to pleading for women's rights. "A
male-dominated Legislature should not be making decisions about the

bodies of women," said one legislator. Another begged his colleagues "to try and be a little more sensitive . . . to the needs of women." Such appeals were hopeless. "When you provide for rape, incest and life of the mother," one pro-exceptions legislator explained, "then that means that the only [remaining step] is abortion on demand, and I'm totally opposed to that." [110]

Within five hours, both the house and senate overrode the veto. It was the first time a Louisiana governor's veto had been overturned. Roemer called the new law "totally unfair to women who have been brutalized and raped." All he had wanted, he said, was "to shut down the window of abortion and still honor women in the one thing that makes America different—some choices in their lives." [111]

Terri Bartlett's smile gave way to rage. "This Legislature doesn't care enough; it doesn't know enough; it doesn't love enough to know what . . . they just did to the women and families," she fumed. The message of the override, she said, is that "this state doesn't care about women." [112]

Nor did the state seem to care about the unborn offspring of rape or incest. The day after the override, Jenkins implored his colleagues to help him suspend the exceptions. They refused. Theriot and Bares disowned his effort. The Catholic bishops urged him to drop it. Many pro-life lawmakers told him they would oppose it. The speaker of the house grumbled that Jenkins was making trouble and taking "the limelight away from the celebrants." [113]

Jenkins wasn't celebrating. He stood alone on the floor of the house, begging his colleagues to recall the words of Matthew: "Take heed, Jesus said, that you do not despise even one of these little ones." Into the awful silence, Jenkins pleaded, "I hear a little voice that says, 'Come back, don't forget me, don't leave me, find me, protect me, let me live.' " [114]

There was much talk among feminists that summer and fall of unseating pro-life legislators in Louisiana's 1991 elections. NOW launched a project to recruit, fund, and advise female challengers. NOW's national office supplied start-up money, volunteers, and a professional campaign coordinator. Other pro-choice groups joined the campaign. "Louisiana legislators will discover they were profoundly mistaken in believing that they could deny women their most fundamental rights," promised Planned Parenthood's Faye Wattleton. She warned that "the people of Louisiana will see them on election day." [115]

The uprising failed to materialize. Women ran for nine seats in the Senate but picked up none. In the House, they lost thirty of thirty-seven races. Jenkins, NOW's top target, was challenged by the female president of the pro-choice coalition he had battled in the legislature. She portrayed him as a pro-life extremist and an overripe career politician. Jenkins pummeled her with ads that called her a "radical" and linked her to NOW, gay rights groups, and other out-of-state liberals. He won easily. Afterward, she lamented that "in almost every one" of the contests in which women ran, "the male candidates chose to attack their opponents as radical feminists." [116]

Roemer, too, ran for reelection that fall. His challengers, led by Edwin Edwards and state representative David Duke, the former Klansman, denounced his veto of the abortion ban. Pro-choice activists predicted that the veto would inspire women throughout Louisiana to campaign for Roemer. A new organization, Women for Roemer, promised to deliver his reelection. Roemer framed the election as a choice between reform and regression to an ugly past represented by Duke and Edwards. His television ads ended with the plea, "Don't turn the clock back now." [117]

Duke outflanked Roemer on the right. He campaigned against taxes and welfare bums and promised to be tougher on crime than any other candidate. On election day, he took enough conservative votes from Roemer to squeeze Roemer out of a Duke-Edwards runoff. Hours after the polls closed, Roemer appeared before the media to concede defeat. He wore the face of a condemned man. His parting words were, "I'm at peace." [118]

CHAPTER 8

The Right to Choose Life

For three decades, abortion activists have waged war in the United States in defense of two rival principles: a woman's right to choose and an unborn child's right to life. Each side, in its resolve to defeat the other, has enlisted the aid of pro-family, anti-tax voters who worship neither of these principles.

Pro-choice activists have advertised government noninterference as a way to protect the right of husbands and parents to participate in abortion decisions. Pro-life activists have promoted consent and notification laws on the same grounds. Pro-choicers have defended abortion as a means of preventing additional births and welfare expenses. Pro-lifers have attacked abortion funding by framing it as a welfare expense.

In short, activists on both sides have sold their policies to voters as a means to safeguard the rights not of women or unborn children but of husbands, parents, businesses, and taxpayers. What happens, then, when the demands of husbands, parents, businesses, and taxpayers threaten the interests of pregnant women *and* unborn children?

That question has long been obscured by the myth that the abortion debate is simply a clash between woman and unborn child. Many women are pressured by boyfriends, husbands, parents, or employers to abort their pregnancies. Many others face similar pressure from taxpayers in the form of financial penalties for bearing children while on welfare.

As a constituency inattentive to such predicaments emerges victorious from the abortion war, what will become of a woman's right to choose life?

BOSTON, MASSACHUSETTS
OCTOBER 23, 1989

The nightmare began a week before Halloween. "My wife's been shot. I've been shot," said the caller. He was on his car phone and couldn't identify his location, but police found him within ten minutes. He had taken a .38-caliber slug in the abdomen. His wife, slumped beside him, had taken one in the head. An ambulance rushed her back to the hospital where the couple had finished a prenatal class minutes earlier. Doctors delivered her baby, eight weeks premature and starved of oxygen, by cesarean section. By 3:00 A.M. Carol Stuart was dead. Her baby lived another two weeks.[1]

The husband, Charles Stuart, survived his wound. He told police that he and his wife (both white) had been shot by a tall black man. Newspapers recounted the couple's dreams of parenthood. "Christmas birth of baby was to cap an idyllic life," wept the *Boston Herald*. Police accosted and searched hundreds of black men. Charles Stuart eventually fingered one man in a lineup. At that point, his brother, under pressure from friends and siblings who knew the truth, told police that Stuart himself had fired the shots. The next day, Stuart jumped to his death.[2]

The Stuart case sparked a nationwide outcry. How could city officials have moved so hastily and overzealously to find a black culprit? The question of race consumed so much attention that a question of sex went unnoticed. Soon after Stuart's suicide, friends indicated that his wife's pregnancy might have triggered his decision to kill her. They told investigators that he had dreaded the birth of his child, deeming it a threat to his professional ambitions.[3]

Testifying before a grand jury a week after the suicide, a friend revealed that four months earlier, Stuart had solicited him to kill Stuart's wife. According to the friend's account, Stuart told him that he had pressured his wife to get an abortion but that she had refused. Apart from the prospect of another mouth to feed, Stuart had worried that his wife would quit her job to take care of the baby. Without her income, his dreams of starting his own business would collapse. The investigation of the murder eventually turned up several plausible motives. But as to why

Stuart had chosen that moment to kill his wife, the evidence clearly indicated that he had done so to get rid of her baby.[4]

Amid the media frenzy over the Stuart case, not a single news story called attention to the abortion angle. The concept of abortion being coerced, particularly by a woman's own husband, defied conventional wisdom. Coercion, as the press understood it, was employed against abortion by the government, not in favor of abortion by a family member. But Charles Stuart was by no means the first man to pressure his wife or girlfriend to end her pregnancy. Nor was he the last to kill a woman for resisting.

Pressure from boyfriends and husbands to abort was a problem familiar to abortion clinic counselors. In 1987 a study by Planned Parenthood's Alan Guttmacher Institute found that 23 percent of abortion patients said they were having the procedure in part because their husbands or boyfriends wanted it. Among eighteen- and nineteen-year-old women, that figure soared to nearly 30 percent.[5] While the National Right to Life Committee was campaigning for a "husband's or boyfriend's right to have a say" in women's abortion decisions, husbands and boyfriends were steering 350,000 women toward abortions each year.

Among these hundreds of thousands of cases, only the few that culminated in public crimes attracted news coverage. Soon after the Stuart murder, a California man whose former girlfriend had refused to submit to an abortion was charged with beating her in order to kill her four-month fetus. He succeeded. In Florida, an attorney put out a contract on his girlfriend's life, explaining that her insistence on carrying their child to term over his objections would cripple his career. In Massachusetts, an ex-convict smothered his girlfriend to death for rejecting his abortion demand. In Arizona, professional basketball player Jerrod Mustaf invoked the Fifth Amendment and his cousin went to jail for killing Mustaf's pregnant former girlfriend, who allegedly had rejected Mustaf's instructions to get an abortion. By comparison, a secretary in Kentucky got off easy: her boss, who had paid her $20,000 to abort a pregnancy he had caused, merely took her to court for failing, as it were, to deliver.[6]

The most notorious criminal case involving coerced abortion was the 1994 trial of a Virginia woman, Lorena Bobbitt, for severing her husband's penis. Among the torrent of abuses that allegedly precipitated her attack, Bobbitt testified that her husband, on discovering in early 1990 that she was pregnant, had threatened to abandon her unless she submitted to an abortion. "Essentially, he told her she had to make a choice—either him or the baby," a defense psychiatrist testified. Bobbitt's husband confirmed that his objections had led her to choose the abortion and that she had regretted it. But he insisted that she had "agreed" to it.[7]

The Bobbitt trial illustrated a common paradox. First, the man's pressure on the woman to abort was part of a pattern of abuse that included violence. Bobbitt testified convincingly that her husband had raped her, though he insisted it was just rough sex, and a jury, perhaps feeling he had been punished enough, declined to convict him.[8] Second, in the public mind, what distinguished the abortion from these other abuses was that it was "a choice" and that the woman, in her partner's words, had "agreed" to it. From a conservative pro-choice viewpoint, the familial and economic consideration that had dictated Bobbitt's abortion decision—her husband's threat to abandon her to single motherhood—wasn't coercion. As long as the government stayed out of it, her choice was free.

If men could force abortions on their wives or girlfriends by threatening to withdraw support, parents could do the same to their daughters. This tradition, as old as abortion itself, wasn't challenged until 1981, when the *Mary P.* case came before a New York City family court.

Mary P. was fifteen years old and three months pregnant. Her mother petitioned Judge Daniel Leddy Jr. to remove Mary from her home and place her elsewhere on the grounds that Mary was "incorrigible, ungovernable or habitually disobedient." Her mother gave several examples, but the one that caught Leddy's attention was, Mary "is pregnant and refuses to have an abortion." Mary repeated in court, as she had throughout her pregnancy, that she wanted to carry the child to term. Leddy concluded that Mary's mother had taken her to court "to force compliance with the parental directive" to abort the pregnancy.[9]

Quoting from *Roe v. Wade* and subsequent decisions, Leddy affirmed and applied three principles. First, legalized abortion rested on a theory of reproductive autonomy that also implied a right to give birth.[10] Second, this right belonged not to a private institution—the family, headed by one or both parents—but to the individual. Therefore, it could be exercised by the individual against that institution:

> In the instant case, the petition assumes an absolute parental veto over a child's decision to give birth. Quite obviously, if the right to abort is within the zone of privacy protected by the Fourteenth Amendment, the right to

give birth exists there as well. . . . [P]arents may not utilize the state court system to exercise or enforce a blanket veto over their daughter's fundamental right to give birth. . . . [I]t is the child who has the ultimate right to decide. Children are not the chattel of their parents. Rather, they are citizens in their own right, endowed with certain fundamental freedoms of which they may not be divested by parental fiat. The right to give birth is among those freedoms.[11]

Third, Mary's rights obliged the government to intervene on her behalf:

[T]he Court believes that additional safeguards should be taken to insure that there is no further parental interference with Mary's stated determination to give birth. . . .
    Accordingly, in order to protect Mary's constitutional right to give birth, the Court herewith issues an Order of Protection to her. . . . The petitioner-mother is ordered not to interfere with Mary's determination to deliver her child nor to attempt to force Mary to have an abortion.[12]

If Mary P.'s vindication was uncommon, her plight wasn't. In the Guttmacher Institute's 1987 study, nearly 30 percent of minors seeking abortions attributed their decisions in part to the fact that their parents wanted them to have abortions. A 1991 Guttmacher study of teenage abortion patients amplified this pattern. On learning of their daughters' pregnancies, parents favored abortion over childbirth by a 4 to 1 ratio. By the time of the abortion, the ratio of preference rose to 10 to 1. Mothers, fathers, and boyfriends were all more likely to encourage abortion than to encourage childbirth. More than a quarter of the mothers tried to persuade their daughters to abort; only 7 percent encouraged childbirth. Aside from stress on their parents, the most common repercussion the girls reported after disclosing their pregnancies wasn't that they were beaten or punished or even that they became uncomfortable living at home but that their parents were forcing them to have an abortion.[13]

Abortion pressure took various forms. In 1994 an Oregon grand jury charged fifty-five-year-old Dorothy Carr with kidnapping for whisking her grandson's former girlfriend out of high school to an abortion clinic. The girl claimed that this had been done against her will, but Carr insisted that the girl had chosen the abortion. Carr said that she had simply confronted the girl with her options, making clear that the boy could pay for the abortion and reminding the girl, if she bore the child, "My grandson and his mother and I will be involved in your life for the next 18 years." Immediately on being told that the girl would agree to the abortion, Carr had swept her out of school and driven her to the clinic. Carr's daughter, the boy's mother, admitted that after learning of the pregnancy, she had phoned the girl at home, threatening to "charge her with contributing to the delinquency of a minor." While the episode wasn't exactly kidnapping, it was hardly free choice.[14]

A more egregious case of parental coercion became public in Los Angeles in 1991, when a judge blocked an abortion on a seventeen-year-old girl who opposed the procedure.[15] The girl said that when she informed her parents that she wanted to keep her baby, they had "freaked out," protesting that she would shame them and destroy her life. Without consulting her, they had planned an abortion and, to prevent her boyfriend from dissuading her, had secluded her in hotel rooms during the days leading up to the abortion. "I want the baby," the girl told reporters. "My parents have a tremendous amount of control over what I do. I should have been stronger, but I just gave up."

Her boyfriend turned to a local pro-life group, which referred him to a conservative Christian public interest law firm. A day before the abortion was to be done, the firm's attorneys secured a court order to block it. When they arrived with the order, the girl was on the operating table awaiting the abortion. The judge got the girl and her parents to agree to a permanent injunction forbidding any abortion "against her will and without her free and voluntary and informed consent." The parents stopped trying to pressure the girl to have an abortion, and she and her boyfriend decided to marry.

Despite having sought the aid of pro-lifers, the girl's boyfriend recognized that the case boiled down to a struggle between two interpretations of choice: "Her parents made it clear that it was not her choice, that it was their choice to make." Likewise, one of the pro-life attorneys who handled the case concluded, "The significant thing is that the parents were forced to realize that they have no choice in the matter and they could not force the daughter to acquiesce to their choice."

Yet this assumption that parents deserved a "choice in the matter" was precisely what pro-life activists had cultivated in their campaigns for parental consent laws. Pro-choice activists, too, were in an awkward position: Having demanded that judges and bureaucrats stay out of abortion decisions, they now had to explain why the judge's intervention to stop the abortion was a victory for their cause.

By challenging teenagers' competence, activists on both sides had undermined girls' authority. Pro-lifers had attacked their competence to choose abortion; pro-choicers had attacked their competence to choose parenthood. As a NARAL official put it, "[A]ny minor who is too immature to decide to have an abortion is certainly not mature enough to be a mother." That argument reached its treacherous conclusion in the complaint of a Boston woman who, several months after the resolution of the Los Angeles case, found herself in a similar confrontation with her pregnant daughter. "She can't even get her ears pierced without my permission," the woman protested. "She has to have my permission to get an abortion. But when it comes to having a baby, we have no say." [16]

In a society dominated by parental anxiety and alarmed by teen motherhood, how long will it be before this demand for a parental "say" in teenagers' childbearing decisions becomes law?

The family wasn't the only private institution that could smother the right to choose life. Employers could do the same. In 1984 a three-judge panel of the D.C. circuit court of appeals addressed this problem in the case of *OCAW v. American Cyanamid*. Robert Bork wrote the court's opinion; Antonin Scalia joined it. [17]

Employees at the American Cyanamid company's plant in Willow Island, West Virginia, were routinely exposed to certain chemicals on the job. The company decided that it couldn't feasibly reduce this exposure to levels that were safe for fetuses. Instead, it devised a "fetus protection policy" for female employees. In 1978 Glen Mercer, an official at the plant,

> told the women that once the fetus protection policy was fully implemented the plant would have only about seven jobs for fertile women in the entire facility. Approximately thirty women were then employed at the Willow Island plant. Apart from the women who obtained those seven positions, Mercer said that female employees who failed to undergo surgical sterilization by May 1, 1978, would be terminated. [18]

Some women chose sterilization in order to keep their jobs; others refused. In 1979 the Occupational Health and Safety Administration (OSHA) classified the sterilization policy as a workplace hazard and fined American Cyanamid for imposing it. But OSHA's Review Commission overturned the penalty on the grounds that the policy wasn't a "hazard" at the "place of employment." The commission reasoned, "An employee's decision to undergo sterilization in order to gain or retain employment grows out of economic and social factors which operate primarily outside the workplace. The employer neither controls nor creates these factors as he creates or controls work processes and materials." [19]

Bork agreed. "The company was charged only because it offered women a choice," he concluded. It had "offered an option of sterilization" and had "let the women decide for themselves which course was less harmful to them." The company couldn't be held responsible for an "employee reaction to the employer's policies." Nor could it be held responsible for a sterilization "option" that was "exercised outside the workplace." [20]

That same year, the United Auto Workers (UAW) sued the Johnson Controls company for violating the civil rights of its female employees. At issue was the company's policy "that women who are pregnant or who are capable of bearing children will not be placed into jobs involving lead exposure or which could expose them to lead through the exercise of job bidding, bumping, transfer or promotion rights." [21]

The case principally concerned sex discrimination, but when it reached the Supreme Court in 1990, it sparked a debate about the relationship between choice and life. In its brief to the Court, Johnson Controls argued that to avoid injuries to unborn children—and the financial liability that would ensue—employers must sometimes override their workers' choices:

> The company has a legal duty to avoid injuries to the unborn. . . . And contrary to the UAW's assertion that an employer might discharge this duty simply by cautioning its employees about the risks and leaving the choice entirely to them . . . the employer's duty runs *directly* to the fetus (or potential fetus); a parent (or potential parent) can neither waive that duty nor assume the risk on behalf of the child. [22]

At this level of abstraction, the economic interests of employers coincided with the welfare of the unborn. For that reason, two pro-life organizations filed briefs in support of Johnson Controls. "Employers are uniquely well-situated and ethically compelled to contribute to protecting their employees' offspring," argued the U.S. Catholic Conference. Concerned Women for America agreed: "As society and the courts increasingly recognize the interest of unborn children, it would be unjust not to permit employers to do the same." [23] Companies such as Johnson Controls would protect the unborn, if only the government would let them.

But in the real world, Johnson Controls' fetal protection policy, like American Cyanamid's policy, produced effects perversely contrary to its pro-life rationale. It forced women into sterilizations and even abortions. This was made clear by testimony from employees who had complied with the Johnson Controls policy. One woman, echoing many others, recalled that she had been told, "[I]n order to keep my job I would have to be sterilized." [24] Another described the mutilation of her liberty, her dignity, and her body:

> I had asked in one of our meetings [with management] whether my husband's vasectomy was adequate protection against my becoming pregnant and was told that it was not. According to the company's representative, I could still fool around and get pregnant.
>   I decided to have the sterilization because I needed to keep my job. . . . I was 26 years old when I was sterilized and the realization of what I had done didn't hit me until two or three weeks after the operation. . . . Both my second husband and I would have very much liked to have had a child together. In fact I tried to have the operation reversed, but was not successful.[25]

There was nothing pro-life or pro-family in these bitter sacrifices. Far more ghastly was the plight of women who were already pregnant when their employers imposed policies to "protect" their unborn children. One woman recalled how, three months into her pregnancy, her shop steward and her company's personnel director had advised her in a private meeting "that the only way [she] could get [her] job back would be to lose the baby." [26] Not that anyone was forcing an abortion on her. The choice was entirely hers.

Recognizing this version of "choice" as a sham, the nation's four leading pro-choice groups signed on to a brief in support of the UAW and the right to choose life. The brief, written by the ACLU, argued that women shouldn't have to "sacrifice the right to have a family in order to work." In attached statements, NOW and Planned Parenthood construed the case as a question of "reproductive rights." NARAL affirmed its commitment "to guaranteeing women the full range of reproductive choices, including the right to bear children without economic sanctions." [27]

The Court's decision, handed down on March 20, 1991, was a victory for pro-choice liberals. Writing for the Court, Justice Blackmun decreed, "Decisions about the welfare of future children must be left to the parents who conceive, bear, support and raise them rather than to the employers who hire those parents." [28]

Still, in a competitive marketplace in which pregnancy and maternity threaten every company's bottom line, pressure to abort persisted. Even cash-strapped government agencies were susceptible. In May 1989 seven officers or former officers of the New York City Corrections Department alleged that the department had routinely instructed pregnant officers to get abortions or quit. Two of the women alleged that the department's director of health management had threatened to fire them if they refused to abort. A third reported that a nurse in the department had warned her that she would lose her job unless she got an abortion.[29]

By the time these women sued the city for federal civil rights violations in January 1990, the city's investigators had implicated four officials in the scandal, and eighteen officers or former officers had signed on as plaintiffs. The lawsuit alleged that women who had resisted pressure to abort or resign had subsequently been intimidated and harassed. The attorney for the plaintiffs asserted that department officials had applied this pressure in order to avoid the cost of maternity leave benefits and of reassigning pregnant officers to safe duties.

In April 1991 the city settled the case for $2.2 million. By then, twenty-two plaintiffs were involved. Mayor David Dinkins promised that under a new department policy, "no correction officer need feel that she must have an abortion to keep her job."

A more typical kind of pressure surfaced in 1993, when Margaret Bonnell, an apartment rental agent in Tampa, sued her employer for pregnancy discrimination. Bonnell had earned raises and commendations over a two-year tenure with the firm until March 1992, when she learned, to her delight, that she was pregnant. According to Bonnell, when she approached her boss with the news and proposed to discuss maternity leave, her boss "strongly suggested abortion" and even offered to locate an abortionist.[30]

Bonnell resisted, and the pressure began to build. Her boss and her colleagues tried to persuade her to get an abortion. "It was never stated if you don't get an abortion you'll be fired, but it was insinuated," Bonnell later recalled. She surmised that the company wanted to end her pregnancy for two reasons. One was to avoid a maternity leave. The other was that if she gave birth, she said, "I wouldn't be useful to them anymore like I was when I was single and able to move from office to office on a day's notice."

The pressure reached a crescendo five months into Bonnell's pregnancy, when her boss plunked a basket of pennies on her desk and told her colleagues it was an "abortion fund." A former tenant in the building confirmed that the boss had approached her with the basket and asked her to contribute to the fund. Two weeks later, Bonnell was fired.

When the case went to trial in March 1994, Bonnell's office mates insisted that they had only given her advice, not orders. The firm's lawyer argued that Bonnell's colleagues had merely shared their views and that their behavior had "nothing to do with the company." Such conversations couldn't be called coercive. Anyway, they were private.

The jury disagreed and awarded Bonnell nearly $85,000. But she was the exception. She told reporters that she had seen other employees at her workplace get fired after becoming pregnant and that she had fought her legal battle to end that practice. Furthermore, after losing her job and being kicked out of her company-owned apartment, she had ended up on welfare, a single woman raising an illegitimate child on the public tab.

In that respect, she had stumbled from one battleground to the next. By early 1994 lawmakers, urged by angry taxpayers, were cracking down on welfare mothers. Several states wanted to stop adjusting welfare grants to family size. No longer would they increase payments to women who bore additional children while on the dole. Their rationale was the same as that of Bonnell's employer: Why should they accommodate every expensive, self-indulgent private choice? If taxpayers, like employers, refused to subsidize a woman's maternity, was that a violation of her right to choose to bear children—or an exercise of their own freedom to choose not to support her?

VISALIA, CALIFORNIA
JANUARY 2, 1991

"Your application for probation is granted."

Those words, addressed to Darlene Johnson by Judge Howard Broadman, were welcome news. Instead of a jail sentence for beating her kids, Johnson—young, black, and pregnant—was getting three years' probation. But there was a catch.

"Are you on welfare?" Broadman asked.

"I was," said Johnson.

"And you will be again, right?" he pressed.

"Yeah," she admitted.

"Do you want to get pregnant again?" he asked.

"No," she replied.

"Okay," said Broadman. "As a condition of your probation, you know, this new thing that's going to be available next month, you prob-

ably haven't heard about it. It's called Norplant." Johnson knew nothing about it. "It's a thing that you put into your arm and it lasts for
five years," Broadman explained. "Well, it's like a birth control pill." He
paused to elicit her consent. "What do you think about that?"

"Okay," said Johnson.

"I'd like you to complete some program of being a good mom before
you get pregnant again," Broadman continued. "You shouldn't have any
kids until we get you squared away." The judge concluded, "[W]ith your
permission, I'm going to impose that as a condition of probation." The
contraceptive implant, he noted, could be removed at his discretion,
thereby restoring Johnson's fertility. "This is not forced sterilization," he
said. That practice, he assured her, had ended long ago.[31]

Had it? Here in California's Central Valley, the tradition of steriliz-
ing "undesirables" hung in the background like the indelible rim of the
Sierra Nevada. In the heyday of the eugenics movement, half of the
United States had authorized compulsory sterilizations of imbeciles,
criminals, addicts, and others deemed unfit to reproduce. But one state's
shame eclipsed all others. Of the roughly sixty thousand mandatory
sterilizations performed in the United States between 1900 and 1960,
California accounted for one-third.[32]

With its dual traditions of left- and right-wing radicalism, California
often led the nation's revolutions in social engineering. In the early years
of the crusade to purify humanity through controlled procreation, California performed more than three-fourths of the nation's compulsory
sterilizations.[33] In 1966, while President Lyndon Johnson was launching
the Great Society, Californians were electing a new governor, Ronald
Reagan, whose promise to get tough on welfare recipients would later
help to catapult him to the presidency. In 1978 California kicked off a
nationwide backlash against big government by passing Proposition 13,
an initiative to cut property taxes.

Tension between taxpayers and welfare mothers persisted long after
the state modified its sterilization laws in 1951. In 1965 a Los Angeles
judge assigned probation to a twenty-year-old Hispanic woman who
had been convicted of driving the getaway car for a robbery. The woman,
who already had two children and was carrying a third, had been on
public assistance since her first pregnancy.

Among his conditions of probation, the judge forbade the woman to
add any more children to the welfare rolls. "[Y]ou are not to become

pregnant until after you become married," he told her. "You have already too many [children]. . . . If you insist on this kind of conduct you
can at least consider the other people in society who are taking care of
your children. You have had too many that some others are taking care
of other than you and the father." A year later, when the woman turned
up pregnant, the judge ordered her to prison, calling her "irresponsible"
for "foisting obligations upon others." [34]

Not until 1979 did California finally rescind its law authorizing involuntary sterilizations. Three years afterward, a judge in Santa Cruz
County threatened to imprison a woman who had malnourished her children if she got pregnant during her five-year probation. An appeals court
ruled that the threat amounted to an abortion order. Small wonder that
by 1984, the predicted year of George Orwell's totalitarian nightmare,
the sociologist Kristin Luker reported a suspicion among California pro-
life activists that abortion was being promoted by "politicians who want
to cut welfare rolls" and "eugenicists who want only the 'best' babies
born." [35]

Judge Broadman seemed the latest heir to this tradition. In 1988,
when a woman who planned to get a hysterectomy came before him in
a divorce case, he warned her, "[I]f you don't get the hysterectomy, start
school, I am going to reduce your [child] support, I am going to make
you go out and get a job." In September 1990 he imposed a five-year
birth control regimen on a thirty-year-old mother of five as a condition
of her probationary sentence for drug abuse. [36]

This was the inauspicious history into which Darlene Johnson found
herself thrust. Her contribution to it was the misfortune of appearing
for her sentencing hearing three weeks after Broadman learned of a new
birth control device called Norplant, which consisted of six capsules.
Once implanted in a woman's arm, the capsules gradually released a
hormone into her body. They prevented pregnancy for up to five years,
or until a doctor removed them. Aside from its efficacy, what distinguished Norplant from pills, condoms, and diaphragms was that the
woman didn't have to think about it. Its operation was involuntary.

For that reason, Johnson's court-appointed attorney, Charles Rothbaum, came before the judge a week after her sentencing hearing to
plead that Norplant was unconstitutional as a condition of probation.
Rothbaum claimed that the right to privacy established in *Griswold* and
Roe entailed a "right to procreate" as well as a right to abortion. He
argued that the judge had deprived Johnson of that right by extracting

her consent to Norplant in a "coercive context," that is, under threat of imprisonment.

Broadman dismissed the argument. Though Johnson sat before him visibly upset, he insisted that she had offered her "willing, knowing, voluntary acceptance of the probationary terms." Furthermore, he maintained that her right to procreate could be "limited" because she had "shown herself incapable of caring for children." [37] She was a criminal and as such had forfeited many of her rights.

In this declaration of Johnson's parental incompetence, Rothbaum caught a whiff of something else. After the hearing, he pointed out that Broadman had issued his Norplant order only after certifying that Johnson was on welfare. Rothbaum also alleged that he had once heard Broadman tell the district attorney that welfare mothers shouldn't be permitted to bear more than two children. "I think that's what's going on here," said the attorney. [38]

The controversy over Norplant and welfare had by this time been boiling for nearly a month. On December 10, 1990, the Food and Drug Administration approved Norplant for sale in the United States. Two days later the *Philadelphia Inquirer* published an editorial entitled "Poverty and Norplant — Can Contraception Reduce the Underclass?" Reasoning that "foolproof contraception could be invaluable in breaking the cycle of inner city poverty," the editorial proposed "a major effort to reduce the number of children, of any race, born into such circumstances."

"No one should be compelled to use Norplant," said the editorial. "But there could be incentives to do so. What if welfare mothers were offered an increased benefit for agreeing to use this new, safe, long-term contraceptive? Remember, these women already have one or more children." The *Inquirer*'s editorial board concluded that while some aspects of this policy were discomforting, "we're made even more uncomfortable by the impoverishment of black America and its effect on the nation's future." [39]

The editorial triggered a storm of outrage within and beyond the *Inquirer*'s offices. Four days after it appeared, an *Inquirer* columnist, Steve Lopez, compared it to the rhetoric of the racist demagogue David Duke. Lopez reported that after the editorial appeared, angry *Inquirer* staffers had looked into Duke's past and found that "sure enough, Duke suggested cutting 'the proliferation of the underclass'—his code word for blacks—through birth control. This would involve 'a series of rewards' for the more 'responsible' practitioners." According to Lopez, editorial department staffers had brushed aside this resemblance by replying "that David Duke says things many people think about but are afraid to say publicly." [40]

On December 23, under fire, the editorial department surrendered. The *Inquirer* apologized for having proposed "incentives" to get poor women to accept Norplant. "Our critics countered that to dangle cash or some other benefit in front of a desperately poor woman is tantamount to coercion," wrote the editors. "They're right." [41]

The *Inquirer* uproar complicated the thicket of questions surrounding Darlene Johnson's sentence. It was hard enough, given the public's loathing of criminals, to persuade people that offering a convicted felon a choice between jail and Norplant was unduly coercive. It was harder still to persuade people that offering a poor woman extra money for accepting Norplant was coercive. After all, it wasn't the state's fault that she was poor.

Within days of Johnson's sentencing, the ACLU entered the case on her behalf. "A plea bargain is so inherently coercive that reproductive decisions cannot constitutionally be part of the package," argued an ACLU official. "Even if it's presented as a choice, how voluntary can it be if the government has that block of cement over your head?" [42] Four days later, after Broadman spurned Johnson's appeal, Planned Parenthood president Faye Wattleton wrote an essay in the *Los Angeles Times* denouncing Johnson's "coercive" sentence.

Making a case against the *Inquirer*'s proposal was a trickier task. Wattleton reasoned that offering extra welfare money to poor women in exchange for submitting to Norplant was no different from the Indian government's offer of free portable radios to women who agreed to be sterilized. She also knew that Planned Parenthood's founder, Margaret Sanger, had collaborated with eugenic racists during the 1920s. Wattleton chose a different course:

> As an African-American, I have spent 20 years fighting to ensure that no person is forced into any reproductive decision through societal pressures, through denial of comprehensive health services or by force of law. . . .
> It is immoral and inhuman to coerce the childbearing decisions of any individual—either by compelling the use of contraception or by denying it. American or not, wealthy or not, white or not—every woman and man deserves the knowledge and the means to make healthy, private choices, free from bribery and manipulation. [43]

Other pro-choice activists followed suit. In a *Los Angeles Times* commentary, the director of NOW's Legal Defense and Education Fund linked Darlene Johnson's sentence to a pattern of attacks on the "right to procreate."[44] In an appellate brief on Johnson's behalf, the ACLU added, "[A]ny government coercion to have or refrain from having a child violates the same fundamental right: individual choice in reproduction. . . . Thus, the order that Johnson submit unwillingly to hormonal contraception as the price of probation is constitutionally equivalent to an order that she submit unwillingly to an abortion."[45]

Some pro-lifers sensed the same peril. Gary Bauer, president of the Family Research Council, warned that "any coercive use of Norplant or other contraceptives sets a dangerous precedent." The *Inquirer*'s proposal "to pay . . . welfare recipients" to accept Norplant was "reprehensible," wrote Cal Thomas, former vice president of the Moral Majority. "[H]ow long will it be," he asked, "before the use of contraceptives is forced on welfare recipients of whatever color?"[46]

In this way, Norplant separated pro-lifers, such as Bauer and Thomas, from critics of *Roe* who cared more about defining choice in conservative terms. The legal scholar Bruce Fein typified the latter faction. In October 1990 Fein summarized the conservative pro-choice argument against liberal abortion rights legislation:

> The Freedom of Choice Act is a fourfold denigration of liberty: It makes the fetus a plaything for the whims of pregnant females, including sex selection; it tramples the liberty of parents over the rearing of their offspring; it squelches the religious freedom of doctors and nurses to satisfy the abortion preferences of others; and it invades the rights of state voters to self-government on abortion matters through initiatives or the election of state officials.[47]

So when, three months later, Judge Broadman extracted Darlene Johnson's "permission" to be surgically equipped with Norplant, Fein ignored the implications for unborn life. He defended Broadman with the same logic Robert Bork had applied to American Cyanamid's sterilization policy. In a gesture of "magnanimity," Fein argued, Broadman had "offered" Johnson an "alternative" to jail. Johnson, in turn, had "voluntarily agreed to the implant." If Norplant seemed "too draconian or intrusive," Fein suggested, Johnson "could have accepted a prison term, along with the loss of reproductive choice that it entails."[48] The provision of options, no matter how bad, qualified her choice as free.

In Visalia, the California town where Johnson was sentenced, Broadman's order drew applause. One resident, expressing an opinion shared by many others, argued in a letter to the local newspaper that the judge should have ordered Johnson permanently sterilized. A few months later, in another child abuse case, Broadman asked a Hispanic defendant whether she would accept Norplant as a condition of probation. When her lawyer said no, the judge handed her a four-year prison term.[49]

Johnson was relieved of her Norplant sentence in June 1991, when California's attorney general, prompted by the ACLU, authorized a higher court to remove that condition of her probation, on the grounds that her consent to it hadn't been "knowing and voluntary."[50] By then, however, Norplant had caught the fancy of Pete Wilson, the state's Republican governor. Wilson, a pro-choice fiscal conservative, was determined to prevent unwanted births. And there were plenty of births the taxpayers of California didn't want.

During spring 1991, Wilson brought up Norplant in several conversations with state legislators. In May he told the *Los Angeles Times* that the state would provide Norplant to teenage girls and drug abusers. A reporter asked whether Wilson might mandate Norplant for addicts. "Frankly, we haven't decided," said the governor.[51]

A *Los Angeles Times* poll showed that Californians overwhelmingly favored the idea. After being told that Norplant was "surgically implanted under a woman's arm" and would "prevent pregnancy for up to five years," the respondents were asked: "Do you approve or disapprove of making the Norplant device mandatory for drug-abusing women of child-bearing age?" More than 60 percent said they approved. Only half as many disapproved. Even most liberals endorsed the idea.[52]

Even if implanted with consent, Norplant's automatic long-term efficacy made it a trap for any woman who couldn't afford to pay for its removal. A southern California woman found that out later in 1991, when she went to a doctor to have the device taken out. The removal fee was $75 per capsule. She failed to come up with more than $75, so the doctor removed only one of the six capsules. He made his incision in such a way that none of the other capsules could be extracted through it.[53]

While Governor Wilson hesitated to push Norplant on unfit mothers, other politicians forged ahead. In January 1991, four weeks after Darlene Johnson's Norplant sentence and seven weeks after the *Inquirer* editorial, Kansas state representative Kerry Patrick introduced a bill that would offer $500 to women on welfare in exchange for accepting Norplant. In a second bill, he proposed to mandate Norplant as a condition of probation for women convicted of possessing cocaine or heroin.

The probation bill drew an immediate outcry from pro-choice activists. NARAL's lobbyist in Kansas, Peggy Jarman, called it "frightening" and "disgusting." By comparison, the incentive bill seemed innocuous. Representatives of NOW and Planned Parenthood reacted favorably. "If it is voluntary and if the state is going to pay for the procedure," said a NOW official, "I don't have any serious problems with it." Only the ACLU of Kansas rejected the idea of using cash to lure poor women. "It's not voluntary," said the state ACLU director. "It's coercion." [54]

Patrick dismissed such liberal nonsense. Given a choice between their fertility and an extra $500, he argued, poor women were "wise enough to make that decision for themselves." If a woman later changed her mind and wanted the implant removed, she would have to find the money herself. Under Patrick's proposal, the state wouldn't bail her out. [55]

Patrick promoted both bills with the same rationale. The purpose of the probation bill was to prevent the births of addicted babies who would saddle taxpayers with enormous medical expenses. Likewise, the incentive bill would save the state about $43 million. "The total cost to the taxpayers of Kansas to provide just basic public assistance to the mother and until the time that the child is legally an adult is approximately $205,000," Patrick argued. "If you add in the cost to the taxpayers to educate that child, the total cost runs over $285,000. The creation of this program has the potential to save the taxpayers millions of their hard-earned dollars." [56]

Pro-choice activists began to smell trouble in Patrick's reasoning. His cost-saving rationale was too broad; his conception of free choice was too narrow. Two weeks later, when the incentive bill came up for a hearing, other pro-choice groups joined the ACLU in opposing it. Kansas NOW called the $500 offer "a form of coercion." Jarman, echoing Faye Wattleton, labeled it "bribery and manipulation" and compared it to the economic blackmail of the 1970s, when reproductive decisions had been "coerced with threats of withholding welfare payments, and other penalties." [57] The president of Planned Parenthood of Kansas added, "The incentive program is clearly coercive and is meant to be that way. To offer a woman who monthly lives on less money than she needs a $500 bonus to choose a particular form of contraception is coercion." [58]

The hearing was a remarkable display of unity. But one witness made

it vastly more remarkable. "Kansas once led the nation in forcefully ster-
ilizing patients in our institutions and prisons," the witness testified.
Patrick's "coercive" bill, she warned, was "a step back toward those
days." With those words, Pat Goodson, the president of Right to Life of
Kansas, concluded her testimony and asked legislators to kill the bill.[59]
Terror had succeeded where trust had failed. Pro-life and pro-choice activists had been driven into a desperate alliance.

Eight hundred miles to the south, state representative David Duke of
Louisiana watched the Norplant debate in Kansas with particular interest. Years earlier, as president of the National Association for the Advancement of White People, Duke had proposed cash payments to welfare recipients in exchange for submitting to sterilizations. In 1989 and
1990, after winning election to the Louisiana legislature, he had devoted
his energies to slashing welfare benefits and rescinding government programs that favored blacks.[60]

Duke had made welfare reform the central issue of his 1990 campaign for the U.S. Senate. His principal television ad in that campaign
had proposed three such reforms. Two, testing welfare recipients for
drug abuse and making them work for their money, had been tried elsewhere. But the third reform was new: Women would stop receiving extra money to offset the cost of children they conceived while on welfare.
Taxpayers would no longer subsidize what Duke's forebear, George
Wallace, had called "breeding children as a cash crop."[61]

Duke captured nearly 60 percent of the white vote and came within
six points of winning that race. The next year he ran for governor, again
on a platform of restricting welfare. In late April, three months after
Kerry Patrick's legislation appeared in Kansas, Duke filed a copycat bill
that would pay $250 to any woman on welfare who accepted Norplant.
Noting that "every child who is born into the welfare system will cost
the state a minimum of $100,000," Duke argued that his bill would
"save the taxpayers tens of millions a year." Like Patrick, he stressed
that his plan was "voluntary."[62]

Duke made the political animus behind this fiscal logic far more obvious than Patrick had. A day after unveiling his bill at the state capitol,
Duke told supporters at a gubernatorial campaign rally, "Just like in my
Senate race, the most important issue is [that] we have a rising welfare
state that is causing most of the crime and is straining the educational
system." The growth of this welfare monster, he told the crowd, was

caused by "a birthrate that's higher than your birthrate—the ones who work and produce something."[63]

Three weeks later, arguing for the bill at a committee hearing, Duke reiterated that children born to welfare mothers were a major cause of crime. A citizen who supported Duke also testified. "How long can we spend taxpayers' money on irresponsible people?" she demanded. "We're sick and tired of working for other people. If you're not going to work, you can at least refrain from bringing other people into the world."[64]

The Kansas and Louisiana bills died in committees, but the crusade against welfare births had been launched. In April 1991, two months after news of the Kansas bill reached the national press, a package of six welfare reform bills was filed in New Jersey. One of the bills incorporated the idea proposed by Duke in his 1990 Senate campaign. It would halt the practice of increasing each family's welfare subsidy to accommodate its growth. A woman who bore another child while on welfare would have to make do with the same money as before.[65] No state had ever tried this idea, which became known as a family cap. Its message to women was, if you can't support another child on your own, don't give birth.

To pro-life activists, one corollary of this message was instantly and horribly clear: If you get pregnant, abort the child. Alarmed that the cap might pressure women to seek abortions, the New Jersey Right to Life Committee and the New Jersey Catholic Conference denounced the bill and threatened to sue the state if it became law. The Catholic Conference declared it "unconscionable that our state government tells a pregnant woman on welfare that it will pay her to have an abortion, but it will not help pay to ensure that the baby is fed and clothed if she chooses not to abort it."[66]

To pro-choice activists, the case against the family cap was equally clear. Like the Norplant bills in Kansas and Louisiana, the New Jersey bill used economic forces to manipulate women's childbearing decisions. Indeed, it was more coercive than Norplant incentives, since it employed blackmail rather than bribery.

That concern, among others, prompted the state chapters of NOW, the ACLU, and the League of Women Voters to oppose the bill. A NOW attorney presented their objections to a legislative committee. The family cap, she argued, would make New Jersey "the first state in nearly

30 years to deny poor women and their families subsistence-level public assistance grants based on women's child-bearing decisions." Three decades had passed since Georgia, Louisiana, and Mississippi tried to use such threats to make unwed mothers relinquish their illegitimate children and stop having sex. NOW's attorney urged New Jersey lawmakers not to "turn back the clock to the dark days when states routinely used subsistence-level benefits to coerce women's personal, constitutionally-protected decisions." [67]

From a conservative standpoint, such talk was nonsense. Nature, not the state, dictated that the economic penalty for procreation was another mouth to feed. Taxpayers had no duty to rescue women from that penalty. When a liberal activist complained at a New Jersey assembly hearing that the family cap was coercive, the bill's author, Democratic majority leader Wayne Bryant, reminded her, "There is not a constitutional right to welfare in this country." [68]

Later, when the family cap reached the floor of the assembly, Bryant defended the bill in emphatically pro-choice terms:

> What this does is give welfare recipients a choice. They can either have the additional children and work to pay the added costs, or they can decide not to have any more children. It's their call and a decision that puts them in the same position as anyone else in mainstream America who must choose among options. [69]

It was hard to argue with this logic, harder still to argue with Bryant. When critics insinuated that Bryant's proposal was a copy of Duke's, the assemblyman had to smile. For all his wealth and connections, Bryant represented the poorest city in the state. And he was black.

Though he rejected the notion of a right to welfare, Bryant never spoke of the family cap as a way to save taxpayers money. He described it as a means of instilling responsibility and liberating poor people from the "slavery" of welfare. He insisted that the cap was inseparable from job training and educational assistance. [70] But as the family cap matured from an idea to a bill to a law to a prototype of welfare reform, Bryant lost control of it. Other politicians commended and commandeered it. They changed its meaning and its purpose.

On November 5, 1991, New Jersey held midterm legislative elections. Furious at a tax hike imposed by Democrats, voters swept them out. Most Democratic bills were doomed in this environment, but welfare reform was an exception. On January 8, 1992, six days before the Democrats were to relinquish control of the assembly, Bryant's family cap coasted through on a vote of 51 to 3.[71] Five days later, on the last night of the session, it ran into resistance on the senate floor. The bill's opponents agreed that welfare mothers should be deterred from bearing children. But they thought it was unfair, in the words of one senator, to "penalize the children . . . who didn't ask to be brought into this world." Likewise, a child welfare activist complained that the cap "penalizes that child who really didn't have any choice in that situation."[72] Choice, responsibility, penalty. Children deserved mercy for all the reasons women didn't.

As in Arkansas and Louisiana, liberal activists in New Jersey chose not to challenge the idea that women ought to suffer the consequences of sex. Instead, they exploited that idea by defending women who hadn't consented to sex. As one activist pointed out at a press conference, even "victims of rape or incest" would be "punished" by the cap.[73]

It was at this point that Governor Jim Florio intervened. Florio, a Democrat, had been elected with Doug Wilder in the pro-choice rout of 1989. His subsequent tax hike had decimated his party in the 1991 elections. Humbled by that setback, Florio promised to cooperate with the GOP. The family cap seemed a good place to begin. On that final night of the session, Florio dispatched three aides to the senate floor to twist arms and squeeze the bill through.[74]

The next day, the new legislature was sworn in. Republicans took control of both houses, promising to slash spending and taxes. Speaking from the assembly podium, Florio assured voters that they had put him "back on track." He promised to limit spending and "not stand in [the] way" of economic growth.[75]

"Government must give people more freedom to make choices," said Florio. It must leave women "to choose how to handle their own reproductive health." Republican lawmakers applauded. The next day, Florio cited the same principle to justify the family cap. The decision about how to support a child should be left to the parents who chose to bring it into the world, the governor said. "[T]hey make that decision."[76]

Pro-life, pro-choice, civil rights, and welfare activists implored Florio to veto the cap. But on January 21 he signed it into law. Working parents, Florio observed, had to earn more money or cut expenses in order to afford children. "Those on assistance will have to make the same choices."[77]

Liberals bristled at this libertarian theory of choice. The columnist Anna Quindlen attacked the premise, advanced by Florio and others, "that middle-class people don't get government subsidies for additional kids." These parents received "tax credits and deductions" for each new child, she noted.[78] Libertarians regarded these deductions as government noninterference: The state was simply taking less money from taxpayers. But to liberals, the question was why the state should accommodate taxpayers and not the dependent poor.

A day after signing the bill, Florio attended a luncheon honoring *Roe*. He signed a decree establishing Freedom of Choice Day and accepted an award from pro-choice activists for defending abortion rights. He credited the award to voters who shared his belief that in decisions about childbearing, "government intrusion into our lives is not acceptable." The activists stood and applauded.[79]

Eleven days later, Florio traveled to Washington, D.C., for a meeting of the National Governors Association. He used the conference to promote New Jersey's welfare reforms. Although Bryant accompanied him, Florio became the spokesman for the reforms. On February 2 Florio and Bryant outlined the reform package before the national press. In the afternoon, Florio peddled the reforms to a panel of governors.

Florio repeated Bryant's argument that the reforms would liberate welfare clients from "a prison of perpetual dependency." But he understood that in a climate of tight budgets and taxpayer revolt, some of his colleagues might find the fiscal arguments for welfare reform more persuasive. To them, Florio offered a different rationale: "Forget the humanitarian aspects. Forget the desire to preserve the family. The question is, can this economy, in our state and all across the country, afford the anchor around our neck of such a substantial portion of our population that is not contributing to a productive economy?"[80]

Among the governors who sat through Florio's presentation, none spoke up against the cap. At the White House the next day, Florio asked President Bush to press federal regulators to approve New Jersey's reforms. Bush pledged his support.[81] Florio and Bryant also visited Capitol Hill to pitch their reforms to a Senate subcommittee. The welfare scholar Charles Murray followed them to the microphone with an appeal to end Aid to Families with Dependent Children altogether:

> Let government policy start from the premise that to bring a baby into the world when one is not emotionally or financially equipped to be a parent is not just ill-advised, not just inimical to the long-term interests of the mother. It is profoundly irresponsible. It is wrong.

> Now, government cannot and must not intervene pro-actively in the decision to have a baby. Nothing I am suggesting has any bearing on notions of giving people licenses to have babies, or telling people we are going to take the babies away from them.
>
> What government can do is say it will no longer be a party to this behavior. . . . The children remain innocent victims, and the government will do what it can. . . . But the government will no longer try to help the innocent children by subsidizing the parents who made them victims.[82]

This was the crowning synthesis of pro-choice conservatism. Many defenders of abortion wanted to stop the multiplication of the underclass. Many critics of abortion wanted poor women to face the consequences of careless sex. Both goals could be accomplished by getting the government out of family life. And what about the unborn? What would the family cap do to them? Senator Pat Moynihan, Democrat–New York, put the question to Bryant and Florio: "Will there be more abortions?" Bryant gave the same answer that had attracted libertarian voters to Florio and Wilder in 1989. The choices families faced were none of the government's business, said Bryant. "Whether they decide to have a child, have abortions, use condoms—that is their personal decision." [83]

On December 9, 1991, while the New Jersey assembly was considering Bryant's bills, Pete Wilson unveiled his own welfare reform plan in suburban Los Angeles. Wilson's plan would institute a family cap and slash welfare benefits by as much as 25 percent. It would also give Wilson sweeping powers to cut the budget in the event of a legislative deadlock. He offered the plan directly to voters as a ballot measure.[84]

As his interest in mandatory Norplant suggested, Wilson's motives for welfare reform strayed far from Bryant's. Bryant's proposal included job training and significant subsidies for education; Wilson's didn't. Bryant called his bill the Family Development Act; Wilson called his ballot measure the Taxpayer Protection Act. Bryant announced his plan at a nonprofit education and employment training center; Wilson announced his plan at a chamber of commerce. Bryant described his proposal as a way to nurture self-reliance among the poor; Wilson described his proposal as a way to cut the state budget and protect the wallets of the middle class.

"California taxpayers are paying far more than their share of the nationwide costs of welfare," Wilson said. "That's not fair to our taxpayers. That's not fair . . . to the merchants and small business people." The family cap, he suggested, would "end the insidious incentive we are giving single mothers, especially teen-age girls, to continue having children out of wedlock." The audience of businesspeople applauded throughout his speech. The Howard Jarvis Taxpayers Association, named for the Californian who had launched the taxpayer backlash of the 1980s, endorsed Wilson's plan. More than twenty other taxpayer organizations followed suit.[85]

On January 8, 1992, Wilson devoted most of his State of the State address to the welfare proposal. He told middle-class parents that in the "competition" for state funds, their schools were being "crowded out" by welfare recipients. He offered voters "a clear choice" as to which group should get the money. Five days later, speaking to another business audience, Wilson advertised his initiative as an extension of the Jarvis tax rebellion.[86]

At the end of the month, Wilson arrived in Washington, D.C., for the national governors' meeting. At every opportunity—a speech to the National Press Club, an interview on CBS, a visit to the White House—he trumpeted his assault on welfare. Like Florio, he presented his plan to the governors' roundtable on February 2. Several governors approached him to request copies of the plan.[87]

Three days after Wilson announced his proposal, opponents in California launched a campaign to defeat it. As in New Jersey, religious groups and welfare advocates led the opposition. And as in New Jersey, the family cap earned the governor an additional enemy: the pro-life movement.

On January 3 Jan Carroll, legislative director of the California Pro Life Council, wrote Wilson a memo asking him to withdraw parts of his plan:

> Two provisions of your proposed welfare initiative are most alarming to those of us who are sensitive to societal pressures to abort rather than to nurture and care for the youngest members of our families, our unborn children. . . .
> [The family cap] proposal does not merely bring subtle pressure to abort. . . . [T]he state would by sheer economics force some mothers to obtain free abortions from Medi-Cal rather than to attempt to absorb the costs of the new child into an already meager subsistence. . . .
> This shocking provision is analogous to the kinds of financial disincentives offered in Communist China, which issues vouchers to those who are allowed to conceive and denies state benefits to children born without

vouchers—benefits which are available to others such as food, clothing—
even education.[88]

A year earlier President Bush had authorized political asylum for
refugees who fled China to escape its one-child policy. But that kind of
coercion couldn't happen in the United States—could it? In the Pro Life
Council's March newsletter, the group's director, Brian Johnston, underscored that question:

> Like Wilson, China's family planners are also "cutting back on expenses."
> A family who has more than one child may get no "food coupons" for sub-
> sequent children. . . .
>   Governor Wilson may scoff at the documented stories of forced abortion
> in China. . . . [But f]or a poor woman who is pregnant the choices are
> simple—free government abortion or the denial of help for her child. In
> polite company, such choices are known as "coercion." [89]

In addition to the family cap, Carroll advised Wilson to scrap a second welfare-reform provision:

> The Teen Pregnancy Disincentive affords support to minors who bear
> children only if they remain at home with their parents or legal guardian.
> At least two common situations do not seem to be taken into considera-
> tion here.
>   First you have the parents who may not fit someone's description of
> abusive or unfit, but nevertheless insist on abortion if their minor daughter
> intends to stay at home. If the minor wants to have her baby, rather than
> abort, does she have to prove her parents are unfit? . . .
>   It is constantly impressed upon pro-lifers that all families are not ideal—
> as if we didn't know. This proposal surely does not take that fact of life into
> consideration. What is needed is greater flexibility, not a system so rigid
> that it forces a young mother to kill her unborn child.[90]

For five years, Carroll and her colleagues had defended California's parental consent law against the argument that teenagers shouldn't have to
go to court to disqualify their parents from vetoing their childbearing
decisions. Now they were challenging parental authority and demanding government subsidies.

Contrary to the accusation that they ignored the welfare of already
born children, pro-life activists raised that concern vigorously in their
campaign against Wilson's plan. Speaking at an elementary school on
February 11, Cardinal Roger Mahony, Catholic prelate of Los Angeles,
protested that the plan would exacerbate child poverty. Archbishop John
Quinn of San Francisco charged that the family cap would "force poor

women to have abortions and to make cruel choices in order to take care of their already born children." The director of the California Catholic Congress added, "We call on those who consider abortion a matter of choice to join us. This is not choice. This is coercion." [91]

In an analysis published soon afterward in the *Sacramento Bee,* the California sociologist Carol Joffe concluded that "an internal struggle is developing within conservatism over what might be called the right to procreation."

> It is now common practice at anti-abortion crisis pregnancy centers across the country for the staff to help their clients enroll in government programs such as Aid to Families with Dependent Children—certainly a heresy for a group rooted in the conservative movement.
>
> Welfare conservatives, meanwhile, have been pushing policies that would dramatically restrict poor women's ability to choose childbearing. Among their proposals: financial penalties for AFDC recipients who have additional children; forbidding unmarried teenage mothers to receive welfare assistance directly; requiring contraceptive use as a condition for receiving welfare or providing financial incentives for such use. . . .
>
> The challenge that welfare conservatives are mounting against procreative freedom presents the pro-choice movement with an opportunity to clarify the meaning of choice itself. The pro-choice movement can now make clear what is often lost in the daily battles over abortion: Reproductive freedom involves far more than abortion; it encompasses the right to choose childbearing as well.[92]

A few pro-choice advocates heeded this advice. In Orange County, they formed an anti–family cap alliance with pro-life activists who counseled and sheltered pregnant women. In Los Angeles, Jewish and Protestant clergy joined forces with Cardinal Mahony to fight the cap. The state's Catholic bishops remained the cap's most vocal critics.[93]

The ballot measure eventually died because of misgivings about a clause that granted the governor emergency budget powers. Had pro-choice and pro-life activists faced a referendum on the family cap alone, however, they would certainly have been crushed. A poll taken early in 1992 showed that by a margin of more than twenty points, Californians agreed that the state should "not increase the amount of welfare payments to low-income families with dependent children when they have additional children." [94]

Local politicians in both parties scrambled aboard the welfare reform bandwagon. In the seven weeks after Wilson outlined his reforms, all five Democrats running for California's two U.S. Senate seats agreed that benefits should be slashed. In April Democratic leaders in the state senate proposed a family cap and other welfare cuts, bragging that their scheme would save taxpayers more than $500,000. "Imitation is the highest form of flattery," gloated a Wilson aide. The family cap, along with the rest of the Democratic package, sailed through the senate on a 27 to 10 vote a month later.[95]

The issue soon spread to the presidential campaign. In the last week of July, the two principal candidates swept through southern California. Flanked by Wilson, President Bush announced his national welfare reform plan. Bush's aides distributed a fact sheet boasting that he had approved Wilson's proposal to encourage "responsible childbearing."[96]

Bush asserted in his speech that "millions" of welfare recipients had "never learned the simple values of hard work and responsibility." He urged voters to support welfare reform in order to "save the most endangered species in California, the taxpayer." Toward that end, he welcomed the family cap: "[T]oo many Americans, many on welfare, are having children they can't afford, can't support, just aren't ready for, and we have to do something about it. The system has to find a way to do something about that. We're allowing States to decide if it's time to say, 'No more money if you have another child.' Let some try that."[97]

Bill Clinton took a similar position. He declined to endorse the family cap but stipulated that he would let states implement it. Advocates for the cap were correct, he argued, that "the average working family doesn't get an increase in income when they have an increased number of kids." In July Clinton told Republicans and Reagan Democrats in California that he was more fiscally conservative than Bush and would make welfare "a second chance, not a way of life." Welfare reform became the centerpiece of Clinton's message to swing voters. In television ads, he pledged "to end welfare as we know it."[98]

The family cap quickly swept the country. In 1992 it was introduced in more than a dozen states. Bush authorized the first cap in Wisconsin in April 1992. Eight months later, after Clinton ousted Bush, the incoming governor of Arkansas announced that he, too, would install a cap. A year later, Clinton authorized the cap in Georgia. By 1994 half the states were considering it.[99]

Resistance by pro-life and pro-choice activists largely proved futile. In Arkansas a NOW official objected that the cap would increase abortions. The Wisconsin Catholic Conference delivered the same warning to pro-life governor Tommy Thompson. In Maryland, lobbyists called the cap pro-abortion and anti-choice. A Maryland Right to Life official likened the cap to China's one-child policy. In Nebraska, a pro-life law-maker unsuccessfully begged his colleagues to spare the unborn by scut-tling the cap.[100]

Victories were rare. Michigan Right to Life defeated the cap by single-handedly reversing the votes of twenty-seven conservative state repre-sentatives. More common was the outcome in Georgia, where Governor Zell Miller bragged about ramming the cap through over the objections of the ACLU. "We cannot reward people for their own personal deci-sions at the cost of the taxpayer," said Miller.[101]

Polls taken in late 1993 and early 1994 showed that roughly two-thirds of Americans favored the family cap. Several states pressed for federal permission to adopt it. Republicans and moderate Democrats lobbied Clinton to issue a blanket waiver allowing any state to institute a cap. Clinton's Welfare Reform Task Force advised him that the cap would save $500 million. Pro-choice and pro-life groups warned the task force that they would fight it, but on May 26, 1994, Clinton agreed to the blanket waiver. "We think it is very important to discourage ad-ditional births on welfare," an aide explained.[102]

A few days later, a legislative conference committee took up the family cap in California. Welfare lobbyists worked with pro-choice and pro-life advocates to quash the measure. Casey McKeever, the state's top welfare rights activist, set up a lobbying pipeline through which NOW collabo-rated with pro-life assemblyman John Vasconcellos to strip the family cap from a state budget deal. McKeever told NOW's attorneys that they owed their success to Vasconcellos, "a strong supporter of the poor as well as an opponent of abortion." [103]

The victory proved short-lived. Lawmakers rejected the deal, and leg-islative leaders spent the last week of June negotiating a new package with the governor. Wilson and the two Republican leaders demanded deeper welfare cuts, including a family cap, while the two Democratic leaders pushed for tax increases instead. On July 1 the five men negoti-ated all day and most of the night in Wilson's office. Finally, the Demo-crats accepted the family cap.[104]

Welfare advocates tried to stop the cap. In an appeal to pro-life law-makers, McKeever distributed an anti-cap fact sheet from the New Jer-sey Right to Life Committee. A cap in California, he warned, would "encourage abortions which might not otherwise occur." The associate director of the California Catholic Conference protested that the legis-lature was "saying poor women can't have children." [105]

Their appeals fell on deaf ears. On July 4 the senate overwhelmingly passed the cap. The house followed suit, and on July 8 Wilson signed it into law. Liberals groused that assembly speaker Willie Brown and senate president Bill Lockyer, the Democratic bosses who had struck the budget deal, had sold out the poor. What about the children hurt by the cap? And what about women forced into abortions? Such complaints exhausted Lockyer's patience. Given the state's money shortage, he explained, the budget deal was as good as the poor could get. His closing proverb summed up the debate: "Beggars can't be choosers." [106]

CHAPTER 9

The Era of Big Government

In the weeks that followed Bill Clinton's election to the presidency, several leading pro-life strategists essentially surrendered the twenty-year struggle to outlaw abortion. Representative Vin Weber, a Minnesota Republican, conceded that voters had "resolved the issue." Cal Thomas, former vice president of the Moral Majority, told his colleagues to "face the reality that government is unlikely to turn around on this issue" and advised them to work not to outlaw but to influence each woman's abortion decision. Former secretary of education Bill Bennett counseled the GOP to withdraw its demand for a constitutional ban on abortion in deference to America's "pro-choice" majority.[1]

On January 22, 1993, the third day of his presidency and the twentieth anniversary of *Roe v. Wade,* Clinton ordered the end of five federal pro-life policies, starting with the ban on abortion counseling at federally funded clinics. Kate Michelman rejoiced, "[W]e've turned the corner" to "a new day for choice in America." Eleanor Smeal of the Feminist Majority called it "the end of an era" of pro-life tyranny. Speaker of the House Tom Foley declared Clinton's election "the most important victory in the last twenty years" for abortion rights. The *Washington Post* and the *Boston Globe* proclaimed "a new era" of pro-choice supremacy. The *New York Times* announced, "The Abortion Tide Turns."[2]

Had any of these activists, politicians, or editorialists fully understood the role of conservative public opinion in the events of the past seven years, they would have recognized that the abortion rights movement was arriving not at a new frontier but at the end of its tether.

The tether jerked taut immediately after Clinton's election, as conservative pro-choice Republicans ousted liberal pro-choice Democrats in two special elections for the U.S. Senate. The first casualty, Senator Wyche Fowler of Georgia, was a cosponsor of the federal Freedom of Choice Act (FOCA), which aimed to prohibit abortion restrictions in the states. While Fowler declared himself "unequivocally pro-choice" in the fashion of 1990 Georgia gubernatorial loser Andrew Young, Fowler's Republican challenger, Paul Coverdell, adopted the posture of Young's nemesis, Governor Zell Miller. Coverdell endorsed parental notice, opposed federal financing of abortions, and rejected FOCA.[3]

Pro-choice and pro-life conservatives united behind Coverdell. Despite his refusal to endorse a ban on abortion, the National Right to Life Committee spent $15,000 on his behalf. The Christian Coalition distributed one million leaflets blasting Fowler's support of "abortion on demand." Pro-lifers mounted a substantial radio ad campaign highlighting the candidates' differences over FOCA and abortion funding. Their help proved crucial to Coverdell's victory. "A lot of Christian voters made a sophisticated calculation," explained Christian Coalition director Ralph Reed. "Although Mr. Coverdell did not agree with them on the right to life, on the votes he would be asked to cast in the U.S. Senate, he was largely in line with their own position."[4]

Republican Party chairman Haley Barbour promised to repeat this feat in Texas, where Democratic senator Bob Krueger faced a challenge from Republican Kay Bailey Hutchison. Krueger, like Fowler, was a cosponsor of FOCA. He favored abortion subsidies for the poor and opposed federally mandated parental involvement. Hutchison, like Coverdell, agreed that abortion should be legal but endorsed parental consent and opposed federal funding of "elective" abortions. She condoned abortion funding only for victims of rape or incest.[5]

Pro-choice activists implored pro-choice voters to reject Hutchison. Television ads aired by Krueger and Voters for Choice, a national abortion rights PAC, dismissed Hutchison as "multiple choice," not pro-choice. NARAL and its Texas affiliate also backed Krueger. Far from apologizing, Hutchison touted these complaints from the left as proof of her moderation. She won the support of national Republican pro-choice groups and demolished Krueger by a 2 to 1 margin. Barbour advertised her victory and Coverdell's as harbingers of the GOP's new pragmatism on abortion.[6]

In Washington, D.C., illusions of a new era of pro-choice liberalism began to crumble. Satisfied that the legal right to abortion was politically secure, moderate pro-choice voters and financial contributors lost interest in the issue. The percentage of poll respondents who deemed abortion one of the country's most urgent issues plunged almost to zero. NARAL's membership and income fell by one-third. Planned Parenthood had to cut its budget by one-fourth.[7]

Abortion rights activists planned a three-stage campaign to replace the prevailing libertarian system with a more expansive pro-choice regime. First, they would repeal the Hyde amendment—named after its sponsor, Representative Henry Hyde—which banned federal funding of abortions. Next, they would pass FOCA. Finally, they would secure coverage of abortions under Clinton's national health insurance proposal.

The first stage of the campaign opened on March 30, when the White House confirmed that Clinton would omit the Hyde amendment from his budget proposal. In explaining the omission, aides never defended a poor woman's right to abortion. Instead, they couched Clinton's position in terms of states' rights and victims' rights. "This is just a matter of for 16 years, the federal government flat out prohibiting states from spending money to pay for abortions, whether or not they're medically necessary," said White House spokesman George Stephanopoulos. "The President feels that that goes too far."[8]

Clinton was recycling the 1986 Arkansas strategy—reducing abortion rights to a negative proposition, with a sharp distinction between abortions for rape victims and abortions for convenience. White House aides stressed that whereas Republicans sought to ban abortions nationwide, even for victims of sex crimes, Clinton's only concern was "to preserve the flexibility of the states" in administering Medicaid. While announcing the Hyde amendment's removal, administration officials told the press that Clinton wouldn't object to congressional restrictions on abortion funding and that he expected to end up with a compromise that would finance abortions only in cases of rape or incest. Clinton would later endorse this distinction explicitly: "It's one thing to say that the taxpayers should not pay for a legal abortion that arises from a poor woman's own decision. That's one thing. Quite another to say the same rules apply to rape and incest."[9]

Pro-lifers responded by accusing Clinton of imposing big government on taxpayers. "AL GORE WAS RIGHT," blared the headline over the Christian Coalition's full-page ad in the April 22 *Washington Post*. Displaying a 1987 letter in which Gore had trumpeted his opposition to federal financing of abortions, the ad noted, "A new CBS/New York Times poll shows that 72% of the American people oppose taxpayer funded abortion. They agree with the Al Gore who once said taxpayers should not be forced to pay for the taking of human life." [10]

Clinton soon invited a leading exponent of this view into his circle. In an April 19 column in *U.S. News & World Report,* Republican strategist David Gergen cautioned Clinton against "opening the floodgates to universal abortion on demand, funded by taxpayers." Instead, Gergen lauded the example of President Carter, who had supported the Hyde amendment on the sensible premise that "the government should stay out of a woman's decision, not blocking her but not encouraging her, either." In yielding to pro-choice "absolutists," Gergen warned,

> the administration threatens to ride roughshod over the sensibilities of most Americans struggling somewhere in between. . . . Where most Americans have drawn the line is on paying for other people's abortions, especially abortions on demand. In an ABC–*Washington Post* survey last year, 69 percent of those polled said the federal government should not pay "for an abortion for any woman who wants it and cannot afford to pay." [11]

Clinton read Gergen's column regularly and took his advice seriously. Six weeks after the abortion column appeared, he hired Gergen as his White House counselor, in part to shed the liberal image of his administration's first months. Thereafter, to the bitter disappointment of pro-choice activists, Clinton neither lobbied Congress against the Hyde amendment nor intervened to rescue the beleaguered Freedom of Choice Act. [12]

Despite the resonance of their anti-tax message, Hyde and his allies soon realized that they were being drowned out by pro-choicers' emphasis on rape. According to their vote count, if they insisted that the Hyde amendment continue to ban abortion funding even in cases of rape or incest, they would lose. So they exempted such cases, as Louisiana pro-lifers had done. [13]

As in Louisiana, the concession paid off. On June 30 the House voted 255 to 178 to renew the Hyde amendment. Pro-choice lawmakers were dumbfounded. Even the freshman class, elected on the ostensibly pro-choice tide of 1992, backed the amendment. Freshmen who had run on pro-choice platforms and who in some cases had taken campaign money from pro-choice groups voted for the amendment. So did a quarter of the women in the House. "I don't think government ought to be involved in the area of reproduction, and that includes financing," explained Karen Thurman, a Florida Democrat whom pro-choice activists had supported in 1992. As for the activists' disappointment with her position, Thurman replied, "I have a responsibility to my constituents." [14]

Pundits were baffled. "Just when the pro-choice forces in this country thought they were on a roll, there was a stunning setback today," exclaimed NBC's Tom Brokaw. Other journalists called the news "jarring" and "shocking." "The year of the woman just went down the chute," lamented Representative Pat Schroeder, a Colorado Democrat. "Everybody thought this was a much more pro-choice Congress," said Schroeder. "We found out we were wrong." Planned Parenthood president Pam Maraldo concurred: "Now that we have a pro-choice White House, a pro-choice Congress, we expected a stronger social conscience. We expected a little less of the 'Let them eat cake' philosophy toward poor women." [15]

Yet that was the philosophy of the hour. In an essay soon afterward, Michelman reflected on the disintegration of the pro-choice coalition. "Hopes were high after the November election" that Clinton and Congress would enact the pro-choice agenda, she recalled.

> Barely a few months later, those hopes have given way to uncertainty. . . . The debate over the Hyde Amendment was typical; opponents of choice are mounting a relentless drive to divide and conquer America's pro-choice majority. . . . They count on women of means not to care if poor women are forced to choose between compulsory childbirth and back alleys. . . . The challenge for pro-choice America is to show that we do care. [16]

Next on the agenda was the Freedom of Choice Act. FOCA had been introduced in Congress every year since *Webster*. Each year, pro-choice lawmakers and activists had presented it as a modest codification of *Roe*. And each year, pro-life activists had branded it a radical distortion of *Roe*. It would knock down state parental notice laws, they charged, and it would "force" states "to pay for abortions without restriction." [17]

Pro-choice lawmakers had scheduled hearings on FOCA early in 1992, hoping to force President Bush to veto what they saw as a popular bill. But popularity proved elusive. Pro-lifers brandished polls indicating that FOCA, by challenging popular abortion restrictions, threatened to alienate huge majorities of Americans. NRLC released a survey showing that adults opposed FOCA when told that it would prohibit parental notice laws.[18]

Pro-choice pragmatists appreciated the perils of this attack. They renounced any suggestion that they were proposing, through FOCA, to encroach on parents' or taxpayers' rights.[19] NARAL political director James Wagoner explained this renunciation as a tragic but necessary evasion of pro-life "wedge" issues such as public funding and parental involvement:

> If you look toward the statements of the authors of the Act, they've made clear that funding is not covered by the Act. Funding wasn't covered in *Roe*, and the pro-choice movement knows fully that to obtain funding, which is a major goal of the movement, we have to move that with separate legislation. . . . In addition, the issue of mandated parental involvement laws was also not mentioned in *Roe*. And I know [FOCA's] authors got a Congressional Research Service opinion which basically stated that the Freedom of Choice Act would not overturn these laws in the states. I have to make absolutely clear that we intend to do everything we can to fight these laws in the states and to try to overturn them at the state level because we view them as so damaging.[20]

But these assurances weren't enough. Fearful that the bill would override parental consent laws and other restrictions, conservative pro-*Roe* legislators turned their backs on it. Senate majority leader George Mitchell added language permitting state restrictions on public funding and abortions for teenagers, but that, too, proved insufficient. Unable to muster enough votes to defeat additional weakening amendments, FOCA's congressional managers refused to bring the bill to the House floor for debate. That fall, the bill languished and died.[21]

FOCA's troubles laid bare the abortion rights movement's dilemma. The purpose of a federal pro-choice bill was to block restrictions that state legislatures favored. Legislatures favored these restrictions largely because voters favored them. And because voters favored them, members of Congress demanded that FOCA be amended to permit them. FOCA could pass Congress only by shedding any pretense of challenging the status quo.

This dilemma opened a public rift in the abortion rights movement in June 1992. NOW backed away from FOCA on the grounds that Mitchell and other pragmatists were accepting amendments that unduly compromised the rights of minors and poor women. The election of a pro-choice president in November intensified this quarrel by encouraging the ambitions of pro-choice purists. NOW, the Fund for a Feminist Majority, Americans for Democratic Action, and the Center for Reproductive Law and Policy repudiated FOCA. Instead, they demanded a bill that would also strike down parental involvement laws and public funding bans.[22]

The purists, among them Pat Schroeder and NOW president Patricia Ireland, made three points. First, they complained that by accommodating every restriction that was too popular to resist, FOCA had become toothless. Even FOCA's supporters saw some truth in this objection.[23]

Second, the purists worried that by purporting to guarantee abortion rights while abdicating public funding and the autonomy of minors, FOCA would sever the latter goals from the pro-choice agenda. It would engrave in federal law the conservative understanding of abortion rights. Kathryn Kolbert, the legal strategist who had led the fight against Pennsylvania's restrictions in *Casey,* warned that FOCA might "end up defeating the long-term interests of young women and poor women." Schroeder agreed. She tried to kill the pragmatists' loophole for parental involvement laws, fearing that it would encourage states that didn't yet have such laws to adopt them.[24]

Third, the purists believed that education could dissolve public support for abortion restrictions. Kolbert was unfazed by survey results demonstrating that support. "When given additional information, people change their point of view," she submitted. To prove her point, she cited the success of the pro-choice advertising campaign against Oregon's parental notice ballot measure in 1990.[25] She neglected to mention that the ad campaign had equated the parental notice measure with the abortion ban accompanying it on the ballot.

Pragmatists disputed each of these points. NARAL and Planned Parenthood, joined by the National Women's Political Caucus, the National Women's Law Center, the Women's Legal Defense Fund, and most pro-choice congressional leaders, concluded that Congress would never pass a liberal version of FOCA. Education might improve the political climate in the long run, but in the short run, the votes weren't there. Michelman called the purists' demands "unrealistic." Representative Barney Frank, a Massachusetts Democrat whose sister, Ann Lewis, had tutored Michelman in politics during her first years in Washington, insisted that FOCA wouldn't pass without a provision acknowledging parents' authority over teenagers' abortions. When Schroeder and her allies tried to kill this compromise, Frank accused them of "the worst self-defeating leftist purism." [26]

Nor did the pragmatists agree that FOCA's compromises rendered it pointless. Even if it failed to enlarge abortion rights, it would prevent a rollback. Michelman, always steeled for the worst, warned her allies that absent such restraint, states would continue to tighten their laws. Her deputy, James Wagoner, cited the same threat at the federal level. Without a compromise allowing states to require parental notice, Wagoner argued, Congress might mandate such a requirement everywhere. To underscore that threat, he pointed out that in 1991 the Senate had voted 92 to 8 to require parental notice at all federally funded family planning clinics. [27]

It was folly, the pragmatists reasoned, to pass up this chance to enshrine in federal law the core of their agenda. Michelman calculated that the inclusion of public funding would turn too many members of Congress against FOCA. And in the long run, she and her allies believed, the bill's passage would build momentum for extending abortion rights to the young and the poor. [28]

By May 1993 pro-choice vote counters realized that even with loopholes for parental involvement laws and public funding bans, Congress was prepared to amend FOCA to accommodate further restrictions such as waiting periods and bans on abortions in public hospitals. Speaker Foley announced that as things stood, FOCA wouldn't be considered. Then came the June 30 vote on the Hyde amendment, shattering the confidence and solidarity of the abortion rights movement. Several black congresswomen, led by Senator Carol Moseley-Braun, an Illnois Democrat, deserted the FOCA coalition. By summer's end, FOCA's supporters pronounced it dead. [29]

On September 28, despite concerted lobbying by Michelman and her colleagues, the Senate easily passed the revised Hyde amendment. Michelman called it "a horrible, bitter disappointment" and conceded that postelection expectations of a rollback of conservative abortion policies had been naive. "It's not a great new era," agreed Schroeder. After the vote, the columnist Ellen Goodman summarized a lesson of the abortion rights movement's seven-year emphasis on privacy and government interference: "The result of the abortion wars has been a two-tier reproductive health care system. One for the poor, one for the rest. One public and the other private." [30]

Pro-choice activists had one last chance to close the gap between public and private, by securing coverage of abortions under Clinton's national health insurance plan. The plan proposed to integrate public and private health care. Everyone would have to carry health insurance. The federal government would dictate a basic package of benefits that all insurers must include. This package would apply to the privately employed middle class as well as to the dependent poor. To thwart conservatives' portrayal of the plan as a tax-funded government program, Clinton enlisted the private sector to fund and administer it. Employers would pay most of their workers' premiums. Insurance companies would continue to collect premiums and pay for claims.

This public-private fusion offended libertarian sensibilities on both sides of the abortion fight. Officers of NRLC protested that if the basic benefits package covered abortions, the plan would "force people to pay their health premiums to fund new abortions" and would "compel private insurers and private employers to provide abortion services."[31] Hyde summarized the conservative pro-choice case against the plan:

> No insurance company could refuse to cover abortion in its policies. No individual would be able to purchase health insurance that did not cover abortion. No state could prohibit abortion coverage, as several do now. . . . And needless to say, there would be taxpayer funding of abortion on demand in Medicaid and other programs.
>   This is what's called "pro-choice."[32]

Conversely, abortion rights activists complained that if the basic benefits package omitted abortions, the government would be confiscating a benefit currently included in two-thirds of the country's private insurance policies. Michelman objected that "all of us who now have [abortion] covered under private health insurance plans would lose it. We're no longer talking about poor women and federal funds; we're talking about all women." NARAL and Planned Parenthood harped on this threat. James Wagoner even accused pro-lifers of trying to use national health insurance as a vehicle to eradicate abortion coverage.[33]

NARAL gloated over the salience of this threat to the middle class. Harrison Hickman produced a new poll and focus groups showing that middle-class women, who had largely sat out the Hyde amendment fight, wouldn't so easily abide a government health plan that removed the abortion coverage they enjoyed under their private insurance policies. Planned Parenthood vice president Bill Hamilton concurred: "Congress has always screwed poor women because they are powerless. But take this away from their wives, daughters and country club colleagues, and there will be a howl." [34]

The White House agreed. "The politics of health care is different from the politics of Medicaid," reasoned a senior Clinton aide. "This is not a 'poor people's issue.' This affects the entire middle class." Bill and Hillary Clinton reminded middle-class voters that a stripped-down national health benefits package could leave them worse off than before. When asked whether the benefits package should cover abortions, the Clintons invariably replied that the government "shouldn't take away from people some right they now have in their health insurance plan." [35]

As they articulated this threat, pro-choice activists relied on their anti-government message. Michelman raised the prospect of the White House "allowing the politicians" in each state "to make decisions" as to whether insurers would cover abortions. Another NARAL official declared, "Politicians and strangers do not have the right to choose any woman's coverage for her." Pam Maraldo complained that delegating the question of abortion coverage to a national commission would subject women to the "vagaries of a politicized body." Congress shouldn't "be able to pick and choose the services that are best for American women," said Maraldo. [36]

This entire line of argument was suicidal. Clinton's plan was predicated on lawmakers and bureaucrats choosing basic medical services for which all Americans would be insured. If citizens feared to entrust their "right to choose" insurance coverage to these "politicians," the safest course was to junk Clinton's scheme altogether. Pro-choice strategists had correctly discerned that by laying down the premise of a unified health care system for the poor and the middle class, the plan forced middle-class voters to finance abortions for the poor in order to retain abortion coverage for themselves. But the conclusion was no more obligatory than the premise. And it was that premise—unified national health care—that gave way under a barrage of ads whose language came straight out of NARAL's playbook.

On September 8, 1993, the Health Insurance Association of America, representing the insurance industry, launched the first of its "Harry and Louise" television spots. "The government may force us to pick from a few health care plans designed by government bureaucrats," said the ad's narrator. "If we let the government choose, we lose." A month later, the Republican National Committee followed with a television ad attacking "Bill Clinton's government-run system and his 100 new government bureaucracies." Citizens for a Sound Economy (CSE), a conservative think tank, chimed in with commercials in which doctors denounced "government intrusion into our medical system" that would "take away the right of the patient" to choose private medical care.[37] Another ad aired by CSE in spring and summer 1994 argued, "What most politicians are proposing would mean a big increase in bureaucracy, tax increases, loss of jobs, waiting lines, limiting your right to choose doctors, rationed medical care. Some politicians want to force this on you and your family. . . . Mandated universal coverage. Fancy words for government-controlled health care."[38]

Over several months, these and other ads focusing on "government," "bureaucracy," and "choice" turned public opinion against the Clinton plan. Between January and July 1994 the plan's net margin of support plunged from an advantage of 19 percentage points to a 15-point deficit. As the public soured, so did Congress.[39]

Clinton and his allies groped for compromises to shed the plan's big-government image. To protect the individual's right to choose not to pay for abortions, they floated the idea of requiring companies to offer each employee a choice between one insurance policy that covered abortions and another policy that didn't. Pro-lifers objected that this scheme just replaced government coercion of individuals with government coercion of employers. They preferred a compromise, adopted by the Senate Finance Committee, that gave employers the right to refuse to insure abortions altogether.[40]

Pro-choice advocates balked at the committee's solution. "Why should your employer be able to impose his conscience or her conscience on you?" asked Schroeder. A Planned Parenthood lobbyist made the same point during a parallel debate in Maryland: "We haven't wanted legislators or politicians to make this decision, and we don't want employers to make this decision either."[41]

At this point, the game was up. Only the government could prevent employers from dictating their workers' insured medical options, and thanks to the ceaseless derision to which abortion rights activists had added their voices, the government's authority lay in ruins. Pro-choicers had affirmed the sovereignty of private enterprise when, as in the case of abortion clinic regulation, it served them well. Now that it served them ill, they were stuck with it.

The death of the Clinton plan also taught a larger lesson. In the plan's final weeks, Clinton and Democratic leaders in Congress thought they might yet save it by separating and privatizing its treatment of abortion. They hoped that this would appease people who feared paying for others' abortions, as well as people who feared losing their own abortion coverage.[42] But these overtures accomplished nothing, because the fears they sought to allay transcended abortion. Americans worried about subsidizing dubious expenses for other people and about losing control of their own medical care. Abortion didn't kill the Clinton plan. Conservatism did.

On November 8, 1994, voters finished the job, sweeping Democrats out of both houses of Congress and most of the governorships they had held. Democrats lost eight seats in the Senate and fifty-two seats in the House. All eleven women running for governor that day went down to defeat. Into Congress and the nation's governorships poured a tide of men such as Governor George Pataki (R-N.Y.), Governor Tom Ridge (R-Pa.), and Senator Bill Frist (R-Tenn.), who stood for the right to choose abortion, the right to choose whether one's daughter could have an abortion, and the right to choose not to pay for anyone else's abortion.

Republican congressional leaders made clear that they would confine the abortion fight to issues of public funding. Their commander, House Speaker Newt Gingrich, described the American consensus as "pro-choice but anti-abortion." During their first year in power, often with Clinton's acquiescence, the Republicans exterminated the vestiges of pro-choice liberalism. They barred federal employees' health insurance from covering abortions. They outlawed the use of American military hospitals for abortions on U.S. servicewomen and dependents of soldiers stationed abroad. They banned federal funding of abortions for federal prisoners. And they eliminated 35 percent of U.S. aid to international family planning programs.[43]

By February 1995 every prominent Republican presidential candidate other than Pat Buchanan had assured voters that he wouldn't seriously pursue a constitutional ban on abortion. Instead, the candidates focused their abortion comments on the rights of parents and taxpayers. "I would not do it again," Senate majority leader Bob Dole replied when asked about his previous support for a constitutional ban. "I think there are other things we can do as far as parental notification." Dole's rival, Senator Phil Gramm, agreed: "We are not going to have a unity of purpose on [abortion]. And if we are going to unify the party, we have to unify it on the issue of passing the decision-making from the government to the family."[44]

Protecting taxpayers and passing responsibility to families meant, among other things, welfare reform. That was the message of another presidential candidate, Governor Pete Wilson. Having pioneered the use of financial penalties to deter undesirable births, Wilson was taking his crusade nationwide. "The argument shouldn't be about whether you are pro-choice or pro-life," he declared in 1994. "The argument ought to be about how you stem the tide of illegitimacy." In 1995 Wilson warned of the "unhappy correlation" between a hypothetical pregnant fourteen-year-old girl "and the thug she'll produce who'll become the triggerman in a teen gang." In 1996 he ordered California agencies to stop providing prenatal care to illegal immigrants. In 1997 he offered a plan to "encourage" welfare recipients to surrender their children for adoption. Pro-choice activists and child welfare advocates condemned the plan, but moral conservatives applauded it.[45]

The Norplant craze that had taken root in California under Wilson spread throughout the nation. Judges in Texas and Florida prescribed the birth control implant to women in conjunction with plea bargains for child abuse or neglect. Six states considered legislation to require Norplant for any woman on public assistance. Three others considered using financial incentives to achieve the same result. In Oklahoma, a pro-life legislator offered to pay welfare recipients $5,000 in exchange for sterilization. Medicaid administrators established an unofficial policy of paying for the insertion of Norplant in any poor woman who wanted it but refusing to pay for its removal if the woman changed her mind.[46]

The family cap, promoted by Wilson, proved even more popular. Voters favored the cap by margins of 2 to 1 or better, though whites were considerably more enthusiastic than blacks. In 1994 Republicans in Congress proposed to mandate family caps nationwide. Some advocated eliminating all cash payments to unwed mothers under the age of twenty-one and channeling the money instead to state agencies that would presumably offer conditional aid to these mothers. Another popular idea was the "illegitimacy bonus," a financial reward to states that reduced births out of wedlock. All three provisions were incorporated in Republican welfare reform legislation.[47]

As in California, the federal fight over welfare reform forced pro-life and pro-choice activists into an awkward alliance. Testifying before Congress, Michelman related how, after being deserted by her first husband, she had discovered that she was pregnant and had been "forced onto welfare" to feed and clothe her children. In such a circumstance, she observed, the family cap would "leave some women with no choice but to have an abortion." Many pro-lifers agreed.[48]

The debate over welfare reform, like the debate over abortions for rape victims, divided pro-lifers from their usual allies in the pro-family movement. In 1990 and 1991, when Louisiana lawmakers had discussed whether to exempt rape victims from a ban on abortions, moral conservatives had split along religious lines: Catholics had advocated compromise, whereas Protestants had held out for the absolute sanctity of life. This time the roles were reversed.

The Protestant-dominated groups—the Christian Coalition, the Family Research Council, Concerned Women for America, Eagle Forum, and the Traditional Values Coalition—were determined to restore and reinforce the self-supporting two-parent family. On this view, the government should encourage childbearing within such families and discourage childbearing outside them. Toward that end, these groups demanded that the welfare bill include the family cap, the ban on aid to unwed mothers, and the illegitimacy bonus.

The Catholic-dominated groups—the U.S. Catholic Conference, the National Right to Life Committee, the American Life League (ALL), and Feminists for Life—were determined never to cause the destruction of human life. They believed that the three provisions advocated by their colleagues encouraged such destruction and for that reason opposed them. "A plan to deny funding to one group of mothers because of their age and because of their economic situation suggests that no one really minds if babies conceived out of wedlock and in poverty die by abortion, so long as we can curtail illegitimate births," worried ALL president Judie Brown. NRLC president Wanda Franz added a further objection: "Denying small cash benefits to the child . . . will not only do little to reverse the cultural breakdown, but may, in fact, accelerate it by making life ever less valued."[49]

During the first year of the Republican Congress, the two pro-life factions waged an internecine war. In the first round of the welfare debate, the purists insisted that the illegitimacy bonus should be scrapped and that if cash payments to unwed teen mothers were capped or eliminated, states should be allowed either to give these girls vouchers for their babies' needs or to send cash to the girls' parents for that purpose. When Republican leaders in the House failed to accommodate them, the purists engineered a revolt. Liberal House Democrats, joined by a splinter group of pro-life Republicans, came within six votes of killing the bill.[50]

In the second round of debate, the competing pro-life factions rallied behind competing presidential candidates. The purists backed a moderate welfare reform bill offered by Senator Dole. The pro-family groups backed a stricter bill offered by Senator Gramm. The pro-family faction successfully pressured Dole to add the family cap and illegitimacy bonus to his bill. But the purists, led by the Catholic bishops, hatched another revolt that tore the cap out of the bill.[51]

The war among pro-lifers extended to a simultaneous debate over parental rights. In 1995 moral conservatives introduced the Parental Rights and Responsibilities Act, which would prohibit government interference in parents' decisions. Pro-family groups supported the bill, but pro-life activists balked. "It would permit the parents to coerce their minor daughters to obtain an abortion and [prohibit] state agencies from interfering," protested NRLC legislative director Douglas Johnson.[52] This was the same objection that NRLC's California affiliate had offered in 1992 when Wilson proposed to require teen mothers to live with their parents in order to get welfare.

Congress resolved the welfare issue in summer 1996. Pro-family groups won a provision similar to Wilson's: States would deny welfare to any child whose unmarried teenage mother failed to stay in school and live with an adult. States would also compete for the illegitimacy bonus, but any increase in abortions would count against them. The family cap would remain optional. No family would be permitted to receive welfare for more than two years at a time, or five years over a lifetime. States could shorten these time limits as they saw fit.

The House and Senate passed the bill overwhelmingly. On August 22, 1996, Clinton signed it into law, abolishing America's sixty-one-year-old guarantee of aid to poor children. "Today, we are ending welfare as we know it," he announced. In his reelection ads, Clinton pointed out that he had signed a bill against gay marriage, favored "curfews and school uniforms to teach our children discipline," and "required teen mothers on welfare to stay in school or lose benefits."[53]

While Clinton courted pro-choice conservatives, a coalition led by NARAL and Planned Parenthood sought a mandate for abortion funding. In a television ad, the coalition told voters, "Fifty times, this Congress has voted to restrict choice: prohibiting American servicewomen from getting abortions in U.S. military hospitals; denying low-income victims of rape and incest access to an abortion." The coalition's print ads continued: "Restrictions, waiting periods, consent laws—every month new controls by government, more harassment, fewer choices for women." But few voters regarded these restrictions as threats to their freedom of choice. Among those who cast their 1996 presidential ballots primarily on the basis of abortion, exit polls indicated that Clinton won only a third.[54]

Unable to ban abortion and unwilling to hurt themselves trying, Republicans adopted two new strategies. One was to defend the unborn child's life only when it coincided with the woman's choice. The other was to move the abortion debate out of the woman's body. The vehicle for this move was a rare method of terminating pregnancies, usually late in the second trimester. The doctor would dilate the cervix, pull the fetus feet-first from the womb, and then—with the fetus's head still lodged inside the woman—puncture, drain, and compress its skull to complete the extraction. An Ohio physician, Martin Haskell, advertised this method at a conference of abortionists in 1992. NRLC obtained a copy of Haskell's paper outlining the procedure. Pro-life activists brought it to the attention of Representative Charles Canady, Republican-Florida, who filed legislation to outlaw the practice.[55]

Canady and his team invented a new name for the procedure. Haskell had called it "dilation and extraction." The pro-lifers called it "partial-birth abortion." In reality, the delivery was artificial and premature. But in pro-life imagery, it was natural and full term. The baby was emerging into the world, only to be stopped, stabbed, and crushed. This was no mere abortion. It was a brutally thwarted "birth."

The distinction was legally and politically important. In a footnote to *Roe*, the Supreme Court had stipulated that its invalidation of Texas's law against abortions didn't address a separate statute that banned procedures "during parturition of the mother" to destroy "a child in a state of being born and before actual birth, which child would otherwise have been born alive." Based on that footnote, pro-life legal scholars advised Congress that partial births could be banned even if standard abortions couldn't. In public forums and congressional debates, pro-life lawmakers and activists, who otherwise tended to describe fetuses as "unborn" or "preborn," distinguished victims of the partial-birth procedure as "being born," "mostly born," or "four-fifths born." [56]

Mindful of public sympathy for the right to choose abortion, pro-life strategists separated the two issues. In a letter to Clinton, Catholic cardinals and bishops pointed out that 65 percent of pro-choice voters opposed the partial-birth procedure. "That the child is mostly born makes it different from abortion," argued Helen Alvare, spokeswoman for the

U.S. Catholic Conference. "To many, this makes it seem more like infanticide than abortion, and they bring a different judgment to it." Another pro-life activist agreed: "We're not really talking about abortion here. We're talking about a baby that's two-thirds born." [57]

In addition to the qualms raised by the fetus's relative maturity, the extraction of the intact fetus rendered the pro-choice conceptual framework irrelevant in two ways. Temporally, it separated the abortion—the termination of the pregnancy by removal of the fetus—from the stabbing and skull vacuuming that ensured the fetus's death. Spatially, it separated the fetus from the privacy of the womb. "If you still believe this little baby is a part of the woman's body, then your ignorance is invincible," said Hyde. Senator Rick Santorum, Republican-Pennsylvania, underscored the difference: "There may be a medical need to terminate a pregnancy, but there is never a need to kill the baby." [58]

The distinction between abortion and the destruction of the "partially born" fetus persuaded dozens of pro-choice politicians to endorse the ban. In May 1996 Senator Pat Moynihan, Democrat–New York, concluded, "This is just too close to infanticide. A child has been born, and it has exited the uterus, and what on earth is this procedure?" Pro-lifers quoted Moynihan far and wide, inviting other pro-choice politicians to follow him. "I'm pro-choice, but this goes above and beyond what anybody would think of as an abortion," said a Democratic leader of the Maryland legislature. The director of Republicans for Choice, Representative Scott McInnis of Colorado, campaigned avidly against the procedure. [59]

Republican presidential nominee Bob Dole emphasized the same distinction in his campaign against Clinton. "A partial-birth abortion blurs the line between abortion and infanticide and crosses an ethical and legal line we must never cross," Dole said. He added, "Regardless of your views on abortion—pro-life or pro-choice—we've got to end this partial-birth abortion." Vice presidential nominee Jack Kemp and other Republicans pressed the same argument. Polls indicated that many pro-choice voters bought it. While the proportion of voters who supported the right to choose abortion and called themselves pro-choice never fell below 52 percent, the proportion of voters who favored a ban on partial births peaked at 71 percent and never fell below 54. It wasn't enough to save Dole, but analysts agreed that the issue hurt Democrats in several House and Senate contests. [60]

Most important, the partial-birth issue allowed Republicans to mollify pro-lifers while conceding the right to abort pregnancies in the womb. Dole routinely dodged questions about a general abortion ban by changing the subject to partial births. With characteristically clumsy honesty, he cited polls to justify this diversion: "Eighty percent of the people oppose that procedure." Aides conceded that Dole was otherwise avoiding the abortion issue because voters preferred Clinton's pro-choice position. Other Republicans capitulated overtly. Kemp promised that the abortion ban proposed in the Republican platform "would not pass" and that the party would confine its anti-abortion activity to "persuasion." Gingrich agreed that in the absence of public support, a ban was out of the question. "You can't just change the law," he said.[61]

Fearing an incremental assault on all abortions, pro-choice activists groped for a persuasive defense of the partial-birth procedure. Some women obtained it for understandable reasons: Their pregnancies had gone awry and, in the opinions of their doctors, might injure or kill them or prevent them from bearing future children unless terminated in this way. Most, however, had no medical reason for having postponed the decision so far into pregnancy. Often, the woman's excuse—she was young and afraid to tell her parents, or she had failed to scrape together the cash to pay for an abortion earlier—was related to the parental involvement laws and public funding bans with which pro-lifers had wall-papered the country. But pointing this out was futile.

As Hyde and Santorum had recognized, the peculiarities of the procedure made it difficult to defend as a matter of privacy or freedom. If the pregnancy had to be ended by premature delivery, why not induce labor and expel the fetus alive, assuming that it could survive briefly, instead of mutilating it? The only conceivable answers to that question were medical, not ideological. Consequently, pro-choice activists stressed that the decision should be left to doctors. They spoke often of the woman's health but seldom of her autonomy. "Women do not choose to have late-term abortions," argued Representative Nita Lowey, Democrat–New York. "Late-term abortions occur as a result of medical necessity." Michelman agreed: "The issue is, doctors must have the autonomy to make decisions."[62]

Superficially, this argument was shrewd. Polls showed that many voters who refused to entrust abortion decisions to women were willing to entrust them to doctors. For years, pro-choice groups had finessed this trust gap by rhetorically attaching a woman's autonomy to her doctor's consent. The risk was that the two principles might come apart. That had happened in Florida in 1989 and 1990, when clinic operators thwarted legislation to protect women from unsafe abortions. And it happened again in May 1997, when the American Medical Association (AMA) joined politicians in endorsing legislation to ban partial births.

On May 14 the AMA stated in writing that it took no position on the ban. Backstage, however, Republican lawmakers were negotiating with Dr. Nancy Dickey, chair of the AMA's board of trustees. According to a subsequent AMA internal report, the organization was "determined to cut a deal with the Congressmen." The AMA wanted doctors to be insulated from criminal penalties and to be judged by their peers before any criminal proceedings were initiated. The lawmakers agreed to amend the ban accordingly.[63]

On May 19 the AMA sent Gingrich a wish list of Medicare reforms. Most of the proposals would be incorporated in Republican legislation two weeks later. They protected doctors' fees, limited their malpractice liability, and allowed them to refer patients to companies from which they profited. On the same day, the AMA's board endorsed the ban on partial births. The AMA's official rationale, later challenged by the internal report, was that the procedure "has no history in peer reviewed medical literature or in accepted medical practice development." Dickey added that because the procedure was "broadly disfavored" in polls, the AMA couldn't defend it.[64]

Even before the discovery of the doctors' simultaneous Medicare lobbying, pro-choicers reacted with disgust to the amendments secured by the AMA. "It looks like the doctors took care of themselves and not the women," grumbled Senator John Chafee, Republican–Rhode Island. Michelman accused the AMA of selling out women in exchange for congressional support on other issues. "I find it incredible that the AMA is welcoming intrusion by politicians into the doctors' professional decision making," she fumed.[65] Her complaint was misconceived. The doctors were protecting their right to make professional decisions. The decisions they were choosing to protect, however, concerned fees and self-referrals, not abortion rights—and this choice of priorities was itself a professional decision.

The authority of the medical profession, long championed by pro-choice activists, now became their nemesis. Pro-life senators and activists made the AMA's endorsement their principal argument for the ban. The next day, the bill picked up seven votes in the Senate, bringing it within three votes of the sixty-seven needed to override a veto. Clinton held the measure at bay, arguing that it lacked sufficient exceptions to protect women's health. In the meantime, most states enacted similar legislation.[66]

In the states, as in Congress, opponents of partial births distinguished them from abortions in the womb. As Dickey put it in the AMA's May 1997 endorsement letter, "The bill has no impact on a woman's right to choose an abortion consistent with Roe vs. Wade. Indeed, the procedure differs materially from other abortion procedures, which remain fully available, in part because it involves the partially delivered body of the fetus which is outside the womb." In a fact sheet distributed to lawmakers a month later, the AMA added, "The 'partial birth' gives the fetus an autonomy which separates it from the right of the woman to choose treatments for her own body." [67]

In Missouri, pro-lifers wrote this distinction into law. In January 1999 they filed legislation outlawing "infanticide," which they defined to include the killing of "a partially born living infant" or "a living infant aborted alive." The bill's purpose, according to the activist who drafted it, was to "draw the line between infanticide and legal abortion." As the bill moved through the Missouri legislature, lawmakers deleted its reference to "aborted" infants and inserted language exempting from prosecution "any person who performs or attempts to perform a legal abortion if the act that causes the death is performed prior to the child being partially born." [68]

The result was a bill that mentioned abortion only in the context of affirming its legality. It appeared to be pro-choice. In a radio ad, proponents suggested that the procedure they were proposing to ban wasn't an abortion, since it occurred outside the womb. Pro-choicers challenged this distinction, but both houses of the legislature passed the bill by lopsided margins and overrode the governor's veto.[69]

Were supporters of such bans serious about the distinction between abortions and partial births? In October 1999, a month after the Missouri bill became law, Senator Tom Harkin, Democrat-Iowa, put them to the test. During a debate on the federal ban, he offered an amendment declaring that *Roe* "secures an important constitutional right" and "should not be overturned." Harkin's colleagues passed his amendment by a vote of 51 to 48 and then turned around and approved the partial-birth ban by a vote of 63 to 34.[70] The amendment, designed to expose the assault on partial births as an assault on *Roe,* proved the opposite. The pro-choice majority, as defined by itself, remained intact.

Shifting the debate out of the womb, through partial-birth legislation, was just one way to bypass the pro-choice majority. Another way was to exempt women from laws against fetal destruction. Pro-lifers embarked on the latter course in July 1999, when Representative Canady, the original sponsor of the partial-birth ban, joined representatives Lindsey Graham, Republican–South Carolina, and Chris Smith, Republican–New Jersey, to file the Unborn Victims of Violence Act (UVVA). Again, NRLC had a hand in drafting the bill.[71]

Under UVVA, anyone who killed or injured a child "in utero" would be punished, short of execution, as though he had killed or injured the child's mother. A man who beat his wife and caused her to miscarry, for example, would be prosecuted for the child's death as well as the wife's injuries. But one category of killers was excluded. "Nothing in this section shall be construed to permit the prosecution . . . of any woman with respect to her unborn child," said the bill. The same exemption extended to anyone who performed "an abortion for which the consent of the pregnant woman has been obtained."[72]

Excluding women from abortion prosecutions wasn't a new idea. As the debate in Louisiana had illustrated, pro-lifers were unwilling to treat women as deliberate killers of their children. But UVVA didn't just exempt women from laws against abortion. It exempted abortion from laws protecting fetuses. This wasn't the usual sexist rationalization. It was a purely political concession. The right to life would no longer challenge the right to choose.

At a House hearing on July 21, 1999, Graham emphasized that UVVA was "not about abortion." Instead, he maintained, it was "about violence against women, violence against the unborn, and holding violent criminals accountable." Proponents of UVVA, like proponents of the partial-birth ban, argued that their legislation was compatible with *Roe*. "All that the [Supreme] Court held in *Roe* was that Texas could not override the rights of the pregnant woman," Notre Dame law professor Gerard Bradley testified. "It is consistent with *Roe* to say the following: As to the rest of the world—that is, to all persons, all individuals other than the pregnant woman and those cooperating with her—a legislature is entitled to recognize the unborn as a person with a right to life."[73]

Indeed, the right to life would now piggyback on the right to choose. "Please write to your U.S. Representative—even if he or she is pro-abortion—to urge the lawmaker to support and co-sponsor the Unborn Victims of Violence Act," NRLC told its members on August 10. Among the points NRLC suggested "you may want to make" was this: "Lawmakers who call themselves 'pro-choice' should support the bill because it protects babies who are injured or killed *contrary to* the choice of their mothers." When the bill reached the House floor on September 30, pro-life lawmakers repeated this point. Representative James Hansen, Republican-Utah, called the bill "the epitome of protecting the right to choose." [74]

In the House debate, pro-lifers labeled their opponents anti-choice. "We are going to divide the pro-choice and pro-abortion people today," Graham declared. He had a point. Lawmakers had ignored the right to choose life when it required welfare subsidies, and they had hesitated to protect it against domestic brutality by intruding into people's homes. But the violence Graham and his allies described, much of it perpetrated by thugs and strangers, was far more compelling than the subtle pressure of family caps and manipulative boyfriends. This wasn't just a choice issue. It was a crime issue. In his final words before the vote, Graham implored his colleagues to "prosecute criminals who want to take babies away from women who have chosen to have them." [75]

Pro-choice lawmakers recognized UVVA's long-term threat. By treating feticide as homicide, albeit by a third party, it laid the groundwork for a right to life that could eventually be asserted against the right to choose. To prevent that outcome, they offered a substitute that would impose the same penalties but would treat the assault as a crime against the woman rather than the fetus. The substitute narrowly failed, but it gave Clinton enough political cover to issue a veto threat that kept UVVA, despite its passage in the House by eighty votes, at bay for the rest of his presidency.[76]

While probing for ways to get around the pro-choice majority, pro-lifers also found ways to exploit it. In 1997 they devised a plan to make parental rights a federal issue. Studies suggested that thousands of girls were evading parental involvement laws by traveling to states in which the laws were either absent or enjoined. Clinics in the destination states advertised that they could perform abortions without telling parents.[77] To plug this loophole, Congress would have to step in.

The poster child for the new campaign was Crystal Lane, a twelve-year-old Pennsylvania girl whose eighteen-year-old boyfriend had gotten her drunk and had impregnated her while she was out cold. Crystal didn't want to tell her mother, so she turned to her sister and to her boyfriend's family. The boyfriend's mother, Rosa Hartford, drove Crystal to a New York clinic and paid for her abortion. The boyfriend later pled guilty to statutory rape. Hartford was convicted of interfering with the custody of a child, but the verdict was overturned because of improper jury instructions.[78]

Pro-lifers recognized the case as a public relations bonanza. At their prodding, Senator Spencer Abraham, Republican-Michigan, and Representative Ileana Ros-Lehtinen, Republican-Florida, crafted the Child Custody Protection Act (CCPA), which would prohibit adults from transporting girls across state lines to evade laws requiring parental involvement in abortion. The culprit could face a one-year jail term, a $100,000 fine, and a civil suit by the girl's parents. NRLC previewed the bill for reporters on January 22, 1998. On May 13 Gingrich, Senate majority leader Trent Lott, and other Republicans spoke at a press conference promoting it.[79]

A week after the press conference, Ros-Lehtinen presented the bill at a Senate hearing. The issue, she explained, was a woman's right to choose:

> Pro-abortionists scream at us about every woman's right to an abortion; about how it is a woman's right to make a choice, and how it is a woman, and only a woman, who has rights over her own body. In response to that I say, yes, it is about rights, HR 3682 is all about women's rights. The right of every mother in this nation to protect her child from the biased and selfish hand of a stranger. The right of every mother to protect her relationship between herself and her daughter.[80]

A month later, Ros-Lehtinen told the *Washington Post*, "We're not framing it as a pro-life issue, we're framing it as a parental rights issue." House majority leader Dick Armey agreed that abortion was irrelevant: "If I had someone bringing kids across state lines for tonsillectomies, I'd be equally outraged."[81] In the GOP's weekly radio address on July 18, Ros-Lehtinen portrayed CCPA as just another in a series of laws protecting parents and kids from predators.

> This Republican Congress also created the V-chip so that parents can block their children's access to materials that they deem inappropriate. . . . Just as we pursued sexual predators who prey on children through the Internet, just as we've cracked down on drug dealers who corner our children at school, we must punish those who put our daughters in physical danger simply because they won't take responsibility for the pregnancies that they create.[82]

Pro-choicers raised familiar objections. They pleaded that laws couldn't make families communicate. They labeled CCPA the Teen Endangerment Act. They said pro-lifers were chipping away at abortion rights for all women.[83] These arguments proved no more effective against CCPA than they had proved against parental involvement laws.

But CCPA wasn't just another parental involvement law. It regulated interstate commerce. In that respect, it challenged free enterprise and states' rights. Those two principles protected an industry dear to conservatives—guns—and liberals didn't hesitate to exploit the contradiction. Planned Parenthood and the ACLU cautioned that CCPA could set a precedent for federal regulation of firearms. Pro-choice lawmakers underscored that point in a July 15 House floor debate. Five days later, a *Post* editorial warned conservatives that CCPA was "a dangerous game. Should the federal government be able to criminalize crossing state lines [to] purchase guns?"[84]

The other twist CCPA added to the parental rights debate was that it didn't target minors. It targeted the adults who assisted them. This neutralized the usual pro-life argument that girls contemplating abortions needed adult supervision. Pro-choicers could point out—and did—that for girls who were determined to get abortions without telling their parents, adult supervision was exactly what CCPA precluded. Again and again, Planned Parenthood, NARAL, and NOW emphasized that girls were "vulnerable" and that CCPA would force them to "go it alone."[85]

But the same twist also neutralized the pro-choice argument that girls were entitled to make their own decisions. One way or another, in every case to which CCPA applied, an adult was involved. By emphasizing the vulnerability of girls and the importance of adult supervision, pro-choicers affirmed that this was necessary. The apparent, if not logical, implication was that the consulted adult would guide the girl's choice. The question was who that adult would be.

This was the conflict pro-lifers wanted: parents versus outsiders. Given that choice, there were many reasons to side with parents. On May 21, a day after presenting CCPA to the Senate, Ros-Lehtinen reminded her House colleagues, "Nowhere in the Constitution does it say that a stranger has more rights to parent and oversee the welfare of my child than I have. Parents know the medical history of their child; a stranger does not. Parents know a child's reaction to pressure of this nature. Parents are capable of comforting their children in their greatest time of need; a stranger is not."[86]

Above all, parents deserved a presumption of sovereignty. A stranger who took their daughter to another state was, in a sense, a thief. As Ros-Lehtinen put it in her radio address, Rosa Hartford had "robbed a mother of her rights to protect her child." More clearly than any other pro-life legislation, CCPA posed the question: Who decides? You or them?

Recognizing that they were on the losing end of that question, pro-choicers turned to the scenario they had often raised against parental involvement laws: incest. Among girls who refused to divulge pregnancies to their parents, they asserted, one in three had been physically, emotionally, or sexually abused by a family member. CCPA might force some of those girls to consult the abusers who had impregnated them.[87]

But the adult-versus-adult framework of the CCPA debate confounded that argument, too. While sexual abuse by a girl's parents was possible, sexual abuse by the adult who spirited her away for an abortion was far more likely. Every girl subject to a parental involvement law was a minor. Her boyfriend was almost certainly older. Sex between a minor and an adult was, by definition, statutory rape. If the boyfriend transported the girl to the abortion or helped to arrange her transportation, he was at least technically covering up a crime.

Gingrich and Lott made much ado of this point. Other conservatives described CCPA as a measure to stop sexual predators and "child molesters."[88] Testifying before the House and Senate, Crystal Lane's mother hammered the word *rape:*

> My child was provided alcohol, raped and then taken out of state by a
> stranger to have an abortion. This stranger turned out to be the mother of
> the adult male who provided the alcohol and then raped my 12-year-old
> daughter while she was unconscious. The rapist's mother arranged and
> paid for an abortion . . . to destroy evidence—evidence that my 12-year-
> old daughter had been raped.[89]

Even in cases in which no rape was involved, pro-lifers could accuse the transporting adult of kidnapping. Lane's mother leveled that charge at Hartford. The founder of Mothers Against Minors' Abortions extended it to every adult covered by CCPA.[90]

In sum, pro-choicers couldn't defeat CCPA by complaining about parental coercion or parental sex crimes, because sex crimes and coercion were more common among boyfriends and other adults who escorted girls to abortions. With CCPA, as with UVVA, pro-lifers had a point. They were standing up, in some cases, for the right to choose life. "Many teenage girls are impregnated by adult men" who "put heavy pressure on their immature partners to dispose of the problem as quickly as possible," observed the *Chicago Tribune* columnist Steve Chapman. "Is that what abortion rights advocates call 'freedom of choice'?"[91]

Given the impossibility of winning a debate between parents and out-siders, the only plausible strategy for defeating CCPA was to blur the distinction between them. In place of the boyfriends and "strangers" whose crimes pro-lifers denounced, pro-choicers shifted the debate to sisters, aunts, and grandparents. They argued that this circle of relatives had the pregnant girl's best interests at heart and that CCPA should be amended to let them help the girl get an abortion.[92]

This strategy had almost always failed against parental involvement laws. No matter how close the relatives were for whom pro-choicers sought exceptions, they weren't parents. Aunts and grandmothers might not be sufficiently involved in the girl's life. Sisters might not be mature enough. None of these relatives bore ultimate responsibility for the girl. As long as the question was who should decide, parents would prevail.

But that wasn't the only question at stake. The flaw in CCPA was that it separated "Who decides?" from the related question of whether women who got abortions would be treated as criminals. In 1989 and 1990 those two arguments—"Congressman Jones wants to take away your right to choose and send women to jail"—had beaten pro-lifers. With CCPA, pro-lifers had captured the first argument. But their emphasis on prosecution put them on the wrong end of the second argument. It was one thing to say that a girl's grandmother had no right to circumvent the girl's parents by driving the girl to an abortion clinic. It was another thing to throw the grandmother in jail. Pro-choicers brought up this scenario repeatedly, tugging at their colleagues' unease about locking up family members. As Representative Lowey put it in the House floor debate, "Under this legislation grandmothers will be jailed for helping their granddaughters, aunts imprisoned for assisting their nieces, brothers for aiding their sisters, all in the name of so-called family values. What will the police do? Set up granny checkpoints to catch grandmothers helping their granddaughters? Will we have dogs and searchlights at State borders to lock up aunts and uncles?"[93]

This critique didn't kill CCPA, but it threw up two obstacles that blocked the bill's path. It gave Clinton a safe reason to oppose the bill. Pro-lifers knew from his record that Clinton was sympathetic to paren-tal notice laws. In a letter to Congress on June 17, White House chief of staff Erskine Bowles said Clinton would support CCPA if it were "properly crafted." The letter irked pro-choicers who had hoped Clin-ton would threaten to veto the bill, but it outlined several changes the president wanted. Chief among them was an exception for family members.[94]

The same objection gave pro-choice lawmakers a basis to vote against CCPA. When House Republicans refused to consider amendments, 150 representatives voted against the bill. That was enough to sustain a veto, making clear that the bill would die unless relatives were exempted from prosecution. Senate Republicans took the same hard line against amendments, and on September 22 Senate Democrats filibustered the bill to death.[95]

The Republican push for parental rights didn't stop at abortion. In 1996 Representative Ernest Istook, Republican-Oklahoma, launched a campaign to require parental consent for minors seeking birth control at federally funded clinics. Istook framed the issue as families versus government, appealing to taxpayers and parents. "If mama says no, Uncle Sam should not wink and say yes," he argued.[96] In a House floor debate on July 11, 1996, Istook complained,

> We are spending $200 million a year of our Federal tax money, one-third of which goes to provide contraceptives, condoms, birth control pills, and related services to teenagers, to minors, with neither the knowledge nor the consent of their parents. . . .
>
> [T]his vote is going to show whether we believe in families and family responsibility or in Government taking over the major aspects of what we teach our children. President Clinton says: Government does not raise children; families do. I say to my colleagues, Then show you mean it.[97]

Unable to defeat Istook's proposal outright, opponents offered alternative language requiring the clinics to "encourage family participation in the decision of the minor to seek family planning services." The alternative prevailed by thirty-nine votes.[98]

A year later, Istook and Representative Don Manzullo, Republican-Illnois, returned with a slicker pitch. They offered to require parental notice rather than consent, and they built their case around a villain in the mold of Rosa Hartford. The villain was William Saturday, a junior high school teacher who, during a sexual relationship with a fourteen-year-old student, had taken the student to a public health clinic for contraceptive injections.[99] To the issues of parental rights and public funding, the Saturday case added a third angle: sex crimes. As Istook explained to his colleagues on September 9, 1997,

> Studies in recent years have shown that 60 percent of young women who have sex before the age of 15 were coerced by males an average of 6 years older than them. . . . Sexual predators who prey on young women [can] keep the relationship going, because they simply take them to a Title X

clinic, a Federal clinic, where they are given the contraceptives and their parents are never told about it. A situation that under the laws of almost any State in the country would be illegal, that might be labeled sexual abuse or child abuse or molestation or statutory rape, is totally ignored.[100]

Istook had raised the ante. To meet it, his opponents offered to require clinics not only to "encourage family participation" but also to "provide counseling to minors on how to resist attempts to coerce minors into engaging in sexual activities." This time, even with the additional requirement, the alternative language prevailed by just nineteen votes.[101]

On the third try, Istook got through. On October 8, 1998, by a twenty-four-vote margin, the House adopted his parental notice requirement. Unable to kill the requirement in public, opponents buried it offstage in a House-Senate conference committee.[102]

In 1999 Republicans shifted from parental rights to public funding. They targeted U.S. aid to family planning organizations that promoted abortion rights overseas. A year earlier Congress had voted to prohibit such aid as part of a bill that would have paid U.S. dues to the United Nations. In response, Clinton had vetoed the bill. By November 1999 the standoff was becoming dangerous. If the United States didn't pay its dues by the end of 1999, it would lose its vote in the UN General Assembly.[103]

Congressional leaders refused to withdraw the prohibition. "It's about the issue of using taxpayer money to fund abortions," said a spokeswoman for House majority leader Armey. In early November Clinton's chief of staff assured pro-choicers that Clinton wouldn't back down. But a few days later, Clinton agreed to sign the funding ban into law. In exchange, Congress agreed to pay the UN dues, review the ban the following year, and grant Clinton authority to waive the ban until then. Use of the waiver would automatically reduce the total allocation for family planning.[104]

The White House boasted that since the president could tinker with the ban's implementation, in practice, Clinton had conceded almost nothing. What he had conceded was a principle: Funding of pro-choice organizations would be presumed illegal unless the president intervened. The party that controlled the White House would control the purse strings. Pro-choice activists were furious. "This is not a compromise," said Michelman. "This is capitulation."[105]

Having established a precedent for the funding ban, the House passed it again in July 2000. Clinton aides promised that the president wouldn't give in again, but nobody believed them. On October 24 the White House cut another deal. Republicans agreed to lift the funding ban after February 15, 2001, and Clinton agreed to honor it until then.[106] By that time, a new president—either Vice President Al Gore or Texas governor George W. Bush—would be in office.

The new deal multiplied the wager made in the old one. The president would call the shots. If Gore won, he would restore funding to the family planning groups. If Bush won, he would ban it. Michelman welcomed the deal but worried that it was "a bit tenuous." Once more, pro-choice liberalism would square off against pro-choice conservatism. Representative Nancy Pelosi, Democrat-California, summarized the mood of the hour. "Everybody's betting on the election," she said.[107]

CHAPTER 10

Fatal Position

In 1978 a young businessman ran for Congress in West Texas. "I'm not for the federal funding of abortions," he told the Lubbock *Avalanche-Journal*. According to the newspaper, the candidate said he opposed a constitutional amendment outlawing abortion "and favor[ed] leaving up to a woman and her doctor the abortion question." The candidate was George W. Bush.[1]

A decade later, having lost that race, Bush watched his father grapple with the storm of *Webster*. In Texas, he helped Clayton Williams to battle Ann Richards in the gubernatorial race of 1990. "Instead of sitting back and waiting for the [abortion] issue to come to him, I think Claytie is going to go right after her and point out to people that she is on the extreme left wing," Bush predicted.[2] Williams did just that, hammering Richards for opposing parental consent. After Williams lost, liberals gloated that his strategy had failed. Bush set out to prove them wrong. In 1994 he would seek the same office, run on the same themes, use the same abortion tactics, avoid Williams's gaffes, and win.

Bush proposed to cut welfare spending, deregulate schools, and lock up criminals. He sketched a power struggle between government and families, pledging to broaden parental rights and tighten the leash on teenagers. Juvenile offenders would be dealt with severely. Teenage welfare mothers would have to live with their parents. Schools would be barred from distributing condoms. Parents would be offered vouchers to wrest their children from education bureaucrats. Minors would be al-

lowed to have guns if and only if their parents consented. It wasn't hard
to extend this logic to abortion. With mechanical consistency, Bush declared the criminalization of abortion a moot issue and changed the subject to parental notice. "I view that as a family rights issue," he said.[3]

Richards toed the liberal pro-choice line—"There are no ifs, ands
or buts on this issue with me"—and assailed Bush for his nominal position, mysteriously acquired since 1978, that abortion should be outlawed. "This election is about whether or not government is going to get
in and mess around in your private life," she told voters. But *Casey* had
dissolved fears that abortion might be banned, and Bush seemed an implausible crusader for such a policy. His father, mother, and wife had re-
coiled from the issue with obvious distaste.[4]

On the campaign trail, Bush featured his mother. Two months before
the election, she went on tour to promote *Barbara Bush: A Memoir*. In
the book, she declared, "For me, abortion is a personal issue—between
mother, father and doctor. If a minor is involved you can add parents
to that list." When asked about abortion, George W. Bush replied, "My
mother and I agree on parental consent. Ann Richards does not agree
with that. Most Texans agree with me on that." [5]

The state's leading pro-life groups fell into line, endorsing Bush's focus on parental rights and calling Richards "out of touch with mainstream Texans" on that issue. On November 8 the strategy paid off. Bush
won by the biggest margin in a Texas gubernatorial race in twenty years.
A survey taken afterward found that on parental notice, school vouchers, and gun control, Texans preferred Bush's positions to Richards's.[6]

Bush was the perfect synthesis of the lessons of the past eight years. He
was pro-life and pro-choice, pursuing popular restrictions while reducing the prohibition of abortion to an inconsequential statement of principle. "The United States Supreme Court has settled the abortion issue.
There will be abortions in Texas and the rest of the United States," Bush
assured pro-choice voters in 1994. He added, "We require parental consent for other surgical decisions—why should we make an exception in
this case?" [7]

Every two years, as pro-choicers and pro-lifers warred over the Republican platform, Bush soothed both sides. He defended the abortion-
banning language pro-lifers had fought to put in the document. Meanwhile, he signaled to pro-choicers that the platform meant nothing. In
1994, when he was asked about his difference with the Texas Republican platform—namely, that he would permit abortion in cases of rape

or incest—Bush said he hadn't read the platform. In 1998 he shrugged, "Platforms are statements of principles. If I disagree with certain parts of the platform, I just move on and campaign." [8]

Bush opposed efforts to strip the abortion plank from the GOP's national platform, explaining that "it's very important for the Republican Party to be viewed as the pro-life party." But he showed no interest in making the document binding on Republican candidates, much less the public. In the name of tolerance and local control, he spurned proposals to require that the Republican vice presidential nominee be pro-life and to cut off GOP aid to candidates who wouldn't ban partial-birth abortions. In private, Bush reportedly ridiculed abortion opponents. [9]

Pro-lifers forgave Bush's toothless view of the platform because when it came to controlling teenagers, empowering parents, and restricting state funding, he delivered. In 1995 he signed into law bills that stiffened sentences for juvenile offenders, extended the application of teen curfews, allowed the imposition of school uniforms, and expanded the ability of parents to choose their children's schools. Two years later Bush secured budget language forbidding the use of state money to provide birth control to minors without their parents' consent. When Planned Parenthood protested that teenagers should be able to get confidential medical care, Bush shot back, "I view this as a parental-rights issue." [10]

In 1997 Bush appointed a new Texas health commissioner, Reyn Archer, who had served in his father's administration as chief advocate of the ban on federally funded abortion counseling. When Archer decided to stop funding new school-based health clinics, Bush stood by him. The decision was "very much in line with the family values message of Governor Bush," since the clinics "refuse to give assurances that they will not engage in abortion counseling or family planning counseling," said Bill Price, the state's top pro-life lobbyist. In 1999 Bush signed legislation prohibiting teenagers from getting their bodies pierced without their parents' written approval. [11] And that year Bush finally won the prize that would clear his path to the Republican presidential nomination: a law requiring parental notice for abortion.

Richards and Democrats in the state senate had blocked parental notice for years. In 1994 Bush ousted Richards; two years later he targeted the state senate. In June 1996 he lambasted Texas Democrats for failing to state a platform position on parental consent. "I think the waffling on parental consent by the Democrat[ic] Party indicates they are against it and they are not willing to take a position that the vast majority of Texans believe in," Bush said. "It's an extreme position not to allow parents to be involved, to have consent, in a minor daughter's decision. . . . I'm prepared to make it an issue." [12]

In November 1996 Republicans captured the state senate. Prodded by Bush, they passed a parental notice bill. Opponents in the house derailed it with a parliamentary maneuver, so Bush made it an issue in his reelection campaign. At the 1998 Texas Republican convention, he pledged to make parental consent a "major legislative plank" in his second term. He trounced his challenger with more promises of tax cuts, welfare reform, aid to private schools, and a war on juvenile crime. [13]

Bush's landslide victory solidified his standing as the Republican presidential front-runner. In his State of the State address on January 27, 1999, he urged Texas legislators to use his potential candidacy to showcase a bipartisan agenda of "limited government, local control, strong families and personal responsibility," including parental notice. By March 7, when he opened the exploratory phase of his campaign, he had formulated a three-step answer to any abortion query. Fielding his first question on that subject, he nodded to pro-lifers in principle (the GOP should maintain a "pro-life tenor"), winked to pro-choicers in practice (banning abortions is "hypothetical"; "our party is big enough for good people to be able to disagree"), and changed the subject to restrictions favored by pro-choice Republicans: mandating parental notice, abolishing public funding, and outlawing partial-birth abortions. The next day, Bush repeated the formula in an interview with the Associated Press: the nod ("I'm a pro-life person"), the wink ("America is not ready to ban abortions"), and the pivot to parental involvement. [14]

Several Republican presidential candidates—Gary Bauer, Pat Buchanan, Steve Forbes, and Alan Keyes—pounced on Bush's equivocation. Bauer protested that Bush was "operationally pro-choice" and represented a new breed of politicians who "say they are pro-life and then the inevitable next word is 'but,' and every word after that explains that nothing can be done." In response, Bush noted that something could be done and was being done: With Bush's emphatic support, parental notice legislation was moving through the Texas legislature. On May 25, as the state senate gave the bill its final approval, Bush placed a phone call to the senate floor to congratulate the bill's sponsor, state senator Florence Shapiro. [15]

Bush and Shapiro were adamant that girls notify parents rather than grandparents, aunts, or adult siblings. When opponents tried to amend the bill to let girls consult these other relatives instead, Shapiro replied,

"This is not a grandmother's right or an aunt's rights bill. This is a parental rights bill." As for ministers or counselors, Shapiro scoffed, "I call that triple bypass. You bypass the parents, then the judiciary, and now give this to the clergy." Bush agreed. "I am not comfortable with alternative bypasses," he said. As a last resort, opponents offered an amendment that would let a girl consult a close relative other than her parents if she hadn't lived with either parent for thirty days. "This is for the parents who have walked away from responsibility," the amendment's sponsor pleaded. But that amendment, too, was rejected.[16]

On June 7, four days before embarking on his debut tour of Iowa and New Hampshire, Bush staged a ceremony in Dallas to sign the bill. He made clear that it involved more than one issue. "I believe that government can encourage—like they do in all other kinds of medical decisions—for minor daughters to interface with their parents," Bush said. He also renewed his call for a ban on state funding of abortions.[17]

On the campaign trail, Bush continued his Texas Three-Step, paying lip service to an abortion ban while effectively ruling it out and focusing instead on popular restrictions. In New Hampshire a week after his signing ceremony, Bush refused to pledge to appoint Supreme Court justices who would overturn *Roe*. While envisioning a world free of abortions, he added, "I'm talking about an ideal world, and we don't live in an ideal world right now. So in the meantime . . . we need a leader to bring people to understand the importance of banning partial-birth abortion, having parental notification laws and not spending taxpayer money on abortion."[18]

In a speech to the Christian Coalition and an interview on *Meet the Press,* Bush emphasized the Texas parental notice law. As for banning abortion, he assured *Meet the Press* viewers, "The country is not ready for a constitutional amendment. There is no chance, at this moment, that there'd be a two-thirds vote out of the House and the Senate." Bush's spokeswoman added that he would abolish "the use of taxpayer money to promote abortions in foreign countries." In the presidential primary debates, Bush stuck to his tripartite message. Would he preserve the GOP's pro-life platform plank? Yes. Would he pledge to appoint only pro-life judges to the Supreme Court? No. What would he do to reduce abortions? Notify parents, ban partial-birth abortions, teach abstinence, and promote adoption.[19]

By late January Bush had assuaged both sides. Pro-lifers would get their platform and help from the White House on politically feasible restrictions. Pro-choicers would retain abortion as an option for adults who could afford it. On January 20, when Bush was asked what a friend or relative should do if she were impregnated by rape, he replied, "It's up to her." Two days later he told reporters that the details of an abortion ban would "be up to the Congress, if America is ever ready for a constitutional amendment." [20] The "when" of patience had faded to the "if" of acquiescence.

While other Republican candidates decried Bush's capitulation, the pro-life establishment rallied around him. Weary after eight years under an avowedly pro-choice president and alarmed by the prospect of another four, NRLC defended Bush's pro-life credentials and chastised his rivals for doubting him. Pat Robertson endorsed Bush's "incremental approach," reasoning that a constitutional ban was unrealistic and that the governor "needs to be portrayed as a centrist candidate." Robertson's former righthand man, Ralph Reed, attributed Bush's strength on the right in part to "a desire on the part of a growing number of pro-life and pro-family leaders to insure that their own political position is in accordance with the political reality." [21]

Political reality intruded sooner than these pragmatists expected. The candidate who caught fire in the primaries wasn't Forbes, Buchanan, or another pro-lifer to Bush's right. It was Senator John McCain of Arizona, who ran straight down the middle, drawing independents and Democrats into open Republican primaries. Like Bush, McCain courted pro-lifers by reminding them of his support for parental consent, a ban on partial-birth abortions, and restrictions on public funding. Like Bush, he assured pro-choicers that he wouldn't prohibit previability abortions for paying adults. [22]

There was one notable difference, however. While Bush's striptease stopped short of admitting that he was subordinating pro-life ends to pro-choice means, McCain's went all the way. "Certainly in the short term, or even the long term, I would not support repeal of *Roe vs. Wade*," McCain declared in August 1999. Instead, he pledged "to work with both pro-life and pro-choice Americans so that we can eliminate the need for abortions." Such naked surrender horrified pro-lifers. It "sounds like something Kate Michelman would say," sputtered Darla St. Martin, NRLC's associate director. [23]

As the religious right turned against McCain, independents and conservative Democrats rallied to him. By the eve of the New Hampshire primary, he posed the principal threat to Bush's nomination. Bush operatives looked for an opportunity to derail the insurgent. On January 26 they thought they'd found it. A reporter asked McCain whether, if his fifteen-year-old daughter, Meghan, got pregnant, he would "tell her that she could not get an abortion." McCain said he wouldn't. "This would be a private decision that we would share within our family and not any-one else," said the senator. "The final decision would be made by Meg-han with our advice and counsel."[24]

Within minutes, McCain's aides realized he had blundered. The sen-ator placed a phone call to the traveling press corps to revise his answer. "This is a family decision," he said. "The family decision will be made by the family, not by Meghan alone. Other than that, I believe that it is a private family matter." At a campaign stop afterward, McCain reiter-ated that the decision as to what his daughter would do about a preg-nancy was "a family decision, not her decision." "[My wife] and I will make that decision," he said.[25]

McCain's fumble and recovery were misconstrued on all sides. Afraid of being tagged a liberal, he refused to admit that the position he had just articulated was pro-choice. "I don't think it is the pro-choice posi-tion to say that my daughter and my wife and I will discuss something that is a family matter that we have to decide," the senator protested, borrowing NARAL's language without acknowledgment. Meanwhile, the press missed the significance of McCain's correction. Comparing McCain's answers to those given by Dan Quayle in 1992, reporters sug-gested that both men had retreated from their pro-life voting records.[26] Nobody pointed out the more salient resemblance: McCain, like Quayle, had distinguished his position from that of the left not by demanding a ban on abortion but by insisting that parents call the shots.

Bush's supporters also misread McCain's remarks. NRLC political director Carol Tobias suggested that McCain wasn't really pro-life, be-cause "he is saying he supports overturning *Roe vs. Wade* but he is not saying when." Bush spokesman Ari Fleischer challenged McCain to ex-plain his inconsistency.[27] But the inconsistency was no less true of Bush. He, too, refused to say when *Roe* should be overturned. Bush and NRLC hadn't exposed McCain's hypocritical tolerance of abortion. McCain had exposed theirs.

On February 1 McCain trounced Bush in New Hampshire. Within hours, Bush's strategists gathered in a hotel room in South Carolina, the next important primary state, to plot McCain's destruction. Resolving to paint McCain as a liberal, they mapped out the help they could ex-pect from friendly interest groups. "Right to Life will do radio," one strategist told the team. Three days later, staffers from NRLC's national office showed up at a board meeting of the local NRLC affiliate, South Carolina Citizens for Life (SCCL), to urge the board to support Bush. One board member resigned, accusing NRLC of coercion and pointing out that Bush had refused to pledge to appoint pro-life judges. But on February 9 SCCL, joined by a National Right to Life PAC, endorsed Bush and announced a campaign of radio ads, mailings, and phone calls urging pro-lifers to vote for him.[28]

Pro-life groups had been running ads against McCain for weeks. The reason, according to NRLC legislative director Douglas Johnson, was that McCain, while wearing "the badge of pro-life," was courting pro-choicers by "signaling he would be no threat to the status quo." But Bush was playing the same game. Moreover, the third candidate still in the race, Alan Keyes, was unambiguously pro-life. Why should pro-lifers vote for Bush? In their radio ads, NRLC and SCCL gave no reason other than that they and Hyde had endorsed Bush.[29] But that begged the question. Why had they endorsed Bush?

In a Bush campaign ad aired on conservative radio programs and de-livered by phone to one hundred thousand pro-life households, Hyde gave his answer. Alluding to McCain's belief that the platform should be changed—but not mentioning that the change would only allow abor-tions in cases of rape or incest—Hyde told listeners, "It has been sug-gested that changes be made to the party platform on the life issue. I'm totally opposed to these changes. . . . George W. Bush agrees. I am en-thusiastically supporting Gov. Bush for president. He has a strong pro-life record in Texas." And what did that record consist of? "A parental notification bill that is a model for the nation," said Hyde.[30]

With that, the pro-life establishment joined Bush's three-step dance. Bush's defense of the platform was sufficient. It didn't matter that on the point in question—exceptions for rape and incest—Bush, like McCain, disagreed with the platform. It didn't matter that Bush had said he felt free to ignore the platform. It didn't matter that Bush had said he would leave the implementation of such a ban to Congress, "if America is ever ready." The only substantial deed or commitment required of Bush was the parental notice law he had signed. On February 18 pro-life South Carolinians went to the polls and buried McCain. For all practical pur-poses, Bush had become the Republican nominee, and pro-life pragma-tism and pro-choice conservatism had become indistinguishable.

Meanwhile, Democrats were debating Bill Clinton's legacy. Clinton had repudiated the left by emphasizing fiscal discipline, welfare reform, and deference to parents on moral issues. At the same time, he had defended middle-class entitlements against the Gingrich revolution. Had the triumph of 1996 debunked the lessons of 1994? Had Clinton made the world safe for liberalism?

Former senator Bill Bradley, Democrat–New Jersey, wagered that the answer was yes. He entered the presidential race on a platform of universal health care, campaign finance reform, and gun control. Vice President Al Gore took a more cautious approach. He entered the race with an agenda of limiting suburban sprawl, helping parents to protect their kids from smut, "working more closely with faith-based organizations," and "giving people the skills and knowledge to succeed in their own right." [31]

Gore's record on abortion matched his moderate platform. In 1984 he had cautioned that "any proposed constitutional amendment [to ban abortion might] put the federal government in the middle of some situations where I don't think the majority of Tennesseans want the federal government to be involved." On the same anti-government grounds, he had voted repeatedly in Congress to prohibit public funding of abortions under Medicaid or federal employee health plans. Forcing taxpayers to fund abortions "violates the relationship between the government and the individual," Gore explained in a 1980 letter. Six years later, he told the *Washington Monthly,* "It is quite correct that a position like mine in opposition to the federal funding of abortion results in unequal access to abortions on the part of poor women. Nevertheless, I feel the principle of the government not participating in the taking of what is arguably human life is more important." [32]

As he approached the 1988 Democratic presidential primaries, Gore stopped voting for abortion funding restrictions. His public posture, however, remained libertarian. He denied that such restrictions affected freedom of choice. "I have never supported restrictions on the ability of the woman to make a choice in having an abortion," he insisted. Campaigning for the vice presidency in 1992, Gore repeated that freedom and funding were separate issues and that he opposed tax-funded abortions. In the White House, he stayed in the background as pro-lifers used his own words, expressed in a 1987 letter, to win reinstatement of the Hyde amendment.[33]

Launching his presidential campaign in June 1999, Gore repeated the libertarian formula: "Responsible men and women must make their own most personal decisions based on their own consciences, not government interference." Two months later he ducked a *Des Moines Register* survey question about abortion funding. An aide said Gore had long opposed the practice because "government should not be involved in those decisions." While Gore's media adviser claimed that Gore endorsed Medicaid-funded abortions, his press secretary said that Gore supported current law allowing Medicaid to pay for the procedure in cases of rape or incest.[34] That language, while allowing liberals to infer that Gore would go further, suggested to conservatives that he wouldn't.

Bradley recognized Gore's double game and attacked it. Pointing to Gore's voting record and evasive statements, the former senator charged that the vice president wasn't really pro-choice. Forced to defend himself to a liberal electorate, Gore withdrew his equivocation. "I have come to believe that because poor women deserve the same constitutional right to safe, legal abortions that more affluent women have, they need Medicaid funding so they can make that decision for themselves," said Gore. When Clinton agreed to sign the ban on U.S. aid to family planning organizations that promoted abortion rights overseas, Gore's aides told the media that Gore had opposed the deal.[35]

Two weeks after Gore edged out Bradley in New Hampshire, NARAL endorsed the vice president. The endorsement, which Gore parlayed into television ads, destroyed Bradley's favorite line of attack. Bradley campaign manager Gina Glantz, a veteran of NARAL's "Who Decides?" campaign, was outraged. Gore's position was no better than Bradley's, and Gore's lifetime voting record was, by NARAL's rating system, vastly inferior.[36] NARAL had never taken sides in a presidential primary before. Why now?

One explanation, repeated by Michelman to numerous reporters, was that the threat of losing abortion rights under a Republican president was too grave to let Bradley "divide pro-choice voters" over the alleged sincerity of Gore's conversion to abortion funding. The other explanation, given to the *Washington Post* by unidentified NARAL officials, was that NARAL expected Gore to win the nomination and wanted to gain his favor. "We believe he can win," NARAL PAC cochair Richard Gross told the *Post*. "We do not believe Bradley can win." According to Gross, NARAL's survey research—conducted by Gore's pollster, Harrison Hickman—had prompted the endorsement by underscoring the damage Bradley's abortion attacks were inflicting on the vice president.[37]

Michelman's sole complaint against Bradley was that his questions about Gore's sincerity were dishonest. But Michelman never answered those questions or reconciled Gore's rhetoric with his record. Instead, the endorsement clarified a pattern of disregard for the policy distinctions on which the dispute focused. In 1989 NARAL had endorsed Doug Wilder, despite his conservative interpretation of abortion rights, because no liberal alternative was available. In 1990, when Andrew Young offered NARAL a liberal alternative to Zell Miller, NARAL had refused to take sides. Now, in the Gore-Bradley race, NARAL was taking sides against the candidate who claimed the more liberal position. Only one principle applied to all three cases: NARAL didn't want to let "divisions" over abortion funding or parental consent damage its relations with the candidate most likely to win.

On February 26, a week after NARAL and NRLC finished off Bradley and McCain, Nebraska attorney general Don Stenberg filed a brief at the Supreme Court in the case of *Stenberg v. Carhart*. Officially, the question at stake was whether states could ban partial-birth abortions. Unofficially, that question turned on two others. The first was whether partial births were abortions. The second was whether decisions about the safety of alternative abortion procedures should be made by states or by each woman's doctor.

Stenberg told the Court that "the public's understanding of what constitutes a legal abortion simply does not include the partial-birth/D&X procedure." That, he argued, was why "pro-choice" legislators in Nebraska and twenty-nine other states had banned partial births: "The general public clearly does not view the procedure as falling within the liberty right protected by *Roe v. Wade* and *Casey* due, in large part, to the fact the child is primarily outside the womb when it is killed." [38]

In a brief filed two days later, NRLC and four other pro-life groups agreed that partial-birth bans were overwhelmingly popular because "Americans do not even regard the partial-birth procedure as within the realm of what they consider to be 'abortion.'" In abortion, the fetus was killed and removed in the same act. In the partial-birth, or D&X, procedure, the removal of most of the fetus preceded the killing. The right "to terminate a pregnancy is protected by *Roe* and *Casey*," NRLC and its allies conceded. But that right—"the right to empty the womb—does not of necessity include a right to feticide." [39]

On March 29 the Center for Reproductive Law and Policy (CRLP) filed a response on behalf of Stenberg's adversary, Dr. LeRoy Carhart. CRLP rejected the distinction between abortions and partial births. Twice, CRLP described the partial-birth ban as an attempt to limit abortion rights based on the fetus's "location in the woman's body." This was a clever phrase. Since the point of the ban was to move the debate out of the woman's body, the word *in* stripped the word *location* of its significance. In case anyone missed the phrase, CRLP attorney Simon Heller repeated it twice more during the April 25 oral argument.[40]

The parties also disagreed about whether it could sometimes be necessary to perform a D&X, as opposed to another abortion procedure, to safeguard a woman's health. Carhart said it could be; Nebraska said it couldn't. Stenberg asked the Court to accept Nebraska's answer because "where opinions by medical witnesses are in disagreement, the decision regarding the regulation of medical procedures should be left to the state legislature." CRLP replied that doctors should decide, case by case, whether safety issues justified the procedure. "This Court has never permitted a State to substitute its judgment for the physician's about when a woman's health is compromised," CRLP argued.[41] In other words: Who should decide—doctors or politicians?

On June 28 the Court answered both questions. Justice Kennedy, joined by Chief Justice Rehnquist, sided with Stenberg. So did Justice Thomas, in a separate opinion joined by Rehnquist and Justice Scalia. Thomas agreed that the killing of the "partially born" fetus "closely borders on infanticide." Kennedy wrote that the D&X "perverts the natural birth process" and that Nebraska, while banning it, had "protected the woman's autonomous right of choice" regarding abortion. Both justices quoted the AMA's 1997 statement that in a partial birth, unlike an abortion, the fetus was "killed outside of the womb," where it had "an autonomy which separates it from the right of the woman to choose treatments for her own body."[42]

Justice Breyer, writing for Justices Ruth Ginsburg, O'Connor, Souter, and Stevens, disagreed. "We do not understand how one could distinguish" a partial birth from an abortion based on Nebraska's definitions, Breyer concluded. Nor could the majority accept Stenberg's claim that the Nebraska law "distinguishes between the overall 'abortion procedure' itself and the separate 'procedure' used to kill the unborn child." Therefore, the law banned conventional abortions, in violation of *Roe* and *Casey*.[43]

Furthermore, said Breyer, the appropriateness of medical procedures depended on "particular cases" in which doctors' opinions "often differ." Accordingly, "*Casey* requires the statute to include a health exception when the procedure is 'necessary, in appropriate medical judgment, for the preservation of the life or health of the mother.'" Nebraska's law lacked such an exception. The dissenters disputed that this was essential. By letting the doctor perform a D&X "whenever he believes it will best preserve the health of the woman," Kennedy protested, "the Court awards each physician a veto power over the State's judgment that the procedures should not be performed." [44]

The announcement of the Court's decision pushed the abortion/infanticide debate into the presidential campaign. Gore pretended that the case had nothing to do with partial births and everything to do with banning abortions. Noting that the outcome had turned on one vote, he warned that Bush could overturn *Roe* by appointing new justices. Conversely, Bush said nothing about the Court's composition. He defended the people's right not to ban abortion but "to protect children who are in the process of being born." [45]

Gore's effort to ignite a debate about abortion rights failed. *Carhart* had upheld *Roe* and *Casey* and was far less broad. Indeed, Gore's whole strategy of running on Clinton's record was failing. Clinton's scandals were hurting Gore more than Clinton's policies were helping him. As the Democratic convention approached, Gore resolved to separate himself from Clinton and sharpen his contrast with Bush on the issues. There was one obvious way to do both—by demanding new "investments."

Accepting the nomination on August 17, Gore called for "high-quality, universal pre-school" and "a prescription drug benefit for all seniors." He pledged to "move toward universal health coverage," "double the federal investment in medical research," and "fight for the greatest single commitment to education since the G.I. Bill." Clinton had guaranteed family leave; Gore vowed to expand it. Clinton had launched a program to put 100,000 cops on the street; Gore promised 50,000 more. Clinton had defended Social Security; Gore resolved to supplement it with tax-free savings accounts he called "Social Security plus." [46] Gore would point out that Bush's proposed tax cut made it impossible for the governor to match these commitments.

Populism became the theme of Gore's campaign. It united his spending proposals, his insistence on "tax cuts that go to the right people," and his regulatory assaults on polluters and HMOs. "This is not just an election between my opponent and me. It's about . . . whether forces standing in your way will keep you from living a better life," Gore told the convention audience. "That's the difference in this election. They're for the powerful. We're for the people."

This was a radical departure from Clintonism. Clinton had confined his liberalism to the proposition that government wasn't all bad. Government couldn't solve people's problems, he argued, but it could give them the tools to help themselves. Defending his budgets against Republican assault, Clinton never forced voters to choose between the public and private sectors. Government wasn't at war with anybody. The threats to Medicare, Medicaid, education, and the environment didn't come from business or a wealthy elite. They came from radical, arrogant, meddling politicians.

Gore was embracing liberalism not as conservatism's limit but as its antithesis. The alternative to state power, he argued, wasn't freedom but private concentrations of power: "Big Tobacco, Big Oil, the big polluters, the pharmaceutical companies, the HMOs." Left unchecked, these institutions would trample individuals. Government's job was to stop them. "So often, powerful forces and powerful interests stand in your way," Gore told the convention audience. "I've taken on the powerful forces, and as president, I'll stand up to them, and I'll stand up for you." The powerful wanted school vouchers, private health insurance, private retirement accounts, and the biggest tax cuts for the biggest taxpayers. Gore wanted to confine tax cuts to the middle class, reserving the rest of the surplus to upgrade Medicare, Social Security, and public schools. He wanted a referendum on liberalism. And he would get it.

The speech shattered the "Clinton-Gore" marriage, refocused the election on issues, excited liberals, and promised benefits to everyone. Gore rocketed upward. Polls showed that voters preferred Gore's health, education, and tax policies to Bush's. But those polls obscured the same paradox that had rescued abortion rights in the late 1980s: Bush's policies, while weaker than Gore's individually, were stronger collectively. When the question moved beyond taxes, prescription drugs, Social Security, and vouchers to whether voters preferred "larger government with many services" or "smaller government with fewer services," a clear majority chose the latter.[47]

In remarks to California Republicans on September 16, Bush touched on the crucial insight. In Gore's assaults on Big Oil, HMOs, and drug companies, there was one constant: the assailant. "The vice president talks about 'the people versus the powerful,'" Bush observed. "But, in all his plans, who ends up with the power? Who always ends up making the choices? Not the taxpayers, but the tax collectors. Not the senior citizens, but the H.M.O. overseers. Not the parents, or even the teachers, but some distant central office."[48] A campaign against big government would beat a campaign against big business because government was a singular and therefore more obvious concentration of power.

On September 28 Bush went to Green Bay, Wisconsin, and accused Gore not of emulating Clinton but of betraying him. "The vice president's spending plan proposes three times more in new spending than Bill Clinton proposed in 1992," said Bush. "If the vice president gets elected, the era of big government being over is over." Borrowing another Clinton phrase, Bush charged, "My opponent has left the vital center of American politics. He has cast his lot with the old Democratic Party. We have come too far, and learned too much, to go back to the old ways of tax and spend."[49]

That day, as the Christian Coalition gathered for its convention in Washington, D.C., the Food and Drug Administration approved mifepristone, the abortion pill previously known as RU486, for use in the United States. Gore seized the opportunity to reaffirm the right to choose. Bush didn't bite. He criticized the decision but said only that he would "build a culture that respects life." A spokesman asserted that while Bush would review the decision to make sure it hadn't been politically influenced, "the president does not have the authority to order drugs off the market." In videotaped remarks to the coalition, Bush didn't mention mifepristone. "I know good people disagree on this issue, but surely we can agree on ways to value life by promoting adoption and parental notification," he said.[50]

Some pro-lifers grumbled about Bush's evasiveness, but coalition founder Pat Robertson defended it. Addressing the convention, Robertson, too, ignored the FDA's decision. Instead, he talked about big government. The mifepristone announcement "[is] a trap for Bush, and I think he ought to stay out of it, and I will too," Robertson told reporters. "Right now, to play this campaign on abortion would be a tragic mistake." The minister urged his allies to let Bush focus on other issues. "He's got to stay on message," said Robertson.[51]

On September 29 Bush flew home to his ranch, where he taped an ad called "Trust." Smiling into the camera, he explained the principle behind his plans:

> That's the difference in philosophy between my opponent and me. He trusts government. I trust you. I trust you to invest some of your own Social Security money for higher returns. I trust local people to run their own schools. . . . And if schools continue to fail, we'll give parents different options. I trust you with some of the budget surplus. I believe one-fourth of the surplus should go back to the people who pay the bills. My opponent

proposes targeted tax cuts only for those he calls 'the right people.' . . .
We should help people live their lives but not run them. Because when we
trust individuals, when we respect local control of schools, when we empower communities, together we can ignite America's spirit and renew our
purpose.

On October 3 Bush met Gore in Boston for their first debate. Forty-
seven million viewers were watching. Gore's agenda "empowers Washington," Bush began. "My vision is to empower Americans to be able to
make decisions for themselves." The difference between Gore's programs and Bush's tax cuts, the governor argued, was "the difference between government making decisions for you and you getting more of
your money to make decisions for yourself."

For the rest of the debate, Bush hammered this message. The one
tricky moment came when he was asked whether he would reverse the
FDA's approval of mifepristone. Bush repeated the Texas Three-Step. He
declared himself pro-life, denied that the president could reverse the
FDA, cautioned that pro-lifers had to "change a lot of minds" before
changing laws, and switched the subject to parental consent.

"Here's the difference," Gore replied. "He trusts the government to
order a woman to do what he thinks she ought to do. I trust women to
make the decisions that affect their lives, their destinies and their bodies." For a flickering moment, Gore seemed on the verge of realizing that
the theme he had just invoked was larger and more powerful than the issue. And then the moment was over.

Two days after the debate, "Trust" hit the airwaves in nineteen states.
Bush followed it with commercials that warned, "Gore's proposing
three times the new spending President Clinton proposed." On the trail
and in the debates, Bush repeated these charges. Gore's message of choice
on abortion was obliterated by Bush's message of choice on everything
else. As Bush put it in his speech to the California GOP, "[Gore] says he
believes in health care choices, and he has made yours for you. If you
want prescription drugs, that's a private matter between you and your
Washington bureaucrat." [52]

In those two weeks, Gore lost the election. Nearly every independent
poll showed him leading before the debates and then slipping about six
net percentage points to a deficit. Among liberals, Gore's margin fell
fewer than five points in Gallup's tracking survey. Among moderates
and conservatives, it fell nearly ten. When asked in an October 13–15

Wall Street Journal–NBC survey whether the country's problems should be resolved by "government" or by "individuals, businesses, and other institutions," voters chose the latter by 62 to 23 percent.[53]

The same polls that showed a preference for smaller government showed Gore losing that dimension of the campaign. In *New York Times*–CBS surveys from mid-September to late October, Gore's net margin closely tracked his ideology index—the percentage of voters who saw him as conservative, minus the percentage who saw him as liberal. From October 1 to October 21 the index fell five points, and Gore's net margin fell six. Another way to measure Gore's image was to subtract the percentage of voters who thought he wanted bigger government from the percentage who thought he wanted smaller government. In the July *Washington Post*–ABC survey, that index stood at minus 33. By October 9 it had plunged to minus 53. During the same period, Bush's index on the same question rose from 18 to 37. When asked in the October 9 *Post* survey which candidate they trusted to hold down the size of government, voters chose Bush by 54 to 33 percent.[54]

On October 24, battered and humbled, Gore went to Little Rock, Arkansas, to renounce big government. Trailing two weeks before election day in a state that Clinton had won twice and that his prodigal heir desperately needed, Gore still believed in a place called hope. Maybe some of the magic Hickman had found there in 1986 was still alive. Maybe if Gore learned the right words, maybe if he spoke them the right way, he could win back voters who had turned against him. Maybe he could become one of them, as Brownie Ledbetter had done. Maybe he, too, could pass from this side of the glass to the other.

"I'm opposed to big government," Gore pleaded in his speech that day. "I don't believe there's a government solution to every problem. I don't believe any government program can replace the responsibility of parents, the hard work of families or the innovation of industry." Failed by his own slogans, Gore reached for Bush's—"I trust ordinary Americans"—and then Clinton's: "We have to give every family the tools and skills to stand up and fight for themselves." He ended with a reactive, scripted, and implausible promise. "As President, I will launch a second wave of reform and change in government: Reinventing Government II," Gore pledged. "I'm proposing the next generation of fiscal discipline and government downsizing."[55]

If Gore couldn't recapture the center, maybe he could mobilize the left. NARAL and other friendly interest groups pursued that strategy, pouring millions of dollars of advertising into states in which Green Party nominee Ralph Nader was siphoning votes from Gore. "If you're thinking of voting for Ralph Nader, please consider: This year, a 5 to 4 Supreme Court decision narrowly protected *Roe v. Wade*," said NARAL's ad. "George Bush would reverse the Court. . . . Bush's goal? Ending legal abortion. Voting for Ralph Nader helps elect George W. Bush." [56]

On November 7 blacks, urbanites, union members, and other reliable Democrats flooded the polls for Gore. Nader supporters defected en masse to the vice president. The Nader states NARAL had targeted—Minnesota, Oregon, and Wisconsin—went to Gore. Liberal America poured out its heart for him. It wasn't enough. The conservative states Clinton had won—Arkansas, Tennessee, and Louisiana—rejected Gore. With peace and prosperity at his back, Gore had managed no better than a razor-thin plurality of the popular vote and a razor-thin defeat in the electoral college. He had tested the limits of liberalism and received his answer.

Exit polls measured the cost of Gore's polarization strategy. Bush's advantage among voters concerned about abortion canceled out Gore's advantage among voters concerned about the Supreme Court. Those issues, in turn, were washed out by larger themes. By 53 to 47 percent, voters said they were more concerned that Gore would go too far in increasing government spending and taxes than that Bush would go too far in reducing needed government programs. Twenty-seven percent of Bush supporters cited Gore's liberalism as a major reason for voting against the vice president. Only 16 percent of Gore supporters cited Bush's conservatism as a major reason they voted against the governor. Twenty-four percent of Bush voters said they approved of Clinton's policies; only 8 percent of Gore voters said they opposed Clinton's policies. By separating his agenda from Clinton's, Gore had lost more votes than he gained. [57]

For weeks, the country was consumed by doubts that Bush had won the election. But another question lingered as well. As a candidate, he had three-stepped his way through the abortion debate. To pro-lifers, he had signaled that he would foster a culture of life. To pro-choicers, he had signaled that he wouldn't outlaw abortion. To pro-choice conservatives, he had signaled that his abortion agenda would match his broader agenda of limiting government and protecting parents and taxpayers.

Could he honor all three commitments as president? If they came into conflict, which would he pursue?

Bush made clear right away that he wouldn't challenge abortion's legality. On January 16, 2001, his nominee for attorney general, John Ashcroft, told the Senate Judiciary Committee, "I accept *Roe* and *Casey* as the settled law of the land." The following day, Ashcroft went further: "I don't think it's the agenda of the president-elect of the United States to seek an opportunity to overturn *Roe*." On January 18 Bush refused to rule out filing a brief against *Roe*, but he suggested that it would be "foolish" to do so. He added, "I don't think we're going to get a constitutional amendment passed. That's for certain." The next morning, Laura Bush said of *Roe*, "I don't think it should be overturned." [58]

On January 22 Bush made equally clear that he would pursue conservative pro-choice restrictions. Exactly eight years after Clinton had lifted the ban on U.S. aid to family planning organizations that promoted abortion rights overseas, Bush reinstated the ban. Pro-choice lawmakers and activists had bet the aid money on the election and had lost it. "[T]axpayer funds should not be used to pay for abortions or advocate or actively promote abortion," Bush declared. When reporters questioned the political wisdom of tackling abortion, Ari Fleischer, now the White House press secretary, replied that "most Americans do not support the use of taxpayer money for these purposes." [59]

On March 29 Bush wrote the funding ban into the Federal Register. The next day, his Department of Health and Human Services (HHS) notified states that the Hyde amendment, which restricted federal Medicaid funding of abortions to cases of rape, incest, or danger to the woman's life, would also apply to mifepristone. The Bush administration would pay "particular" attention to this restriction "in determining a state's compliance" with the law, an HHS official told state Medicaid directors in a letter. The official added that states could apply existing abortion restrictions "such as requirements for parental notification" to mifepristone as well. [60]

Two weeks later, Bush advanced from abortion to birth control. Health insurance plans for federal employees already excluded coverage of abortions. Bush proposed to eliminate a requirement that they cover a variety of contraceptives. On July 17 the House Appropriations Committee blocked this rollback of benefits for middle-class women. Poor women were another matter. Two days after the committee vote, officials told the *Washington Post* that the Bush administration would reject all future requests by states for waivers to extend birth control coverage under Medicaid. Meanwhile, HHS signaled that it would relax limits on parents' access to their children's medical records.[61]

If Bush was serious about respecting the legality of abortion and keeping tax money out of it, how could he fulfill his third pledge, to build a culture of life? The battles of the Clinton years suggested two answers: Bush could link life to choice, defending the fetus only when the woman wanted it, or he could shift the debate out of the woman's body. The simplest vehicle for the linkage strategy was the Unborn Victims of Violence Act, which would punish anyone who killed an unborn child in the course of assaulting its mother. The bill had passed the House in 1999 but had never been taken up by the Senate. On April 24, 2001, Bush endorsed it. Two days later, the House passed it.[62]

Pro-choice groups pounced on the bill. They accused UVVA's sponsors of overlooking the fact that any assault on a fetus took place inside the body of a woman. NARAL, NOW, Planned Parenthood, and the Center for Reproductive Law and Policy blasted UVVA for "ignoring" the woman and focusing instead on the fetus. Michelman and Planned Parenthood president Gloria Feldt pointed out that the bill didn't even mention the injury to the woman.[63]

At the same time, pro-choice groups insisted that whether the woman wanted the child was irrelevant. Any legislation that accorded rights to a fetus was, in Feldt's words, "a direct assault on *Roe.*" *Roe* calculated that in the first two trimesters, a woman's rights outweighed the state's interest in protecting unborn life. To prevent the latter from surpassing the former, pro-choice groups were determined to reduce the value of unborn life to zero. Bloodless language was part of the game. The bill was just a scheme to grant rights to "an entity of pre-natal development," scoffed CRLP. Such rights could lead to "absurd legal ramifications," the organization noted—even "federal benefits" for fetuses.[64]

Two months later, that absurdity became real. In a draft letter leaked to the media on July 5, an HHS official disclosed that under guidelines soon to be proposed by the Bush administration, "an unborn child may be considered a 'targeted low income child' by the state and therefore eligible" for the State Children's Health Insurance Program (SCHIP). Since the program was designed for kids whose parents couldn't afford health insurance, it didn't cover pregnancy-related care for women above a certain age or income level. Under the new rules, said the letter, "regardless of the age of the mother, eligibility for the unborn child may be established, thereby making services including prenatal care and delivery available." [65]

The SCHIP proposal brought to the surface an implicit conflict among Bush's three abortion themes. He was getting serious about fostering a culture of life, serious enough to risk a collision with his other two commitments. In theory, by recognizing fetal rights, UVVA and the SCHIP initiative could lay the groundwork for a challenge to *Roe*. More immediately, however, these initiatives defied family sovereignty and small government. The culture of life was threatening the culture of conservatism.

In the 1999 debate on UVVA, Republicans had talked about punishing thugs who attacked innocent women. But UVVA was also a domestic violence bill. During the April 2001 House debate, the bill's sponsor, Representative Lindsey Graham, admonished his colleagues,

> You talk about an assault on *Roe v. Wade;* I am talking about an assault on Shawana Pace. . . . Her boyfriend, the father, former boyfriend, paid three people $400 to kidnap her and terminate her pregnancy because he did not want to pay child support. . . . She is lying on the floor and they are beating her within an inch of her life, and one of them says, 'Your baby is dying tonight.' . . . Rae Carruth, NFL football player, hired a person to kill his pregnant girlfriend. She refused to have an abortion. He did not want to pay for the child. The hit man charged $5,000 for the mother and $5,000 for the baby, charged him twice. Let us punish him twice. [66]

If UVVA was an admission of public responsibility for halting domestic violence, the SCHIP plan was an admission of public responsibility for health and welfare. An HHS spokesman later told reporters that under Reagan, conservatives had abolished public health insurance coverage for unborn children because they thought women were having kids just to get welfare and Medicaid. Bush was reversing that decision, the spokesman said. [67]

Bush was also reversing himself. In his 1994 campaign for governor, he had run a television ad pledging to throw people off welfare after two years. "And during that period of time, if you choose to have additional children, that's your right," Bush said in the ad. "But no more taxpayer monies to do so." When Bush tried to push a family cap through the Texas legislature in 1995, the Texas Right to Life Committee and the Texas Catholic Conference opposed the idea. "It's not right to force a woman [to] get an abortion because you have two kids and you're on welfare," said the Catholic Conference's executive director. Nevertheless, in 1997 Bush renewed his push for the cap, instructing legislators to "make sure our welfare system changes behavior." [68]

By 1998 the evidence showed that both sides were right. The family cap did change behavior, and part of that change was an increase in abortions. Researchers hired by the state of New Jersey found that New Jersey's cap had led to 14,000 fewer births and 1,429 more abortions than would have taken place otherwise. Republican governor Christie Whitman—whose 1997 reelection NOW, unlike NARAL, had refused to support because of the cap—ignored the abortion figures and welcomed the decline in births. "The message of personal responsibility is working," she concluded. [69]

Bush, Whitman, and other pro-choice conservatives didn't focus on the abortion spike. What they focused on was curtailing the welfare population. By 2001 nearly half the states had family caps. Pat Robertson even defended China's one-child policy, which pro-lifers had likened to the family cap. "If every family over there was allowed to have three or four children, the population would be completely unsustainable," Robertson argued on CNN on April 16, 2001. "They're doing what they have to do. I don't agree with the forced abortion, but I don't think the United States needs to interfere with what they're doing internally in this regard." [70]

Robertson's comments outraged Michelman. She had testified against the family cap in 1995, arguing that it was anti-choice. What galled her about Robertson's CNN interview was that it conveyed equal indifference to unborn life. "The only thing he is consistent about is his opposition to the right of women to choose," she charged. [71]

But Michelman faced a similar test of principle. Yes, by granting rights to the fetus, the SCHIP plan posed an indirect risk to *Roe*. Yes, the proposal mentioned no increase in money for SCHIP. Yes, the official who had drafted it had also engineered Bush's assault on birth control funding. [72] But the risk to *Roe* was marginal, pregnancies were worth covering regardless of what happened to birth control, and the money for covering them could be leveraged more easily once everyone agreed on the idea.

The SCHIP proposal wasn't just a stunt to embarrass pro-choicers. It was a repudiation of the logic of the family cap. The government was going to tell low-income women that if they got pregnant, their medical expenses would be covered. Nor would they have to worry about insuring the resulting children. According to the draft, once the fetus qualified for coverage, "a separate eligibility determination would not be required after birth." In the words of one pro-life activist, the proposal offered "real choice—the choice of being the healthy mother of a healthy baby, even when money is a problem."[73] The question was whether pro-choice groups would embrace and improve the proposal or whether the only thing they were consistent about was opposing the right to life.

The answer came promptly. Every major pro-choice organization attacked the proposal. Planned Parenthood threatened to sue the government to block it. "Bush is seeking to score political points with the most anti-choice extremists in his party—those who want to criminalize legal abortion by any means possible," Michelman scoffed.[74] Pro-choice activists opposed the plan because pro-lifers supported it. The activists would tolerate no threat to *Roe,* no matter how small the risk or how great the benefit to choice and life. They would protect legal abortion by any means possible.

Rather than insure the fetus, pro-choicers proposed to extend SCHIP to insure the woman. They noted that Bush's SCHIP plan, like UVVA, overlooked the fact that the fetus was inside a woman. Michelman accused Bush of "bypassing the pregnant woman." Feldt said the plan "carves women and their health right out of the picture."[75] But pro-choice groups couldn't explain why a program designed for children would extend more logically to adults than to fetuses. Nor, in the absence of a direct threat to *Roe,* could they explain why, even if their approach was better, Bush's should be rejected. There was only one solid reason to oppose Bush's plan. As NARAL explained,

> [I]t could actually do harm to women by pitting them against the program's "patients"—the embryos. Under this proposal, would a pregnant woman with cancer be able to access potentially life-saving radiation treatment or chemotherapy, since such treatment could harm the embryo? . . . This proposal reveals the Administration's troubling belief that a woman is merely a vessel for carrying a pregnancy.[76]

In rejecting Bush's offer of state-funded reproductive health care, the abortion rights movement had raised a question: In what sense, other than opposing the right to life, was the movement pro-choice? This was the answer: The movement opposed the SCHIP proposal because medical guarantees to the fetus alone endangered the woman carrying it. The movement's concern had always been the woman—her body, her safety, her autonomy. Without her, choice could mean anything: parental rights, spousal rights, taxpayers' rights, property rights. She was the movement's anchor, the "you" in "you or them."

Because choice was anchored to the woman, the simplest way for pro-lifers to circumvent it was to keep moving the debate out of the woman's body. They had tried to do that with the partial-birth ban but had fallen one vote short in the Supreme Court. Justice O'Connor had told them how to get that vote: broaden the health exception and distinguish the D&X procedure more clearly from other kinds of abortion. They were willing to do the latter but not the former. For the time being, the par-tial-birth issue was dead.[77]

If partial births weren't sufficiently distinct from abortions, what about whole births? What if the fetus came all the way out of the woman, completely separating the termination of pregnancy from the killing? To pose that question, Representative Charles Canady, chief sponsor of the partial-birth ban, filed the Born-Alive Infants Protection Act in April 2000. The bill granted personhood to any member of the human spe-cies upon

> the complete expulsion or extraction from its mother of that member, at
> any stage of development, who after such expulsion or extraction breathes
> or has a beating heart, pulsation of the umbilical cord, or definite move-
> ment of voluntary muscles, regardless of whether the umbilical cord has
> been cut, and regardless of whether the expulsion or extraction occurs as a
> result of natural or induced labor, cesarean section, or induced abortion.[78]

In July 2000, three weeks after their defeat in *Carhart,* pro-lifers con-vened a House hearing on the born-alive bill. They summoned Gerard Bradley, the same law professor who had testified a year earlier that UVVA didn't "override the rights of the pregnant woman." Bradley made the same point about the born-alive bill. "This bill is not about pregnant women. It's about protecting people born after pregnancy has been terminated," he testified. "[T]he bill codifies or affirms what *Roe* and all the cases have been saying, that abortion refers to terminating a pregnancy and has really nothing to do with terminating children."[79]

Would abortion rights groups extend their defense of the choice to kill beyond the woman's body? They would. CRLP dismissed the born-alive bill as "another anti-choice initiative to open a public debate on 'infanticide.'" NOW said the bill would "limit a woman's right to make complex and private decisions regarding termination of pregnancy."[80] In a statement released on the day of the hearing, NARAL defended the freedom to choose to kill a nonviable fetus even if the fetus was no longer inside the woman and even if the freedom in question was that of the doctor, not the woman:

> This bill also attempts to inject Congress into what should be personal and private decisions about medical treatment in difficult and painful situations where a fetus has no chance of survival. It could also interfere with the sound practice of medicine by spurring physicians to take extraordinary steps in situations where their efforts may be futile and when their medical judgment may indicate otherwise.[81]

NARAL eventually backed down, but NOW didn't. For the next two years, NOW complained that the bill created fetal rights, promoted " 'infanticide' rhetoric," and, in the view of some physicians, "would obligate doctors to provide increased care to newborns in cases where there is no hope of survival." [82] These principles—minimizing the value of nascent human life, defining pro-choice victory as pro-life defeat, and opposing government interference in a utilitarian calculus outside the woman's body—would govern the pro-choice movement's response to the next issues of the abortion war: stem cells and cloning.

The medical world was abuzz over human embryonic stem cells, known as ESCs. They could be grown perpetually in laboratories, turned into various types of cells such as marrow or liver, and transplanted into patients to cure diseases. But to obtain these cells, scientists had to destroy the rudimentary embryos that bore them. Thousands of such embryos were left over from in vitro fertilizations. Supporters of ESC research argued that these embryos were going to be thrown out anyway. Opponents argued that no human individual, even an early embryo, should be destroyed to save another.

On August 9, 2001, Bush announced that he would limit federally funded ESC research to cell lines already derived. No additional embryos could be destroyed as part of such research. Every major pro-choice organization attacked the decision. NARAL questioned why pro-life groups opposed the research, since the early embryo "has never been placed or implanted in a uterus," and "none of the research involves abortion or aborted fetal tissue." NOW made the same points, expressing amazement that stem cells were "being portrayed as an abortion issue" by pro-lifers. "Babies do not grow in petri dishes," observed former NOW president Patricia Ireland. "They grow inside a real live human being." [83]

NOW and NARAL had it backward. The fact that pro-lifers were fighting for unborn life outside the womb suggested not that they were disingenuous but that they were sincere. They really were pro-life, not just anti-abortion. On the other hand, if stem cell research wasn't an abortion issue and if the embryos at stake had never been implanted in women, the mystery wasn't why pro-life groups were involved in the stem cell debate. The mystery was why pro-choice groups were involved.

Strategically, there were two reasons. One was that pro-choice activists saw stem cell restrictions, along with UVVA and Bush's SCHIP plan, as part of a scheme to inflate the value of embryos. "All of these machinations have a political goal . . . limiting birth control and abortion," said NOW's new president, Kim Gandy. The other reason was that pro-choicers saw an opportunity to hurt pro-lifers politically. On stem cells, pro-lifers had picked a fight with millions of families facing degenerative diseases. NARAL, NOW, CRLP, and Planned Parenthood made sure those families knew that "anti-choice" groups were behind the opposition.[84]

Together, these two reasons formed a utilitarian argument that had nothing to do with a woman's autonomy. The embryo was nothing; the patient was everything. "We're talking about the difference between 16 or 32 cells that will never on their own become a human being, versus human beings who are already born," said Ireland. "I don't find that a moral dilemma." Another NOW activist pointed out that choice was irrelevant: "Whether your own political beliefs are pro-choice or pro-life, the real issue here is increasing the quality of life for thousands of people who are alive and with us today."[85]

Abortion rights groups sprayed this argument around as though it were a simple extension of a woman's primacy over her fetus. It wasn't. In abortion, the unborn child was inside the body of the person whose primacy was being asserted. In stem cell harvesting, it was outside. By overlooking this difference, pro-choicers committed the same fallacy for which they had rebuked Bush in the SCHIP debate: They ignored the location of the unborn child. Ireland's inference that the embryo fertilized in vitro wasn't a baby because "babies do not grow in petri dishes" underscored this blindness. The absence of a baby in the dish was a moral question. The absence of a woman—the person for whom NOW purported to speak—was a certainty.

Why did ESC research merit advocacy by organizations dedicated to women, reproductive rights, or planned parenthood? NARAL claimed that the research could help in "increasing contraceptive choices" and "treating and preventing some forms of infertility." NOW said it could promote "women's health" by, among other things, "creating tissue banks" for transplants.[86] These were certainly benefits to health and reproductive freedom. But the women who would get these benefits weren't the women who would furnish the embryos. From the stand-point of the embryo's mother, the population for whose sake NOW and NARAL promoted ESC research wasn't you. It was them.

The activist who saw this problem most clearly was Judy Norsigian, di-rector of the feminist collective that had produced the famous women's health book *Our Bodies, Ourselves.* Norsigian didn't oppose ESC re-search in principle. Her concern was the direction in which the biotech-nology industry was pushing that research. To grow tissues that would match patients genetically and to mass-produce cells for experiments, scientists wanted to create embryos by cloning. That would pose "enor-mous risks to women and children's health," Norsigian told a House committee on June 20, 2001. Six weeks later, in a *Boston Globe* op-ed, Norsigian and Stuart Newman, a cofounder of the Council for Respon-sible Genetics, cautioned that "women whose eggs are harvested for cloning have to be treated with hormones to induce superovulation, pos-sibly putting them at increased risk of ovarian cancer with no benefit to themselves." [87]

Norsigian, Newman, and other leftists feared the creeping influence of contracts, economic coercion, mass production, and genetic engineer-ing. They warned of "the commoditization of women's bodies" and "the utilization of human eggs and embryos for experimental manipulations and as items of commerce." If biotech companies were allowed to im-plant cloned embryos, Newman and Norsigian wondered, what would happen to a woman who wanted "to terminate a pregnancy involving some company's 'property?'" [88] Banning implantation posed even uglier possibilities. Richard Doerflinger, a spokesman for the National Con-ference of Catholic Bishops, asked the House committee,

> If the government allows use of cloning to produce human embryos for re-search but prohibits initiating a pregnancy, what will it be requiring people to do? If pregnancy has already begun, the only remedy would seem to be government-mandated abortion—or at least, jailing or otherwise punishing women for remaining pregnant and giving birth. . . . It would be as "anti-choice" as it is "anti-life." [89]

NARAL said nothing about these problems. Like other pro-choice groups, it was silent about cloning. As for genetic screening, it was enthusiastic. NARAL promoted embryo research as a means of "developing techniques for the pre-implantation genetic diagnosis of inherited diseases[,] . . . thereby providing in vitro fertilization candidates with the ability to screen for genetic defects prior to embryo implantation." Weeding out inferior embryos was just another choice. Norsigian saw the issue differently. At the House hearing, she warned of a descent into "eugenics."[90] In the *Globe,* she and Newman rejected an asserted right to choose genetic traits:

> Advocates of human reproductive cloning and other forms of inheritable genetic modification have attempted to appropriate the language of reproductive rights to support their case. But there is an immense difference between seeking to end an unwanted pregnancy and seeking to create a genetically duplicated or modified human being. It is an unfortunate consequence of the rise of the new genetic technologies that "reproductive choice" is increasingly taken to include the right to manipulate the genetic composition of the next generation.[91]

It didn't take long for genetic screening to turn on its feminist proponents. In May 2001 the ethics committee of the American Society of Reproductive Medicine (ASRM) had conditionally approved a technique for selecting a child's sex. The technique involved separating sperm prior to conception. It was effective but not perfect. Three of every ten couples who wanted a boy got a girl; three of every twenty couples who wanted a girl got a boy.[92] There was an obvious way to eliminate these unwanted outcomes—by screening after conception. A clinic could fertilize several eggs in vitro, pick an embryo of the correct gender, and get rid of the others. The only thing standing in the way was ethics.

NARAL promoted the postconception technique, known as preimplantation genetic diagnosis (PGD), as a means of eliminating "inherited diseases" and "genetic defects." It was already approved for screening out embryos of either sex in families that might pass down a serious inherited disease through that sex. Dr. Norbert Gleicher, chair of a chain of fertility clinics, had a number of clients who didn't carry such a disease but felt they had too many kids of one sex or not enough of the other. They were willing to pay an extra $3,000 or so to get rid of embryos of the wrong sex.[93] That was sort of a defect, wasn't it?

Gleicher took the question to his company's ethics committee, which concluded that it was not only ethical but also imperative to offer PGD for this purpose. So Gleicher put the question to the ASRM ethics committee. In late September, John Robertson, the committee's acting chairman, sent Gleicher a letter affirming that a clinic "might ethically offer preimplantation genetic diagnoses" for the sake of "gender variety" in a family. Gleicher announced that he would begin selling the service immediately.[94]

Norsigian, Newman, and other left-feminists denounced the decision. In a letter to ASRM on January 15, 2002, they noted:

> Nearly concurrent with Robertson's approval of PGD for sex selection, ads placed by American fertility practitioners offering both pre- and post-conception sex selection have targeted the South Asian community in North America. . . . Those marketing this "service" to South Asians are surely aware that sex selection in India disfavors female children, capitalizing on the strong son preference and overall gender discrimination. . . . PGD presents serious ethical dilemmas precisely because it is so often difficult to distinguish medical from non-medical conditions. Allowing PGD for "gender variety" is a clear example of a non-medical application. Preselecting traits such as sex opens the door to embryo selection based on other non-medical traits, and constitutes a major step toward the "designing" of children.[95]

On February 7 the ASRM ethics committee retreated. Robertson sent Gleicher a letter advising him that the use of PGD to weed out boys or girls for the sake of variety "should be discouraged." Three weeks later, however, the committee defended a geneticist's use of PGD to eliminate embryos that carried a gene for early-onset Alzheimer's disease. Some ethicists complained that filtering out embryos over a flaw that wouldn't appear until the age of forty crossed the line into "designing our descendants." But a spokeswoman for the ASRM committee said the procedure was acceptable.[96]

By July 2002 dozens of clinics were selling PGD in the United States. Nearly two thousand embryos tested in this way had been brought to term. Since in vitro fertilization typically produced embryos in bunches, presumably many thousands more had been deemed inferior and frozen or destroyed. No law restricted the uses to which PGD could be put. Some doctors casually admitted to helping clients eliminate male or female embryos for nonmedical reasons. "What is medical need?" one clinic operator asked the *Los Angeles Times*. "Isn't the right to happiness and health a part of that?"[97]

The stem cell debate took a similar turn. In July 2001 the House of Representatives voted to ban the cloning of human embryos, whether for reproduction or for therapeutic research. Reproductive cloning was judged unsafe and abhorrent; research cloning was condemned on the grounds that no human embryo should be created for the purpose of destroying it to benefit others.[98] In the months that followed, powerful lobbies representing the biotechnology industry and patients who could benefit from cloning-based research went to work to stop the Senate from passing a similar ban.

Pro-choicers were happy to see pro-life activists pitted once more against millions of patients and their families. But because the cloning lobby needed the votes of pro-life senators and didn't want to polarize the issue, most pro-choice activists kept their mouths shut. Those who spoke up for research cloning argued that it would advance women's health. Only a few expressed what they feared—that restrictions on cloning might lead to restrictions on abortion. Pro-lifers were "objecting to cloning on the same grounds they use to object to women making reproductive decisions," the Religious Coalition for Reproductive Choice warned in November 2001.[99] In July 2002 the *American Prospect* concluded,

> [T]he cloning issue boils down to abortion politics by other means. . . . [R]ight-to-life opposition to research cloning should be classified alongside the Bush administration's controversial draft regulations to cover embryos and fetuses under the Children's Health Insurance Program and the House's 2001 passage of the Unborn Victims of Violence Act—both of which were widely viewed as indirect attempts to roll back abortion rights.[100]

From UVVA to SCHIP to cloning, pro-choice liberals were still dead set against Bush's culture-of-life agenda. To defeat it, they were willing to team up with biotech entrepreneurs and conservative lawmakers in defense of manufacturing human embryos outside the womb for their parts. They were even willing to pretend that cloned human embryos were neither cloned, nor human, nor embryos.

On April 24, 2002, Hollywood activists launched a pro-cloning ad campaign featuring Harry and Louise, the couple whose commercials for the insurance industry had torpedoed the Clinton health care plan. In the opening ad, Harry, referring to research cloning, asked, "Is it cloning?" Louise replied, "No! It uses an unfertilized egg and a skin cell."[101] The ad didn't mention that all clones were created this way and that in principle the absence of fertilization wouldn't prevent the birth of a cloned baby any more than it had prevented the birth of Dolly the sheep.

Many proponents who admitted that human cloning was cloning refused to admit that the consequent developing entity was human. A cloned embryo "is no different than a clump of blood cells," Senator

Dianne Feinstein, Democrat-California, asserted in a June 14 speech on the Senate floor. She concluded, "An unfertilized egg is not capable of becoming a human being." Senator Orrin Hatch, Republican-Utah, said he was "not sure that human being would even be the correct term" for a born human clone.[102]

Feinstein and Hatch didn't propose to permit the destruction of cloned human embryos. They proposed to mandate it. To prevent women from giving birth to cloned babies, they stipulated that embryos created for research had to be discarded within two weeks. In legislation filed on May 1, they called the cloned human embryo a "product of nuclear transplantation" and prescribed a fine of at least $1 million and a jail sentence of as much as ten years for anyone who implanted this product in "a uterus or the functional equivalent of a uterus." The bill demanded forfeiture of "any property, real or personal, derived from" such implantation.[103]

On May 15 the U.S. Justice Department told Congress that the bill could entail forfeiture of cloned fetuses and might require a "government-directed attempt to terminate a cloned embryo in utero." But the Senate was unmoved. By late June the cloning ban was dead, and fifty-eight senators, nearly all of them supporters of Roe, had signed on to Feinstein's embryo termination bill. Delegates to NOW's national convention gave the bill one last push. Noting that research on embryos might "benefit women" and that "the leading opponents of such research [were] anti-abortionists," the delegates pledged that NOW would "actively support" research cloning.[104]

On August 5 Bush signed the Born Alive Infants Protection Act into law. NOW dismissed it as a "ploy," but NARAL declined to criticize the measure. Two weeks later the Bush administration unveiled a program to promote public awareness of embryo "adoption." The originator of the idea, pro-choice Republican senator Arlen Specter, argued that leftover in vitro embryos shouldn't be used for research if donors and recipients were willing to give them life. But Michelman warned that by elevating the status of embryos, the program might advance the "effort to roll back Roe." [105]

In late September the administration released its regulation extending SCHIP medical coverage to fetuses. The final version encompassed pregnant illegal immigrants, to whom federally subsidized health care was otherwise unavailable. Pro-choice and feminist activists called the new coverage "fake," "sham," and "anti-choice." Gloria Feldt accused Bush of making SCHIP "a weapon against women." These attacks on the policy were foolishly spiteful, but suspicion of the administration's motives proved valid. A few days after issuing the regulation, HHS secretary Tommy Thompson withdrew his support for legislation that would have extended SCHIP more fully to pregnant women.[106]

In October HHS revised the charter of its Advisory Committee on Human Research Protections, adding embryos to the list of "human subjects" whose welfare had to be safeguarded in medical experiments. Michelman accused the administration of "politicizing medical research at [the] expense of women's health." Summarizing the pro-choice community's all-out war against legal respect for the unborn, she charged, "[F]reedom of choice is disappearing as rights are bestowed on embryos and fetuses."[107]

Six days later, the war turned against her on both fronts. In the midterm elections, NARAL lost eight of the nine Senate races it had targeted, leaving Republicans in clear control of Congress and the White House for the first time since *Roe*. Democrats gave up hope of blocking the partial-birth ban. Republicans prepared to follow suit with two pro-life bills—UVVA and a ban on cloning—and several conservative pro-choice bills, led by CCPA, restrictions on international family planning funds, and legislation protecting the right of doctors, nurses, and hospitals to abstain from abortions.[108]

Which way would abortion rights activists turn? Would they confront the culture of life or the culture of conservatism? Thirty years after *Roe* and sixteen years after the dark days of Arkansas, they had come nearly full circle. They had saved *Roe*, but in the streets and in their souls they had lost the struggle to define it.

Notes

SOURCES AND ABBREVIATIONS

This book rests on three layers of research. I began with public records: federal and state government documents, newspaper and magazine articles, television and radio news broadcasts, and press releases. Next, I interviewed participants in the events mentioned in these records. Finally, I obtained private documents that substantiated points or themes drawn from interviews or public records. As far as possible, I relied on written material. Where necessary, I filled in gaps by interviewing participants and checking each person's recollections against others' recollections and against written records. Occasionally, when accounts couldn't be reconciled, I relied on the same standards by which testimony is evaluated in court: which witness had the clearer memory, which seemed more honest, which had a motive to lie or distort.

The notes identify public records and private documents that support specific passages. They identify interview sources simply as "interviews," because I've promised various sources confidentiality. Press releases are identified by sponsoring organization, title, and date. Memorandums are identified by author, subject line, addressees, and date. "Contemporaneous notes" and "contemporaneous records" refer to documents that I can't cite by name or author because of confidentiality.

Most periodicals and broadcast news sources are cited by abbreviation. For example, *WP* 5/9/91 12A refers to the *Washington Post,* May 9, 1991, page 12A, and *MTP* 10/22/89 refers to NBC's *Meet the Press,* October 22, 1989. All page numbers refer to the first section of the newspaper unless a different section is specified. Periodicals with short titles—*Time, Parade,* and *Newsday*—are unabbreviated, as are broadcast programs such as CNN's *Crossfire,* NBC's *Today,* CBS's *60 Minutes,* and ABC's *20/20.* When the *Abortion Report,* a digest of periodicals and broadcast news, is cited parenthetically next to another source—

for example, Ft. Wayne *Journal-Gazette* 8/31/90 (*AR* 8/31/90 #5)—this means that a digest of the article can be found in the designated section of that day's *Abortion Report*. Books, which are cited by the author's surname and page number (e.g., Bronner 142), are fully identified in the bibliography.

The following is a list of abbreviations and the periodicals or broadcast programs to which they refer. All sources are published or broadcast daily unless otherwise specified.

AAS	*Austin American-Statesman* (Tex.)
ABCN	*ABC World News Tonight*
AC	*Atlanta Constitution* (or *Atlanta Journal-Constitution* [*AJC*])
AD	*Arkansas Democrat*
ADG	*Arkansas Democrat-Gazette*
ADT	*Alexandria Daily Town Talk* (La.)
AG	*Arkansas Gazette*
AJ	*Atlanta Journal*
AP	Associated Press
AR	*Abortion Report*
ATC	*All Things Considered* (NPR)
ATW	*This Week* (ABC TV)
AzR	*Arizona Republic*
BG	*Boston Globe*
BH	*Boston Herald*
BN	*Birmingham News* (Ala.)
BR	*The Record* (Bergen County, N.J.)
BRM	*Morning Advocate* (Baton Rouge, La.)
BRS	*State Times* (Baton Rouge, La.)
BS	*Baltimore Sun*
CBST	*This Morning* (CBS TV)
CD	*Congress Daily*
CDM	*Charleston Daily Mail* (W. Va.)
CM	*Concord Monitor* (N.H.)
CO	*Charlotte Observer*
CR	*Congressional Record*
CS	*The State* (Columbia, S.C.)
CSM	*Christian Science Monitor*

CT	*Chicago Tribune*
DFP	*Detroit Free Press*
DMN	*Dallas Morning News*
DN	*Detroit News*
DP	*Denver Post*
EN	*Evans & Novak* (CNN TV, weekly)
FB	*Fresno Bee* (Calif.)
FLN	*Fort Lauderdale News & Sun-Sentinel*
FPP	*Family Planning Perspectives* (monthly)
FTN	*Face the Nation* (CBS TV, weekly)
FTU	*Florida Times-Union* (Jacksonville)
FWS	*Star-Telegram* (Ft. Worth, Tex.)
GN	*Greenville News* (S.C.)
GNR	*Greensboro News & Record* (N.C.)
GRP	*Grand Rapids Press* (Mich.)
GS	*Gainesville Sun* (Fla.)
HC	*Houston Chronicle*
HCt	*Hartford Courant*
HP	*Houston Post*
IS	*Idaho Statesman*
JMO	*John McLaughlin's One-on-One* (NBC TV, weekly)
KCS	*Kansas City Star*
KCT	*Kansas City Times*
KG	*Kalamazoo Gazette* (Mich.)
LAT	*Los Angeles Times*
LCJ	*Louisville Courier-Journal* (Ky.)
LKL	*Larry King Live* (CNN TV)
LSJ	*Lansing State Journal* (Mich.)
LT	*Legal Times* (weekly)
MA	*Montgomery Advertiser* (Ala.)
MH	*Miami Herald*
MJ	*Milwaukee Journal*
MLN	*McNeil-Lehrer NewsHour* (PBS TV)
MST	*Star-Tribune* (Minneapolis, Minn.)

MTP	*Meet the Press* (NBC TV, weekly)
NBCN	*NBC Nightly News* (TV)
NPR	National Public Radio
NYD	*New York Daily News*
NYP	*New York Post*
NYT	*New York Times*
OCR	*Orange County Register* (Calif.)
OS	*Orlando Sentinel*
OWH	*Omaha World-Herald* (Neb.)
PBP	*Palm Beach Post* (Fla.)
PG	*Phoenix Gazette* (Ariz.)
PI	*Philadelphia Inquirer*
PO	*Oregonian* (Portland, Ore.)
PP	*Pittsburgh Press* (Pa.)
PPFA	Planned Parenthood Federation of America
PTL	*Prime Time Live* (ABC TV, weekly)
RMN	*Rocky Mountain News* (Denver, Colo.)
RNL	*Richmond News-Leader*
RNO	*Raleigh News & Observer*
RTD	*Richmond Times-Dispatch*
SB	*Sacramento Bee*
SDU	*San Diego Union-Tribune*
SFC	*San Francisco Chronicle*
SFX	*San Francisco Examiner*
SJ	*Shreveport Journal* (La.)
SJM	*San Jose Mercury-News*
SL	*Star-Ledger* (Newark, N.J.)
SLP	*St. Louis Post-Dispatch*
SPT	*St. Petersburg Times*
ST	*Shreveport Times* (La.)
SU	*Sacramento Union*
TD	*Tallahassee Democrat* (Fla.)
TNR	*The New Republic* (weekly)
TnT	*Trenton Times* (N.J.)

TP   *Times-Picayune* (New Orleans, La.)

TT   *Tampa Tribune* (Fla.)

TW   *Tulsa World* (Okla.)

UL   *Union Leader* (Manchester, N.H.)

USA   *USA Today*

USN   *U.S. News & World Report* (weekly)

VP   *Virginian-Pilot* (Norfolk, Va.)

WCP   *Weekly Compilation of Presidential Documents*

WE   *Wichita Eagle* (Kan.)

WP   *Washington Post*

WSJ   *Wall Street Journal*

WT   *Washington Times*

CHAPTER 1: A PLACE CALLED HOPE

1. The account of the focus group is based on interviews and Hickman-Maslin Research, "Recent Poll and Focus Groups" (memo to Planned Parenthood), 10/10/86.

2. The account of the Central High School showdown is based on *AG* 9/22–29/57.

3. Lydia Neumann, "The Arkansas Campaign to Defeat Amendment 65" (memo to PPFA Public Affairs Retreat Participants), 11/26/84.

4. *FPP* July–August 1985, 157. See also *DP* 11/8/84 1A.

5. *RMN* 11/5/84 49.

6. *FPP,* op. cit., 157.

7. The postelection quotes and analysis are taken from *FPP,* op. cit., 157, 159.

8. All data and quotations from the survey report are taken from Tubby Harrison, *Nationwide Study* (report to Linda Davidoff et al.), 5/2/84. Emphasis in original.

9. All quotations from the speech are taken from Lynn Paltrow, "Legal Overview of the Arkansas Proposed Constitutional Amendment" (speech text), 5/31/86.

10. *AG* 10/18/84 13A.

11. Neumann, op. cit.

12. The preceding and following quotes are taken from *Campaigns & Elections,* September–October 1987, 28.

13. *RNO* 8/15/00 A1.

14. *WP* 6/10/84 A3, *LAT* 2/7/85 15.

15. Philip W. Dyer and R. Harrison Hickman, "American Conservatism and F. A. Hayek," *Modern Age* (Fall 1979): 385, 391.

16. Ibid., 386.

17. All data and quotations from the survey report are taken from Hickman-Maslin Research, "Executive Summary" (report to Planned Parenthood of Greater Arkansas), April 1986; and Hickman-Maslin Research, final survey questionnaire for Planned Parenthood of Greater Arkansas, March 7–12, 1986.

18. Kurjiaka's letter was addressed to state senator Travis Miles on 2/3/86. For the NOW ads, see *AD* 11/2/86 28A, *AG* 11/2/86 15A.

19. For examples of the prenatal care argument, see *AD* 9/27/86 3B, *AD* 10/10/86 2B, *AG* 10/10/86 19A, *AD* 10/19/86 15A, *AG* 10/19/86 15A. The fund-raising letter was sent by Virginia Vollmer to "Fellow Nurses in Arkansas."

20. *AG* 7/9/86 7A. See also *AD* 9/14/86 1B.

21. For examples of the parental authority argument, see *AD* 7/1/86 1A, *AG* 9/16/86 3A, *AG* 10/14/86 1B, *AD* 10/14/86 2B, *AG* 10/16/86 3A, *AD* 11/3/86 1A. For the husband consent argument, see Mary Heinzel, letter to the editor, *Waldron News*, 8/21/86.

22. Harrison, *Nationwide Study*, xii.

23. For examples of the rape argument, see *AD* 10/10/86 2B, *AG* 10/10/86 19A, *AG* 10/26/86 5B, *AG* 10/29/86 1A, *AG* 11/2/86 15A.

24. *AG* 12/9/85 18A.

25. *AG* 1/26/86 3B.

26. Jim Lair, *Carroll County Tribune*, 9/26/86.

27. *AG* 10/28/86 11A.

28. *AG* 9/29/86 8A.

29. For Kurjiaka's radio commentary, see *AG* 7/16/84 3A. Her letter, "Sample Letter for Opponents of Amendment 65 to Mail to Newspaper Editor," is undated.

30. *AG* 10/13/84 3A, *AG* 11/12/85 1B, *AG* 9/25/86 3A, *AD* 9/25/86 3E.

31. Hickman-Maslin Research, final survey questionnaire for Planned Parenthood of Greater Arkansas, September 22–24, 1986; Hickman-Maslin Research, "Recent Poll and Focus Groups"; *AD* 10/14/86 6B, *AD* 10/21/86 3B.

32. *AD* 10/26/86 6B, *AG* 10/26/86 5B.

33. *AD* 10/29/86 1A.

34. *AD* 11/1/86 2D, *AG* 11/1/86 8A.

35. *AG* 11/6/86 1A.

36. *AG* 11/7/86 3A, *AD* 11/6/86 7A; PPFA Executive Committee, "Arkansas" (resolution), 12/5/86.

37. *AG* 11/6/86 1A.

CHAPTER 2: PRIVACY AND PREJUDICE

1. The account of the focus group is based on *WP* 8/26/87 A4a, *WP* 9/13/87 A39, Pertschuk 133, Hickman-Maslin Research, "Alabama Focus Groups on the Bork Nomination" (memo to NARAL), 8/28/87, and interviews. For the quote from Senator Kennedy, see *WP* 7/2/87 A1.

2. For Michelman's discussion of her trip to Selma, see *MA* 2/15/90 1A.

3. *MA* 9/12/87 2A, *MA* 8/16/87 1C, *MA* 7/6/87 2C.

4. *MA* 3/5/87 1A, *NYT* 3/5/87 A12.

5. *BN* 10/8/87 5D, *MA* 7/13/87 6A, *MA* 7/23/87 13A, *MA* 7/8/87 1C.
6. *MA* 8/9/87 1B, *MA* 8/8/87 1B.
7. Alabama Code 1975, § 26-21-1 (1987 Supp.).
8. Michelman has also discussed her abortion in *PI* 2/15/86 1C; *AC* 10/4/88 1D, *BG* 12/31/89 1; *Salem* (Ore.) *Statesman Journal* 10/18/90 1C; WP 7/19/93 A15; and written testimony to the Minnesota House Health and Human Services Committee, 2/28/90.
9. *Legislative Journal,* Pennsylvania House of Representatives, 11/15/83, 1802.
10. *PI* 10/6/84 1A.
11. The preceding and following quotations are taken from "Remarks of Kate Michelman" (speech text), 1/22/86. Much of the speech is reproduced in *NARAL News* (February 1986): 2.
12. Michelman, letter to Senator Joseph Biden, 8/13/86.
13. The preceding and following quotations are taken from Michelman, "Public Funding Strategy—Rape & Incest" (memo to NARAL affiliates), 6/23/86.
14. *WP* 8/16/86 A9, *AC* 9/11/86 C12.
15. The account of the conference presentations is based on interviews and contemporaneous records.
16. The account of the Hickman-Michelman relationship is based on interviews and contemporaneous records.
17. Michelman, form letter to U.S. senators, 1/21/87; Hickman-Maslin Research, "Arkansas Abortion Initiative" (memo to Kate Michelman), 1/14/87.
18. *Public Opinion* (May–June 1987): 4.
19. NARAL, "Working Document on the Reproductive Bill of Rights," 5/20/87, 2–3.
20. *WP* 7/11/87 A2, *NYT* 7/9/87 A24; Michelman, "One Justice away from Injustice" (press release), 7/13/87.
21. The preceding and following quotations are taken from Michelman's speech text, 7/11/87.
22. Michelman, text of closing remarks, 7/12/87, 2.
23. *WP* 7/2/87 A1; Pertschuk 129, 257–58.
24. For more on Michelman's and Lewis's roles in the coalition, including the genesis of the NARAL focus groups, see Pertschuk 55, 128, 129, 132, 158, 256.
25. Hickman-Maslin Research, "Focus Groups on the Bork Nomination" (memo to NARAL), 8/6/87, 3–4; Hickman-Maslin Research, "Alabama Focus Groups on the Bork Nomination."
26. Pertschuk 135; *WP* 10/24/87 A16; Marttila & Kiley, Inc., "A Survey of Attitudes toward the Supreme Court and the Bork Nomination," 9/10/87, 6, Tables 9, 11.
27. Alliance for Justice, "Message" (memo to Grassroots Leadership), 8/28/87, 4, 6–7.
28. *LAT* 9/1/87 13, WP 9/14/87 A9; People for the American Way, "Gregory Peck" (ad video), 1987.

29. *Nomination of Robert H. Bork* (hearings, U.S. Senate Judiciary Committee), September 1987, 34, 44, 149.

30. *WP* 7/3/87 A4, *WP* 8/12/87 A1, *WP* 10/24/87 A16, *NYT* 7/9/87 A1, *WP* 7/9/87 A1; Bronner 142–43.

31. *WP* 10/24/87 A16; *Nomination of Robert H. Bork,* op. cit., 96, 114–20, 320, 696, 710–12, 1297; *NYT* 9/17/87 C26.

32. Michelman and Duke, "Op Ed on the Bork Nomination" (unpublished essay), 10/6/87, 3.

33. *AC* 9/6/87 D1; Michelman, "Life, Liberty, and Presidential Politics" (unpublished essay), June 1987.

34. *WP* 8/7/87 A18, *WP* 9/25/87 A18, *WP* 10/2/87 A1, *WP* 10/16/87 A10.

35. *WP* 9/15/87 A13, *WP* 10/4/87 A12; McGuigan 78–79.

36. *WP* 7/11/87 A2, *WP* 9/22/87 A1, *WP* 10/2/87 A1.

37. *MA* 9/4/87 2A; "Statement of the Civil Liberties Union of Alabama," 9/17/87, 1; Alabama New South Coalition, "Block Bork" (flyer), 1987.

38. *WP* 10/4/87 A12; *Time* 7/13/87 13; *MA* 9/12/87 1A.

39. *BN* 9/20/87 6B, *BN* 9/18/87 10A; Bronner 180.

40. *MA* 9/18/87 2A, *BN* 7/12/87 1B, *WP* 9/7/87 A1.

41. *Nomination of Robert H. Bork,* op. cit., 78; *BN* 9/15/87 1A.

42. *Nomination of Robert H. Bork,* op. cit., 289–93; *BN* 9/17/87 3B.

43. *BN* 9/20/87 6B, *BN* 10/9/87 20A.

44. Bronner 294; *MA* 10/23/87 2A.

45. Eleven senators explicitly opposed Bork in the name of conservatism. Aside from Heflin, those who cited Bork's past socialism were Breaux, Johnston, Nunn, Reid, and Sasser. See *CR,* September 29 to October 9 and October 21 to 23, 1987. For the quotations in this paragraph, see *CR* 10/6/87 26512 and *CR* 10/13/87 27344.

46. *WP* 10/4/87 A1; Bronner 289.

47. *WP* 10/4/87 A1, *WP* 10/8/87 A18, *WP* 10/24/87 A16, *NYT* 10/8/87 A34; Bronner 285, 289.

48. The seven exceptions to the fifty-eight were Senators Burdick, Exon, Matsunaga, Melcher, Reid, Sarbanes, and Warner. The five who implied sympathy for abortion rights were Cranston, Chafee, Dodd, Kerry, and Packwood. The other exceptions among the eighteen were Boren and Hollings. Those who expressed hostility to abortion included Breaux, Exon, Johnston, and DeConcini. See *Congressional Record,* op. cit.; *NYT* 10/24/87 1.

49. *Nomination of Robert H. Bork* (Judiciary Committee report), 10/13/87, 30; *CR* 10/6/87 26512, *CR* 10/23/87 29110.

50. *Bellotti v. Baird,* 443 U.S. 622; *Harris v. McRae,* 448 U.S. 297; *Bowers v. Hardwick,* 478 U.S. 186; *NYT* 6/27/87 32, *NYT* 8/26/98 A1.

51. *Nomination of Robert H. Bork* (hearings), op. cit., 150, 3906.

52. Ibid., 95, 130, 313, 440.

53. Ibid., 119, 242, 1298. See also Bronner 124.

54. *Dred Scott v. Sandford,* 60 U.S. 393; *Nomination of Robert H. Bork,* op. cit., 314, 315, 321.

55. *Nomination of Robert H. Bork,* op. cit., 300.

56. Ibid., 382; *CR* 6/12/64 13664.

57. *BN* 10/6/87 1A, *MA* 10/11/87 1B.

58. *BN* 10/7/87 2A, *BN* 10/8/87 2A, *MA* 10/8/87 3C.

59. *Nomination of Robert H. Bork,* op. cit., 5284–85.

60. *WP* 7/31/87 A3e, *WP* 9/16/87 A21; *Federal Register* 9/1/87 33210.

CHAPTER 3: WHO DECIDED

1. Michelman, "Priority Mail Wiregram" (form letter), 10/9/87.

2. *ABA Journal* 1/1/88, 33.

3. NARAL, request for proposals, October 1987.

4. Hickman-Maslin Research and American Viewpoint, *Analytical Report,* 1/18/88, 1–2.

5. American Viewpoint and Hickman-Maslin Research, NARAL survey results (pretest), December 1987, Question 27; NARAL survey results (final), December 1987, Question 15.

6. Hickman-Maslin Research, "Public Attitudes Concerning Reproductive Policy" (memo to NARAL), 11/2/87, 6.

7. *Analytical Report,* op. cit., 21.

8. NARAL, "Strategic Recommendations on the Issue of Reproductive Choice for Governor Michael Dukakis," 9/7/88, 2–3.

9. Harrison Hickman, "Abortion in the Presidential Campaign" (memo to Kate Michelman), 9/1/88, 1–2.

10. "Strategic Recommendations," op. cit., 6.

11. *WP* 9/26/88 A19.

12. *NYT* 9/27/88 A1, *BG* 9/27/88 12.

13. "NARAL Responds to Bush Views on Abortion" (press release), 9/27/88.

14. Michelman, "Why Can't George Bush Hear Women's Voices?" (speech text), 9/28/88, 2–3, 5.

15. Michelman, "Heeding the Warnings" (speech text), 10/11/88, 3–4.

16. *WP* 11/9/88 A29.

17. Brownie Ledbetter, letter to Harrison Hickman, 8/23/88; Hickman-Maslin Research, "Recent Survey Results" (memo to Planned Parenthood of Greater Arkansas), 9/27/88, 1–2, 4–5; Ledbetter, notes from briefing by Hickman, 1988, 1–2.

18. *AG* 10/29/88 1A, *AG* 11/4/88 1B, *AG* 11/4/88 3B.

19. Ledbetter, "Planned Parenthood's Effort to Effect Voter Attitudes in the 1988 Election" (private report), 1988, 2; *AG* 11/10/88 9B.

20. NARAL, "Analysis of State Election Results—1988," December 1988, 5; Nancy Broff, "Political Post Election Analysis," December 1988, 1.

21. *NYT* 1/10/89 B5.

22. Michelman, "Emergency Action Mobilization Campaign" (memo to NARAL Friends), 12/23/88, 1–2; NARAL, "National Mobilization Campaign" (memo to Affiliates), 12/23/88.

23. "Statement of Kate Michelman," 1/9/89.

24. Hickman-Maslin Research, "Tampa Focus Groups" (memo to Kate Michelman), 1/28/89, 2–4.

25. Videotape of the focus group. For another firsthand account, see *BG* 2/19/89 1.

26. Hickman-Maslin Research, "Birmingham Focus Groups" (memo to Kate Michelman), 2/16/89, 1–2. Emphasis in original.

27. Hickman-Maslin Research, "Recommended Messages" (memo to Page Gardner), 2/21/89, 3–4.

28. Podesta Associates, "Communications Strategy" (memo to NARAL), 3/17/89, 3.

29. Ibid.; Blumenthal, "NARAL Campaign Plans: Proposed Campaign Theme" (memo to Nikki Heidepriem), 3/13/89, 2.

30. Ibid.

31. *WP* 4/5/89 B3, *BG* 4/10/89 1, *NYT* 4/10/89 A1–B6, *WP* 4/10/89 B1, *PI* 4/10/89 4A; "Talking Points for NARAL Press Advance Team at April 9 March" (undated).

32. NARAL, *Campaign Update,* 4/15/89.

33. *FTN* 4/9/89, *ATW* 4/23/89, *Today* 7/12/89.

34. Podesta Associates, op. cit., 2.

35. Hickman-Maslin Research, "Talking Points" (memo to NARAL), 3/22/89, 1–2.

36. NARAL, "Voices" (videotape), 1989.

37. NARAL, *The Voices of Women,* 1989, 4.

38. "Brief for Amici Curiae Women Who Have Had Abortions and Friends of Amici Curiae," *Webster v. Reproductive Health Services,* 1989, 4, 5, 7, and Appendixes A, B, and C.

39. The account of Frank Greer's and Kim Haddow's backgrounds and roles in the campaign is based on *WP* 3/23/92 D1 and interviews.

40. Greenberg-Lake, "The Right to Decide" (report to NARAL), 4/19/89, 9–10.

41. Ibid., 4–5.

42. NARAL, "Dr. Gerstley," "Back Alley," and "Snapshot" (ad videos), 1989.

43. NARAL, "April 26th Speak-Outs—Messages and anticipated questions from the media" (memo to NARAL Affiliates), 4/24/89.

44. NARAL, "Talking Points for May 15 House Parties," 5/5/89.

45. *NYT* 4/27/89 B12.

46. *Maher v. Roe,* 432 U.S. 464; *Harris v. McRae,* 448 U.S. 297.

47. *NYT* 4/27/89 B12.

48. Ibid.

49. "Statement of Kate Michelman," 4/26/89.

50. *Webster,* 492 U.S. 509–10.

51. Ibid., 520–21, 538, 532.

52. "Statement of Kate Michelman," 7/3/89, 1.

53. "Statement of Kate Michelman," 1/9/89; "Statement of Kate Michelman," 7/3/89.

54. "Statement of Kate Michelman," 7/3/89, 2–3.

55. NARAL, "Face of America" (ad video), 1989.

CHAPTER 4: THE NEW MAINSTREAM

1. *WP* 3/15/89 C7, *RTD* 3/15/89 B1.

2. The account of Goldman's and Donilon's backgrounds and plans is based on interviews, contemporaneous records; *WP* 10/31/89 A23, *WP* 11/12/89 A1; Yancey 95–99; Edds 127, 131, 134, 150.

3. *RNL* 4/10/89 1.

4. *RNL* 4/22/89, *VP* 4/22/89 B1.

5. Marshall Coleman, letter to Virginia ministers, 6/5/89.

6. "Vote . . . to Protect the Virginia Family" (flyer).

7. *RTD* 7/4/89 B1; Edds 148.

8. *RTD* 7/6/89 B1; Edds 149.

9. *WP* 7/8/89 B5, AP 7/6/89.

10. *VP* 7/16/89 A1; Edds 152–54.

11. *WP* 10/31/89 A23, *WP* 11/12/89 A1; Edds 127; interviews.

12. *WP* 9/5/89 D1, *VP* 9/5/89 D5; Edds 182.

13. *WP* 7/12/89 D3, *Time* 7/17/89 64.

14. "NARAL's Policy Statement on Minors' Access," 1984.

15. Dawn Johnsen and Marcy Wilder, "Pro-Choice Legislative Strategy for Minor's Access to Abortion Services" (memo to NARAL Staff and Consultants), 9/5/89, 1–2.

16. Page Gardner, "NARAL Political Plan" (memo to Strategic Team), 9/11/89, 1–5, 7, 12.

17. Paul Goldman, "Abortion Ad Script" (memo to Frank Greer and Mike Donilon), August 1989.

18. *VP* 9/20/89 A1, *RTD* 9/20/89 B1; and video of the ad.

19. Interviews; Edds 191, 203. For another poll that confirmed the shift, see *VP* 9/21/89 A1.

20. Podesta Associates and Martin and Glantz, "Strategy for Virginia Media and Grassroots Campaign on Marshall Coleman's Position on Choice Issues" (memo to NARAL Strategy Group), 9/20/89, 2.

21. Podesta Associates, "Virginia Media Update" (memo to NARAL Strategy Group), 9/28/89.

22. Gardner, op. cit., 4; Gardner, "Discussion Document for NARAL's Political Direction," 10/3/89, 8; *AR* 10/13/89 #32, *AR* 10/25/89 #32; NARAL flyer, October 1989.

23. *WT* 10/29/90 B3, *WP* 10/27/90 B1.

24. *WP* 10/31/88 A1.

25. Edds 222.

26. "Virginia Media Update," op. cit.; draft ad scripts; *WP* 10/5/89 A8.

27. *WP* 10/18/89 D7, *RTD* 10/22/89 C5, *AR* 10/23/89 #7.

28. George Bush, "Letter to Members of the Senate Appropriations Committee on Federal Funding for Abortion," 10/17/89 (*WCP* 10/17/89 1560).

29. NARAL, Planned Parenthood, et al., "Publicly Funded Abortions for Women Who Have Been Sexually Assaulted," September 1989; *WP* 10/22/89 A11, *NYT* 10/22/89 68.

30. See *Congressional Record,* October 17–25, 1989. CR 10/19/89 25166, CR 10/25/89 25827; CR 10/25/89 25812, CR 10/25/89 25819; CR 10/25/89 25817, CR 10/19/89 25169, CR 10/25/89 25818, CR 10/17/89 24764, CR 10/25/89 25825.

31. CR 10/25/89 25819, CR 10/25/89 25825.

32. CR 10/25/89 25817.

33. Ibid., CR 10/17/89 24769, CR 10/25/89 25821, CR 10/25/89 25815, CR 10/20/89 25412.

34. CR 10/19/89 25169.

35. CR 10/25/89 25818.

36. CR 10/25/89 25824.

37. CR 10/25/89 25829.

38. WP 10/24/89 B1; Edds 215.

39. WP 11/2/89 A1, RTD 11/3/89 A1, WP 11/3/89 A1.

40. *Nightline* 11/7/89 (transcript), 5–7.

41. "CBS News/New York Times Virginia Exit Poll" (press release), 11/7/89, 8.

42. *Nightline* 11/7/89, 7.

CHAPTER 5: TRIAGE

1. "Statement of Kate Michelman," 11/8/89, 1–2.

2. *NARAL Guide for Candidates and Campaigns,* 1990. All quotations from the *Guide* can be found on 1–3.

3. Celinda Lake, "Abortion in the Partisan Context" (memo to EMILY's List), January 1990, 4.

4. "Statement of Kate Michelman," 1/22/90; AR 3/1/90 #2.

5. Lake, op. cit., 5.

6. For example, see *BG* 12/17/89 1, *NYT* 9/29/89 A13; *Time* 7/9/90 22; *WSJ* 7/13/90 A10, AR 12/4/89 #91, AR 1/19/90 #91.

7. WP 12/21/89 A8. See also CT 3/25/90 2 (sec. 2C), NYT 6/18/90 A18.

8. Sandra Faucher and Darla St. Martin, *A 1990 Handbook for Political Candidates,* 1990, 46.

9. Ibid., 20–21.

10. Ibid., 37, 28.

11. WT 11/6/89 F4.

12. WFAA-TV 3/1/90 (AR 3/6/90 #34); *State Journal-Register* 2/21/90 (AR 2/27/90 #32); PI 9/4/90 3B, WP 11/2/90 A6.

13. CSM 7/27/90 7; BS 7/28/90 5A; (Ft. Wayne, Ind.) *Journal-Gazette* 8/31/90 (AR 8/31/90 #5).

14. AR 10/13/89 #1, CS 2/14/90 1A; *Newsday* 6/26/90 14.

15. DMN 5/27/90 1A, (Lubbock) *Avalanche-Journal* 5/27/90.

16. AAS 7/1/90 B1, DMN 7/4/90 12D.

17. DMN 5/27/90 1A.

18. AAS 7/1/90 BB1, DMN 5/27/90 1A, DMN 7/8/90 42A, DMN 9/9/90 1J.

19. DMN 4/5/90 22A; transcript of the ad.

20. *Ohio v. Akron Center for Reproductive Health,* 497 U.S. 502; *Hodgson v. Minnesota,* 497 U.S. 417.

21. *Hodgson,* 462, 464, 465, 472.

22. Ibid., 471, 473.

23. Proceedings before the Supreme Court of the United States (transcript), *Hodgson,* 11/29/89, 24, 27.

24. *Hodgson,* 483–85, 501.

25. Ibid., 483.

26. Brief for Cross-Respondents, *Hodgson,* 10/14/89, 31–32.

27. Proceedings, *Hodgson,* op. cit., 3, 11.

28. *Hodgson,* op. cit., 450, 457.

29. Ibid., 422–23, 453.

30. *LCJ* 9/28/90 B3.

31. *DMN* 6/26/90 17A, *DMN* 11/7/90 1A, *MJ* 12/3/90 (*AR* 12/10/90 #5), *Wisconsin State Journal* 3/27/92 1D.

32. *GNR* 2/19/90 B2, *GNR* 5/27/90 D1, *RNO* 5/27/90 1A.

33. NARAL press release 7/30/90 (*AR* 7/31/90 #1); *RNO* 7/31/90 3B, *CO* 8/14/90 1B; "Ten Times" (ad video), 1990.

34. *GNR* 7/31/90 B3, *RNO* 8/15/90 1A, *WP* 10/5/90 A1.

35. *CO* 8/16/90 1B, *WP* 11/1/90 A1.

36. *GN* 4/25/90 1C.

37. *HP* 1/30/90 A11, *SLP* 2/12/90 4B, *PI* 9/1/90 3B, *NYT* 11/9/89 A28, *OCR* 9/16/89 B5, *MH* 8/9/90 1A, *LCJ* 2/25/90 1B, *MH* 4/20/90 5B, *BH* 6/29/90 8, *CT* 6/30/90 5; New Hampshire NARAL PAC release, May 1990 (*AR* 5/23/90 #5).

38. Ray Briscuso press release (*AR* 8/27/90 #4); *OWH* 4/26/90 18, WFAA-TV 3/1/90 (*AR* 3/6/90 #34), *OS* 7/20/89 B3, *AR* 4/19/90 #3, *AzR* 7/8/90 B1. In California, Pete Wilson defeated Dianne Feinstein. In Colorado, Hank Brown defeated Josie Heath.

39. *LT* 3/16/92 1, *WP* 4/4/92 D1.

40. *HCt* 4/24/90 B11.

41. *WT* 8/2/90 A5; *USA* 6/27/90 10A; "Yard Calls Court Decisions 'A Tragedy for Our Young Sisters" (NOW press release), 6/25/90.

42. *CS* 1/18/90 12A, *CS* 2/14/90 1A.

43. *CS* 2/15/90 1A, *GN* 2/15/90 1A, *CS* 2/22/90 1B, *GN* 2/22/90 1A.

44. *CDM* 2/23/90 1A.

45. *CDM* 2/23/90 1A, *CDM* 2/27/90 2A, *CDM* 3/9/90 1A, *CDM* 3/10/90 1A, *CDM* 3/12/90 7A, *CDM* 3/15/90 1A, *CDM* 3/16/90 1A, *Charleston Gazette* 3/13/90 1B.

46. *AC* 6/13/90 A6, *WT* 6/13/90 A3.

47. *AC* 8/18/88 1B, *AC* 10/1/88 1D, *AC* 4/3/89 D2.

48. *AC* 5/1/89 B1, *AC* 7/4/89 A1, *AC* 7/8/89 1C.

49. "GARAL Political Endorsements—July 17, 1990 Primary Races" (pamphlet), 1990; *Marietta Daily Journal* 4/1/90 1B.

50. *AC* 7/8/90 F1, *AC* 7/12/90 D1, *AC* 7/31/90 B1; "Freedom" (ad video), 1990.

51. *AJ* 5/24/90 E1, *AC* 7/31/90 B1.

52. *AC* 8/3/90 A6.

53. *AC* 8/3/90 A1, *AJ* 5/24/90 E1, *AC* 7/12/90 D1, *AC* 8/15/90 A10.

54. *AJ* 5/24/90 E1; interviews.

55. *NYT* 9/21/76 27, *NYT* 7/13/77 1, *WP* 1/23/79 A1.

56. "Statement of Kate Michelman at the Rosie Jimenez Memorial Service in Atlanta," 10/3/88; Page Gardner, "Discussion Document for NARAL's Political Direction," 10/3/89, 19.

57. "NARAL-PAC Criteria for Support of Candidates," 1/10/90, 1–2.

58. Andrew Young, "PAC Information Questionnaire" (NARAL), 3/9/90.

59. *AC* 5/2/90 A8, *AC* 5/22/90 D4; "Georgia Pro-Choice Elections Committee Candidate Report Card," October 1990; *AC* 5/1/89 B1, *AC* 11/20/89 C1, *AC* 8/7/91 D1.

60. Hickman-Maslin Research, "Missouri Abortion Survey Results" (memo to NARAL and Missouri Alliance for Choice), 11/7/89, 12, 15.

61. *KCT* 1/18/90 A1, *SLP* 1/18/90 1A, *SLP* 6/11/90 1B.

62. *SLP* 1/18/90 1A; STOP!PAC press release, 1/17/90.

63. *KCS* 5/17/90 C4, *SLP* 6/11/90 3A, *SLP* 1/18/90 1A, *SLP* 5/16/90 2B; STOP!PAC press release, 1/17/90.

64. *KCS* 6/10/90 B3, *SLP* 1/18/90 1A, *SLP* 1/22/90 1B, *SLP* 4/12/90 4C. *SLP* 6/12/90 1A; Kathryn Kolbert, letter to Alison Gee, 1/25/90, 1–2.

65. *SLP* 6/8/90 1A.

66. *KCS* 6/11/90 B3, *SLP* 6/11/90 1B; STOP!PAC press release, 6/10/90 (*AR* 6/12/90 #5).

67. *KCS* 6/10/90 B3, *KCS* 6/11/90 B3, *SLP* 1/18/90 1A, *SLP* 6/8/90 1A, *SLP* 6/9/90 3A, *SLP* 6/12/90 1A.

68. *KCS* 6/10/90 B3, *SLP* 6/12/90 1A, *SLP* 6/13/90 1B; STOP!PAC press release, 6/10/90 (*AR* 6/12/90 #5); *SLP* 6/8/90 1A, *SLP* 6/11/90 1B.

69. *KCS* 6/12/90 A1, *KCS* 7/6/90 A1, *SLP* 5/18/90 1A, *SLP* 6/13/90 1B, *SLP* 7/6/90 1A.

70. *PO* 1/28/90 C1, *AR* 11/19/90 #1, *PO* 1/25/90 C3, *PO* 4/27/90 D8, *AR* 11/19/90 #1, *PI* 3/15/92 F1.

71. *PO* 9/4/90 A1, *PO* 8/10/90 E6.

72. *PO* 10/15/90 A8, *PO* 10/28/90 E10, *PO* 10/26/90 C6, *PO* 11/3/90 E5, *PO* 11/4/90 A23, *PO* 11/5/90 A8.

73. *PO* 10/26/90 C6, *PO* 9/11/90 C16.

74. *PO* 3/3/90 D4.

75. Jeanette Fruen Turk, "Campaign Status Report #1" (memo to All Interested Parties), 3/19/90, 2; *PO* 4/27/90 D8.

76. *PO* 8/4/90 D4, *PO* 10/16/90 B6, *PO* 11/2/90 E12, *PO* 11/8/90 D4.

77. *DFP* 9/8/88 3A, *DFP* 7/4/89 10A.

78. *DFP* 11/9/88 1A.

79. *DFP* 9/16/88 4A, *DN* 11/4/88 1A.

80. *DN* 10/2/88 1A, *DFP* 9/8/88 3A, *LSJ* 9/8/88 1B, *GRP* 9/8/88 D4.

81. *DN* 9/8/88 3B, *DN* 9/8/88 3A, *GRP* 9/8/88 D4, *DN* 10/2/88 1A, *DN* 11/2/88 1A, *DN* 11/8/88 3B, *KG* 9/16/88 A1.

82. *DFP* 11/6/88 3A, *DFP* 9/8/88 3A, *DFP* 9/16/88 4A, *DN* 10/2/88 1A, *LSJ* 11/10/88 1A, *DN* 11/10/88 3A, *DN* 12/3/88 1B.

83. *DFP* 7/4/89 10A, *DN* 7/12/89 1A.

84. *DFP* 7/13/89 1A, *DFP* 10/9/89 3A, *AR* 10/13/89 #1, *DN* 10/11/89 3B.

85. *DN* 10/26/89 1A, *DFP* 10/26/89 1A, *DFP* 11/5/89 1A, *DN* 12/6/89 1A, *DN* 10/18/89 1A, *LSJ* 10/26/89 1A.

86. *DN* 11/4/89 7B, *DN* 11/25/89 1B, *DN* 12/3/89 23A.

87. *DN* 12/6/89 1A, *DFP* 11/5/89 1A, *DN* 12/7/89 1B. For polls, see also *DN* 7/9/89 1A (77 percent would require parental notice, and 66 percent would require notification of a woman's husband or male partner).

88. *LSJ* 2/24/90 1A, *LSJ* 2/27/90 4A.

89. *DN* 2/27/90 6A.

90. *DN* 2/27/90 3D, *DN* 3/22/90 3B, *GRP* 9/13/90 A1, *DN* 8/6/90 1A.

91. *DN* 8/6/90 1A, *DN* 3/22/90 3B, *DN* 9/7/90 1B, *DN* 9/13/90 1A.

92. *DN* 9/7/90 1B, *LSJ* 9/13/90 1A, *AR* 9/13/90 #1, *DN* 10/18/89 1A.

93. *DFP* 7/4/89 10A, *DN* 10/27/89 4B, *LSJ* 2/24/90 1A, *DN* 10/11/89 3B, *DN* 11/6/88 7C.

94. *LSJ* 2/15/90 1A, *GRP* 9/13/90 A1, *LSJ* 1/23/90 5D, *LSJ* 2/12/90 5A, *DN* 2/13/90 1B.

95. *DN* 2/13/90 1B, *DN* 2/15/90 1B, *AR* 2/26/90 #34.

96. *KG* 9/13/90 A1, *GRP* 9/13/90 A1.

97. *DN* 9/25/90 2B (see also NARAL press release, 11/2/90), *DN* 11/8/90 1A, *AR* 11/14/90 #14.

CHAPTER 6: MIDDLE GROUND

1. *PI* 4/5/91 1A, *PI* 4/6/91 1A, *PI* 4/7/91 1A, *PI* 4/14/91 1C.

2. *PP* 8/25/91 A10.

3. *PP* 8/25/91 A10, *LAT* 11/4/91 A5, *PI* 5/9/91 1A.

4. *CT* 8/15/91 5; *Allentown* (Pa.) *Morning Call* 8/25/91 (*AR* 8/27/91 #8); *AR* 10/31/91 #8.

5. *Rust v. Sullivan,* 500 U.S. 173; *WP* 10/31/90 A9.

6. 500 U.S. 201–2.

7. Ibid., 201, 203.

8. *PI* 11/30/91 9A, *PI* 12/6/91 1B, *PI* 4/16/92 B8.

9. *Planned Parenthood v. Casey,* 947 F.2d 689, 697, 698, 719; *Akron v. Akron Center for Reproductive Health,* 462 U.S. 453.

10. *Petition for a writ of certiorari, Casey,* 11/7/91, i; *WP* 2/23/92 M24.

11. *Parade* 5/17/92 4–5; CBS News release 7/12/92 (*AR* 7/13/92 #13); *AR* 10/10/91 #1.

12. *USA* 6/30/92 1A, *Times-Mirror* poll release 5/8/92 (*AR* 5/8/92 #15), *AR* 10/10/91 #1; *WP* 7/1/92 A4; Wirthlin Group survey, January 1992 (*AR* 1/23/92 #12); *WP* 7/1/92 A4; *Parade* 5/17/92 4–5; *SL* 5/10/92 6 (*AR* 5/11/92 #1).

13. *WSJ* 4/22/91 B1.

14. *Time* 2/3/92 16.

15. *WCP* 1/22/92 143.

16. *WCP* 3/3/92 391, *WT* 3/4/92 A4.

17. *WT* 4/26/92 A3.

18. *USA* 4/22/92 15A.

19. *WT* 6/12/92 A8.

20. *MTP* 6/7/92.

21. *AD* 11/4/88 3B, *AD* 2/12/89 3B. See chapter 1.

22. *AG* 2/12/89 1B.

23. *AG* 2/14/89 3A, *AG* 2/17/89 4A.

24. *AG* 10/12/89 1A.

25. *AG* 3/15/90 1A, *AG* 10/4/90 6B.

26. *Time* 1/17/94 28.

27. *AG* 7/15/91 1A, *AG* 8/14/91 8A, *AG* 7/16/91 1B, *AG* 7/17/91 1B, *AD* 7/16/91 1A, *AD* 7/17/91 1B, *AD* 10/11/91 12A, *AG* 10/11/91 3A, *WT* 9/27/92 A6, *WP* 8/3/92 A19; Bill Clinton, "NARAL Presidential Questionnaire," 11/5/91, 3. Also see *ADG* 3/9/92 1A.

28. *ADG* 3/9/92 1A, *ATW* 2/16/92 (*AR* 2/17/92 #1)

29. *UL* 2/12/92 46.

30. *JMO* 3/15/92 (*AR* 3/16/92 #11), *MTV* 6/16/92 (*AR* 6/17/92 #7).

31. *Today* 4/6/92; *NYT* 4/4/92 8, *NYT* 4/9/92 A20.

32. *MTP* 5/3/92, 20/20 5/29/92.

33. *Brief for Petitioners and Cross-respondents, Casey,* 3/6/92, 35, 19; *Brief for Respondents, Casey,* 4/6/92, 28.

34. *Brief for Focus on the Family, et al., Casey,* 4/6/92, 4; *Brief for Petitioners,* op. cit., 45.

35. *Brief for Focus on the Family,* op. cit., 4, 12–13.

36. *Brief for Petitioners,* op. cit., 56–57.

37. *RTD* 3/24/92 B1, *PI* 4/21/92 C1, *USA* 4/22/92 1A, *WSJ* 4/15/92 A22, *USA* 4/23/92 1A.

38. *Planned Parenthood v. Casey,* 505 U.S. 833.

39. Ibid., 869, 867.

40. Ibid., 833, 881.

41. Ibid., 874, 877.

42. Ibid., 877, 899–900.

43. Ibid., 954, 966.

44. Ibid., 974–75.

45. Ibid., 896–98.

46. ABC, CBS, CNN, NBC, 6/29/92.

47. *MLN* 6/29/92, CNN 6/29/92, *NBCN* 6/29/92, *Nightline* 6/30/92.

48. CNN 6/29/92, *MLN* 6/29/92, *Crossfire* 6/29/92, *ATC* 6/29/92, *CBST* 6/30/92, *NBCN* 6/29/92.

49. *MLN* 6/29/92, NBC 6/29/92.

50. *ATW* 7/5/92. All other quotes come from the designated television programs and newspaper front pages, 6/29/92 and 6/30/92.

51. *WT* 6/30/92 A9.

52. *CBSN* 6/30/92.

53. "An Evening with Bill Moyers," 7/7/92 (*AR* 7/8/92 #11).

54. *HC* 7/1/92 A8, *WP* 7/2/92 A10, *MTP* 7/5/92.

55. *CBST* 7/13/92; Ad Hoc Committee in Defense of Life press release, 7/10/92 (*AR* 7/13/92 #2); *ATW* 7/12/92, *WT* 7/24/92 A5.

56. *LKL* 7/22/92; *LAT* 7/24/92 A22, *AC* 7/23/92 A8.

57. *Dateline* 8/11/92, *ATW* 8/16/92; *NYT* 8/21/92 A14, *LAT* 8/21/92 A10.

58. *EN* 8/15/92, *MTP* 8/23/92.

59. *PTL* 8/27/92, *FTN* 8/30/92; *LAT* 9/9/92 A1.

60. *LAT* 7/24/92 A22, *Newsday* 7/24/92 5, *TW* 7/25/92 A20.

61. *MTP* 7/19/92, *LKL* 7/22/92, *EN* 8/8/92, *ATW* 9/13/92, *MTP* 9/20/92; *AR* 9/28/92 #11, *WP* 10/14/92 A17, *PI* 9/25/92 A4.

62. *ATW* 8/23/92, *PTL* 8/27/92; *NYT* 8/6/92 A20; *ATW* 8/16/92.

63. *LKL* 10/4/92.

64. All of the Rodham excerpts are reprinted in *WP* 8/24/92 A15.

65. *WSJ* 3/13/92 A10.

66. *WP* 3/31/92 A6, *WT* 4/1/92 A1.

67. *WP* 8/13/92 A16, *LAT* 8/13/92 A1.

68. Speech text, AP 8/17/92.

69. Speech text, AP 8/19/92.

70. *DMN* 8/9/92 22A, *WP* 11/9/92 A9, *SLP* 9/30/92 10A; *LKL* 10/5/92, *PTL* 10/29/92.

71. *The Whoopi Goldberg Show*, 9/23/92 (*AR* 9/24/92 #11); *AR* 9/28/92 #11, *WP* 10/14/92 A17.

72. *Colorado Statesman* 3/13/92 (*AR* 3/23/92 #6), *Tucson Citizen* 8/25/92 3C, *MH* 10/9/92 1B, *OS* 8/10/92 A4.

73. *BS* 10/9/92 1C, *BS* 10/18/92 1H, *BS* 11/1/92 1B, *BS* 11/1/92 3J.

74. *BS* 10/14/92 16A.

75. *AzR* 9/18/92 A1, *PG* 9/18/92 B5, *PG* 9/22/92 A1, *AzR* 9/23/92 A1, *PG* 9/23/92 A1.

76. *PG* 9/23/92 A1, *AzR* 10/20/92 B1, *PG* 10/21/92 B1.

77. *PG* 10/22/92 A21, *PG* 10/21/92 B1, *AzR* 10/27/92 B1.

78. *PG* 10/22/92 B1. For more on Goldwater's role, see *AzR* 8/7/92 A1, *PG* 10/1/92 B4.

79. *PG* 10/22/92 B4.

80. *AzR* 11/5/92 A5, *BS* 11/5/92 1B; *Harrisburg* (Pa.) *Patriot* 7/2/92 A8, *Pittsburgh Post-Gazette* 6/29/92 (*AR* 6/30/92 #2), *WT* 8/31/92 D1.

CHAPTER 7: VICTIMS AND VILLAINS

1. *TP* 5/16/90 B3, *BG* 5/17/90 1, *BRS* 5/17/90 1B, *BRS* 5/18/90 1A, *ST* 5/18/90 1A, *TP* 5/18/90 A6.

2. *TP* 11/29/89 B1, *BRS* 5/17/90 1B, *TP* 5/19/90 A1.

3. *BRS* 5/18/90 1A, *BG* 5/17/90 1, *WP* 4/24/90 A25.

4. *TP* 11/30/89 B1, *BRS* 5/14/90 1A.

5. *BG* 5/17/90 1, *TP* 5/19/90 A1.

6. *BRS* 7/4/89 1A, *TP* 7/7/89 B1.

7. *TP* 9/9/90 B5, *AC* 6/21/91 A3, *TP* 8/6/91 A1.

8. *TP* 10/1/89 A36, *BRS* 1/12/90 2B.

9. *WP* 6/27/90 A3.

10. *TP* 6/19/90 B5.

11. *TP* 6/19/90 B5, *WP* 6/30/93 A3, *BRS* 6/28/90 8A, *TP* 6/28/90 B1, *TP* 7/3/90 C1, *ST* 7/4/90 10A, *TP* 7/4/90 B1.

12. *CR* 5/20/87 13129; H.R. 555 (99th Cong., 1st sess.), 1; *CR* 5/8/85 11147; H.J. Res. 104 (100th Cong., 1st sess.), 2; *CR* 2/25/87 4089.

13. H.J. Res. 101; *CR* 6/16/83 16092; H.J. Res. 379; *CR* 6/19/86 14742; *TP* 2/27/90 B2; Buddy Roemer, letter to Mrs. Flo Alexander, 10/21/80; *BRS* 7/1/90 9A; *CR* 11/15/83 32683.

14. *CR* 12/7/81 29710, *CR* 4/22/82 7579, *CR* 9/30/82 26407; H.R. 3541 (97th Cong., 1st sess.), 10–11; *CR* 7/9/81 15268.

15. *BRS* 4/23/90 2B, *TP* 12/9/90 A1, *NYT* 1/20/91 20, *WSJ* 9/6/91 A1, *LAT Magazine* 10/13/91 18, *TP* 4/17/90 A1.

16. *BRS* 10/31/82 4B, *TP* 6/10/84 25.

17. *BRS* 7/25/83 1B, *TP* 6/17/83 1.

18. *TP* 6/10/84 25, *BRS* 11/26/86 4A; "Jenkins promoting Senate campaign," *Bunkie Record,* 3/2/78.

19. Sarvis and Rodman 30–33.

20. *NYT* 8/3/89 A18, *NYT* 9/29/89 A1, *WP* 10/7/89 A6, *BG* 3/29/90 18, *IS* 3/31/90 1A, *IS* 4/1/90 1A, *WP* 6/15/90 A22.

21. *IS* 3/30/90 4A.

22. *IS* 3/24/90 10A, *IS* 3/20/90 1A, *IS* 3/30/90 4A.

23. *IS* 3/20/90 6A, *IS* 3/30/90 1A.

24. *IS* 3/31/90 1A, *LAT* 3/31/90 A1.

25. *IS* 3/31/90 1A, *WP* 3/31/90 A1, *NYT* 3/31/90 1; Michelman, "On Idaho Governor Cecil Andrus' Veto of an Extreme Anti-Choice Law" (NARAL press release), 3/30/90.

26. Minutes, House Administration of Criminal Justice Committee, 6/6/90, 5.

27. *SJ* 1/23/90 6A, *ST* 4/18/90 3A.

28. For example, see *BRS* 6/3/90 8A, *ADT* 6/15/90 A5.

29. *NYT* 6/27/90 A14.

30. *SJ* 1/23/90 6A.

31. *ST* 6/14/90 5A, *NYT* 6/27/90 A14, *ST* 7/1/90 9B.

32. *ST* 7/4/89 1A.

33. For examples of Rothrock's conservative language, see *SJ* 1/22/90 7A and Robin Rothrock, letter to "Dear Senator," 4/9/90.

34. "Statewide poll confirms that Louisiana voters don't want additional restrictions on abortion" (LCRF press release), 5/29/90.

35. Voters for Choice press release, 7/27/89 (*AR* 7/28/89 #12); *WP* 10/7/89 A6, *NYT* 8/3/89 A18; *NYT*-CBS poll, July 25–28, 1989, Question 6.

36. *NYT* 9/29/89 A1.

37. Minutes, Senate Committee on Health and Welfare, 6/4/90, 9, 11–13.

38. Ibid., 7, 10–11.

39. Minutes, House Committee on Administration of Criminal Justice, 6/6/90, 8.

40. *ST* 6/19/90 3A.

41. *State v. Selman,* 300 So.2d 467 (1974); *Selman v. Louisiana,* 428 U.S. 906 (1976); Minutes, 6/6/90, op. cit., 6. The analysis of Jenkins's position is based on his statement in *Official Journal of the Proceedings of the House of Representatives of the State of Louisiana,* 1973, 783 (6/11/73); his vote on S.B. 400 (death penalty for homosexual rape) (ibid., 1975, 2698); and his remarks in *TP* 6/12/73 1 and *BRM* 5/12/92 8A (death penalty for drug trafficking).

42. *ST* 4/4/90 12A.

43. Minutes, 6/6/90, op. cit., 39, 8, 17–18, 28.

44. *Louisiana Statutes Annotated—Revised Statutes* (1986), 14:87(2); Jenkins and Cross, "Response to Governor's Veto on House Bill 1637," 7/6/90, 3.

45. Minutes, House Committee on Administration of Criminal Justice, 6/7/90, 8–9; "Statement of Sally O. Donlon," 6/7/90, 1 (also, audiotape of the hearing).

46. *TP* 6/24/90 A10.

47. *TP* 6/8/90 A1.

48. *BRS* 6/5/90 5A, *BRS* 6/15/90 14A, *BRS* 6/18/90 1A, *BRS* 6/19/90 8A, *ST* 6/28/90 1A.

49. All quotes from the ad are in *BRS* 6/13/90 7A.

50. *WP* 9/9/87 D10a.

51. *BRS* 6/15/90 14A, *TP* 6/15/90 A1, *NYT* 6/15/90 A13, *ST* 6/15/90 1A.

52. *ADT* 6/15/90 A1.

53. *ST* 6/15/90 1A.

54. *ST* 6/15/90 1A, *WP* 6/15/90 A1.

55. Minutes, Senate Committee on Health and Welfare, 6/20/90, 5, 17.

56. Ibid., 9, 11.

57. Ibid., 29, 48, 25, 18.

58. *ST* 6/27/90 1A; Minutes, 6/20/90, op. cit., 58–60.

59. *ST* 6/21/90 1A, *TP* 6/21/90 A1; Minutes, 6/20/90, op. cit., 62.

60. *TP* 6/27/90 A1, *ST* 6/27/90 1A.

61. *USA* 6/27/90 3A, *BRS* 6/27/90 1A, *WP* 6/27/90 A3.

62. *ST* 6/27/90 1A, *TP* 6/27/90 A1, *BRS* 6/27/90 1A.

63. *TP* 6/27/90 A1.

64. *BRS* 6/28/90 8A.

65. Buddy Roemer, letter to house clerk Alfred Speer (veto message on H.B. 1637), 7/6/90.

66. Jenkins and Cross, 7/6/90, op. cit., 5.

67. Ibid., 6–7.

68. *TP* 7/7/90 A1.

69. *ST* 7/8/90 1A, *TP* 7/8/90 A1, *ST* 7/8/90 2A.

70. *ST* 7/8/90 1A.

71. The account of last-minute pro-life lobbying and conversion of the flag bill is based on interviews; *ST* 7/8/90 1A, *ADT* 7/9/90 A1, *BRM* 7/9/90 1A, *TP* 7/9/90 A1, *AC* 7/10/90 A3, *WP* 7/10/90 A3.

72. *ST* 5/29/90 1A, *ADT* 7/9/90 A1, *ST* 7/10/90 2A, *TP* 7/9/90 A1.

73. *BRS* 7/9/90 1A, *AC* 7/10/90 A3, *ST* 7/10/90 1A, *TP* 7/10/90 A1.

74. *BRM* 7/28/90 1A, *BRS* 7/30/90 9A, *LAT* 7/31/90 A16.

75. *LAT* 7/31/90 A16.

76. *NYT* 7/13/90 A9, *TP* 7/12/90 A1.

77. For text of the veto message, see *BRS* 7/27/90 6A, *ST* 7/28/90 1A.

78. "Governor Roemer's Personal Statement on HB 1331" (Roemer press release), 7/27/90. See also *TP* 7/28/90 A1.

79. "Governor Roemer's Personal Statement," op. cit.

80. *AC* 7/28/90 A3, *NYT* 7/28/90 1, *WP* 7/28/90 A1, *ST* 7/28/90 1A.

81. *BRS* 7/27/90 1A, *LAT* 7/28/90 A1, *BRS* 7/27/90 6A, *BRM* 7/28/90 1A, *TP* 7/28/90 A10, *TP* 7/31/90 A1, *WP* 7/28/90 A1.

82. *TP* 9/9/90 B5, *NYT* 8/3/89 A18, *WP* 10/7/89 A6. Also see *NYT* 8/3/89 A18, *NYT* 9/29/89 A1, *WP* 10/7/89 A6, *BG* 3/29/90 18.

83. *CT* 3/22/90 1 (sec. 2C); Citizens for Mulligan, "Trapped" (brochure), 1990; Citizens for Mulligan, "Penny Pullen's 10 worst votes" (brochure), 1990.

84. *PI* 10/24/90 1B.

85. Script of the ad (*AR* 3/22/90 #8).

86. *Argus Leader* (newspaper, Sioux Falls, S.Dak.) 2/8/91 1A, *Forum* (newspaper, Fargo, N.Dak.) 3/28/91 A1, *CDM* 7/21/91 3B, and NARAL press release, 5/27/91 (*AR* 5/28/91 #12); *MJ* 10/20/92 A7, *NYT* 10/18/92 51; NARAL press release, 5/21/92 (*AR* 5/22/92 #7); NARAL press release, 10/18/92 (*AR* 10/20/92 #11); DNC press release, 10/23/92 (*AR* 10/26/92 #15); *LCJ* 10/21/92 B3; Geri Rothman-Serot campaign press release, 10/13/92 (*AR* 10/20/92 #9); Steve Lewis campaign press release 10/2/92 (*AR* 10/6/92 #12); *NYT* 10/26/92 B6.

87. Script of the ad.

88. *RNO* 8/15/90 1A, *CO* 8/16/90 1B.

89. *LAT* 8/17/90 A39; *NYD* 10/18/92 19, *NYT* 10/18/92 51, *NYD* 10/22/92 18; *LKL* 8/17/92. For the complete history of Quayle's retreat, see Dan Quayle, letter to constituent, 2/1/82; *BG* 11/3/88 28, *LAT* 11/3/88 22, *WP* 11/3/88 A30; *LKL* 7/22/92, *MTP* 9/20/92, *CBST* 9/24/92; *NYD* 9/25/92 23, *WP* 10/14/92 A17; *JMO* 10/18/92.

90. See, for example, *AC* 7/10/91 C3, *AR* 2/7/91 #5, *BH* 5/31/92 12.

91. *Nightline* 10/12/90; *AC* 2/3/90 A21, *USA* 6/27/90 10A.

92. Jim Mattox, written response to questionnaire, *AR* 8/23/89 #1.

93. *RNO* 4/21/90 1B.

94. *BG* 5/29/91 23, *BH* 5/29/91 6.

95. *ST* 4/28/91 19A, *TP* 5/10/91 A1, *ST* 5/14/91 1A.

96. *NYT* 7/9/90 A1, *NYT* 6/23/91 12, *ST* 4/28/91 19A, *TP* 5/10/91 A1, *ST* 5/14/91 1A, *TP* 4/16/91 B3, *BRS* 4/25/91 7A, *ST* 4/25/91 3A, *TP* 4/25/91 B8.

97. *BRS* 4/30/91 13A, *ST* 5/19/91 15A.

98. "Statement of Louisiana Catholic Bishops," 5/19/91, 1; Minutes, House Committee on Administration of Criminal Justice, 5/9/91, 13, 11, 27.

99. Minutes, Senate Committee on Health and Welfare, 5/29/91, 25, 28, 42–43; *ST* 5/30/91 1A.

100. Minutes, 5/29/91, op. cit., 28, 42–43.

101. *BRS* 5/30/91 1A, *TP* 5/30/91 A1.

102. Minutes, Senate Committee on Health and Welfare, 5/30/91, 7–9.

103. *BRS* 5/30/91 1A, *ST* 5/31/91 1A, *ST* 6/1/91 3A.

104. *ST* 5/14/91 1A.
105. *BRM/BRS* 6/1/91 1A, *BRS* 5/10/91 1B, *TP* 5/11/91 A1, *TP* 5/31/91 A1.
106. *BRM* 6/2/91 1A, *BRS* 6/5/91 1A; *Official Journal of the Proceedings of the Senate of the State of Louisiana,* 1991, 777–83 (6/4/91).
107. *TP* 6/15/91 A1.
108. The entire text of the veto message is in *BRM/BRS* 6/15/91 8A and *ST* 6/15/91 4A.
109. *ST* 6/16/91 1A, *TP* 6/16/91 A1.
110. *ST* 6/18/91 4A, *TP* 6/19/91 A1, *ST* 6/19/91 4A.
111. *ST* 6/19/91 1A, *TP* 6/19/91 A1, *NYT* 6/19/91 1.
112. *BRS* 6/19/91 4A.
113. *BRS* 6/19/91 1A, *BRS* 6/20/91 1B, *TP* 6/20/91 A1, *ST* 6/21/91 4A.
114. *BRS* 6/21/91 1A.
115. *ST* 5/19/91 15A, *ST* 6/23/91 3A, *TP* 8/6/91 A1; "Planned Parenthood Challenges Louisiana Abortion Law" (Planned Parenthood press release), 7/10/91, 2.
116. *TP* 8/6/91 A1, *BRM* 11/17/91 11A, *TP* 11/17/91 B1.
117. *TP* 6/20/91 A8, *TP* 6/23/91 B7, *TP* 9/5/91 B4, *TP* 10/20/91 A1.
118. *TP* 10/20/91 A1, *BRM* 10/21/91 1A, *BRM* 10/20/91 1A, *ST* 10/20/91 1A, *ST* 10/20/91 17A, *TP* 10/21/91 A8.

CHAPTER 8: THE RIGHT TO CHOOSE LIFE

1. For the initial reports on Stuart, see *BG* 10/24/89 1, *BG* 10/25/89 1.
2. *BH* 10/25/89 6, *BG* 1/5/90 17, *BG* 1/6/90 21, *BG* 1/5/90 1.
3. *BG* 1/11/90 1, 22.
4. *BG* 1/13/90 27, *BG* 11/3/91 1, *BG* 2/1/90 1, *BG* 1/28/90 1.
5. *FPP* August 1988 170.
6. *LAT* 12/27/89 B1, *BH* 8/25/93 10, *AzR* 9/18/98 A1, *LCJ* 6/22/91 A1.
7. *WP* 9/24/93 D1, *WP* 1/15/94 A1, *AP* 1/18/94, *CNN* 1/19/94.
8. *WP* 11/11/93 A1, *NYT* 11/11/93 A18.
9. *In re Mary P.,* 444 NYS 2d 545–46 (11/25/81).
10. Ibid., 547.
11. Ibid., 547–48.
12. Ibid.
13. *FPP* August 1988 170–71; *FPP* September–October 1992 203–5.
14. *PO* 4/28/94 A1, *PO* 8/31/94 A1, *PO* 9/11/94 L1, *PO* 10/3/95 A1.
15. The account of the Los Angeles episode is based on *LAT* 6/18/91 B1 and *OCR* 1/12/91 A3.
16. *AP* 10/4/93 (*AR* 10/4/93 #3); *BG* 8/14/91 21.
17. For background, see *OCAW v. American Cyanamid,* 741 F.2d 444.
18. Ibid., 446.
19. Ibid., 447.
20. Ibid., 445, 449.
21. *UAW v. Johnson Controls,* 499 U.S. 192.
22. Brief for Respondent, *Johnson Controls,* 7/19/90, 27.

23. Brief of the United States Catholic Conference as amicus for respondent, *Johnson Controls,* 7/17/90, 13; Brief amicus of Concerned Women for America for respondent, 7/19/90, 17.

24. Brief Amici Curiae in Support of Petitioners by American Civil Liberties Union et al., *Johnson Controls,* 6/1/90, A42.

25. Ibid., A51–A53.

26. Ibid., A40–A41.

27. Ibid., 15, A21, A28, A18.

28. 499 U.S. 206.

29. The account of the New York City episode is based on *NYT* 5/24/89 B3, *WT* 1/11/90 A5, *NYT* 4/18/91 B1.

30. The account of the Bonnell episode is based on *TT* 3/23/94 FM1 and *SPT* 3/23/94 1B.

31. Reporter's Transcript, *People vs. Johnson* (Tulare Superior Court, Calif., 1990), 1/2/91, 6–8.

32. *Conservatorship of Valerie N. v. Valerie N.,* 219 Cal. Rptr. 392, 409. See also *LAT* 5/31/91 E1; Kevles 114, 116.

33. Ibid.

34. *People vs. Dominguez,* 65 Cal. Rptr. 292.

35. California Probate Code § 1951 (1999); *People v. Pointer,* 199 Cal. Rptr. 357–66; Luker 156.

36. *FB* 1/10/91 A1.

37. Reporter's Transcript, Motion to Modify Sentence, *People vs. Johnson,* 1/10/91, 3–22; *FB* 1/11/91 A1, *Times-Delta* (Visalia, Calif.) 1/11/91 1A.

38. *NYT* 1/10/91 A20, *Times-Delta,* op. cit.

39. *PI* 12/12/90 18A.

40. *NYT* 12/21/90 A20, *PI* 12/16/90 1B.

41. *PI* 12/23/90 4C.

42. *NYT* 1/10/91 A20.

43. *LAT* 1/13/91 M7.

44. *LAT* 3/3/91 M1.

45. Appellant's Opening Brief, *People vs. Johnson,* 4/25/91, 61; *SB* 4/26/91 B2.

46. *WP* 1/4/91 A1, *AzR* 12/30/90 C5.

47. *WT* 10/16/90 G1.

48. *USA* 2/4/91 8A.

49. *USA* 2/4/91 8A, *LAT* 3/3/91 M5, *SB* 6/18/91 B3.

50. Respondent's Brief, *People vs. Johnson,* 6/3/91, 5.

51. *LAT* 5/17/91 A1.

52. *LAT* 5/27/91 A1.

53. *SB* 12/16/91 A1.

54. *WE* 2/1/91 1D.

55. *WE* 2/13/91 1D.

56. *WE* 2/1/91 1D.

57. *WE* 2/13/91 1D, *KCS* 2/13/91 C8; Testimony, House Federal and State Affairs, State of Kansas, 2/12/91, Attachment #11, Attachment #14, 1–2.

58. Testimony, op. cit., Attachment #9, 1.

59. Ibid., Attachment #13, 2; KCS 2/13/91 C1.

60. *ST* 5/24/91 2A, *ST* 5/22/91 21A, *TP* 7/15/90 B1. See *BRS* 5/1/91 1A and *ST* 5/12/91 for Duke's confirmation that his bill was modeled on the Kansas bill.

61. *TP* 7/13/90 B4, *AzR* 3/8/98 J1.

62. *BRS* 10/8/90 1A, *ST* 4/30/91 1A, *BRS* 5/1/91 1A, *ST* 5/3/91 1A.

63. *ST* 5/4/91 13A.

64. *BRS* 5/24/91 12A, *ST* 5/24/91 2A.

65. *NYT* 4/9/91 B4.

66. *SL* 1/16/92 1.

67. *SL* 1/14/92 1.

68. *NYT* 9/4/91 B1.

69. *NYT* 1/14/92 A1.

70. *NYT* 9/4/91 B1, *NYT* 6/26/92 B5, *TnT* 1/21/92 A4.

71. *SL* 1/9/92 1.

72. *SL* 1/14/92 1, *NYT* 4/9/91 B4.

73. *SL* 1/18/92 4.

74. *SL* 1/16/92 1, *TnT* 1/14/92 A1.

75. *SL* 1/15/92 1.

76. *TnT* 1/19/92 A1, *SL* 1/16/92 1.

77. *NYT* 1/18/92 25, *SL* 1/16/92 1, *SL* 1/18/92 4, *SL* 1/22/92 1.

78. *NYT* 1/22/92 A21.

79. *SL* 1/23/92 1, *TnT* 1/23/92 A6.

80. *BR* 2/3/92 A5, *SL* 2/3/92 1.

81. *LAT* 2/5/92 A3, *SL* 2/4/92 1.

82. *Changes in State Welfare Reform Programs* (Hearings, Senate Subcommittee on Social Security and Family Policy), 2/3/92, 46.

83. Ibid., 10; *SFC* 2/4/92 A8.

84. For accounts of Wilson's speech and proposal, see *SB* 12/10/91 A1 and *LAT* 12/10/91 A1. For contrasts with Bryant's presentation, see *NYT* 4/9/91 B4, *NYT* 9/4/91 B1, *NYT* 6/26/92 B5, *SB* 2/9/92 A3, *SL* 1/22/92 1, *TnT* 1/21/92 A4.

85. *LAT* 12/10/91 A1, *SB* 10/18/92 A1.

86. *LAT* 1/9/92 A1, *SFC* 1/9/92 A6, *LAT* 1/14/92 A3.

87. *LAT* 2/5/92 A3, *SB* 2/1/92 A6, *SB* 2/4/92 A1, *SB* 2/9/92 A3.

88. Janet Carroll, "Proposed Welfare Reform Initiative" (memo to Gov. Pete Wilson), 1/3/92, 1. The memo was released to the media on January 15. See *SFC* 1/16/92 A13, *SB* 1/16/92 A3, *SDU* 1/16/92 A3.

89. *California ProLife News* (March 1992): 3.

90. Carroll, op. cit., 1–2.

91. *LAT* 2/12/92 B3, *SFC* 2/12/92 A15, *SB* 2/13/92 B5.

92. *SB* 7/28/92 B5.

93. *OCR* 4/4/92 A3, *LAT* 10/24/92 B5. For examples of the bishops' criticism, see *SFC* 8/4/92 A13, *OCR* 8/15/92 B3.

94. *SB* 10/13/92 A4, *SB* 10/27/92 A3, *SFC* 11/4/92 A12, *SFC* 2/4/92 A8, *SB* 10/4/92 A1.

95. *SB* 1/26/92 A14, *LAT* 4/9/92 A1, *OCR* 5/22/92 A3.

96. *WCP* 7/31/92 1363, *SDU* 8/1/92 A1.

97. Ibid., 1360–61.

98. *NYT* 5/23/92 8, *SL* 5/23/92 1, *LAT* 7/27/92 A17, *USA* 9/10/92 12A, *LAT* 10/8/92 A1, *CT* 10/8/92 12.

99. *AC* 4/11/92 A7, *ADG* 12/3/92 1A, *AC* 11/2/93 A1.

100. *ADG* 12/4/92 13A, *BG* 4/21/92 3, *WT* 3/28/94 A1, *BS* 2/12/94 2B, *OWH* 3/30/94 1.

101. *GRP* 6/2/94 A1, *AC* 2/8/93 A8, *AC* 4/30/93 E1.

102. *USN* 12/13/93 32; *LAT* 6/15/94 A14, *BS* 3/17/94 14A, *LAT* 3/27/94 A1, *NYT* 5/26/94 A14; *Time* 6/20/94 29; *LAT* 5/26/94 A1, *NYT* 5/26/94 A14.

103. Casey McKeever, "Child Exclusion in California" (memo to Martha Davis and Jodie Levin-Epstein), 6/20/94; McKeever, "Conference Issues—Item 5180" (memo to Members of Joint Budget Conference Committee), 6/2/94.

104. *SJM* 6/24/94 3B, *SDU* 7/1/94 A3, *LAT* 7/2/94 A1, *SFC* 7/2/94 A1, *SJM* 7/2/94 1A.

105. McKeever, "AFDC 'Maximum Family Grant'—AB473—OPPOSE" (memo to members of the legislature), 7/5/94; SB 7/9/94 A12.

106. *SB* 7/5/94 A1, *SB* 7/9/94 A1, A12, *LAT* 7/2/94 A1, *SFC* 7/2/94 A1.

CHAPTER 9: THE ERA OF BIG GOVERNMENT

1. *MST* 12/15/92 1A, *RTD* 1/25/93 A9, *PI* 3/4/93 A12, *Daily Oklahoman* 3/4/93 A14.

2. *DMN* 1/23/93 1A, *PI* 1/22/93 A3; *AR* 1/25/93 #3; *BG* 1/23/93 A16, *WP* 1/26/93 A16, *NYT* 1/23/93 A20.

3. *TP* 11/29/92 B7.

4. *AJC* 5/8/93 B4; *AR* 12/1/92 #2; *AJC* 1/27/93 A5.

5. *AAS* 1/14/93 B2, *HC* 4/28/93 A24, *MTP* 5/16/93; *EN* 5/29/93.

6. *DMN* 5/20/93 1A, *DMN* 5/22/93 42A, *HC* 1/23/93 27A, *HC* 2/3/93 15A, *HP* 4/28/93 A23, *DMN* 4/30/93 1A, *DMN* 5/16/93 1A, *DMN* 6/3/93 1A, *KCS* 9/12/93 B1, *DMN* 10/24/93 1J.

7. *LT* 5/3/93 5, *NYT* 4/17/93 A7.

8. *SFX* 3/30/93 A1.

9. *CT* 3/30/93 A3; *ABCN* 3/30/93, *NBCN* 3/30/93; *WCP* 7/3/95 1122.

10. *WP* 4/22/93 A19.

11. *USN* 4/19/93 74.

12. *NYT* 7/15/93 A1; *TNR* 10/11/93 10.

13. *WP* 7/15/93 A17, *WP* 7/29/93 A24.

14. *CR* 6/30/93 H4329–30; *Plain Dealer* (Cleveland, Ohio) 7/11/93 9A, *WP* 7/12/93 A4; *AP* 7/3/93.

15. *NBCN* 6/30/93, *CNN* 6/30/93; *BG* 7/3/93 A22; *AP* 7/1/93.

16. *WP* 7/19/93 A15.

17. *WP* 3/4/92 A4, *WP* 3/5/92 A8, *WT* 3/5/92 A3, *WT* 6/12/92 A8; *Freedom of Choice Act of 1991* (Hearings, Senate Committee on Labor and Human Resources), 5/13/92, 3, 5, 7, 9, 13, 19, 20, 21, 63.

18. *Freedom of Choice Act of 1991*, op. cit., 7, 49, 63–65, 72.

19. Ibid., 39, 47, 48, 50, 52.

20. *AR* 2/14/92 #11.

21. *NYT* 7/31/92 A11, *WP* 8/6/92 A21.

22. *SU* 2/16/93 A1, *USA* 2/24/93 4A, *NYT* 4/7/93 A22, *NYT* 7/3/93 A6, *Sun-Times* (Chicago, Ill.) 7/9/93 A1, *SLP* 7/18/93 1B.

23. *USA* 2/24/93 4A, *NYT* 4/2/93 A16.

24. *SU* 2/16/93 A1, *NYT* 4/2/93 A16.

25. *SU* 2/16/93 A1.

26. *SU* 2/16/93 A1, *NYT* 4/2/93 A16, *SLP* 7/18/93 1B, *CM* 7/21/93 A1, *BG* 4/21/93 A3.

27. *NYT* 4/2/93 A16, *CSM* 12/1/92 A1.

28. *CM* 7/21/93 A1, *NYT* 7/17/93 A18.

29. *BG* 4/21/93 A3, *LAT* 5/20/93 A16, *WP* 7/15/93 A17, *WT* 7/7/93 A1, *NYT* 9/16/93 A18, *SLP* 6/17/93 12A, *CS* 7/9/93 A1.

30. *AP* 9/28/93; *BS* 9/30/93 9A, *BG* 9/30/93 A15.

31. *TW* 11/7/93 N6, *TP* 3/17/93 A2.

32. *WT* 9/17/93 A23.

33. *LAT* 4/14/93 A1, *WT* 2/14/94 A3.

34. *AR* 8/30/93 #9, *AR* 5/10/94 #1, *AR* 10/1/93 #6.

35. CBS 5/27/93 (*AR* 5/27/93 #8); *PO* 9/8/93 A11, *WP* 5/19/93 A1; NPR 5/21/93 (*AR* 5/21/93 #1), CBS 9/14/93 (*AR* 9/15/93 #10), *Nightline* 9/23/93 (*AR* 9/24/93 #1), CNN 9/23/93 (*AR* 9/24/93 #1); *WT* 10/1/93 A15, *LAT* 5/28/93 A1.

36. *AR* 8/30/93 #9; *RMN* 6/17/94 57A; *BG* 2/23/94 A1, *Cincinnati Enquirer* 6/22/94 B2.

37. For transcripts of the ads, see American Health Line 10/22/93 and 3/25/94.

38. Ad script, 5/31/94; *TP* 6/1/94 A8.

39. CNN-USA-Gallup poll (*AR* 7/19/94 #12).

40. *CD* 7/19/94, *WP* 7/2/94 A9.

41. *Nightline* 7/13/94 (*AR* 7/14/94 #1); *BS* 10/28/93 12A.

42. *BG* 7/20/94 A1, *USA* 8/10/94 4A.

43. *FTN* 4/9/95, *MTP* 5/7/95; *AR* 12/6/95 #2; *WP* 12/1/95 A1, *NYT* 2/11/96 A33, *SPT* 2/16/96 12A, *WP* 1/27/96 A8.

44. *NYT* 9/17/94 A9, *AP* 2/7/95, *Today* 12/4/95; *MTP* 12/17/95; *BG* 2/8/95 A10.

45. *SFX* 7/14/94 A14, *LAT* 7/13/94 (*AR* 7/13/94 #3), *RMN* 6/24/95 32A, *LAT* 11/2/96 A1, *LAT* 1/10/97 A1, *LAT* 1/10/97 A3.

46. *SPT* 7/22/93 4B, *HC* 10/6/93 A21, *MST* 9/18/94 1A, *DO* 8/12/94 A10, *TW* 8/12/94 N12.

47. *USN* 12/13/93 30; *LAT* 4/21/94 A1; *AR* 6/22/94 #5; *AC* 8/28/94 E1, *WT* 4/29/94 A4, *WP* 4/29/94 A37, *WP* 3/1/95 A14.

48. *Contract with America: Welfare Reform, Part II* (Hearings, House Subcommittee on Human Resources), 2/2/95, 823–75.

49. *AR* 3/23/95 #1; *WT* 5/1/95 A6.

50. *LAT* 1/31/95 A19, *WP* 2/1/95 A4, *NYT* 3/5/95 A24, *NYT* 3/19/95 A1, *LAT* 3/22/95 A19, *WSJ* 3/22/95 A18, *NYT* 3/23/95 A1, *WP* 3/23/95 A12, *WSJ* 3/23/95 A16.

51. *WT* 7/26/95 A8, *WT* 8/3/95 A10, *WP* 8/9/95 D1, *RTD* 9/3/95 A16, *WP* 9/9/95 A8, *LAT* 9/14/95 A1.

52. *WT* 6/28/95 A1, *RMN* 6/28/95 28A.

53. *NYT* 7/24/96 A1, *NYT* 8/1/96 A1, *NYT* 8/23/96 A1, *WT* 10/16/96 A3, *WP* 11/3/96 A32.

54. *AR* 8/7/96 #9, *AR* 10/11/96 #8; *LAT* 11/6/96 A1.

55. *WT* 4/18/93 A4, *WP* 7/24/93 A17, *WP* 9/17/96 A1.

56. *Roe v. Wade,* 410 U.S. 113, footnote 1; *WT* 4/23/96 A16, *WP* 9/13/96 A3, *USA* 3/11/97 1D, *CT* 3/21/97 A3.

57. *AR* 4/17/96 #1; *York* (Pa.) *Daily Record* 3/18/97 A8, *Bangor Daily News* 4/3/97.

58. *NYT* 9/20/96 A22, *NYT* 5/18/97 A17.

59. *NYP* 5/3/96 A2, *WT* 2/24/97 C3, *RMN* 4/6/97 4B.

60. *NYT* 4/11/96 A1, *SPT* 11/4/96 4A; *AR* 3/19/96 #12; *USA* 5/22/96 8A, *USA* 8/13/96 17A; *AP* 5/19/97.

61. CNN 10/10/96; *WT* 9/8/96 A1; *MTP* 10/6/96, *LKL* 10/17/96.

62. *NYT* 3/21/97 A1, *NYT* 5/15/97 A14, *NYD* 4/11/96 A51, *WP* 6/14/95 A4.

63. *NYT* 12/4/98 A27, *NYT* 5/20/97 A1, *LAT* 5/20/97 A1, *WP* 5/20/97 A1, *WP* 5/30/97 A7.

64. Ibid.; *Modern Healthcare* 5/26/97 2.

65. *LAT* 5/20/97 A1, *NYT* 5/20/97 A1.

66. Ibid.; *NYT* 5/21/97 A1, *LAT* 5/21/97 A1, *LAT* 2/11/99 A5.

67. *WP* 5/20/97 A1; AMA Board of Trustees Fact Sheet on H.R. 1122, June 1997.

68. H.B. 427; *WP* 9/23/99 A9; Senate Substitute #3 for House Bills 427, 40, 196, and 404.

69. *KCS* 8/20/99 B3, *KCS* 9/17/99 A1, *SLP* 9/17/99 A1.

70. *CR* 10/20/99 S12886, *CR* 10/21/99 S12961, S12997.

71. H.R. 2436 (introduced 7/1/99); *AP* 7/22/99.

72. H.R. 2436.

73. *Unborn Victims of Violence Act of 1999* (Hearing, House Subcommittee on the Constitution), 7/21/99, 26, 117–18.

74. "Action Alert," *National Right to Life News,* 8/10/99; *CR* 9/30/99 H9060.

75. *CR* 9/30/99 H9045, H9071.

76. *CR* 9/30/99 H9047, H9072–73; *NYT* 10/1/99 A20.

77. Spencer Abraham et al., news conference on CCPA, 5/13/98 (transcript); *WT* 6/16/98 A21.

78. *PPG* 5/14/98 A13, *Weekly Standard* 7/27/98 7.

79. S. 1645 (introduced 2/12/98), H.R. 3682 (introduced 4/1/98); Statement by Douglas Johnson, NRLC Federal Legislative Director, 1/22/98; Abraham, op. cit.

80. *Child Custody Protection Act* (Hearing, Senate Judiciary Committee), 5/20/98 (transcript).

81. *WP* 6/21/98 A2.

82. Republican Response to President's Weekly Radio Address, 7/18/98 (transcript).

83. Statement by Gloria Feldt, 5/13/98; *NYT* 5/29/98 A20, *BG* 7/9/98 A15.

84. *WP* 6/21/98 A2; *CR* 7/15/98 H5511, 16, *WP* 7/20/98 A16.

85. Statement by Gloria Feldt, op. cit.; *WP* 6/21/98 A2, *HCt* 6/23/98 A1, *BG* 7/9/98 A15.

86. *Child Custody Protection Act* (Hearing, House Subcommittee on the Constitution), 5/21/98, 36.

87. AP 6/17/98; *BG* 7/9/98 A15.

88. Abraham, op. cit.; Republican Response, op. cit.; Family Research Council, "Minors Should Not Be Abused in 'Interstate Commerce'" (release), 9/23/98.

89. *Child Custody Protection Act,* House, op. cit., 58.

90. Ibid., 60, 65.

91. *CT* 7/16/98 A21.

92. Statement by Gloria Feldt, op. cit.; *BG* 7/9/98 A15; *CR* 7/15/98 H5513–16.

93. Ibid.

94. *WP* 6/21/98 A2, *CD* 6/24/98, *WP* 7/19/98 A4.

95. *CR* 7/15/98 H5540, *CR* 9/22/98 S10703–4.

96. *NYT* 6/28/96 A33.

97. *CR* 7/11/96 H7353.

98. *CR* 7/11/96 H7349, H7366.

99. *CT* 7/15/97 A4, *CT* 9/11/97 A4.

100. *CR* 9/9/97 H7053.

101. *CR* 9/9/97 H7053, H7079–80.

102. *CR* 10/8/98 H10148; *CD* 9/21/99.

103. *CR* 3/10/98 H956, H982; *NYT* 10/22/98 A3.

104. *NYT* 11/11/99 A18, *NYT* 7/14/00 A16, *NYT* 11/15/99 A1.

105. *NYT* 11/15/99 A1, *WP* 11/15/99 A1, *NYT* 11/16/99 A1.

106. *NYT* 7/14/00 A16, *NYT* 10/25/00 A1, *LAT* 10/25/00 A20.

107. *NYT* 10/25/00 A1, *LAT* 10/25/00 A20.

CHAPTER 10: FATAL POSITION

1. *Nation,* 7/3/00, 5.

2. *DMN* 7/1/90 30A.

3. *DMN* 11/9/93 1A, *HC* 11/7/93 A5.

4. *DMN* 10/22/94 32A, *DMN* 10/28/94 1A, *DMN* 9/25/94 46A.

5. *DMN* 9/27/94 1C, *DMN* 10/28/94 1A.

6. *AAS* 5/8/94 C3, *FWS* 6/5/94 A1, *DMN* 11/10/94 1A, *DMN* 2/26/95 45A.

7. *AAS* 5/8/94 C3.

8. *DMN* 6/18/94 42A, *FWS* 6/13/98 A1.

9. *DMN* 6/12/96 15A, *DMN* 5/18/96 30A, *DMN* 1/13/98 4A, *DMN* 1/17/98 30A, *NYT* 10/29/00 A1.

10. *FWS* 9/5/95 A1, *DMN* 8/20/97 25A.

11. *DMN* 9/2/98 34A, *HC* 7/1/97 A1, *DMN* 8/29/99 1A.

12. *AAS* 6/12/96 B1.

13. *HC* 6/3/97 A15, *FWS* 6/13/98 A1, *DMN* 11/4/98 1A.

14. *DMN* 1/28/99 1A; *AP* 3/8/99; *FWS* 3/8/99 A1.

15. *DMN* 3/10/99 30A, *DMN* 6/24/99 25A, *WP* 4/14/99 A1, *DMN* 3/11/99 1A, *DMN* 5/26/99 1A.

16. *DMN* 5/21/97 24A, *DMN* 3/18/99 1A, *DMN* 5/20/99 27A, *DMN* 5/22/99 1A.

17. *DMN* 6/8/99 3A.

18. *WP* 6/16/99 A19.

19. *DMN* 10/2/99 1A; *MTP* 11/21/99; *NYT* 11/16/99 A1; debate transcripts 12/2/99, 12/13/99, 1/10/00.

20. Transcript of Bush remarks at Pella Centra College, Iowa, 1/20/00; *WP* 1/23/00 A9.

21. *DMN* 3/21/99 31A, *DMN* 11/21/99 1A, *NYT* 6/21/99 A1.

22. *AP* 8/24/99; *WP* 1/27/00 A8.

23. *SFC* 8/20/99 A3, *SFC* 8/25/99 A3, *FWS* 2/10/00 A15.

24. *BG* 1/27/00 A1.

25. *WP* 1/27/00 A8; *AP* 1/26/00.

26. *BG* 1/27/00 A1; *AP* 1/26/00.

27. *AP* 8/24/99; *WP* 2/15/00 A1.

28. *Time* 2/14/00 26; *AP* 2/7/00, *AP* 2/9/00; *BG* 2/9/00 A15.

29. *MJ* 2/13/00 1A; "McCain: Facts" (radio ad script), February 2000.

30. *WP* 2/15/00 A1, *ATC* 2/15/00.

31. Speech transcript, 6/16/99; *SLP* 9/13/99 A7.

32. *Nashville Banner* 9/17/84; letter to constituent 9/10/80; *Washington Monthly* 11/86 43. The most recent Gore votes took place on 9/22/83, 10/11/83, 6/27/84, and 10/24/85.

33. *NYT* 2/25/00 A1, *WSJ* 8/15/00 A1; constituent letter 7/23/87; *MTP* 2/21/88; see chapters 6 and 9.

34. Speech transcript, 6/16/99; *Des Moines Register* 8/8/89 2B, *WP* 8/13/99 A4; *AP* 8/12/99.

35. *NYT* 2/12/00 A13, *NYT* 11/16/99 A1. Bradley's attacks on Gore's abortion position began in *AP* 8/11/99 and continued for six months.

36. *WP* 2/16/00 A14; Statement from Gina Glantz, 2/15/00.

37. *AP* 2/15/00; *WP* 2/16/00 A14, *RMN* 2/20/00 43A, *WP* 3/1/00 A7.

38. Brief of Petitioners, *Stenberg v. Carhart*, 2/26/00, 4–5, 29–30.

39. Brief of Amici Curiae National Right to Life Committee et al., *Carhart*, 2/28/00, 9–11.

40. Brief of Respondent, *Carhart*, 3/29/00, 1–2, 19; official transcript, *Carhart*, 4/25/00, 26, 44.

41. Brief of Respondent, op. cit., 47; Brief of Petitioners, op. cit., 46.

42. *Stenberg v. Carhart*, 530 U.S. 983, 1007, 962–63, 979.

43. Ibid., 938–39, 943.

44. Ibid., 937–38, 964.

45. *NYT* 6/29/00 A26; Governor Bush Statement on Supreme Court Ruling on Partial-Birth Abortion, 6/28/00.

46. The entire text of Gore's speech can be found in *WP* 8/18/00 A30.

47. *Washington Post*–ABC News poll, Oct. 6–9, 2000, Question 11 (trend data included).

48. *NYT* 9/17/00 A22.

49. *WT* 9/29/00 A1.

50. *NYT* 9/29/00 A1, *NYT* 10/1/00 A22.

51. *LAT* 9/30/00 A16, *WSJ* 10/2/00 A2.

52. AP 10/5/00, AP 10/11/00; *NYT* 9/17/00 A22.

53. The cited question from the Oct. 13–15 WSJ-NBC survey is Question 14. Gore's decline in the Gallup tracking poll among liberals (4.6 net percentage points), moderates (8.6), and conservatives (9.6) was measured by comparing (A) the averages for Bush and Gore from the Sept. 11–13 sample to the Oct. 2–4 sample with (B) their averages from the Oct. 4–6 sample to the Oct. 26–28 sample. For Gore's decline, see September and October polls by NYT-CBS, WP-ABC, WSJ-NBC, *Newsweek*, *Time*-CNN, and Reuters-MSNBC.

54. The ideology indices cited are based on *NYT*-CBS and *WP*-ABC data but were not calculated by those organizations.

55. *WP* 10/25/00 A18, *LAT* 10/25/00 A12; speech transcript.

56. *WP* 10/26/00 A24, *NYT* 10/27/00 A29.

57. Voter News Service exit poll, 11/7/00, Questions L, M, O, and R.

58. *WP* 1/17/01 A4, *WSJ* 1/18/01 A4; Fox News 1/18/01; *Today* 1/19/01.

59. *LAT* 1/23/01 A1.

60. *Federal Register* 3/29/01 17303; Penny R. Thompson, letter to State Medicaid Directors, 3/30/01; *WP* 3/31/01 A9.

61. *WP* 4/12/01 A29, *WP* 7/18/01 A6, *WP* 7/20/01 A6, *WP* 7/7/01 A6.

62. Statement of Administration Policy on H.R. 503, 4/24/01; *WP* 4/27/01 A1.

63. Statement of Kate Michelman, 4/26/01; statement by Gloria Feldt, 3/22/01; CRLP, "Statement of Opposition to H.R. 503," 3/13/01; "NOW Denounces House Passage of Unborn Victims of Violence Act," 4/26/01.

64. Fox News 4/25/01; "Statement of Opposition to H.R. 503," op. cit.; CRLP, "U.S. House Passes Legislation Threatening Reproductive Rights," 4/26/01; CRLP, "The 'Unborn Victims of Violence Act,'" May 2001.

65. *NYT* 7/6/01 A1, *WSJ* 7/6/01 A10.

66. *CR* 4/26/01 H1644.

67. *LAT* 2/1/02 A30.

68. *HC* 9/22/94 A24, *DMN* 5/16/95 17A, *AAS* 1/29/97 A8.

69. *WP* 11/3/98 A7, *WP* 10/31/97 A1.

70. *WT* 3/18/01 A1; CNN 4/16/01; *WP* 4/18/01 A11.

71. *WP* 4/18/01 A11.

72. *WSJ* 7/6/01 A10, *WP* 7/30/01 A1.

73. *NYT* 7/6/01 A1, *LAT* 7/7/01 A12.

74. AP 7/6/01; Statement of Kate Michelman, 7/6/01; "NOW President-elect Kim Gandy Blasts Bush Plan to Cover Fetuses, Ignore Moms," 7/6/01.

75. Michelman, "President Bush Plan to Insure the 'Unborn' Is Part of a New 'Stealth Front' in the War on the Right to Choose" (memo to Editors and Editorial Writers), 7/12/01; Statement by Gloria Feldt, 7/6/01.

76. NARAL, "Bush Administration Proposal to Make 'Unborn Children' Eligible for SCHIP Is Part of Stealth Campaign to Undermine Abortion Rights" (fact sheet), February 2002.

77. *WSJ* 4/27/01 A20.

78. H.R. 4292, as introduced, 4/13/00.

79. *Born-Alive Infants Protection Act of 2000* (Hearings, House Subcommittee on the Constitution), 7/20/00, 123.

80. CRLP, *Reproductive Freedom News,* Sept. 2000; Elizabeth Liu, "Supreme Court Shows Vulnerability with Close Decisions," *National NOW Times,* summer 2000.

81. NARAL, "*Roe v. Wade* Faces Renewed Assault in House," 7/20/00; *CR* 9/26/00 H8158.

82. "Statement of NARAL on the Born Alive Infant Protection Act," 6/13/01; NOW, "Another Fetal Rights Bill May Surface" (Legislative Updates), Feb. 2001; NOW, "Activists: Send Comments on 'Fetal Personhood' by May 6," 4/1/02.

83. NARAL, "Human Embryo Research" (fact sheet), 1/22/02; NOW, "Promising Stem Cell Research Now Threatened" (Legislative Updates), Feb. 2001; *Hardball* (CNBC), 8/9/01.

84. "NOW President-elect Kim Gandy Blasts Bush Plan to Cover Fetuses, Ignore Moms," op. cit.; "President Bush Plan to Insure the 'Unborn' Is Part of a New 'Stealth Front' in the War on the Right to Choose," op. cit.; *Reproductive Freedom News,* op. cit.; Statement by Gloria Feldt, 8/9/01.

85. Fox News 8/9/01, Rebecca Farmer, "'Fetal Rights' Initiatives Concern Abortion Rights Supporters," *National NOW Times,* fall 2001.

86. "Human Embryo Research," op. cit.; "Promising Stem Cell Research Now Threatened," op. cit.

87. "Human Cloning Prohibition Act of 2001" (hearing, House Subcommittee on Health), 6/20/2001; *BG* 8/3/01 A23.

88. *SFC* 8/9/01 A1, *BG* 8/3/01 A23; "Human Cloning Prohibition Act of 2001," op. cit.

89. "Human Cloning Prohibition Act of 2001," op. cit.

90. Ibid.; "Human Embryo Research," op. cit.

91. *BG* 8/3/01 A23.

92. AP 9/28/01.

93. Ibid.; "Human Embryo Research," op. cit.; *Chicago Sun-Times* 11/6/01 A20.

94. AP 9/28/01; *NYT* 9/28/01 A16.

95. Nahar Alam et al., letter to J. Benjamin Younger, M.D., 1/15/02.

96. *NYT* 2/16/02 A16; AP 2/28/02.

97. *LAT* 7/23/02 A1.

98. *NYT* 8/1/01 A1.

99. Women's E-news, 6/9/02; "Cloning Embryos Should Not Be Considered

an Abortion Issue" (Religious Coalition for Reproductive Choice release), 11/26/01.

100. *American Prospect,* 7/15/02, 10.

101. CuresNow, "Confused" (ad video), 4/24/02.

102. CR 6/14/02 S5580; Statement of The Hon. Orrin Hatch, 2/5/02.

103. CR 6/14/02 S5580; WP 6/6/02 A3; S. 2439 (filed 5/1/02).

104. Statement of Daniel J. Bryant before the House Subommittee on Criminal Justice, Drug Policy, and Human Resources, 5/15/02; CR 6/14/02 S5581; National Right to Life Action Alert 7/8/02; National NOW Times, fall 2002.

105. Legislative Updates (NOW), Aug. 2002; *NYD* 8/6/02 22; AP 8/21/02.

106. Statement of Gloria Feldt, 9/27/02; WP 9/28/02 A4; *LAT* 9/28/02 A23; AP 10/10/02.

107. WP 10/30/02 A1; Statement of Kate Michelman, 10/30/02.

108. WP 10/2/02 A8; WP 11/12/02 A23.

Bibliography

Bronner, Ethan. *Battle for Justice: How the Bork Nomination Shook America.* New York: W. W. Norton, 1989.

Condit, Celeste Michelle. *Decoding Abortion Rhetoric: Communicating Social Change.* Urbana: University of Illinois Press, 1990.

Edds, Margaret. *Claiming the Dream: The Victorious Campaign of Douglas Wilder of Virginia.* Chapel Hill: Algonquin, 1990.

Falik, Marilyn. *Ideology and Abortion Policy Politics.* New York: Praeger, 1983.

Fried, Marlene Gerber, ed. *From Abortion to Reproductive Freedom: Transforming a Movement.* Boston: South End Press, 1990.

Garrow, David J. *Liberty & Sexuality: The Right to Privacy and the Making of Roe v. Wade.* New York: Macmillan, 1994.

Ginsburg, Faye. *Contested Lives: The Abortion Debate in an American Community.* Berkeley: University of California Press, 1989.

Gorney, Cynthia. *Articles of Faith: A Frontline History of the Abortion Wars.* New York: Simon & Schuster, 1998.

Kevles, Daniel J. *In the Name of Eugenics: Genetics and the Uses of Human Heredity.* New York: Knopf, 1985.

Luker, Kristin. *Abortion and the Politics of Motherhood.* Berkeley: University of California Press, 1984.

McGuigan, Patrick B., and Dawn M. Weyrich. *Ninth Justice: The Fight for Bork.* Washington, D.C.: Free Congress Research and Education Foundation, 1990.

Paige, Connie. *The Right to Lifers.* New York: Summit, 1983.

Pertschuk, Michael. *The People Rising: The Campaign against the Bork Nomination.* New York: Thunder's Mouth Press, 1989.

Petchesky, Rosalind Pollack. *Abortion and Woman's Choice*. Boston: North-
eastern University Press, 1984.
Rosenblatt, Roger. *Life Itself: Abortion in the American Mind*. New York: Ran-
dom House, 1992.
Sarvis, Betty, and Hyman Rodman. *The Abortion Controversy*. New York: Co-
lumbia University Press, 1974.
Tribe, Laurence H. *Abortion: The Clash of Absolutes*. New York: W. W. Nor-
ton, 1990.
Yancey, Dwayne. *When Hell Froze Over: The Untold Story of Doug Wilder*.
Dallas: Taylor Publishing Co., 1988.

Index

Indexer:	Patricia Deminna
Text:	10/13 Sabon
Display:	Sabon
Compositor:	G & S Typesetters, Inc.
Printer and binder:	Maple-Vail Manufacturing Group